English Poetry

OF THE *Seventeenth Century*

𝔈𝔫𝔤𝔩𝔦𝔰𝔥 𝔓𝔬𝔢𝔱𝔯𝔶

OF THE *Seventeenth Century*

SELECTED AND EDITED BY

ROBERTA FLORENCE BRINKLEY

ASSOCIATE PROFESSOR OF ENGLISH
GOUCHER COLLEGE

W·W·NORTON & COMPANY, INC.

NEW YORK

FIRST EDITION

PRINTED IN THE UNITED STATES OF AMERICA
FOR THE PUBLISHERS BY THE VAIL-BALLOU PRESS

Preface

THE EDITOR has long felt that there was a need for a collection of poetry limited to the seventeenth century and selected to represent with some degree of fulness the leading figures, types, and ideas of the period. It is the purpose of this volume to afford the student and the general reader a medium between the very comprehensive and the severely limited anthologies. The scope is sufficiently broad to include notable or interesting poems which are not lyrical, as well as the more frequently collected lyrics, and therefore to give a just delineation of the century with its experimentation in structure and types and its wide range of mood. Twenty-five poets have been chosen and an adequate number of poems selected to illustrate their characteristics of thought and style. Figures primarily of the Renaissance, such as Campion or Drayton, have been omitted; but since Spenser's influence parallels the dominance of Jonson and Donne among the Jacobean poets, a group of the followers of Spenser has been included.

The selections are primarily complete poems or large divisions, such as cantos or eclogues; in a few cases, however, it seemed desirable to illustrate ideas or style by excerpts. There are no selections from *Paradise Lost* because the editor feels that the poem should be read in its entirety.

A condensed account of some of the outstanding ideas of the century has been included to give the background in which the various poets developed, and the poets are presented in chronological order so that their relation to the period and the ideas which shaped their thinking may be immediately apparent. The short biographies are an attempt to reach a sane balance between necessary facts and portraiture, with the hope that even sketches of these varied and stimulating personalities will awaken old names into living individuals.

The notes have been kept to a minimum and placed at the bottom of the page for the convenience of the reader.

The bibliography provides a reference list of obvious materials for more detailed study, either as a guide to the student or a time-saver for the teacher.

The editor has prepared the text for the reader inexperienced in the oddities of seventeenth century form and has attempted to remove many of the visual difficulties in reading the poems. The old forms of spelling have been retained only where they affect rhyme or rhythm; in general both spelling and punctuation have been modernized. Elisions, where obvious, have been expanded, and unnecessary capitals and italics have been eliminated.

The editor wishes to express her thanks to the staff of the Library of Congress for their generous cooperation, to Dean Dorothy Stimson of Goucher College and Dr. James W. McManaway of Johns Hopkins University for reading the essay on the period, to Dr. McManaway and Dr. Ray Heffner of Johns Hopkins University for consultation regarding the bibliography, and to her sister, Sarah Gibson Brinkley, for reading all the original material and giving constant advice on the problems of editing.

ROBERTA FLORENCE BRINKLEY

Contents

English Poetry

OF THE *Seventeenth Century*

The Seventeenth Century in England

THE MODERN world evolved in the seventeenth century. The ideas which are the very fibre of our thinking, which seem as though they had existed always, were developed and systematized from an embryonic and chaotic state by the zeal and almost superhuman efforts of the giant intellects that dominate the period. These ideas did not come forth without conflict: the monarchy was overthrown and then restored; the church suffered an upheaval; and religious faith felt the impact of the materialistic view resulting largely from the new science. The very turn of the century is marked not only by an attempt to crush out the new science but also by the beginning of experimental methods. It was in 1600 that Bruno, who accepted and expanded the Copernican idea of the universe, suffered martyrdom and that William Gilbert published the first great scientific work to be published in England, *On the Magnet, on magnetic bodies, and on the earth as a great magnet, a new physiography, demonstrated by many arguments and experiments.* In differentiating between arguments and experiments, Gilbert led the way toward the true scientific method.

The century is marked by a tireless search for truth, regardless of the consequences. Bacon set this keynote when he said, "The inquiry, knowledge, and belief of truth is the sovereign good of human nature." He reasoned against the practice of the schoolmen, who "have withdrawn themselves from the contemplation of nature and experience and sported with their own reason and the fictions of fancy"; he criticized the method of Aristotle, who "did not consult experience in order to make right propositions and axioms, but when he had settled his system to his will, he twisted experience round and made her bend to his system"; and he substituted for these means the scientific method of the wide observation of facts. At the beginning of the century he advanced the idea that man was merely on the threshold of truth and must assume the obligation of adding to the store of the world's knowledge.

The need of more practical means for the discovery of truth was answered by the development of mechanical instruments to insure precision. The first of these was the telescope. It gave evidence to the physical sense which reason alone could not have fathomed, and it revolutionized man's conception of his relation to the universe and to God by furnishing physical evidence of the Copernican theory. The Ptolemaic system had made the earth and man the focal point of the universe and of God's attention. The extent of space was comprised within ten concentric spheres, limited, patterned, accountable. The Copernican system, however, changed the fixed center from the earth to the sun and greatly extended the conception of space, though leaving it still bound by the outer sphere of fixed stars. Bruno, however, in interpreting the Copernican theory, gave evidence that there were no bounds to space and that man is on the smallest of countless universes, whirling in illimitable space about the sun. The sudden projection into infinity staggered man's imagination and necessitated a thoroughgoing readjustment of his ideas. In the first place, the heliocentric theory of the universe was held to be contrary to the Scriptures: it changed the location of heaven and hell and violated the literal interpretation of various passages, which were eagerly cited as evidence against the new theory. In the second place, it revealed that the stars, which according to the old belief governed man's fate by their influence, were other worlds, remote and not concerned about man's affairs. Comets, long held to be miraculous portents of death and disaster, were discovered to have a place in this universe; and their supernatural powers vanished when it was found that their return could be accurately predicted. The old science of astrology had to pass. Speculations arose as to whether other creatures dwelt upon these newly discovered worlds and vied with man for the attention of a God suddenly lost in an infinity of space, and whether voyages could be made to the moon. Comedy, satire, and serious study reflect the different attitudes of thought concerning the possibility of such a voyage and the nature of the inhabitants of the moon. The telescope became increasingly popular, and even literature is full of references to it: in Daniel's masque *The Vision of the Twelve Goddesses,* for example, a sibyl used a telescope to describe the goddesses, who descend from a mountain; and in *Paradise Lost* Milton's recollection of the appearance of the moon's surface as he had seen it through Galileo's telescope in Fiesole was used in figuratively portraying Satan's shield. In Restoration England a private individual might have a telescope on top of his house, as did Pepys, for the entertainment of his friends or join the crowds which gathered to look through the great telescope in St. James's Park. The Royal Society spent much time in improving the instrument and recording observations made under various conditions.

A second mechanical instrument which changed man's thoughts about himself and his world was the microscope. This revealed to him the marvelous perfection of his body in even its most minute organisms, and the structural infinity and complexity of tissue. He learned many things about the structure of the human organs and for the first time became acquainted with the basic facts of modern physiology. The discovery of the capillaries added the final proof to Harvey's theory of the circulation of the blood; the corpuscular composition of the blood was ascertained; and vast realms of living creatures of which man had never dreamed became visible. The microscope led also to the study of plant anatomy and to a classification of plants based upon structure instead of upon a description of external appearance. Furthermore, sex was recognized in plants and the primary facts in plant reproduction were understood. Nature seemed excessive, terrifying in its fecundity. Milton expresses this idea in *Comus* when he speaks of the seas with their "spawn innumerable," the teeming earth, and the air crowded with birds. Man felt overwhelmed by the stupendous sweep of the new cosmos, so crowded with worlds and packed with creatures; and a spirit of melancholy became prevalent. Some would not accept the evidence of the senses; others refused to look through the telescope and the microscope, holding that faith must be preserved even if it meant the denial of actuality. With great humor Galileo wrote to Kepler of a professor of philosophy at Pisa who tried "with logical arguments, as if with magical incantations, to charm the new planets out of the sky." [1]

Donne said that the "new philosophy calls all in doubt," but the disturbing evidence to the physical senses afforded by these two instruments was less significant than the profound shock to faith occasioned by the development of mathematics and the application of the laws of mathematics to astronomy and physics. The importance of the gift of the seventeenth century in mathematical notation can hardly be overemphasized. The innovations range from the simplest symbols, such as $><$, x, $::$, and brackets to the decimal system, algebra, analytic geometry, logarithms, and calculus. Tycho Brahe and Copernicus had been obliged to make their computations through laborious arithmetical processes. If no quick and accurate method of computation had been devised, the century could never have made the steps of progress which it achieved, for the new mathematics made it possible to work out the laws of nature through formulae. The application of mathematical laws to the phenomena of motion led men to see that nature operated by laws which could be depended upon as invariable and to question whether God were necessary to the mechanism of the universe. Descartes argued that there was no place for an active Providence who could interfere in the working of these laws. The development of mathematics also led to greater confidence in reasoning and fuller reliance on the rational. The determination of the unknown from the known, the steps in analytical generalization, the trustworthiness of the law of cause and effect—all these were found valuable not

[1] Quoted by O. Lodge in *Pioneers of Science* (1893), p. 106.

only in science but also in the more abstract realm of philosophy.

In the mental confusion which resulted from the conflict between science and religion, some found a safe retreat in mysticism, where the individual could depend upon the personal experience of religious ecstasy instead of upon the evidence of his senses. Donne in *The Second Anniversary* questions the soul:

> When wilt thou shake off this pedantry
> Of being taught by sense and fantasy? [2]

Browne thinks that faith is strengthened by being challenged, and holds that there are not enough doubts for an active faith to overcome. Direct communion with God will give all one needs to know, and this contact can be secured through contemplation or found revealed in nature and the happy innocence of childhood. Donne, Herbert, and Crashaw are the poets of mystic contemplation; Vaughan and Traherne, of nature and childhood. Milton, on the other hand, holds that the new science is based on theories and that theories are relatively unimportant. Others follow Hobbes in the denial of faith and the acceptance of a purely materialistic philosophy, or Descartes in the separation of faith and reason by the theory of dualism.

In contrast with the disturbance of faith by science was the increased knowledge of the Bible and interest in religious thought resulting from the publication of the King James Version in 1611. The way in which the Biblical phraseology and ideas permeated the thought of the entire century is revealed by the literature of the period. It molds the style of many of the writers in prose, accounting for the sonorous tones of Sir Thomas Browne, Jeremy Taylor, and Milton; it becomes the substance and form of the graphic allegories of Bunyan; it stirs the poets to epic conceptions—*Christ's Victory and Triumph, The Apollyonists, Davideis, Paradise Lost, Paradise Regained;* it bears fruit in a drama conceived

[2] Lines 290–92.

in the classical mold, *Samson Agonistes,* and in a great satire, *Absalom and Achitophel;* and it is the inspiration of the lyric poets—Drummond, Wither, Donne, Herbert, Vaughan, Traherne, Crashaw, Quarles, and Herrick.

Gradually the mind worked its way out of the first re-action of gloom, which led to skepticism on the one hand and to blind faith and retreat into mysticism on the other, and became aware that the new theory of the universe was a stupendous challenge to a broader view and not a destructive attack on faith. A creator who could conceive of the grandeur of an infinity of worlds and originate laws to give order to their motion was a greater god than a being who could conceive of only a limited universe. As man began to discover realms of knowledge of which he had previously been unaware, he saw that apparent lack of order in the world as he knew it might be attributable to man's restricted view and not to the plan. Perhaps there was a rational scheme of which man's puny mind could only dimly conceive. Late in the century Blackmore in his poem *The Creation* phrases the idea that if one could understand the entire system of worlds, faith would be strengthened rather than decreased:

> Would not this view convincing marks impart
> Of perfect prudence and stupendous art?

The idea of ordered systems of worlds was paralleled in the realm of creatures by a revival of the ancient conception of a "scale of nature" or "chain of being." No one species could ascend beyond its link in the chain or usurp the realm of the other, nor could the vegetable world encroach upon the animal. Evidence for such a law lay in the theory that without its existence chaos would prevail.

In this way man once more adjusted himself to the natural world, but he could not find his old complacence. His mental vision had been expanded by the new light it had received, and with enthusiasm and unremitting effort the intellectual leaders set out to explore the powers of the mind and to increase knowledge and understanding. It had become evident that the way to reach truth was through greater accuracy in observations and that to be accurate one must have adequate tools for measurement. The invention of the barometer, thermometer, air pump, and pendulum clock marks other steps of progress in science. Indeed, Robert Hooke, one of the members of the Royal Society, thought it might be possible to gain all knowledge through instruments; and man's ability to invent and discover did appear to be unlimited.

It soon became evident that more could be accomplished through a combination of efforts, and by 1645 a group of interested men were collaborating in their attempt to advance scientific knowledge. This group was known as the "Invisible College" and met first in London during the time of the greatest disturbance of university life in the civil war period, and later divided upon the return of some of the members of the group to Oxford. The London group is associated with Gresham College and forms the nucleus of the Royal Society, which was finally chartered in 1663. By the formal organization of the Royal Society public recognition was made of the national need of cooperation in furthering knowledge. Through correspondence and the visits of foreign scientists cooperation was, indeed, made international. Experiments were performed, inventions demonstrated, and data accumulated; and a careful record of all proceedings was kept in the *Philosophical Transactions*.

As the century advanced it became apparent that scientific principles and laws could be applied to practical affairs. The principle of accuracy and exactness was evidenced even in speech and writing. The Royal Society cultivated "a close, naked, natural way of speaking; positive expressions; clear senses; a native easiness; bringing all things as near the mathematical plainness as they can." Bishop Wilkins, a member of the Society, even attempted to find a symbolic language which would be as exact as is notation in mathematics. The fundamental postulate that certain causes inevitably produce certain results was applied to the study of governments; the laws of statistics were applied by Sir William Petty to population and trade; and the principle of balance, by Harrington to property.

The search for truth was carried over into the realm of human nature, and the study of man's mind and attitudes originated. Types of character were analyzed in the *Character Books* and portrayed by Jonson on the stage. History was interpreted through personality by Bacon in his *Henry VII*. Biographical writing became popular, and the carefully ascertained facts of a person's life were seen to be as essential to the understanding of his nature as was the close noting of his manners and eccentricities which made the more vivid portrait. Anthony Wood's facts and Aubrey's anecdotes were both important; and the blending of the two types of material by Walton marks a notable advance in biographical writing. Lyric writers studied and described the emotions. The old conventional pattern of the chivalrous code and idealistic love between man and woman was ruthlessly destroyed by Donne. He analyzed the actual emotions of love, laying bare the diversity of moods: cynicism and idealism, sensuality and purity, gaiety and despair, self-giving and grasping dominance—all are set forth in his poems. He and all the other religious poets of the age also portrayed such emotional states as resulted from the conflict between doubt and faith or the lure of sin and the desire of the soul for God.

The critical temper of mind was also focused upon the traditional conceptions of the Bible and of history. Spinoza in 1670 argued in his *Tractatus Theologico-politicus* that the miracles of the Old Testament could be explained as the workings of laws that it was possible to determine. Father Simon in *Histoire critique du Vieux Testament* attacked the reliability of Scriptural text. Both works were known in England; the latter was translated into English in 1682 and stimulated Dryden to write *Religio Laici*. In history the attempt to sift fact from legend led into zealous research in the antiquities of Britain. The fabulous account of the settlement of Britain by Brutus, descendant of Æneas, and of the incredible exploits of its heroes, including Arthur, was discarded. The monuments of Britain, old coins, old burial urns, old manuscripts—all could throw light on the past and help to separate truth from fiction. The Antiquarian Society, like the Royal Society, shows the appreciation of cooperative effort. Manuscripts were collected and transcribed; scholars in their enthusiasm frequently worked thirteen and fourteen hours a day at copying materials. Courteous exchange of valuable manuscripts and of transcriptions was made with foreign scholars. The generosity of the great collector of manuscript material is illustrated by the hospitality of Sir Robert Cotton, which made available his library for the constant use of scholars.

One of the most far-reaching results of the new realism was the conflict which immediately originated between authority and freedom. Cromwell's words, "Bethink you that you may be mistaken," might be used as a motto for the intellectuals. Intellectual life had long been based upon the authority of books and abstract theory, not upon the actualities of experience. The method employed by the medieval schoolmen to arrive at truth was the method of deduction from some general principle assumed to be true, but not tested for its truth by observation of fact. Such a method led to emphasis on a process of reasoning founded upon opinion, and often amounted to no more than the spinning out of words. Though Bacon admired the ancients, he saw that truth could be reached only after the mind had been liberated from the bondage of blind acceptance of the principles set up by the ancient writers, particularly Aristotle, and of the method of syllogistic reasoning perfected by the medieval schoolmen. Like Sir Thomas Browne in his *Vulgar Errors,* Bacon set out to meet the "Goliath and Giant Authority." Men should not make the ancients their dictators, he said, for "knowledge derived from Aristotle will at most rise no higher than the knowledge of Aristotle."

Authority, he held, should be tested by reason and experiment; one should not be satisfied merely with theoretical arguments; but with a critical temper of mind, a spirit of inquiry, and a willingness to defer judgment over a period of time, one should observe things as they are and base opinion upon facts, not words. Bacon began a controversy over the relative value of the ancients and the moderns, which centered at first in the fields of science and philosophy but later in the century extended into the realm of literature.

One phase of the conflict between the ancients and the moderns in literature found expression in the new criticism which went back to the ancients for models and standards. The establishment of the neo-classical rules is not due solely to French influence; there is a continuous movement toward a norm from Sidney, through Ben Jonson, to Dryden. This movement is in part an effort to gain the sophistication of maturity. The setting up of social codes, the development of satire, the critical temper of the age, the growing rationalism, the influence of scientific thought—all these contribute to the changing style in literature. The Jacobean and Caroline literature was considered too unrestrained. It was individual and emotional; freedom of expression led to violation of good taste; and imagination and fancy were not sufficiently curbed. Experimentation in verse forms had produced such oddities as stanzas shaped to form altars, crosses, and wings. Waller in his poem on the Earl of Roscommon's translation of Horace expresses the reaction against the literature of the first half of the century:

> Though poets may of inspiration boast,
> Their rage, ill-governed, in the clouds is lost.

The literary world became as weary of such exuberance as the political world of violence, and in both realms there arose the desire for stability. Early in the century Ben Jonson had shown in *Timber* that the classical writers had many valuable suggestions for the English. He pointed the way to the improvement of English literature when he told Drummond that the study of Quintilian would correct the defects of his writing. The scientific point of view also influenced literature: regular and dependable laws had been discovered in nature, and it was thought that laws of composition might be discovered in literature. The only field of research was in the writing of past ages. Jonson does not, however, advocate the "rules" drawn from the medieval interpretation of Aristotle, but a return to the primary sources. These are to be followed "as guides, not commanders," for "we have our own experience, which, if we will use and apply, we have better means to pronounce." In Dryden's *Essay of Dramatic Poesy* the relative values of ancient and modern literature are left balanced. Dryden advocated the analytical study of literature as it is and advanced the idea that although conformity to law generally improved literature, sometimes violation of law, as in the case of Shakespeare, was compensated by other qualities. But even Dryden felt with many others of his age that Shakespeare could be improved, and illustrated his theory by adapting *Antony and Cleopatra*. He did not depreciate native English genius but felt that it would gain by conforming to certain basic laws. He also urged the merits of rhyme on the ground that it acted as a restraint to an over-luxuriant fancy, for he felt that the overflow of the romanticists needed to be limited by the bounds of the closed couplet.

The literary quarrel over the ancients and moderns was not, however, limited to criticism; it found expression again in Sir William Temple's *An Essay upon the Ancient and Modern Learning* (1690) and in Swift's *Battle of the Books* (1704), which took the discussion over into the eighteenth century.

Milton saw that freedom must be given also to the expression of thought and wrote his magnificent *Areopagitica*, protesting the act to re-establish the censorship of the press in 1643. His plea for the freedom of the press is one in principle with his constant plea for liberty—social, intellectual, religious, or political. In this work he establishes the principle upon which the more specialized arguments may be based: "Give me the liberty to know, to utter, and to argue freely, according to conscience, above all liberties." In a glowing defense of man's reason and the cause of truth he argues for freedom of intellectual activity as a foundation for national progress.

In education there was also a definite break with authority —the authority of the medieval scholastic system. Bacon was the first to see that there should be a humanitarian ideal back of learning, and in both *The Advancement of Learning* and the *New Atlantis* he sets forth the ideal that the "gift of reason" is for "the use and benefit of mankind" and that knowledge is "a rich storehouse for the glory of the Creator, and the relief of man's estate." Cowley reiterates this aim in his *Proposition for the Advancement of Experimental Philosophy*. Milton turns the humanistic ideal definitely toward the academic system, defining "a complete and generous education" as "that which fits a man to perform justly, skilfully, and magnanimously all the offices, both private and public, of peace and war."

Even music shows the effect of release from authority— the authority of the church. When the Puritans forbade the use of church music and went about breaking up organs and destroying musical scores, they unintentionally prepared the way for an unprecedented development in secular music. Up to this time music had been dominated by ecclesiastical authority and had been primarily the handmaid of religion. Now musicians could concentrate their attention on the deliberate development of a type of music which would express emotions and states of mind not necessarily religious; and in a period which produced much excellent lyric poetry, it is not surprising to find the poets and musical composers working in close cooperation. Henry and William Lawes, who set to music many of the lyrics of Carew, Lovelace, and Waller, were leading composers of the first half of the century. It was Henry Lawes who suggested to Milton the writing of *Comus* and who composed the musical score for it.

One of the most delightful pictures of the learned Hobbes is that given by Aubrey when he tells us that Hobbes kept the songs of Henry Lawes on his table, "which at night, when he was abed, and the dores made fast, and was sure nobody heard him, he sang aloud, (not that he had a very good voice) but to cleare his pipes . . ." The break with traditional religious concepts, the skeptical and intellectual attitude, made impossible the old mystical expression which had characterized the music of worship, and music became more intellectual, with more emphasis on structure and less on emotion. The experimental temper of the age led to much experimentation in music, which is said to have been encouraged by the king. New types of instruments were invented and old types were improved; the laws of vibration were studied; and new systems of musical theory were devised. Even music-loving Mr. Pepys entertained himself by inventing "a better theory of musique than hath yet been abroad." Purcell, in whom the new music of the century culminates, not only tried all the known forms of music but created new forms. The care for accuracy shown in scientific observation, mathematical precision, and simplicity and clarity of speech and writing, is reflected in the definiteness and repetition of phrase to emphasize design in music, in the attention to form and pattern, and in the prominence given to melody and rhythm.

This conflict between authority and freedom took place not only in literature, the press, education, and music, but also in the civil, religious, and philosophical ideas. King James I had come to England claiming full power by the "Divine Right of Kings." He was "as God" to his subjects and claimed to hold over them the power of life and death. To the people this authority seemed a contradiction of their old laws and personal rights; they held that the law was supreme and that the king contracted with his subjects to see that the law was carried out. In the attempt to establish the precedent of early times, scholars and lawyers turned to a study of the Common Law. Many of the documents, however, were in Anglo-Saxon, and through long neglect that language had been completely lost. The restoration of the vocabulary and grammar is one of the most thrilling of all the miracles of literary achievement. From the likeness of Anglo-Saxon words to the Dutch and from the use of familiar materials, such as the Lord's Prayer and the Ten Commandments, or of the *Æneid* "Scottished," an understanding of the language finally emerged. Parliament, acting on the authority of the supremacy of the law established by this study, swept on to victory with the beheading of Charles I in 1649. To Milton this is "the age of ages, with God standing at the door." Diametrically opposed to this idea of the sovereignty of the law and the responsibility of the king in maintaining his part of the governmental contract is the idea set forth by Hobbes two years later in the *Leviathan*. To him the social contract does not mean mutual responsibility but the delegation, once and for all, of authority to a supreme power. To attain peace and security, the people must focus in the king all authority, both civil and religious, and merge all individual rights in the rights of this all-powerful state or *Leviathan* so established. Certainly Hobbes's theory seemed ratified by the failure of the Commonwealth. Hobbes held that man's nature is naturally evil and that the only check upon it is external law. Milton's explanation for the failure of the Commonwealth, however, is that the nation had not learned that true freedom lay in self-control through the dominance of the power of reason. The removal of external authority therefore led to the substitution of license for liberty. *Paradise Lost* is the literary interpretation of this age. Here Milton shows that true liberty in "right reason dwells," and that without the guidance of reason "all the upstart passions rise," snatching the reins of government in the individual life and bringing about a state of anarchy. Outer authority, he says, is only an indication of the loss of inner authority, the dominance of the rational. Others find an explanation for the chaotic conditions in the rise of the middle class and its insistence upon social equality, an advance which broke the order sustained by the "chain of being." The failure of the Commonwealth necessitated the Restoration, and it seemed that once more authority and the upper classes were dominant. But a nation that had beheaded a king could depose a king; and when the old conflict between authority and freedom was augmented by the fear of Catholicism and its implication of authority in religion, James II had to flee the kingdom. Meanwhile Locke added the support of his great name to the social contract theory, arguing that the supremacy lay in the will of the people. When William of Orange accomplished the bloodless revolution in 1688, the modern nation had already arisen and the major source of power lay in Parliament.

The Parliamentarians, who had fought to gain freedom from the authority of the king, fought also for liberty in religious beliefs and practices. They believed that men had a right to think for themselves in religion; but having overthrown the authority of the church, they themselves would have shown the very intolerance they had put down had not Cromwell restrained them. Under Cromwell general liberty of worship was sustained, including that of the Jews; intolerance was shown only to the Catholics, who represented the power of authority. This breadth of thought was not maintained after the Restoration, and Charles II introduced strict laws against the Dissenters. It was not until the Act of Toleration in 1689 that the separation of the church and the state advocated by Milton really came into being. Locke's *Letter Concerning Toleration* is another landmark in the development of modern thought in its logical distinctions between the provinces of civil government and religion. Beginning with 1689, freedom of worship was granted to all sects except the much-feared Catholics and the "heretical" Unitarians.

When we turn to the conflict between authority and freedom in philosophy, it is again Bacon who hurls the challenge. The first step in the advancement of thought is to rid oneself of all the prepossessions which arise from one's natural predisposition, whether racial or individual, from society and the accepted use of words, and from the accepted systems of philosophy. These he calls the Idols. Slowly, by the inductive method, one may then build up reality. Bacon, however, did not try to enter the theological realm. He kept the regions of reason and faith clearly separate, and so there could be no conflict; the end of reason was knowledge, but the end of faith was wonder. Hobbes, on the other hand, recognized only that to which the senses could testify. The only things which were real were the material. These realities were governed by mechanical laws which could be calculated and understood through the study of mathematics. Descartes, the great French philosopher who shaped much of English thought, started, like Bacon, with the principle that one should doubt all things. He conceded a dual reality of matter and the soul, both of which could be rationally understood. In England much sympathy for the philosophy of Descartes and much opposition to that of Hobbes were found in the group called the Cambridge Platonists. They reconciled the duality of matter and spirit by giving reason the control over the lower realms. Reason is something more than the "Inner Light" of the Quakers or the "Witness of the indwelling Spirit" of the Puritans: it is the very spirit of God, found not in inspired revelation but in a moral law which should be the guiding principle of life. "To follow Reason is to follow God" is the summary of the faith of the Cambridge Platonists as stated by one of their number, John Smith. This belief found realistic expression in a life of positive goodness, recognized as more important than faith in any creed. Milton saw in this rational choice of the good a substitute for the state of innocent goodness in the Garden of Eden, a "Paradise within thee, happier far," and recognized as the "true wayfaring Christian" the one who could distinguish between good and evil and choose good even when his natural desires made evil pleasing to him. Locke approached even more nearly the modern point of view. He broke entirely with traditional knowledge and opinion and set forth the idea that all one can really know is what he learns through experience and his own intellectual effort.

Tools with which to work, freedom from tradition and authority, and confidence in intellectual power were the gifts of this century to mankind. With these in his possession he caught the vision of progress. It is difficult for the modern age to conceive of a time when man looked back to the days of ancient Greece and Rome as the period of perfection and felt that since then the world had been plunging on a downward career toward ultimate destruction. Such, however, was the belief until the changing thought of the seventeenth century prepared the ground for the conception of continuous development. To earlier centuries the increasing age of the world meant only growing remoteness from the vigor of youth. This idea had been fostered by the portrayal of the golden age in classical literature, and it was popularized through the revival of this literature during the Renaissance. The pastorals of Renaissance England are full of it, and Spenser's poetry shows how much it had become a part of the thought of the age. The Christian picture of the state of innocence before the fall of man became colored by the classical representation of the golden age and gained great popularity in Puritan England. The high point of its expression is in the beautiful portrayal of life in the Garden of Eden in *Paradise Lost*. The Puritans held that the process of degeneration had gone on steadily since the fall and would terminate in the destruction of the world. From the ashes would arise like the phœnix (one of the favorite figures of the seventeenth century) a new heaven and a new earth— a golden age to be anticipated in the future.

When James I was welcomed to the throne of England, the poets and pageant makers used the idea that now Astræa would return to earth and a new golden age would be ushered in. There were no remarkable changes, however, and it was soon apparent that after all it was only the "rusty iron age." To men who accepted the idea that they lived in the iron age and that they were not the equals of the ancients, there naturally came the doubt as to whether nature was still capable of producing men with as great ability, either physical or mental, as those of the past. Old tombs were opened and the bones measured, an experiment which established the fact that men had decreased in physical size. The result was that many believed that nature was losing her power and that not only was man degenerating but also that the universe was diminishing, and even that the very plants and animals were becoming smaller than in previous ages. The controversy over the decay of nature was so current in the reign of James I and the early years of Charles I that the question became the subject of books and was used for disputations in the universities. Bishop Goodman in 1616 wrote a book entitled *The Fall of Man, or the Corruption of Nature Proved by Natural Reason,* which was answered by George Hakewill in 1627 with *An Apologie or Declaration of the Power and Providence of God in the World.* Hakewill pointed out that belief in the Providence of God was irreconcilable with belief in the decay of nature. In the following year the subject of the decay of nature was used for disputation at Cambridge; and Milton, in writing the poetical treatment of the subject which was distributed among the audience, *Naturam Non Pati Senium,* argued on the negative.

With the growth of the new science it became apparent that new truths were constantly being reached. Discoveries and inventions were enabling man to attain heights that he had scarcely yet dreamed of. These were marshaled as proof that man was advancing beyond the achievements of the past. There also arose a sense of greater surety, for the laws of nature were found to be invariable and dependable, so that nature could be counted on to carry on her processes without alteration. In the light of the view that knowledge was to be used to meet human needs, man saw that through his own powers he could improve conditions, physical and social, and literally build a "new Jerusalem in England's green and pleasant land."

It was with exhilaration that the giant intellectuals attempted to prove themselves equal to the challenge of progress. There was an intensity of eagerness about their work and a spirit of cooperation in a great task that, together with unusual gifts of genius, proved sufficient to meet the demands that arose. With enthusiasm these men set out to enlarge their own mental horizons: Bacon, perceiving that "the sovereignty of man lieth hid in knowledge," reached forth to take all knowledge for his province; Crashaw wrote of the "large drafts of intellectual day"; and Donne acknowledged a "hydroptic, immoderate desire of human learning." In *The Harmony of the World* Kepler expressed the thankful exultation characteristic of these workers: "That . . . for which I have devoted the best part of my life to astronomical contemplations—at length I have brought to light, and recognized its truth beyond my most sanguine expectations." Traherne sums up the new idea: "From the centre to the utmost bounds of the everlasting hills all is Heaven before God, and full of treasure: and he that walks like God in the midst of them is blessed." [3]

Looking at the progress of this century, one questions why these developments could not have come in the other great age of scientific progress, the period between Pythagoras and Plato in Greece. The seventeenth century, however, fulfilled certain conditions necessary for further advance. There was a change in the type of reasoning: the Greeks turned to the philosophical inquiry of *why* things happen; the seventeenth century studied the more objective question of *how* things happen. Theory was, therefore, replaced by experiment. A convenient and quick system of notation to use in making astronomical computations or in interpreting other phenomena, a system which Greek mathematics had not provided, was developed; and, finally, instruments which made possible more accurate observations were produced. The extraordinary contribution of the century to the history of scientific thought lies back of all the progress in the period and was made possible by the achieve-

[3] *Century of Meditations*, IV, no. 37.

ments of such men as Copernicus, Galileo, Bacon, Harvey, Kepler, Toricelli, Boyle, and Newton. Throwing off the restraining bondage of authority of all sorts and cooperating in organized effort to increase human knowledge, the leaders in thought used the new tools for accuracy and the new standards of precise thought so effectively that they created the idea of progress and challenged succeeding centuries to move forward in invention, discovery, and thought.

CAREW SUMS up Donne's dual nature in the closing couplet of his *Elegy on Donne:*

> Here lie two Flamens, and both those the best:
> Apollo's first, at last the true God's priest.

In his young manhood Donne spent himself in a strange combination of gay profligacy and concentrated study; in his maturity he gave himself with equal intensity to winning the supremacy of the spirit over the ever-conflicting elements of his own nature. We can never understand him; but after more than three hundred years we still feel the spell of his abounding vitality, his dominating mind, and his spiritual perception. We can, therefore, realize how it was that the eccentric power of his poetry imprinted itself upon the verse of the younger poets throughout the century and how it was that the throngs in St. Paul's Cathedral were swayed and purified by his self-searching sermons. The devout dean who wished to garner in the poems of his young manhood to destroy them could not stop their course. Though very few had been published, and these without his consent, the poems had been widely circulated in manuscript, and their tang had already permeated the poems of other writers. It was not, however, until two years after Donne's death that his poems were collected and published.

Born into a Roman Catholic family of distinguished ancestry and considerable wealth, Donne had the training of a gentleman and money to satisfy his extravagant tastes. He had a tutor at home and then studied at Oxford for three years, where his inability to take the required oaths on account of his religion kept him from a degree. His never-sated thirst for learning already urging him on, he probably went to Cambridge for three additional years of study. Even so, he was still in his teens when he returned to London. Handsome, gay, and after he came of age, independently wealthy by the legacy of his father, he led a life of excesses and of

shifting aims. He dipped into law at Lincoln's Inn, gaining
at least legal figures for his poems; and he spent much time
in reading divinity, determined to settle for himself the rela-
tive truth of the Catholic and the Anglican beliefs. He knew
the zeal which the Catholic faith could stir and also its con-
sequences, for many members of his family had suffered
for their religion. In his own time his uncle had been im-
prisoned and then banished, and his brother Henry had died
as the result of imprisonment for his religion. But Donne
had to be intellectually satisfied. St. Augustine, Chrysostom,
and the rest appear as the carved figures of the Saints adorn-
ing some cathedral, and his dissipation as the fantastic gar-
goyles overhanging them.

The exact chronology of Donne's life during these years
is difficult to follow, but at some time between 1592 and
1596 he may have traveled on the Continent.[1] We do know
with some degree of certainty, however, his emotional history
for the period. This is expressed in strange pulsating poems
in which the thought and feeling tear their way through new
rhythms, destroying the smooth lyricism characteristic of
the Renaissance. The earliest dated poems are three satires
of 1593,[2] which, however, remained unpublished until 1633.
These and other early satires give Donne precedence over
Bishop Hall in this field. Donne's satires are portraits of
types; and though in obscurity and roughness they follow
the model of the youthful Latin satirist, Persius, they show
Donne's characteristic closeness of observation and realism
of treatment. His love poems record his free experimentation
in passionate love. Toward women he is utterly cynical;
they are all inconstant, man's torture and the satisfaction of
his passion; therefore he will range where he wills, variety
being "love's sweetest part."

The expedition of Essex to Cadiz afforded Donne both
an escape from a morass of infidelity and an opportunity for
adventure, and so in 1596 Donne was out of England from

[1] Gosse, *Life and Letters*, I, 55–7.
[2] *Ibid.*, p. 28.

June to August. In 1597 he again joined Essex, this time in the unsuccessful Azores Expedition. The expedition was handicapped at the very beginning by a violent storm, which for Donne resulted in a poem of graphic description sent back to his friend, Christopher Brooke. A companion poem, *The Calm,* was produced when the vessel reached the tropics. These two poems mark a departure in lyrical poetry, as they deal with actual details of a real experience. Apparently they made an impression on Ben Jonson, for more than twenty years afterwards, on his visit to Hawthornden, he quoted a part of *The Calm* to William Drummond.

Upon his return to England Donne secured the position of secretary to Sir Thomas Egerton, Lord Keeper of the Great Seal. He soon held an important place in the household, was sent abroad on missions of responsibility, and took part in the exciting events in which the Lord Keeper was involved at home, especially the events connected with the defection of Essex. He was also thrown into contact with Anne More, the niece of Lady Egerton and hostess for her uncle after Lady Egerton's death. The sudden love which Donne gave Anne was far more spiritual than any he had previously experienced. It lasted to the end of his life, giving him a steadfastness he had never before known; and it brought the realization that a love which satisfies is the union of spirit as well as body:

> Love's mysteries in souls do grow,
> But yet the body is his book.

In 1601 Donne's secret marriage to Anne put an end to his promising career. Anne's father was so enraged that he had Donne and the friends who had assisted in the marriage thrown into prison. He also influenced Egerton to dismiss Donne. Donne had spent his inheritance; and when he regained his freedom and Anne, there followed years of financial insecurity. At first they lived with relatives and then secured an uncomfortable little house in Mitcham. Donne himself spent much time in London trying to obtain an opening with some great patron suitable to his learning and ability. His now steadfast love did not prevent despair. Poverty, the continual sickness of a growing family, and delayed preferment weighed down his spirit; perhaps suicide was justifiable—probably during this time he wrote *Biathanatos*, a pamphlet justifying suicide under certain circumstances; perhaps America would offer a new start. Lady Herbert, the mother of George Herbert, found gracious ways to aid the family, and her encouragement sustained his spirit. During this time his knowledge of divinity enabled him to assist Bishop Morton in arguments against the Catholics. Impressed by Donne's great learning and abilities, Bishop Morton offered him an opening in the church, but in spite of his financial need he declined on the ground that his early life had unfitted him for such a calling.

When things were at the worst at Mitcham, a reconciliation was made with Donne's father-in-law, who agreed to furnish a regular allowance as Anne's dowry. Donne's mercurial spirits rose, and procuring suitable clothing to appear among his friends in high places, he again attempted to gain court preferment. At last, quite by chance, a way opened for at least temporary security. Donne won the patronage of Sir Robert Drury by writing an elegy on the death of his young daughter Elizabeth. Sir Robert removed Donne's entire family from the unhealthful Mitcham house to his own home in London. Later Donne accompanied Sir Robert and his wife to the Continent, though Anne, in ill health and depressed by forebodings, tried to dissuade him. To this parting belong *A Valediction Forbidding Mourning* and *Sweetest Love, I Do Not Go*. The intangible bond between Donne and Anne even in their separation is revealed by Donne's vision of Anne's passing through the room bearing a dead child in her arms. The vision was accounted for later when news came that the expected child had died at birth.

Donne returned to Drury House in 1612 and for a while seems to have been comfortable and happy. He was often with his friends, especially in the congenial group gathered around Lucy, Countess of Bedford, at Twickenham Garden. But sickness came and the loss of several children. Finally, when Donne thought surely to receive a place at court through the influence of a powerful patron, the king, who needed Donne's services for the Protestant cause, refused to prefer him in any field but the church. Donne did not immediately accept. His conscience still troubled him, and his faith had felt the impact of the new science. In his period of study in the 1590's he had recognized that truth could not be reached either easily or quickly:

> On a huge hill,
> Cragged and steep, Truth stands, and he that will
> Reach her, about must and about must go,
> And what the hill's suddenness resists win so.
> Yet strive so, that before age, death's twilight,
> Thy soul rest, for none can work in that night.

Donne turned to further study of divinity and after reaching the conclusion that "reason is our soul's left hand, faith her right," was ordained in 1615. He became the king's chaplain and was granted an honorary degree from Cambridge at the king's personal request. For six years he was a popular preacher at Lincoln's Inn, but he aspired to a higher position. Finally the king granted him the deanship of St. Paul's Cathedral.

Anne had died before Donne's ultimate success, and Donne, frequently in ill health, brooded upon death, a subject which had always had a peculiar fascination for him. He designed his own monument and posed for it wrapped in his winding sheet. He kept a painting of this design by his bedside as a perpetual reminder of death. Six weeks before his death he preached his last sermon, *Death's Duel*, and his congregation felt then that he was preaching his own funeral sermon.

Donne's later years were as burning with consecration as his early years with excesses, and all his religious moods are given in the *Holy Sonnets*. He had himself experienced joy in sin, and he had known the extreme agony of repentance. Out of his experience he poured forth his life to reach men as good and as bad as himself. Never fully at peace as was Herbert, whom he had finally won for the church, he constantly argued to rewin his own faith and tortured himself with the fear that his sin was not fully pardoned. He wanted to give his life completely to God, but unable to reach out with confidence, he pleaded with God violently to take possession:

> Batter my heart, three-personed God . . .
> That I may rise and stand, o'erthrow me . . .

His troubled mind, his constant study, and his unflagging zeal wore out a body spent with many sicknesses.

Donne's poetry covers a wide range of types: satires, verse letters, epithalamia, elegies, funeral elegies, lyrics, and divine poems. Of these the most interesting are the love lyrics and the divine poems. Observing his own complex psychology in love and religion, Donne gives in these poems an accurate and realistic portrayal of a variety of moods. He widens the range of love poetry, for he revolts against the Petrarchan convention of idealized love and presents all the conflicting moods of a lover. His analysis of emotional states does not, however, follow the experience; it is a part of it. Emotion and mind seem to work simultaneously, so that even while Donne enjoys or suffers, his keen, quick mind observes and analyzes. T. S. Eliot has compared this state to that of a penitent in the confessional,[3] but Donne has more accurately described it in his phrase, "a naked, thinking heart."

Donne's poetry has many characteristics which are commonly termed "metaphysical." In his life of Cowley, Dr. Johnson gives as the dominant characteristic of metaphysical poetry *"discordia concors;* a combination of dissimilar images or discovery of occult resemblances in things apparently un-

[3] The Percy Turnbull Lectures on Poetry at the Johns Hopkins University, 1933.

like." Donne often produces a mental shock by the odd analogies which he uses, yet his figures are never mere adornment or a conscious exercise of intellectual ingenuity as in the poems of some of his followers; they are the spontaneous expression of his strange and fertile mind. Sometimes his conceits are condensed and enumerated until the mind is taxed by the quick transition from one likeness to another; again they are expanded, as in *A Lecture upon the Shadow,* to the farthest extent Donne's agile wit can push them, and the mind is wearied in pursuing the subtle line of reasoning. These figures are new in material as well as in treatment, for they are not drawn from mythology or sense experience but from Donne's wide reading and his contemporary interests. Donne's exuberant spirit sometimes led him into hyperbole and paradox but frequently resulted in figures of great imaginative stimulation.

In form Donne was frankly experimenting, as his wide structural variety shows. He was deliberately turning away from Elizabethan sweetness and searching for a medium identical in tone with the content. Always dramatic, he frequently startles one into attention. Sometimes he gains his effect by an abrupt beginning, sometimes by a surprising analogy, and again by harsh metrical effects. Especially in the last he reminds one of Browning, who was a great admirer of Donne's poetry.

Though we may analyze in detail the qualities of Donne, we cannot explain his full power. Emotional force, intellectual vitality, and strangeness of style all have their share, but there are flashes of imagination that open up whole vistas of perception and rich harmonies that beat out their peculiar rhythms, which cannot be analyzed. We are sometimes forced to agree with both of Ben Jonson's famous comments: "He esteemeth John Donne the first poet in the world in some things," [4] and "That Donne, for not keeping of accent, deserved hanging"; [5] yet Donne's very phrasing and rhythm

[4] *Conversations,* ed. Laing, VII.
[5] *Ibid.,* I.

seem a part of the vigor and intensity of their author, and dissonance, as well as harmony, forms a part of his perennial fascination.

Song

Go and catch a falling star,
　Get with child a mandrake root,[1]
Tell me where all past years are,
　Or who cleft the devil's foot,
Teach me to hear mermaids singing,[2]
Or to keep off envy's stinging,
　　　　And find
　　　　What wind
Serves to advance an honest mind.

If thou beest born to strange sights,　　　10
　Things invisible to see,
Ride ten thousand days and nights,
　Till age snow white hairs on thee;
Thou, when thou return'st, will tell me
All strange wonders that befell thee,
　　　　And swear
　　　　No where
Lives a woman true and fair.

If thou find'st one, let me know;
　Such a pilgrimage were sweet.　　　20
Yet do not; I would not go,
　Though at next door we might meet.
Though she were true when you met her,
And last till you write your letter,
　　　　Yet she
　　　　Will be
False, ere I come, to two or three.

[1] The mandrake root is forked and therefore supposed to resemble the human body.
[2] The sirens are here identified with the mermaids.

The Indifferent

I can love both fair and brown;
Her whom abundance melts, and her whom want betrays;
Her who loves loneness best, and her who masks and plays;
Her whom the country formed, and whom the town;
Her who believes, and her who tries;
Her who still weeps with spongy eyes,
And her who is dry cork and never cries.
I can love her, and her, and you, and you;
I can love any, so she be not true.

Will no other vice content you?   10
Will it not serve your turn to do as did your mothers?
Or have you all old vices spent, and now would find out
    others?
Or doth a fear that men are true torment you?
Oh, we are not; be not you so;
Let me, and do you, twenty know.
Rob me, but bind me not, and let me go.
Must I, who came to travail thorough you,
Grow your fixed subject because you are true?

Venus heard me sigh this song,
And by love's sweetest part, variety, she swore   20
She heard not this till now, and that it should be so no more.
She went, examined, and returned ere long,
And said, "Alas, some two or three
Poor heretics in love there be,
Which think to 'stablish dangerous constancy.
But I have told them, 'Since you will be true,
You shall be true to them who are false to you.'"

Woman's Constancy

Now thou hast loved me one whole day,
    To-morrow when thou leavest, what wilt thou say?

Wilt thou then antedate some new-made vow?
        Or say that now
We are not just those persons which we were?
Or that oaths made in reverential fear
Of Love, and his wrath, any may forswear?
Or, as true deaths true marriages untie,
So lovers' contracts, images of those,
Bind but till sleep, death's image, them unloose?   10
        Or, your own end to justify,
For having purposed change and falsehood, you
Can have no way but falsehood to be true?
Vain lunatic, against these 'scapes I could
        Dispute, and conquer, if I would;
        Which I abstain to do,
For by to-morrow I may think so too.

The Legacy

When I died last, and, dear, I die
As often as from thee I go,
Though it be but an hour ago,
And lover's hours be full eternity,
I can remember yet that I
Something did say, and something did bestow;
Though I be dead, which sent me, I should be
Mine own executor and legacy.

I heard me say, "Tell her anon,
That my self," (that is you, not I)   10
"Did kill me, and when I felt me die,
I bid me send my heart when I was gone,
But I alas, could there find none,
When I had ripped me and searched where
        hearts did lie;"
It killed me again, that I who still was true
In life, in my last will should cozen you.

' Yet I found something like a heart,
But colors it, and corners had;
It was not good, it was not bad,
It was entire to none, and few had part.   20
As good as could be made by art
It seemed; and therefore for our losses sad,
I meant to send this heart instead of mine,
But oh, no man could hold it, for 'twas thine.

The Message

Send home my long-strayed eyes to me,
Which, oh, too long have dwelt on thee;
Yet since there they have learned such ill,
            Such forced fashions,
            And false passions,
                  That they be
                  Made by thee
Fit for no good sight, keep them still.

Send home my harmless heart again,
Which no unworthy thought could stain;   10
But if it be taught by thine
            To make jestings
            Of protestings,
                  And cross both
                  Word and oath,
Keep it, for then 'tis none of mine.

Yet send me back my heart and eyes
That I may know and see thy lies,
And may laugh and joy, when thou
            Art in anguish   20
            And dost languish
                  For some one
                  That will none,
Or prove as false as thou art now.

Love's Deity

I long to talk with some old lover's ghost,
  Who died before the god of love was born.
I cannot think that he, who then loved most,
  Sunk so low as to love one which did scorn.
But since this god produced a destiny,
And that vice-nature, custom, lets it be,
  I must love her that loves not me.

Sure, they which made him god meant not so much,
  Nor he in his young godhead practiced it;
But when an even flame two hearts did touch,   10
  His office was indulgently to fit
Actives to passives. Correspondency
Only his subject was; it cannot be
  Love till I love her that loves me.

But every modern god will now extend
  His vast prerogative as far as Jove.
To rage, to lust, to write to, to commend,
  All is the purlieu of the god of love.
Oh, were we wakened by this tyranny
To ungod this child again, it could not be   20
  I should love her who loves not me.

Rebel and atheist too, why murmur I,
  As though I felt the worst that love could do?
Love might make me leave loving, or might try
  A deeper plague, to make her love me too;
Which, since she loves before, I am loth to see.
Falsehood is worse than hate; and that must be
  If she whom I love should love me.

The Ecstasy

Where, like a pillow on a bed,
  A pregnant bank swelled up to rest

The violet's reclining head,
   Sat we two, one another's best.
Our hands were firmly cemented
   With a fast balm, which thence did spring;
Our eye-beams twisted, and did thread
   Our eyes upon one double string.
So to entergraft our hands, as yet
   Was all the means to make us one;   10
And pictures in our eyes to get
   Was all our propagation.
As, 'twixt two equal armies, fate
   Suspends uncertain victory,
Our souls, which to advance their state
   Were gone out, hung 'twixt her and me.
And whilst our souls negotiate there,
   We like sepulchral statues lay;
All day, the same our postures were,
   And we said nothing, all the day.   20
If any, so by love refined
   That he soul's language understood,
And by good love were grown all mind,
   Within convenient distance stood,
He, though he knew not which soul spake,
   Because both meant, both spake, the same,
Might thence a new concoction take,
   And part far purer than he came.
This ecstasy doth unperplex
   (We said) and tell us what we love;   30
We see by this it was not sex;
   We see, we saw not what did move;
But as all several souls contain
   Mixture of things, they know not what,
Love these mixed souls doth mix again
   And makes both one, each this and that.
A single violet transplant,
   The strength, the color, and the size,
All which before was poor and scant,

Redoubles still and multiplies. 40
When love with one another so
 Interinanimates two souls,
That abler soul, which thence doth flow,
 Defects of loneliness controls.
We then, who are this new soul, know
 Of what we are composed and made,
For the atomies of which we grow
 Are souls, whom no change can invade.
But, O alas! so long, so far,
 Our bodies why do we forbear? 50
They are ours, though they are not we; we are
 The intelligences, they the sphere.[1]
We owe them thanks, because they thus
 Did us, to us, at first convey,
Yielded their forces, sense, to us,
 Nor are dross to us, but allay.
On man heaven's influence works not so,
 But that it first imprints the air; [2]
So soul into the soul may flow,
 Though it to body first repair. 60
As our blood labors to beget
 Spirits, as like souls as it can,
Because such fingers need to knit
 That subtle knot which makes us man,
So must pure lovers' souls descend
 To affections, and to faculties,
Which sense may reach and apprehend;
 Else a great prince in prison lies.
To our bodies turn we then, that so
 Weak men on love revealed may look; 70
Love's mysteries in souls do grow,
 But yet the body is his book.

[1] According to medieval teaching the heavenly bodies were moved by "intelligences," which controlled them.

[2] In the old astrological conceptions the air transmitted the influence of the stars. The body, says Donne, serves as a like medium for the soul.

And if some lover, such as we,
  Have heard this dialogue of one,
Let him still mark us; he shall see
  Small change when we are to bodies gone.

Lovers' Infiniteness

If yet I have not all thy love,
Dear, I shall never have it all;
I cannot breathe one other sigh to move,
Nor can entreat one other tear to fall;
And all my treasure, which should purchase thee,
Sighs, tears, and oaths, and letters, I have spent.
Yet no more can be due to me
Than at the bargain made was meant;
If then thy gift of love were partial,
That some to me, some should to others fall,   10
  Dear, I shall never have thee all.

Or if then thou gavest me all,
All was but all which thou hadst then;
But if in thy heart since there be or shall
New love created be by other men,
Which have their stocks entire, and can in tears,
In sighs, in oaths, and letters outbid me,
This new love may beget new fears,
For this love was not vowed by thee.
And yet it was, thy gift being general;   20
The ground, thy heart, is mine; whatever shall
  Grow there, dear, I should have it all.

Yet I would not have all yet.
He that hath all can have no more;
And since my love doth every day admit
New growth, thou shouldst have new rewards in store.
Thou canst not every day give me thy heart;
If thou canst give it, then thou never gavest it.

Love's riddles are, that though thy heart depart,
It stays at home, and thou with losing savest it.[1]   30
But we will have a way more liberal
Than changing hearts, to join them; so we shall
    Be one, and one another's all.

The Anniversary

All kings, and all their favorites,
    All glory of honors, beauties, wits,
The sun itself, which makes times, as they pass,
Is elder by a year now than it was
When thou and I first one another saw.
All other things to their destruction draw,
    Only our love hath no decay;
This no to-morrow hath, nor yesterday;
Running, it never runs from us away,
But truly keeps his first, last, everlasting day.   10

Two graves must hide thine and my corse;
    If one might, death were no divorce.
Alas, as well as other princes, we,
Who prince enough in one another be,
Must leave at last in death these eyes and ears,
Oft fed with true oaths, and with sweet salt tears;
    But souls where nothing dwells but love,
All other thoughts being inmates, then shall prove
This, or a love increased there above,
When bodies to their graves, souls from their graves, re-
    move.   20

And then we shall be thoroughly blest,
    But we no more than all the rest;
Here upon earth we are kings, and none but we
Can be such kings, nor of such subjects be.

[1] "Whosoever shall seek to save his life shall lose it; and whosoever shall lose his life shall preserve it." *Luke* 17:33.

Who is so safe as we? where none can do
Treason to us, except one of us two.
　　True and false fears let us refrain;
Let us love nobly, and live, and add again
Years and years unto years, till we attain
To write threescore: this is the second of our reign.　　30

The Good-Morrow

I wonder, by my troth, what thou and I
Did till we loved? were we not weaned till then,
But sucked on country pleasures, childishly?
Or snorted we in the seven sleepers' den? [1]
'Twas so; but this, all pleasures fancies be.
If ever any beauty I did see,
Which I desired, and got, 'twas but a dream of thee.

And now good-morrow to our waking souls,
Which watch not one another out of fear;
For love all love of other sights controls,　　10
And makes one little room an everywhere.
Let sea-discoverers to new worlds have gone;
Let maps to other, worlds on worlds have shown;
Let us possess one world; each hath one, and is one.
My face in thine eye, thine in mine appears,
And true plain hearts do in the faces rest;
Where can we find two better hemispheres
Without sharp north, without declining west?
Whatever dies, was not mixed equally;
If our two loves be one, or thou and I　　20
Love so alike that none do slacken, none can die. [2]

[1] According to legend seven young men of Ephesus, who hid in a cave to escape the persecution of the Christians by Decius, slept on there for two hundred years.

[2] Grierson's note explains ll. 19–21: "If our two loves are *one,* dissolution is impossible; and the same is true if, though *two,* they are always alike. What is simple—as God or the soul—cannot be dissolved; nor compounds, e. g., the Heavenly bodies, between whose elements there is no contrariety."

The Canonization

For God's sake hold your tongue, and let me love;
  Or chide my palsy, or my gout;
  My five gray hairs, or ruined fortune flout;
With wealth your state, your mind with arts improve;
  Take you a course, get you a place,
  Observe his honor, or his grace;
Or the king's real, or his stamped face [1]
  Contemplate; what you will, approve,
  So you will let me love.

Alas! alas! who's injured by my love?   10
  What merchant's ships have my sighs drowned?
  Who says my tears have overflowed his ground?
When did my colds a forward spring remove?
  When did the heats which my veins fill
  Add one more to the plaguy bill?
Soldiers find wars, and lawyers find out still
  Litigious men, which quarrels move,
  Though she and I do love.

Call us what you will, we are made such by love;
  Call her one, me another fly;   20
  We're tapers too, and at our own cost die,
And we in us find the eagle and the dove.
  The phœnix riddle hath more wit
  By us; we two being one, are it.
So, to one neutral thing both sexes fit;
  We die and rise the same, and prove
  Mysterious by this love.

We can die by it, if not live by love,
  And if unfit for tomb or hearse
  Our legend be, it will be fit for verse;   30
And if no piece of chronicle we prove,

[1] The king's face appears on the currency.

We'll build in sonnets pretty rooms;
   As well a well-wrought urn becomes
The greatest ashes, as half-acre tombs,
   And by these hymns all shall approve
   Us canonized for love;

And thus invoke us: "You, whom reverend love
   Made one another's hermitage;
   You, to whom love was peace, that now is rage;
Who did the whole world's soul contract, and drove   40
   Into the glasses of your eyes
   (So made such mirrors, and such spies,
That they did all to you epitomize)
   Countries, towns, courts: beg from above
   A pattern of your love."

The Undertaking

I have done one braver thing
   Than all the worthies did,
And yet a braver thence doth spring,
   Which is, to keep that hid.

It were but madness now to impart
   The skill of specular stone,
When he which can have learned the art
   To cut it, can find none.

So if I now should utter this,
   Others, because no more   10
Such stuff to work upon there is,
   Would love but as before.

But he who loveliness within
   Hath found, all outward loathes,
For he who color loves, and skin,
   Loves but their oldest clothes.

If, as I have, you also do
    Virtue attired in woman see,
And dare love that, and say so too,
    And forget the he and she;   20

And if this love, though placed so,
    From profane men you hide,
Which will no faith on this bestow,
    Or, if they do, deride;

Then you have done a braver thing
    Than all the worthies did;
And a braver thence will spring,
    Which is, to keep that hid.

Elegy XVII

On His Mistress

By our first strange and fatal interview,
By all desires which thereof did ensue,
By our long starving hopes, by that remorse
Which my words' masculine persuasive force
Begot in thee, and by the memory
Or hurts which spies and rivals threatened me,
I calmly beg; but by thy father's wrath,
By all pains, which want and divorcement hath,
I conjure thee; and all the oaths which I
And thou have sworn to seal joint constancy,   10
Here I unswear, and overswear them thus:
Thou shalt not love by ways so dangerous.
Temper, O fair love, love's impetuous rage,
Be my true mistress still, not my feigned page;
I'll go, and by thy kind leave, leave behind
Thee, only worthy to nurse in my mind
Thirst to come back; oh, if thou die before,

My soul from other lands to thee shall soar.
Thy else almighty beauty cannot move
Rage from the seas, nor thy love teach them love,   20
Nor tame wild Boreas' harshness; thou hast read
How roughly he in pieces shivered
Fair Orithyia,[1] whom he swore he loved.
Fall ill or good, 'tis madness to have proved
Dangers unurged; feed on this flattery,
That absent lovers one in the other be.
Dissemble nothing, not a boy, nor change
Thy body's habit, nor mind's; be not strange
To thyself only; all will spy in thy face
A blushing womanly discovering grace.   30
Richly clothed apes are called apes; and as soon
Eclipsed as bright, we call the moon the moon.
Men of France, changeable chameleons,
Spitals [2] of diseases, shops of fashions,
Love's fuellers, and the rightest company
Of players which upon the world's stage be,
Will quickly know thee, and no less, alas!
The indifferent Italian, as we pass
His warm land, well content to think thee page,
Will hunt thee with lust and hideous rage   40
As Lot's fair guests were vexed. But none of these,
Nor spongy hydroptic Dutch shall thee displease,
If thou stay here. Oh, stay here! for, for thee,
England is only a worthy gallery
To walk in expectation, till from thence
Our greatest King call thee to his presence.
When I am gone, dream me some happiness,
Nor let thy looks our long hid love confess,
Nor praise, nor dispraise me, nor bless nor curse
Openly love's force, nor in bed fright thy nurse   50
With midnight's startings, crying out, Oh, oh,

[1] Unable to sigh gently as a lover should, Boreas, the north wind, roughly seized the nymph and bore her away to his home.
[2] Hospitals.

Nurse, oh, my love is slain, I saw him go
O'er the white Alps alone; I saw him, I,
Assailed, fight, taken, stabbed, bleed, fall, and die.
Augur me better chance, except dread Jove
Think it enough for me to have had thy love.

Song

Sweetest love, I do not go
  For weariness of thee,[1]
Nor in hope the world can show
  A fitter love for me;
    But since that I
Must die at last, 'tis best,
To use myself in jest
    Thus by feigned deaths to die.

Yesternight the sun went hence,
  And yet is here to-day;   10
He hath no desire nor sense,
  Nor half so short a way.
    Then fear not me,
But believe that I shall make
Speedier journeys, since I take
    More wings and spurs than he.

O how feeble is man's power,
  That if good fortune fall,
Cannot add another hour,
  Nor a lost hour recall!   20
    But come bad chance,
And we join to it our strength,
And we teach it art and length,
    Itself o'er us to advance.

[1] Written to his wife upon the occasion of Donne's going to the Continent with the Drurys.

When thou sigh'st, thou sigh'st not wind,
  But sigh'st my soul away;
When thou weep'st, unkindly kind,
  My life's blood doth decay.
    It cannot be
That thou lov'st me as thou say'st,   30
If in thine my life thou waste;
  Thou art the best of me.

Let not thy divining heart
  Forethink me any ill; [1]
Destiny may take thy part,
  And may thy fears fulfil;
    But think that we
Are but turned aside to sleep;
They who one another keep
  Alive, ne'er parted be.   40

A Valediction Forbidding Mourning

As virtuous men pass mildly away,
  And whisper to their souls to go,
Whilst some of their sad friends do say,
  "The breath goes now," and some say, "No";

So let us melt, and make no noise,
  No tear-floods nor sigh-tempests move;
'Twere profanation of our joys
  To tell the laity our love.

Moving of the earth brings harms and fears;
  Men reckon what it did and meant;   10

[1] Walton says that Donne's wife held that "her divining soul boded *her* some ill in his absence"; her fears were fulfilled, for while Donne was away, she gave birth to a dead child.

But trepidation of the spheres,[1]
   Though greater far, is innocent.

Dull sublunary lovers' love,
   Whose soul is sense, cannot admit
Absence, because it doth remove
   Those things which elemented it.

But we, by a love so much refined
   That ourselves know not what it is,
Inter-assured of the mind,
   Care less eyes, lips, and hands to miss.   20

Our two souls, therefore, which are one,
   Though I must go, endure not yet
A breach, but an expansion,
   Like gold to airy thinness beat.

If they be two, they are two so
   As stiff twin compasses are two;
Thy soul, the fixed foot, makes no show
   To move, but doth if the other do.

And though it in the center sit,
   Yet when the other far doth roam,   30
It leans, and hearkens after it,
   And grows erect as that comes home.

Such wilt thou be to me, who must,
   Like the other foot, obliquely run;
Thy firmness makes my circle just,
   And makes me end where I begun.

The Funeral

Whoever comes to shroud me, do not harm,
   Nor question much,

[1] The reference is to the explanation of the harmless variation in date of the equinox under the Ptolemaic system.

That subtle wreath of hair which crowns my arm;
The mystery, the sign you must not touch;
    For 'tis my outward soul,
Viceroy to that, which, then to heaven being gone,
    Will leave this to control,
And keep these limbs, her provinces, from dissolution.

For if the sinewy thread my brain lets fall
    Through every part   10
Can tie those parts, and make me one of all,
These hairs which upward grew, and strength and art
    Have from a better brain,
Can better do it; except she meant that I
    By this should know my pain,
As prisoners then are manacled, when they are condemned
        to die.

Whate'er she meant by it, bury it with me,
    For since I am
Love's martyr, it might breed idolatry
If into others' hands these reliques came.   20
    As 'twas humility
To afford to it all that a soul can do,
    So 'tis some bravery
That since you would save none of me, I bury some of you.

The Relique

When my grave is broke up again
Some second guest to entertain,
    (For graves have learned that woman-head
    To be to more than one a bed)
      And he that digs it, spies
A bracelet of bright hair about the bone,
    Will he not let us alone,
And think that there a loving couple lies,
Who thought that this device might be some way

To make their souls, at the last busy day,　　　10
Meet at this grave, and make a little stay?

If this fall in a time, or land,
Where mis-devotion doth command,
Then he that digs us up will bring
Us to the bishop and the king,
To make us reliques; then
Thou shalt be a Mary Magdalen, and I
A something else thereby;
All women shall adore us, and some men;
And since at such time, miracles are sought,　　　20
I would have that age by this paper taught
What miracles we harmless lovers wrought.

First, we loved well and faithfully,
Yet knew not what we loved nor why;
Difference of sex no more we knew,
Than our guardian angels do;
Coming and going, we
Perchance might kiss, but not between those meals;
Our hands ne'er touched the seals,
Which nature, injured by late law, sets free:　　　30
These miracles we did; but now alas,
All measure and all language I should pass,
Should I tell what a miracle she was.

Twicknam Garden [1]

Blasted with sighs, and surrounded with tears,
Hither I come to seek the spring,
And at mine eyes, and at mine ears,
Receive such balms as else cure everything;
But oh, self traitor, I do bring

[1] The country house of Lucy, Countess of Bedford, at Twickenham
is probably meant.

The spider love, which transubstantiates all,
    And can convert manna to gall;
And that this place may thoroughly be thought
    True paradise, I have the serpent brought.

'Twere wholesomer for me that winter did   10
    Benight the glory of this place,
    And that a grave frost did forbid
These trees to laugh and mock me to my face;
    But that I may not this disgrace
Endure, nor yet leave loving, Love, let me
    Some senseless piece of this place be;
Make me a mandrake, so I may groan here,
    Or a stone fountain weeping out my year.

Hither with crystal vials, lovers, come
    And take my tears, which are love's wine,   20
    And try your mistress' tears at home,
For all are false that taste not just like mine;
    Alas, hearts do not in eyes shine,
Nor can you more judge woman's thoughts by tears,
    Than by her shadow what she wears.
O perverse sex, where none is true but she,
    Who's therefore true, because her truth kills me.

A Fever

Oh, do not die, for I shall hate
    All women so, when thou art gone,
That thee I shall not celebrate
    When I remember thou wast one.

But yet thou canst not die I know;
    To leave this world behind is death;
But when thou from this world wilt go,
    The whole world vapors with thy breath.

Or if, when thou, the world's soul, goest,
   It stay, 'tis but thy carcass then;   10
The fairest woman, but thy ghost;
   But corrupt worms, the worthiest men.

O wrangling schools that search what fire
   Shall burn this world, had none the wit
Unto this knowledge to aspire,
   That this her fever might be it?

And yet she cannot waste by this,
   Nor long bear this torturing wrong,
For much corruption needful is
   To fuel such a fever long.   20

These burning fits but meteors be,
   Whose matter in thee is soon spent.
Thy beauty, and all parts, which are thee,
   Are unchangeable firmament.

Yet 'twas of my mind, seizing thee,
   Though it in thee cannot persever;
For I had rather owner be
   Of thee one hour, than all else ever.

An Anatomy of the World [1]

The First Anniversary

There is not now that mankind, which was then,
When as the sun and man did seem to strive
(Joint tenants of the world) who should survive;
When stag, and raven, and the long-lived tree,

---

[1] This poem was written to commemorate the death of Elizabeth Drury and is important as an expression of the idea of the decay of the world and of the skepticism aroused by the new science. The first 111 lines, with their fulsome flattery of Elizabeth Drury, are omitted.

Compared with man, died in minority;
When if a slow-paced star had stolen away
From the observer's marking, he might stay
Two or three hundred years to see it again,
And then make up his observation plain;
When, as the age was long, the size was great;   10
Man's growth confessed, and recompensed the meat;
So spacious and large that every soul
Did a fair kingdom and large realm control;
And when the very stature, thus erect,
Did that soul a good way towards heaven direct.
Where is that mankind now? who lives to age,
Fit to be made Methusalem his page?
Alas! we scarce live long enough to try
Whether a true made clock run right, or lie.
Old grandsires talk of yesterday with sorrow,   20
And for our children we reserve to-morrow.
So short is life that every peasant strives,
In a torn house, or field, to have three lives.
And, as in lasting, so in length is man
Contracted to an inch, who was a span;
For had a man at first in forests strayed,
Or shipwrecked in the sea, one would have laid
A wager that an elephant or whale
That met him, would not hastily assail
A thing so equal to him; now alas,   30
The fairies and the pigmies well may pass
As credible; mankind decays so soon,
We are scarce our father's shadows cast at noon;
Only death adds to our length; nor are we grown
In stature to be men, till we are none.
But this were light, did our less volume hold
All the old text; or had we changed to gold
Their silver; or disposed into less glass
Spirits of virtue, which then scattered was.
But 'tis not so: we are not retired, but damped;   40
And as our bodies, so our minds are cramped;

'Tis shrinking, not close weaving that hath thus,
In mind and body both bedwarfed us.[2]
We seem ambitious God's whole work to undo;
Of nothing He made us, and we strive too,
To bring ourselves to nothing back; and we
Do what we can to do't so soon as He:
With new diseases on ourselves we war,
And with new physic, a worse engine far.
Thus man, this world's vice-emperor, in whom   50
All faculties, all graces are at home
(And if in other creatures they appear,
They're but man's ministers, and legates there,
To work on their rebellions and reduce
Them to civility, and to man's use),
This man, whom God did woo, and loth to attend
Till man came up, did down to man descend;
This man, so great, that all that is, is his,
Oh, what a trifle, and poor thing he is!
If man were anything, he's nothing now;   60
Help, or at least some time to waste, allow
To his other wants, yet when he did depart
With her whom we lament, he lost his heart.
She, of whom the ancients seemed to prophesy,
When they called virtue by the name of *she;*
She, in whom virtue was so much refined
That for allay [3] unto so pure a mind
She took the weaker sex; she that could drive
The poisonous tincture and the stain of Eve
Out of her thoughts and deeds, and purify   70
All by a true religious alchemy;
She, she is dead; she's dead: when thou knowest this,

----

[2] In the first quarter of the century this theory of the decay of the world engrossed many minds. The discussion became so popular that the subject was used for debate at both universities. Milton's *Naturam non pati senium* furnishes the poetical illustration for a fellow-student's disputation. Books were written arguing the subject and philosophic opinion was divided.

[3] Alloy.

Thou knowest how poor a trifling thing man is,
And learn'st thus much by our anatomy,
The heart being perished, no part can be free,
And that except thou feed (not banquet) on
The supernatural food, religion,
Thy better growth grows withered and scant;
Be more than man, or thou'rt less than an ant.
Then, as mankind, so is the world's whole frame   80
Quite out of joint, almost created lame:
For before God had made all the rest,
Corruption entered, and depraved the best;
It seized the angels, and then first of all
The world did in her cradle take a fall,
And turned her brains, and took a general maim,
Wronging each joint of the universal frame.
The noblest part, man, felt it first; and then
Both beasts and plants, cursed in the curse of man.
So did the world from the first hour decay;   90
That evening was beginning of the day,
And now the springs and summers which we see,
Like sons of women after fifty be.
And new philosophy calls all in doubt,[4]
The element of fire is quite put out;
The sun is lost, and the earth; and no man's wit
Can well direct him where to look for it.
And freely men confess that this world's spent,
When in the planets and the firmament
They seek so many new; then see that this   100
Is crumbled out again to his atomies.
'Tis all in pieces, all coherence gone;
All just supply and all relation:

[4] "Copernicus' displacement of the earth, and the consequent dis-
turbance of the accepted mediaeval cosmology with its concentric
arrangement of elements and heavenly bodies, arrests and disturbs
Donne's imagination much as the later geology with its revelation
of vanished species and first suggestion of a doctrine of evolution
absorbed and perturbed Tennyson when he wrote *In Memoriam* and
throughout his life." (Grierson, I, 188–9).

Prince, subject, father, son are things forgot,
For every man alone thinks he hath got
To be a phœnix, and that there can be
None of that kind of which he is, but he.
This the world's condition now, and now
She that should all parts to reunion bow,
She that had all magnetic force alone,   110
To draw, and fasten sundered parts in one;
She whom wise nature had invented then
When she observed that every sort of men
Did in their voyage in this world's sea stray,
And needed a new compass for their way;
She that was best and first original
Of all fair copies, and the general
Steward to fate; she whose rich eyes and breast
Gilt the West Indies, and perfumed the East;
Whose having breathed in this world did bestow   120
Spice on those isles, and bade them still smell so,
And that rich Indy, which doth gold inter,
Is but as single money, coined from her;
She to whom this world must itself refer,
As suburbs, or the microcosm of her,
She, she is dead; she's dead: when thou know'st this,
Thou know'st how lame a cripple this world is;
And learn'st thus much by our anatomy,
That this world's general sickness doth not lie
In any humor, or one certain part;   130
But as thou sawest it rotten at the heart,
Thou seest a hectic fever hath got hold
Of the whole substance, not to be controlled,
And that thou hast but one way, not to admit
The world's infection, to be none of it.
For the world's subtlest immaterial parts
Feel this consuming wound and age's darts.
For the world's beauty is decayed, or gone,
Beauty, that's color and proportion.
We think the heavens enjoy their spherical,   140

Their round perfection embracing all,
But yet their various and perplexed course,
Observed in divers ages, doth enforce
Men to find out so many eccentric parts,
Such divers down-right lines, such overthwarts,
As disproportion that pure form; it tears
The firmament in eight and forty shires,
And in these constellations then arise
New stars,[5] and old do vanish from our eyes;
As though heaven suffered earthquakes, peace, or war,   150
When new towers rise, and old demolished are.
They have impaled within a zodiac
The free-born sun, and keep twelve signs awake
To watch his steps; the Goat and Crab control,
And fright him back, who else to either pole
(Did not these tropics fetter him) might run:
For his course is not round; nor can the sun
Perfect a circle, or maintain his way
One inch direct; but where he rose to-day
He comes no more, but with a cozening line,   160
Steals by that point, and so is serpentine;
And seeming weary with his reeling thus,
He means to sleep, being now fallen nearer us.
So, of the stars which boast that they do run
In circle still, none ends where he begun:
All their proportion's lame; it sinks, it swells;
For of meridians, and parallels,
Man hath weaved out a net, and this net thrown
Upon the heavens, and now they are his own.
Loth to go up the hill, or labor thus   170
To go to heaven, we make heaven come to us.
We spur, we rein the stars, and in their race
They're diversely content to obey our pace.
But keeps the earth her round proportion still?
Doth not a Teneriffe or higher hill

[5] The appearance of a new star in Ophiuchus in 1604 created considerable excitement.

Rise so high like a rock that one might think
The floating moon would shipwreck there and sink?
Seas are so deep that whales being struck to-day,
Perchance to-morrow, scarce at middle way
Of their wished journey's end, the bottom, die: 180
And men, to sound depths, so much line untie,
As one might justly think that there would rise
At end thereof, one of the antipodes.
If under all, a vault infernal be,
(Which sure is spacious, except that we
Invent another torment, that there must
Millions into a straight hot room be thrust)
Then solidness and roundness have no place.
Are these but warts and pock-holes in the face
Of the earth? Think so; but yet confess, in this   190
The world's proportion disfigured is;
That those two legs whereon it doth rely,
Reward and punishment, are bent awry.
And, oh! it can no more be questioned,
That beauty's best, proportion, is dead,
Since even grief itself, which now alone
Is left us, is without proportion.
She by whose lines proportion should be
Examined, measure of all symmetry,
Whom had that ancient seen, who thought souls made   200
Of harmony,[6] he would at next have said
That harmony was she, and thence infer
That souls were but resultances from her,
And did from her into our bodies go,
As to our eyes the forms from objects flow;
She, who if those great Doctors truly said
That the ark to man's proportions was made,
Had been a type for that, as that might be
A type of her in this, that contrary

[6] The doctrine of the harmony of the soul was attributed to Pythagoras. Probably "that ancient" is Aristoxenus, the musician, who we learn from Cicero held that the soul is a harmony.

Both elements, and passions lived at peace   210
In her, who caused all civil war to cease;
She, after whom, what form soe'er we see,
Is discord and rude incongruity;
She, she is dead, she's dead; when thou know'st this,
Thou know'st how ugly a monster this world is;
And learn'st thus much by our anatomy,
That here is nothing to enamor thee;
And that not only faults in inward parts,
Corruptions in our brains, or in our hearts,
Poisoning the fountains whence our actions spring,   220
Endanger us; but if that everything
Be not done fitly and in proportion,
To satisfy wise and good lookers on,
(Since most men be such as most think they be)
They're loathsome too, by this deformity.
For good and well must in our actions meet;
Wicked is not much worse than indiscreet.
But beauty's other second element,
Color and luster, now is as near spent.
And had the world his just proportion,   230
Were it a ring still, yet the stone is gone.
As a compassionate turquoise which doth tell
By looking pale, the wearer is not well,
As gold falls sick being stung with mercury,
All the world's parts of such complexion be.
When nature was most busy, the first week,
Swaddling the new-born earth, God seemed to like
That she should sport herself sometimes, and play,
To mingle and vary colors every day;
And then, as though she could not make enow,   240
Himself His various rainbow did allow.
Sight is the noblest sense of any one;
Yet sight hath only color to feed on,
And color is decayed: summer's robe grows
Dusky, and like an oft dyed garment shows.
Our blushing red, which used in cheeks to spread,

Is inward sunk, and only our souls are red.
Perchance the world might have recovered
If she whom we lament had not been dead;
But she in whom all white, and red, and blue   250
(Beauty's ingredients) voluntary grew,
As in an unvexed paradise; from whom
Did all things verdure, and their luster come;
Whose composition was miraculous,
Being all color, all diaphanous,
(For air and fire but thick gross bodies were,
And liveliest stones but drowsy and pale to her),
She, she is dead; she's dead: when thou know'st this,
Thou know'st how wan a ghost this our world is;
And learn'st thus much by our anatomy,   260
That it should more affright than pleasure thee;
And that, since all fair color then did sink,
'Tis now but wicked vanity to think
To color vicious deeds with good pretense,
Or with bought colors to illude men's sense.
Nor in ought more this world's decay appears,
Than that her influence the heaven forbears,
Or that the elements do not feel this.
The father or the mother barren is:
The clouds conceive not rain, or do not pour,   270
In the due birth time, down the balmy shower;
The air doth not motherly sit on the earth
To hatch her seasons and give all things birth;
Springtimes were common cradles, but are tombs;
And false conceptions fill the general wombs;
The air shows such meteors as none can see,
Not only what they mean, but what they be;
Earth such new worms, as would have troubled much
The Egyptian Mages to have made more such.
What artist now dares boast that he can bring   280
Heaven hither, or constellate anything,
So as the influence of those stars may be
Imprisoned in an herb, or charm, or tree,

And do by touch, all which those stars could do?
The art is lost, and correspondence too;
For heaven gives little, and the earth takes less,
And man least knows their trade and purposes.
If this commerce 'twixt heaven and earth were not
Embarred, and all this traffic quite forgot,
She, for whose loss we have lamented thus,   290
Would work more fully and powerfully on us;
Since herbs and roots, by dying lose not all,
But they, yea ashes too, are medicinal,
Death could not quench her virtue so, but that
It would be (if not followed) wondered at;
And all the world would be one dying swan,
To sing her funeral praise, and vanish then.
But as some serpents' poison hurteth not,
Except it be from the live serpent shot,
So doth her virtue need her here, to fit   300
That unto us; she working more than it.
But she, in whom to such maturity
Virtue was grown, past growth, that it must die;
She, from whose influence all impressions came,
But, by receivers' impotencies, lame;
Who, though she could not transubstantiate
All states to gold, yet gilded every state,
So that some princes have some temperance;
Some counsellors some purpose to advance
The common profit; and some people have   310
Some stay, no more than kings should give, to crave;
Some women have some taciturnity;
Some nunneries some grains of chastity—
She that did thus much, and much more could do,
But that our age was iron, and rusty too,
She, she is dead; she's dead: when thou know'st this,
Thou know'st how dry a cinder this world is;
And learn'st thus much by our anatomy,
That 'tis in vain to dew, or mollify
It with thy tears, or sweat, or blood: nothing   320

Is worth our travail, grief, or perishing,
But those rich joys, which did possess her heart,
Of which she's now partaker, and a part.
But as in cutting up a man that's dead,
The body will not last out, to have read
On every part, and therefore men direct
Their speech to parts that are of most effect;
So the world's carcass would not last, if I
Were punctual in this anatomy;
Nor smells it well to hearers, if one tell   330
Them their disease, who fain would think they're well.
Here therefore be the end. And, blessed maid,
Of whom is meant what ever hath been said,
Or shall be spoken well by any tongue,
Whose name refines coarse lines and makes prose song,
Accept this tribute, and his first year's rent,
Who till his dark short taper's end be spent,
As oft thy feast sees this widowed earth,
Will yearly celebrate thy second birth,
That is, thy death; for though the soul of man   340
Be got when man is made, 'tis born but then
When man doth die; our body's as the womb,
And, as a mid-wife, death directs it home;
And you, her creatures, whom she works upon,
And have your last, and best concoction
From her example and her virtue, if you
In reverence to her, do think it due
That no one should her praises thus rehearse,
As matter fit for chronicle, not verse;
Vouchsafe to call to mind that God did make   350
A last, and lastingest piece, a song. He spake
To Moses to deliver unto all,
That song,[7] because He knew they would let fall
The Law, the Prophets, and the History,
But keep the song still in their memory:
Such an opinion (in due measure) made

[7] The song of Moses, *Deut.* 32.

Me this great office boldly to invade;
Nor could incomprehensibleness deter
Me from thus trying to imprison her,
Which when I saw that a strict grave could do,   360
I saw not why verse might not do so too.
Verse hath a middle nature; heaven keeps souls,
The grave keeps bodies, verse the fame enrolls.

Holy Sonnets

Show me, dear Christ, Thy spouse so bright and clear.
What! is it she which on the other shore
Goes richly painted? or which, robbed and tore,
Laments and mourns in Germany and here?
Sleeps she a thousand, then peeps up one year?
Is she self-truth, and errs? now new, now outwore?
Doth she, and did she, and shall she evermore
On one, on seven, or on no hill appear?
Dwells she with us, or like adventuring knights
First travel we to seek, and then make love?   10
Betray, kind husband, Thy spouse to our sights,
And let mine amorous soul court Thy mild dove,
Who is most true and pleasing to Thee then
When she is embraced and open to most men.

Thou hast made me, and shall Thy work decay?
Repair me now, for now mine end doth haste;
I run to death, and death meets me as fast,
And all my pleasures are like yesterday.
I dare not move my dim eyes any way,
Despair behind, and death before doth cast
Such terror, and my feeble flesh doth waste
By sin in it, which it towards hell doth weigh.
Only Thou art above, and when towards Thee
By Thy leave I can look, I rise again;   10

But our old subtle foe so tempteth me
That not one hour myself I can sustain.
Thy grace may wing me to prevent his art,
And Thou like adamant [1] draw mine iron heart.

Death, be not proud, though some have called thee
Mighty and dreadful, for thou art not so;
For those whom thou think'st thou dost overthrow
Die not, poor Death, nor yet canst thou kill me.
From rest and sleep, which but thy pictures be,
Much pleasure; then from thee much more must flow,
And soonest our best men with thee do go,
Rest of their bones, and souls' delivery.
Thou art slave to fate, chance, kings, and desperate men,
And dost with poison, war, and sickness dwell,   10
And poppy or charms can make us sleep as well
And better than thy stroke; why swell'st thou, then?
One short sleep past, we wake eternally,
And Death shall be no more; Death, thou shalt die.

At the round earth's imagined corners,[2] blow
Your trumpets, angels; and arise, arise
From death, you numberless infinities
Of souls, and to your scattered bodies go;
All whom the flood did, and fire shall, o'erthrow,
All whom war, dearth, age, agues, tyrannies,
Despair, law, chance hath slain, and you whose eyes
Shall behold God, and never taste death's woe.[3]

[1] The meaning is "like a magnet."
[2] "And after these things I saw four angels standing on the four corners of the earth, holding the four winds of the earth. . . ." *Rev.* 7:1.
[3] "Verily I say unto you, there be some standing here, which shall not taste of death, till they see the Son of man coming in his kingdom." *Matt.* 16:28.

But let them sleep, Lord, and me mourn a space;
For, if above all these, my sins abound,   10
'Tis late to ask abundance of Thy grace
When we are there. Here on this lowly ground,
Teach me how to repent; for that's as good
As if Thou hadst sealed my pardon with Thy blood.

As due by many titles I resign
Myself to Thee, O God: first I was made
By Thee, and for Thee, and when I was decayed
Thy blood bought that, the which before was Thine;
I am Thy son, made with Thyself to shine;
Thy servant, whose pains Thou hast still repaid;
Thy sheep, Thine image, and till I betrayed
Myself, a temple of Thy Spirit divine.[4]
Why doth the devil then usurp on me?
Why doth he steal, nay ravish that's Thy right?   10
Except Thou rise and for Thine own work fight,
Oh, I shall soon despair, when I do see
That Thou lovest mankind well, yet wilt not choose me,
And Satan hates me, yet is loth to lose me.

I am a little world made cunningly
Of elements, and an angelic sprite;
But black sin hath betrayed to endless night
My world's both parts, and oh, both parts must die.
You which beyond that heaven which was most high
Have found new spheres, and of new lands can write,
Pour new seas in mine eyes, that so I might
Drown my world with my weeping earnestly,
Or wash it if it must be drowned no more.

[4] "Know ye not that ye are the temple of God, and that the Spirit of God dwelleth in you?" *I Cor.* 3:16.

But oh, it must be burnt! Alas, the fire   10
Of lust and envy have burnt it heretofore,
And made it fouler; let their flames retire,
And burn me, O Lord, with a fiery zeal [5]
Of Thee and Thy house, which doth in eating heal.

This is my play's last scene; here heavens appoint
My pilgrimage's last mile; and my race
Idly, yet quickly run, hath this last pace;
My span's last inch, my minutes' latest point,
And gluttonous death will instantly unjoint
My body and soul, and I shall sleep a space;
But my ever-waking part shall see that face,
Whose fear already shakes my every joint.
Then as my soul to heaven, her first seat, takes flight,
And earth-born body in the earth shall dwell,   10
So fall my sins, that all may have their right,
To where they are bred, and would press me, to hell.
Impute me righteous, thus purged of evil,
For thus I leave the world, the flesh, the devil.

Spit in my face, you Jews, and pierce my side,
Buffet, and scoff, scourge, and crucify me,
For I have sinned, and sinned, and only He,
Who could do no iniquity, hath died:
But by my death cannot be satisfied
My sins, which pass the Jews' impiety;
They killed once an inglorious man, but I
Crucify Him daily, being now glorified.
Oh, let me then, His strange love still admire;
Kings pardon, but He bore our punishment.   10
And Jacob came clothed in vile harsh attire

[5] "For the zeal of thine house hath eaten me up . . ." *Psalms* 69:9.

But to supplant, and with gainful intent;
God clothed Himself in vile man's flesh, that so
He might be weak enough to suffer woe.

Batter my heart, three-personed God; for You
As yet but knock, breathe, shine, and seek to mend;
That I may rise, and stand, o'erthrow me, and bend
Your force, to break, blow, burn, and make me new.
I, like an usurped town to another due,
Labor to admit You, but oh! to no end;
Reason, Your viceroy in me, me should defend,
But is captived and proves weak or untrue.
Yet dearly I love You, and would be loved fain,
But am betrothed unto Your enemy.   10
Divorce me, untie, or break that knot again,
Take me to You, imprison me, for I
Except You enthrall me, never shall be free;
Nor ever chaste, except You ravish me.

A Hymn to God the Father [1]

I

Wilt Thou forgive that sin where I begun,
　　Which is my sin, though it were done before?
Wilt Thou forgive those sins, through which I run,
　　And do run still, though still I do deplore?
　　　　When Thou hast done, Thou hast not done,
　　　　　　For I have more.

II

Wilt Thou forgive that sin which I have won
　　Others to sin? and made my sin their door?

[1] This hymn, later set to music and sung at St. Paul's, was written at the time of Donne's serious illness when he was about fifty. The music is given in Grierson II, 252–4.

Wilt Thou forgive that sin which I did shun
A year or two, but wallowed in a score?
 When Thou hast done, Thou hast not done, 10
 For I have more.

III

I have a sin of fear, that when I have spun
My last thread, I shall perish on the shore;
But swear by Thyself, that at my death Thy Son
Shall shine as He shines now, and heretofore;
 And, having done that, Thou hast done,
 I fear no more.

THE PRE-RESTORATION poetry of the seventeenth century was dominated by three great personalities: Spenser, whose followers, Browne, Drummond, Giles and Phineas Fletcher, and Wither, continued the Elizabethan tradition; and Donne and Jonson, who established new and widely divergent schools of poetry. The two latter poets were agreed in their aim but differed in their method of attaining it. Both felt that the Elizabethan lyric had developed in songlike quality until its very sweetness and spontaneous ease had become cloying, and both wanted to give to this form greater strength and virility. It was Donne's idea to have weightier thought, a conversational tone, and surprising figures: to have something to say and to secure mental alertness by shocking the mind into attention. Jonson, on the other hand, thought that the classical writers provided the proper model and that the mental appeal should come through the calculated effects of balance, compactness, and polish. Donne consciously employed roughness and obscurity; Jonson strove for technical perfection and absolute clarity. Each writer established a school, though many of the poets show the influence of both masters. The religious poets, Herbert, Vaughan, Traherne, and Crashaw, are primarily followers of Donne; Carew, Herrick, Lovelace, and Suckling, who have something of the classic feeling for form and restraint, are known as the "Sons of Ben."

In spite of his wide learning, Jonson had little formal education; the degree of Master of Arts, conferred upon him by both universities, was only in recognition of his independent literary attainments. He had to some extent Donne's "hydroptic, immoderate desire of human learning and languages" and read persistently, taking careful notes. When Jonson's library was destroyed by fire, it was primarily the loss of his voluminous notes that he regretted. Apparently

[1] Briggs, W. D., "The Birth-Date of Ben Jonson," in *Modern Language Notes*, XXXIII (1918), 137–45.

William Camden, Headmaster of Westminster School, inspired Jonson with this love of reading. In a beautiful tribute to his old schoolmaster he says he owed to Camden all his learning. Perhaps Jonson also owed to him the opportunity to use Sir Robert Cotton's magnificent collection of books and manuscripts, for Camden and Jonson were both in the brilliant group which took advantage of Sir Robert's generosity. The learned discussions in this library must have equaled in interest the lighter turns of wit in the famous gatherings at the Mermaid.

But Jonson was no Robert Burton secluding himself from the reality of life. He lived in his own day; and as he went about the streets of London, he created his comedies from the characters and manners that he observed. He presented only the most outstanding characteristic of a person but gave it so much emphasis that he developed a new type of characterization called a "humor." The figures were as recognizable, however, as those in modern cartoons. When some of his contemporaries recognized themselves, trouble arose for Jonson; as he had always been daring and quarrelsome, this difficulty provided only another adventure.

Jonson's nature may have been inherited; we know that he had Scotch borderland blood from his mother. He had not known the influence of his minister father, who died before Jonson's birth; and his stepfather, who was a bricklayer, only stirred him to antagonism by arguing that a strong young lad had better be laying bricks than idling away time at school. Through Camden's interest in him, Jonson had the opportunity to go through Westminster School. But further bricklaying instead of university life followed his completion of this course of study. Adventure began for Jonson when bricklaying could no longer be endured, and he ran away to join the English troops in the Netherlands. There he fought in single combat between the two armies, like an epic hero, and returned to his comrades with the trophies which he had stripped from his slain foe. There was little active service at this time, however, and the routine of army life had no more lure for him than bricklaying. So Jonson again found his long legs of use in getting himself out of the army and back to London.

There he married a woman whom he briefly described to Drummond as "a shrew, but honest," began acting in a company of strolling players, and was soon connected with Philip Henslowe's company. His connection with the theatre led to familiarity with three of the London prisons. He became acquainted with the Marshalsea for daring to complete a satiric comedy, which Thomas Nash had more prudently left unfinished. He knew the Old Bailey on account of killing Gabriel Spencer, a fellow actor, in a quarrel. This time he escaped hanging only by claiming the rights of the old law of "benefit of clergy," which permitted those who could read to go free. His thumb, however, was branded with a *T* so that all who saw him would know of his crime, and his property was confiscated. He was thrown into Newgate for a ridiculous portrayal of the king in *Eastward Ho,* a play in which he collaborated with Marston and Chapman. Only the aid of his distinguished friends saved his ears and nose. In the event of failure, his stern mother prepared a "lusty poison" for him and herself to avoid the shame of his disfigurement.

Quarrels which were less disastrous gave zest to the intervals between his imprisonments. Some of his colleagues among the playwrights were material for comedy which Jonson could not resist. Marston was the first to recognize himself in a ridiculous but unflattering portrait. There followed the War of the Theatres, which lasted for about three years and resulted in some extremely amusing and revealing plays. Jonson had to take many a gibe, but his satirical caricatures of his fellow playwrights more than compensated him until Shakespeare entered the combat. It is said that he gave Jonson such a "purge" that he even gave up writing comedy for a while. Finally, late in his life, the quarrel which had been long brewing between Jonson and Inigo Jones, the great architect for the masques, came to a head. Jones held that the masque should appeal primarily to the senses and that therefore machinery and setting were more important than poetry. Jonson, realizing that the only permanency of these costly entertainments lay in beautiful poetry, claimed precedence for the poet. Jones had the greater influence at this time and succeeded in having Jonson dropped as the composer of court masques.

Jonson's theatrical associations were not, however, entirely abusive and satirical: Shakespeare acted in his plays, the younger playwrights vied with each other in securing the friendship and patronage which entitled them to be "sealed of the Tribe of Ben," and the child-actors at Blackfriars knew his aid and his tenderness. One of the most promising of these boys, Nathan Field, became his especial care; he even helped the little boy with his Latin. His appreciation of the ability of these actors and his personal affection for them are seen in the *Epitaph for Salathiel Pavy*.

The personal magnetism of Jonson drew to him a wide range of friends: King James, who made him poet laureate, Shakespeare, Beaumont, Sir Walter Raleigh, Bacon, Donne, Selden, Herrick, Lord Falkland, and Lucy, Countess of Bedford. The younger poets came under his dominance, and the "Sons of Ben" grew in number and power. The first of the great literary dictators presided at the Mermaid or in the Apollo Room of the Devil Tavern. Herrick writes from Devonshire of the "lyric feasts" where Jonson's verses "outdid the meat, outdid the frolic wine," but Francis Beaumont in a "Letter to Ben Jonson" gives the most famous description of the meetings at the Mermaid:

> . . . What things have we seen
> Done at the Mermaid! heard words that have been
> So nimble and so full of subtle flame,
> As if that every one from whence they came
> Had meant to put his whole wit in a jest
> And had resolved to live a fool the rest
> Of his dull life.

Doing the unusual appealed to Jonson all through his life. He became a Catholic for twelve years and on re-entering the Protestant faith emptied the communion cup to show the sincerity of his conversion; he acted as tutor to the young son of Sir Walter Raleigh on a foreign tour; in 1616 he did what no one before him had ever done—he chose and prepared for publication a folio volume of the writing he wished to be remembered by, calling it his "Works", to the great amusement of his critics; and, most interesting of all, he set out on a walking tour to Scotland in spite of a figure grown somewhat Falstaffian from long sitting in the taverns. John Taylor, the Water-Poet, followed Jonson to Scotland to parody his trip, but found him enjoying distinction in high circles and wrote back to London an appreciative tribute. Jonson's visit to Drummond is recorded in the *Conversations,* which give us much of Jonson's personality and many unrestrained comments on his famous contemporaries.

The death of King James, itself a misfortune to Jonson, was followed by other disasters. He had a stroke of paralysis in 1626; he was in need, and though appointed City Chronologer upon his temporary recovery, he was censured when he became unable to perform his duties and was in danger of losing his job; he produced a new set of plays which failed; Charles I did not call on him for masques; many of his friends, including Camden, died; and he himself was bedridden for a number of years. Except for a group of young men who visited him at his home, few even remembered Jonson until his death in 1637 thronged Westminster Abbey with his old admirers.

Something of the inconsistency of "Rare Ben Jonson" may be seen even in his writings. In drama he created the "comedy of humors"; he satirized contemporary fraudulent practices in such realistic dramas as *Volpone* and *The Alchemist;* he wrote heavy classical tragedy, which had to be further weighted down with footnotes; and he devised masques full of dainty grace and imaginative fancy. Following classical models, he produced lyrics of flawless technique, which he admitted having written first in prose. He set forth many sound critical principles in his prose *Timber*. In range and variety and in literary creativeness ruled severely by art, there is no equal to Ben Jonson.

Oberon, the Fairy Prince

A Masque of Prince Henry's

The first face of the scene appeared all obscure, and nothing perceived but a dark rock, with trees beyond it, and all wildness that could be presented: till, at one corner of the cliff, above the horizon, the moon began to show, and rising, a Satyr was seen by her light to put forth his head and call.

1 *Sat.* Chromis! Mnasil! none appear?
See you not who riseth here?
You saw Silenus, late, I fear.—
I'll prove, if this can reach your ear.
He wound his cornet, and thought himself answered; but was deceived by the echo.
Oh, you wake then! come away,
  Times be short are made for play;
  The humorous moon too will not stay:—
  What doth make you thus delay?
Hath his tankard touched your brain?
  Sure, they're fallen asleep again:
  Or I doubt it was the vain
  Echo, did me entertain.   10
Prove again—
Wound his cornet the second time, and found it.
      I thought 'twas she!
  Idle nymph, I pray thee be
  Modest, and not follow me:
  I not love myself, nor thee.
Here he wound the third time, and was answered by another Satyr, who likewise showed himself.

Ay this sound I better know;
  List! I would I could hear moe.

*At this they came running forth severally, to the number of
  ten, from divers parts of the rock, leaping and making
  antic actions and gestures; some of them speaking, some
  admiring: and amongst them a Silene, who is ever the
  prefect of the Satyrs, and so presented in all their chori
  and meetings.*

2 *Sat.* Thank us, and you shall do so.   20

3 *Sat.* Ay, our number soon will grow.

2 *Sat.* See Silenus! [1]

3 *Sat.* Cercops too!

4 *Sat.* Yes. What is there now to do?

5 *Sat.* Are there any nymphs to woo?

4 *Sat.* If there be, let me have two.

Silen. Chaster language! These are nights
Solemn to the shining rites
Of the Fairy Prince and knights,
While the moon their orgies lights.   30

2 *Sat.* Will they come abroad anon?

3 *Sat.* Shall we see young Oberon?

4 *Sat.* Is he such a princely one,
As you spake him long agone?

Silen. Satyrs, he doth fill with grace
Every season, every place;
Beauty dwells but in his face;
He's the height of all our race.

  Our Pan's father, god of tongue,
Bacchus, though he still be young,   40
Phœbus, when he crowned sung,
Nor Mars, when first his armor rung,
  Might with him be named that day:

---

[1] In the pomps of Dionysus, or Bacchus, to every company of Satyrs
there was still given a Silene for their overseer or governor.

[2] Mercury, who for the love of Penelope, while she was keeping her
father Icarius's herds on the mountain Taygetas, turned himself into
a fair buck-goat; with whose sports and flatteries the nymph being
taken, he begat on her Pan.

He is lovelier, than in May
Is the spring, and there can stay
As little as he can decay.
   Omn. O that he would come away!
   3 Sat. Grandsire, we shall leave to play
With Lyæus [3] now; and serve
Only Oberon.   50
   Silen. He'll deserve
All you can, and more, my boys.
   4 Sat. Will he give us pretty toys,
To beguile the girls withal?
   3 Sat. And to make them quickly fall.
   Silen. Peace, my wantons! he will do
More than you can aim unto.
   4 Sat. Will he build us larger caves?
   Silen. Yes, and give you ivory staves,
When you hunt; and better wine—   60
   1 Sat. Than the master of the vine?
   2 Sat. And rich prizes, to be won,
When we leap, or when we run?
   1 Sat. Ay, and gild our cloven feet?
   3 Sat. Strew our heads with powder sweet?
   1 Sat. Bind our crooked legs in hoops
Made of shells, with silver loops?
   2 Sat. Tie about our tawny wrists
Bracelets of the fairy twists?
   4 Sat. And, to spite the coy nymphs' scorns,   70
Hang upon our stubbed horns
Garlands, ribands, and fine posies—
   3 Sat. Fresh as when the flower discloses?
   1 Sat. Yes, and stick our pricking ears
With the pearl that Tethys wears.
   2 Sat. And to answer all things else,
Trap our shaggy thighs with bells;
That as we do strike a time,
In our dance shall make a chime—

[3] A name of Bacchus, Lyæus, of freeing men's minds from cares.

3 *Sat.* Louder than the rattling pipes 80
Of the wood gods—
  1 *Sat.* Or the stripes
Of the tabor; when we carry
Bacchus up, his pomp to vary.
  Omn. O that he so long doth tarry!
  Silen. See! the rock begins to ope,
Now you shall enjoy your hope;
'Tis about the hour, I know.

*There the whole scene opened, and within was discovered
    the frontispiece of a bright and glorious palace, whose
    gates and walls were transparent. Before the gates lay
    two Sylvans, armed with their clubs, and dressed in
    leaves, asleep. At this the Satyrs wondering, Silenus
    proceeds:*

  Silen. Look! does not his palace show
Like another sky of lights? 90
Yonder with him live the knights,
Once the noblest of the earth,
Quickened by a second birth,
Who for prowess and for truth
There are crowned with lasting youth
And do hold, by Fate's command,
Seats of bliss in Fairyland.
But their guards, methinks, do sleep!
Let us wake them.—Sirs, you keep
Proper watch, that thus do lie 100
Drowned in sloth!
  1 *Sat.* They have ne'er an eye
To wake withal.
  2 *Sat.* Nor sense, I fear;
For they sleep in either ear.[4]
  3 *Sat.* Holla, Sylvans!—sure they're caves
Of sleep these, or else they're graves.

---

[4] For they sleep in either ear. The Latin phrase is, *In utramvis aurem
dormire;* and means to sleep soundly, without any thoughts of care.
Whaley.

4 Sat. Hear you, friends!—who keeps the keepers?

1 Sat. They are the eighth and ninth sleepers!

2 Sat. Shall we cramp them?   110

Silen. Satyrs, no.

3 Sat. Would we had Boreas here, to blow
Off their heavy coats, and strip them.

4 Sat. Ay, ay, ay; that we might whip them.

3 Sat. Or that we had a wasp or two
For their nostrils.

1 Sat. Hairs will do
Even as well: take my tail.

2 Sat. What do you say to a good nail
Through their temples?   120

2 Sat. Or an eel,
In their guts, to make them feel?

4 Sat. Shall we steal away their beards?

3 Sat. For Pan's goat, that leads the herds?

2 Sat. Or try, whether is more dead,
His club, or the other's head?

Silen. Wags, no more: you grow too bold.

1 Sat. I would fain now see them rolled
Down a hill, or from a bridge
Headlong cast, to break their ridge-   130
Bones: or to some river take 'em,
Plump; and see if that would wake 'em.

2 Sat. There no motion yet appears.

Silen. Strike a charm into their ears.

At which the Satyrs fell suddenly into this catch.

> Buz, quoth the blue fly,
>   Hum, quoth the bee:
> Buz and hum they cry,
>   And so do we.
> In his ear, in his nose,
>   Thus, do you see?— [*They tickle them.*   140
> He ate the dormouse;
>   Else it was he.

The two Sylvans starting up amazed, and betaking them-
selves to their arms, were thus questioned by Silenus:
    Silen. How now, Sylvans! can you wake?
I commend the care you take
In your watch! Is this your guise,
To have both your ears and eyes
Sealed so fast as these mine elves
Might have stolen you from yourselves?
    3 *Sat.* We had thought we must have got
Stakes, and heated them red-hot,   150
And have bored you through the eyes,
With the Cyclops, ere you'd rise.
    2 *Sat.* Or have fetched some trees to heave
Up your bulks, that so did cleave
To the ground there.
    4 *Sat.* Are you free
Yet of sleep, and can you see
Who is yonder up aloof?
    1 *Sat.* Be your eyes yet moon-proof?
    1 *Syl.* Satyrs, leave your petulance,   160
And go frisk about and dance;
Or else rail upon the moon:
Your expectance is too soon.
For before the second cock
Crow, the gates will not unlock;
And, till then, we know we keep
Guard enough, although we sleep.
    1 *Sat.* Say you so? then let us fall
To a song, or to a brawl:
Shall we, grandsire? Let us sport,   170
And make expectation short.
    Silen. Do, my wantons, what you please.
I'll lie down and take mine ease.
    1 *Sat.* Brothers, sing then, and upbraid,
As we use, yond seeming maid.

SONG

Now, my cunning lady: moon,
Can you leave the side so soon
　　Of the boy you keep so hid?
Midwife Juno sure will say,
This is not the proper way　　　　　　　　　180
　　Of your paleness to be rid.
But, perhaps, it is your grace
To wear sickness in your face,
　　　That there might be wagers laid
　　　Still, by fools, you are a maid.

Come, your changes overthrow,
What your look would carry so;
　　Moon, confess then, what you are,
And be wise, and free to use
Pleasures that you now do lose;　　　　　190
　　Let us Satyrs have a share.
Though our forms be rough and rude,
Yet our acts may be endued
　　　With more virtue: every one
　　　Cannot be Endymion.

Here they fell suddenly into an antic dance full of gesture
　　and swift motion, and continued it till the crowing of
　　the cock: at which they were interrupted by Silenus.

　　Silen. Stay! the cheerful chanticleer
Tells you that the time is near:—
See, the gates already spread!
Every Satyr bow his head.

There the whole palace opened, and the nation of Faies were
　　discovered, some with instruments, some bearing lights,
　　others singing; and within afar off in perspective, the
　　knights masquers sitting in their several sieges: at the
　　further end of all, Oberon, in a chariot, which, to a loud
　　triumphant music, began to move forward, drawn by

*two white bears, and on either side guarded by three
Sylvans, with one going in front.*

SONG

Melt earth to sea, sea flow to air,   200
   And air fly into fire,
Whilst we in tunes, to Arthur's chair [5]
   Bear Oberon's desire;
   Than which there's nothing can be higher,
Save James, to whom it flies:
But he the wonder is of tongues, of ears, of eyes.

Who hath not heard, who hath not seen,
   Who hath not sung his name?
The soul that hath not, hath not been;
   But is the very same   210
   With buried sloth, and knows not fame,
Which doth him best comprise:
For he the wonder is of tongues, of ears, of eyes.

*By this time the chariot was come as far forth as the face
of the scene. And the Satyrs beginning to leap, and ex-
press their joy for the unused state and solemnity, the
foremost Sylvan began to speak.*

1 *Syl.* Give place, and silence; you were rude too late;
This is a night of greatness and of state,
Not to be mixed with light and skipping sport,
A night of homage to the British court,
And ceremony due to Arthur's chair,
From our bright master, Oberon the fair,
Who with these knights attendants, here preserved   220
In Fairyland, for good they have deserved
Of yond high throne, are come of right to pay
Their annual vows; and all their glories lay

[5] The Tudor sovereigns represented themselves as descendents of
Arthur and held that the long-expected return of Arthur was fulfilled
in the restoration of his race to the throne.

At's feet, and tender to this only great,
True majesty, restored in this seat;
To whose sole power and magic they do give
The honor of their being; that they live
Sustained in form, fame, and felicity,
From rage of fortune or the fear to die.

   Silen. And may they well. For this indeed is he,   230
My boys, whom you must quake at when you see.
He is above your reach; and neither doth
Nor can he think within a Satyr's tooth:
Before his presence you must fall or fly.
He is the matter of virtue, and placed high.
His meditations to his height are even,
And all their issue is akin to heaven.
He is a god o'er kings; yet stoops he then
Nearest a man, when he doth govern men,
To teach them by the sweetness of his sway,   240
And not by force. He's such a king as they
Who are tyrants' subjects, or ne'er tasted peace,
Would, in their wishes, form for their release.
'Tis he that stays the time from turning old,
And keeps the age up in a head of gold;
That in his own true circle still doth run;
And holds his course as certain as the sun.
He makes it ever day and ever spring
Where he doth shine, and quickens everything
Like a new nature: so that true to call   250
Him, by his title, is to say, he's all.

   1 *Syl.* I thank the wise Silenus for his praise.
Stand forth, bright Faies and Elves, and tune your lays
Unto his name; then let your nimble feet
Tread subtle circles that may always meet
In point to him, and figures, to express
The grace of him and his great emperess.
That all that shall to-night behold the rites
Performed by princely Oberon and these knights,

May without stop point out the proper heir 260
Designed so long to Arthur's crowns and chair.

SONG BY TWO FAIES

> 1 *Faie*. Seek you majesty, to strike?
> Bid the world produce his like.
> 2 *Faie*. Seek you glory, to amaze?
> Here let all eyes stand at gaze.
> *Cho*. Seek you wisdom, to inspire?
> Touch then at no other's fire.
> 1 *Faie*. Seek you knowledge, to direct?
> Trust to his without suspect.
> 2 *Faie*. Seek you piety, to lead? 270
> In his footsteps only tread.
> *Cho*. Every virtue of a king,
> And of all, in him, we sing.

Then the lesser Faies dance forth their dance; which ended,
a full SONG *follows by all the voices.*

> The solemn rites are well begun;
> And though but lighted by the moon,
> They show as rich as if the sun
> Had made this night his noon.
> But may none wonder that they are so bright,
> The moon now borrows from a greater light:
> Then, princely *Oberon*, 280
> Go on,
> This is not every night.

Oberon and the knights dance out the first masque dance,
which was followed with this

SONG

> Nay, nay,
> You must not stay,
> Nor be weary yet;
> This is no time to cast away,

Or for Faies so to forget
The virtue of their feet.
Knotty legs and plants of clay
Seek for ease, or love delay, 290
But with you it still should fare
As with the air of which you are.

*After which they danced forth their second masque dance
and were again excited by a*

SONG

1 *Faie*. Nor yet, nor yet, O you in this night blest,
Must you have will, or hope to rest.
2 *Faie*. If you use the smallest stay,
You'll be overta'en by day.
1 *Faie*. And these beauties will suspect
That their forms you do neglect,
If you do not call them forth.
2 *Faie*. Or that you have no more worth 300
Than the coarse and country Fairy,
That doth haunt the hearth or dairy.

*Then followed the measures, corantos, galliards, &c., till
Phosphorus the day-star appeared, and called them
away; but first they were invited home by one of the
Sylvans with this*

SONG

Gentle knights,
Know some measure of your nights.
Tell the high-graced *Oberon*,
It is time that we were gone.
Here be forms so bright and airy,
    And their motions so they vary,
As they will enchant the Fairy
    If you longer here should tarry. 310
Phos. To rest, to rest! the herald of the day,
Bright Phosphorus, commands you hence; obey.

The moon is pale, and spent; and winged night
Makes headlong haste to fly the morning's sight,
Who now is rising from her blushing wars,
And with her rosy hand puts back the stars.
Of which myself the last, her harbinger,
But stay to warn you that you not defer
Your parting longer: then do I give way,
As night hath done, and so must you, to day.   320

*After this they danced their last dance into the work. And
   with a full* SONG *the star vanished and the whole ma-
   chine closed.*

O yet how early, and before her time,
The envious morning up doth climb,
   Though she not love her bed!
What haste the jealous sun doth make,
His fiery horses up to take,
   And once more show his head!
Lest, taken with the brightness of this night,
The world should wish it last, and never miss his light.

Song

To Celia [1]

Drink to me only with thine eyes,
   And I will pledge with mine;
Or leave a kiss but in the cup,
   And I'll not look for wine.
The thirst that from the soul doth rise
   Doth ask a drink divine;

[1] This delicate lyric is based upon material from four letters of
Philostratus, a Greek writer living about 170–245 A. D.
   a. "Drink to me with thine eyes only. Or if thou wilt, putting
the cup to thy lips, fill it with kisses, and so bestow it upon me."
                                              Letter 24.
   b. "I, as soon as I behold thee, thirst, and taking hold of the cup,
do not, indeed, apply that to my lips for drink, but thee."
                                              Letter 25.

But might I of Jove's nectar sup,
   I would not change for thine.

I sent thee late a rosy wreath,
   Not so much honoring thee   10
As giving it a hope, that there
   It could not withered be.
But thou thereon didst only breathe,
   And sent'st it back to me;
Since when it grows, and smells, I swear,
   Not of itself but thee.

Hymn

Queen and huntress,[1] chaste and fair.
Now the sun is laid to sleep,
Seated in thy silver chair,
State in wonted manner keep:
   Hesperus entreats thy light,
   Goddess excellently bright.

Earth, let not thy envious shade
Dare itself to interpose;
Cynthia's shining orb was made
Heaven to clear when day did close: 10
   Bless us, then, with wished sight,
   Goddess excellently bright.

c. "I send thee a rosy wreath, not so much honoring thee, though this also is in my thoughts, as bestowing favor upon the roses, that so they might not be withered."

                               Letter 30.

d. "If thou wouldst do a kindness to thy lover, send back the relics of the roses [I gave thee], for they will smell no longer of themselves only, but of thee."

                               Letter 31.

The translation is that of Richard Cumberland in the *Observer*, No. 74.

[1] At the conclusion of *Cynthia's Revels* Queen Elizabeth is represented in a masque as Cynthia or Diana. This song opens Act V, Scene 3, a scene preparatory to the masque.

Lay thy bow of pearl apart,
And thy crystal-shining quiver;
Give unto the flying hart
Space to breathe, how short soever;
 Thou that mak'st a day of night,
 Goddess excellently bright.

A Song

O do not wanton with those eyes,
 Lest I be sick with seeing;
Nor cast them down, but let them rise,
 Lest shame destroy their being.
O be not angry with those fires,
 For then their threats will kill me;
Nor look too kind on my desires,
 For then my hopes will spill me.
O do not steep them in thy tears,
 For so will sorrow slay me;   10
Nor spread them as distract with fears;
 Mine own enough betray me.

[*Simplex Munditiis*] [1]

Still to be neat, still to be dressed,
As you were going to a feast;
Still to be powdered, still perfumed:
Lady, it is to be presumed,
Though art's hid causes are not found,
All is not sweet, all is not sound.

Give me a look, give me a face,
That makes simplicity a grace;
Robes loosely flowing, hair as free:
Such sweet neglect more taketh me   10

[1] This lyric from *Epicœne* follows the general thought of an anonymous Latin poem.

Than all the adulteries of art;
They strike mine eyes, but not my heart.

FROM *A Celebration of Charis*

Her Triumph

See the chariot at hand here of Love,
   Wherein my lady rideth!
Each that draws is a swan or a dove,
   And well the car Love guideth.
As she goes, all hearts do duty
     Unto her beauty;
And, enamored, do wish, so they might
     But enjoy such a sight,
That they still were to run by her side,
Through swords, through seas, whither she would ride.   10

Do but look on her eyes; they do light
   All that Love's world compriseth!
Do but look on her hair; it is bright
   As Love's star when it riseth!
Do but mark, her forehead's smoother
     Than words that soothe her!
And from her arched brows, such a grace
     Sheds itself through the face,
As alone there triumphs to the life
All the gain, all the good, of the elements' strife.[1]   20

Have you seen but a bright lily grow,
   Before rude hands have touched it?
Ha' you marked but the fall o' the snow
   Before the soil hath smutched it?
Ha' you felt the wool of beaver?
     Or swan's down ever?
Or have smelt o' the bud o' the brier?
     Or the nard in the fire?

[1] Perfection resulted when the four elements were brought into a combination which would overcome their normal strife.

Or have tasted the bag of the bee?
O so white, O so soft, O so sweet is she! 30

FROM *The Sad Shepherd*

Here she was wont to go! and here! and here!
Just where those daisies, pinks, and violets grow:
The world may find the spring by following her,
For other prints her airy steps ne'er left.
Her treading would not bend a blade of grass,
Or shake the downy blow-ball from his stalk!
But like the soft west wind she shot along;
And where she went, the flowers took thickest root,
As she had sowed them with her odorous foot.

On My First Daughter

Here lies, to each her parents' ruth,
Mary, the daughter of their youth;
Yet all heaven's gifts being heaven's due,
It makes the father less to rue.
At six months' end she parted hence
With safety of her innocence;
Whose soul heaven's queen, whose name she bears,
In comfort of her mother's tears,
Hath placed amongst her virgin-train:
Where while that severed doth remain, 10
This grave partakes the fleshly birth;
Which cover lightly, gentle earth!

On My First Son

Farewell, thou child of my right hand, and joy;
My sin was too much hope of thee, loved boy:
Seven years thou wert lent to me, and I thee pay,
Exacted by thy fate, on the just day.
O could I lose all father now! for why

Will man lament the state he should envy—
To have so soon 'scaped world's and flesh's rage,
And, if no other misery, yet age?
Rest in soft peace, and asked, say, "Here doth lie
Ben Jonson his best piece of poetry;   10
For whose sake henceforth all his vows be such
As what he loves may never like too much."

Epitaph on Elizabeth, L. H.

Wouldst thou hear what man can say
In a little? Reader, stay.
Underneath this stone doth lie
As much beauty as could die;
Which in life did harbor give
To more virtue than doth live.
If at all she had a fault,
Leave it buried in this vault.
One name was Elizabeth;
The other, let it sleep with death: 10
Fitter, where it died, to tell,
Than that it lived at all. Farewell!

Epitaph on S[alathiel] P[avy], a Child of Queen Elizabeth's Chapel [1]

Weep with me, all you that read
    This little story;
And know, for whom a tear you shed
    Death's self is sorry.
'Twas a child that so did thrive
    In grace and feature,
As heaven and nature seemed to strive
    Which owned the creature.

[1] One of the child-actors.

Years he numbered scarce thirteen
    When fates turned cruel,   10
Yet three filled zodiacs had he been
    The stage's jewel;
And did act, what now we moan,
    Old men so duly,
As, sooth, the Parcae [2] thought him one,
    He played so truly.
So, by error, to his fate
    They all consented;
But viewing him since, alas, too late!
    They have repented,   20
And have sought, to give new birth,
    In baths to steep him; [3]
But being so much too good for earth,
    Heaven vows to keep him.

FROM [*A Pindaric Ode*]

*To the Immortal Memory and Friendship
of That Noble Pair
Sir Lucius Cary and Sir H. Morison*

It is not growing like a tree
  In bulk, doth make man better be;
Or standing long an oak, three hundred year,
To fall a log at last, dry, bald, and sear:
    A lily of a day
    Is fairer far, in May,
  Although it fall and die that night;
  It was the plant and flower of light.
In small proportions we just beauties see,
And in short measures life may perfect be.   10

[2] The Fates who had control over birth and death.
[3] Medea restored the youth of Jason's aged father by means of a magic bath.

To the Memory of My Beloved
Master William Shakespeare,
And What He Hath Left Us

To draw no envy, Shakespeare, on thy name,
Am I thus ample to thy book and fame,
While I confess thy writings to be such
As neither man nor Muse can praise too much.
'Tis true, and all men's suffrage. But these ways
Were not the paths I meant unto thy praise:
For seeliest ignorance on these may light,
Which, when it sounds at best, but echoes right;
Or blind affection, which doth ne'er advance
The truth, but gropes, and urgeth all by chance;   10
Or crafty malice might pretend this praise,
And think to ruin where it seemed to raise.
These are as some infamous bawd or whore
Should praise a matron—what could hurt her more?
But thou art proof against them, and, indeed,
Above the ill fortune of them, or the need.
I therefore will begin. Soul of the age,
The applause, delight, the wonder of our stage,
My Shakespeare, rise! I will not lodge thee by
Chaucer or Spenser, or bid Beaumont lie   20
A little further to make thee a room: [1]
Thou art a monument without a tomb,
And art alive still while thy book doth live,
And we have wits to read and praise to give.
That I not mix thee so, my brain excuses,
I mean with great, but disproportioned Muses;
For, if I thought my judgment were of years,
I should commit thee surely with thy peers,
And tell how far thou didst our Lyly outshine,
Or sporting Kyd, or Marlowe's mighty line.   30
And though thou hadst small Latin and less Greek,

[1] Shakespeare, buried at Stratford, would not be placed beside the
first three English poets to be buried in Westminster Abbey.

From thence to honor thee, I would not seek
For names, but call forth thundering Æschylus,
Euripides, and Sophocles to us,
Pacuvius, Accius,[2] him of Cordova [3] dead,
To life again, to hear thy buskin [4] tread
And shake a stage; or when thy socks were on,
Leave thee alone for the comparison
Of all that insolent Greece or haughty Rome
Sent forth, or since did from their ashes come.   40
Triumph, my Britain; thou hast one to show
To whom all scenes of Europe homage owe.
He was not of an age, but for all time!
And all the Muses still were in their prime
When like Apollo he came forth to warm
Our ears, or like a Mercury to charm.
Nature herself was proud of his designs,
And joyed to wear the dressing of his lines,
Which were so richly spun, and woven so fit,
As, since, she will vouchsafe no other wit: 50
The merry Greek, tart Aristophanes,[5]
Neat Terence, witty Plautus,[6] now not please,
But antiquated and deserted lie,
As they were not of Nature's family.
Yet must I not give nature all; thy art,
My gentle Shakespeare, must enjoy a part:
For though the poet's matter nature be,
His art doth give the fashion; and that he
Who casts to write a living line must sweat
(Such as thine are) and strike the second heat   60
Upon the Muses' anvil, turn the same,
And himself with it, that he thinks to frame,

[2] Pacuvius and Accius were early Roman tragic poets.

[3] Seneca, who was born at Cordova.

[4] The buskin, the boot worn by Greek tragic actors, and the sock, the light shoe worn by actors in comedy, are used to represent Shakespeare's tragedies and comedies, respectively.

[5] Aristophanes wrote satirical comedies.

[6] Plautus and Terence were writers of Latin comedy.

Or for the laurel he may gain a scorn;
For a good poet's made as well as born.
And such wert thou! Look how the father's face
Lives in his issue; even so the race
Of Shakespeare's mind and manners brightly shines
In his well-turned and true-filed lines,
In each of which he seems to shake a lance,
As brandished at the eyes of ignorance.   70
Sweet swan of Avon, what a sight it were
To see thee in our waters yet appear,
And make those flights upon the banks of Thames
That so did take Eliza and our James!
But stay; I see thee in the hemisphere
Advanced and made a constellation there!
Shine forth, thou star of poets, and with rage
Or influence [7] chide or cheer the drooping stage,
Which, since thy flight from hence, hath mourned like night,
And despairs day, but for thy volume's light.   80

To William Camden

Camden,[1] most reverend head, to whom I owe
All that I am in arts, all that I know
(How nothing's that!), to whom my country owes
The great renown and name wherewith she goes; [2]
Than thee the age sees not that thing more grave,
More high, more holy, that she more would crave.
What name, what skill, what faith hast thou in things!
What sight in searching the most antique springs!
What weight and what authority in thy speech!
Man scarce can make that doubt, but thou canst teach. 10

[7] Belief in astrology was just beginning to wane in the seventeenth century. See "On Lucy, Countess of Bedford," l. 8, for a similar reference.

[1] Camden was headmaster at Westminster School when Jonson was in school. According to some stories, it was Camden who first encouraged Jonson to attend school at all.

[2] Camden's greatest work was *Britannia*, a general survey of England.

Pardon free truth and let thy modesty,
Which conquers all, be once overcome by thee.
Many of thine, this better could than I;
But for their powers, accept my piety.

On Lucy, Countess of Bedford [1]

This morning, timely rapt with holy fire,
  I thought to form unto my zealous Muse
What kind of creature I could most desire
  To honor, serve, and love, as poets use.
I meant to make her fair and free and wise,
  Of greatest blood, and yet more good than great;
I meant the day-star should not brighter rise,
  Nor lend like influence from his lucent seat;
I meant she should be courteous, facile, sweet,
  Hating that solemn vice of greatness, pride;   10
I meant each softest virtue there should meet,
  Fit in that softer bosom to reside.
Only a learned and a manly soul
  I purposed her, that should, with even powers,
The rock, the spindle, and the shears [2] control
  Of destiny, and spin her own free hours.
Such when I meant to feign, and wished to see,
My muse bade Bedford write, and that was she!

To Penshurst [1]

Thou art not, Penshurst, built to envious show,
  Of touch or marble; nor canst boast a row

---

[1] The home of the Countess of Bedford was a frequent resort of the poets. Donne, Chapman, Drayton, and Jonson were among those enjoying her patronage.

[2] Each of the three Fates had a symbol: for Lachesis, who set the length of life, a globe; for Clotho, who spun the thread of life, a spindle; for Atropos, who cut off life, a pair of shears.

[1] Penshurst was the home of the Sidney family, and the scene is still very much as Jonson described it. The picture of home life is particularly pleasing. Sir Robert Sidney, father of Waller's *Sacharissa*, occu-

Of polished pillars, or a roof of gold;
Thou hast no lantern, whereof tales are told,
Or stair, or courts; but stand'st an ancient pile,
And, these grudged at, art reverenced the while.
Thou joy'st in better marks, of soil, of air,
Of wood, of water; therein thou art fair.
Thou hast thy walks for health, as well as sport;
Thy mount, to which the dryads do resort,   10
Where Pan and Bacchus their high feasts have made,
Beneath the broad beech and the chestnut shade;
That taller tree, which of a nut was set
At his great birth where all the Muses met.[2]
There in the writhed bark are cut the names
Of many a sylvan, taken with his flames;
And thence the ruddy satyrs oft provoke
The lighter fauns to reach thy Lady's Oak.
Thy copse too, named of Gamage, thou hast there,
That never fails to serve thee seasoned deer   20
When thou wouldst feast or exercise thy friends.
The lower land, that to the river bends,
Thy sheep, thy bullocks, kine, and calves do feed;
The middle grounds thy mares and horses breed.
Each bank doth yield thee conies; and the tops,
Fertile of wood, Ashore and Sidney's copse,
To crown thy open table, doth provide
The purpled pheasant with the speckled side;
The painted partridge lies in every field,
And for thy mess is willing to be killed.   30
And if the high-swollen Medway [3] fail thy dish,
Thou hast thy ponds, that pay thee tribute fish,
Fat aged carps that run into thy net,
And pikes, now weary their own kind to eat,
As loth the second draught or cast to stay,

pied the castle in Jonson's day and entertained many of the poets.
Waller also wrote a poem on Penshurst and celebrated Lady Dorothy
Sidney in many lyrics.

[2] The acorn was planted on the birthday of Sir Philip Sidney.

[3] The Medway is the river on which the estate is located.

Officiously at first themselves betray;
Bright eels that emulate them, and leap on land
Before the fisher, or into his hand.
Then hath thy orchard fruit, thy garden flowers,
Fresh as the air, and new as are the hours.   40
The early cherry, with the later plum,
Fig, grape, and quince, each in his time doth come;
The blushing apricot and woolly peach
Hang on thy walls, that every child may reach.
And though thy walls be of the country stone,
They are reared with no man's ruin, no man's groan;
There's none that dwell about them wish them down;
But all come in, the farmer and the clown,
And no one empty-handed, to salute
Thy lord and lady, though they have no suit.   50
Some bring a capon, some a rural cake,
Some nuts, some apples; some that think they make
The better cheeses bring them, or else send
By their ripe daughters, whom they would commend
This way to husbands, and whose baskets bear
An emblem of themselves in plum or pear.
But what can this (more than express their love)
Add to thy free provisions, far above
The need of such? whose liberal board doth flow
With all that hospitality doth know;   60
Where comes no guest but is allowed to eat,
Without his fear, and of thy lord's own meat;
Where the same beer and bread, and self-same wine,
That is his lordship's shall be also mine,
And I not fain to sit, as some this day
At great men's tables, and yet dine away.
Here no man tells my cups, nor, standing by,
A waiter doth my gluttony envy,
But gives me what I call, and lets me eat;
He knows below he shall find plenty of meat.   70
Thy tables hoard not up for the next day;
Nor, when I take my lodging, need I pray

For fire, or lights, or livery; all is there,
As if thou then wert mine, or I reigned here:
There's nothing I can wish, for which I stay.
That found King James when, hunting late this way
With his brave son, the prince, they saw thy fires
Shine bright on every hearth, as the desires
Of thy Penates had been set on flame
To entertain them; or the country came, 80
With all their zeal, to warm their welcome here.
What great I will not say, but sudden cheer
Didst thou then make 'em! and what praise was heaped
On thy good lady then, who therein reaped
The just reward of her high housewifery;
To have her linen, plate, and all things nigh,
When she was far; and not a room but dressed
As if it had expected such a guest!
These, Penshurst, are thy praise, and yet not all.
Thy lady's noble, fruitful, chaste withal. 90
His children thy great lord may call his own,
A fortune in this age but rarely known.
They are, and have been, taught religion; thence
Their gentler spirits have sucked innocence.
Each morn and even they are taught to pray,
With the whole household, and may, every day,
Read in their virtuous parents' noble parts
The mysteries of manners, arms, and arts.
Now, Penshurst, they that will proportion thee
With other edifices, when they see 100
Those proud, ambitious heaps, and nothing else,
May say their lords have built, but thy lord dwells.

Ode to Himself

Come leave the loathed stage,
And the more loathsome age,
Where pride and impudence, in faction knit,
Usurp the chair of wit!

Indicting and arraigning every day
    Something they call a play.
  Let their fastidious, vain
  Commission of the brain
Run on and rage, sweat, censure, and condemn;
They were not made for thee, less thou for them.   10

    Say that thou pour'st them wheat,
    And they will acorns eat;
'Twere simple fury still thyself to waste
    On such as have no taste!
To offer them a surfeit of pure bread,
    Whose appetites are dead!
  No, give them grains their fill,
  Husks, draff to drink and swill:
If they love lees, and leave the lusty wine,
Envy them not; their palate's with the swine   20

    No doubt some moldy tale,
    Like *Pericles*,[1] and stale
As the shrieve's crusts, and nasty as his fish—
    Scraps, out every dish
Thrown forth and raked into the common tub,[2]
    May keep up the Play-club:
  There, sweepings do as well
  As the best-ordered meal;
For who the relish of these guests will fit
Needs set them but the alms-basket of wit.   30

    And much good do it you then:
    Brave plush and velvet men
Can feed on orts; and, safe in your stage clothes,[3]

[1] The popular story of Pericles originated in Greece early in the Christian era.

[2] Since Sheriff's set a good table, there would be many scraps, or *orts,* l. 33.

[3] The gallants who secured seats on the stage were dressed to excite the admiration of other spectators.

Dare quit, upon your oaths,
The stagers and the stage-wrights too, your peers,
Of larding your large ears
With their foul comic socks,
Wrought upon twenty blocks;
Which, if they are torn, and turned, and patched enough,
The gamesters share your gilt, and you their stuff.   40

Leave things so prostitute
And take the Alcaic lute;
Or thine own Horace, or Anacreon's lyre; [4]
Warm thee by Pindar's fire:
And though thy nerves be shrunk, and blood be cold,
Ere years have made thee old,
Strike that disdainful heat
Throughout, to their defeat,
As curious fools, and envious of thy strain,
May, blushing, swear no palsy's in thy brain.   50

But when they hear thee sing
The glories of thy king,
His zeal to God and his just awe o'er men,
They may, blood-shaken then,
Feel such a flesh-quake to possess their powers
As they shall cry, "Like ours,
In sound of peace or wars,
No harp e'er hit the stars
In tuning forth the acts of his sweet reign,
And raising Charles his chariot 'bove his Wain." [5]   60

[4] Alcæus was a Greek lyric poet; Horace and Anacreon, Latin.
[5] In the seventeenth century the Great Dipper, or Charlemagne's Wain, was associated with the name of Charles I.

THE BROTHERS, Phineas and Giles Fletcher, have an unusual
interest for the student of literature in that they look back
to one mountain peak in literature and forward to another.
In their stanza forms and in the use of pastoral and allegory,
they were imitating Spenser. Though the new religious and
didactic themes appeared rather quaint in a style fashioned
and embroidered after the Spenserian pattern, they gained
an immediate audience from the admirers of Spenser. But
as Spenser prepared the way for the Fletchers, they, in turn,
prepared the way for Milton; *The Apollyonists* by Phineas
is a precursor of *Paradise Lost* and *Christ's Victory and
Triumph* by Giles, of *Paradise Regained*. The importance of
these poets does not, however, consist solely in their relation
to greater figures; they have written much that is of moving
beauty and independent value.

The Fletcher family was attracted by either the religious
or the literary life, or a combination of both. The grand-
father of the poets was a divine; their father was a sonneteer;
their cousin John, a distinguished dramatist, collaborator
with Beaumont; they themselves were both poets and divines.

Phineas Fletcher began his literary career at King's Col-
lege, Cambridge, when he contributed in 1603 to the collec-
tion of verses published by the university in commemoration
of the death of Queen Elizabeth. In 1614 he wrote a pastoral
play to be acted before King James on his visit to the uni-
versity. Although the king's party left the university before
the play could be produced, the play was given later at
King's College.

After sixteen years at Cambridge, Phineas left the uni-
versity life to become chaplain to Sir Henry Willoughby.
Through Sir Henry he received an appointment to the rector-
ship of Hilgay in Norfolk, where he remained until his death.

Though the composition of his poems belongs to an earlier
period, it was not until he had been settled at Hilgay for
several years that he published any of his work. His *Pisca-*

tory Eclogues are in obvious imitation of Spenser's *Shepherd's Calendar,* except that the pastoral figures are fishermen instead of shepherds. The poet himself is Thyrsil, and his father and other contemporary figures appear under pastoral names. His most ambitious poem is *The Purple Island,* a massive work of most extraordinary conception. The physiology and anatomy of the human body are presented allegorically by the geography of this island, and the intellectual and moral qualities by its warring inhabitants. He strains ingenuity to point out all possible resemblances and in so doing, crowds the mind with pictures. The theme itself is ugly and the allegory far too intricate to be effective, but the treatment is at least curious and fantastic. The poet, representing himself as the shepherd Thyrsil, narrates the story to an eager group of shepherds and shepherdesses, who gather around him day after day through the spring on a hillside near Cambridge. The pastoral setting provides delicate descriptive introductions to the cantos, making a strange contrast with the narrative. The *Locustae* or *Apollyonists* is of particular interest for Milton. The Latin poem with its English paraphrase tells of the fall of the angels under the leadership of Satan. Fletcher represents the forces of Satan as planning a subtle revenge on God by working through the Roman Catholic Church to foment the Gunpowder plot, an idea which Milton used in his youthful *In Quintum Novembris. Paradise Lost* is, however, more heavily indebted than is the earlier poem. Fletcher's magnificent conception of Satan as a powerful and indomitable character, and his picture of Sin as the Porter of Hell gave Milton a suggestion for his portrayal of Satan and for his famous allegory of Sin and Death, the keepers of Hell Gate in *Paradise Lost,* Book II.

These long poems are written in a variation of the Spenserian stanza which simplifies the rhyme yet leaves the stanza definitely reminiscent of Spenser. Frequently Fletcher is very melodious, and Quarles did not hesitate to call him "the Spencer of this age."

The Apollyonists

CANTO I

1

Of men, nay beasts; worse, monsters; worst of all,
Incarnate fiends, English Italianate;
Of priests, O no! mass-priests, priests-cannibal,
Who make their Maker, chew, grind, feed, grow fat
With flesh divine; of that great city's fall,
Which born, nursed, grown with blood, the earth's empress
      sat,
  Cleansed, spoused to Christ, yet back to whoredom fell,
  None can enough, something I fain would tell.
How black are quenched lights! Fallen heaven's a double
      hell.

2

Great Lord, who graspest all creatures in Thy hand,   10
Who in Thy lap layest down proud Thetis' head,
And bindest her white curled locks in cauls of sand,
Who gatherest in Thy fist and layest in bed
The sturdy winds, who groundest the floating land
On fleeting seas, and over all hast spread
  Heaven's brooding wings to foster all below,
  Who makest the sun without all fire to glow,
The spring of heat and light, the moon to ebb and flow,

3

Thou world's sole Pilot, who in this poor isle
(So small a bottom) hast embarked Thy light,   20
And glorious Self and steerest it safe, the while
Hoarse drumming seas and winds' loud trumpets fight,
Who causest stormy heavens here only smile,
Steer me, poor ship-boy, steer my course aright;
  Breathe, gracious Spirit, breathe gently on these lays;

Be Thou my compass, needle to my ways;
Thy glorious work's my freight; my haven is Thy praise.

4

Thou purple whore,[1] mounted on scarlet beast,
Gorged with the flesh, drunk with the blood of saints,
Whose amorous golden cup and charmed feast   30
All earthly kings, all earthly men attaints,
See thy live pictures, see thine own, thy best,
Thy dearest sons, and cheer thy heart that faints.
    Hark! thou saved island, hark! and never cease
    To praise that hand which held thy head in peace;
Else hadst thou swum as deep in blood as now in seas.

5

The cloudy night came whirling up the sky
And scatt'ring round the dews, which first she drew
From milky poppies, loads the drowsy eye.
The wat'ry moon, cold Vesper, and his crew   40
Light up their tapers; to the sun they fly
And at his blazing flame their sparks renew.[2]
    Oh, why should earthly lights then scorn to tine
    Their lamps alone at that first Sun divine?
Hence as false as falling stars, as rotten wood, they shine.

6

Her sable mantle was embroidered gay
With silver beams, with spangles round beset;
Four steeds her chariot drew: the first was gray,
The second blue, third brown, fourth black as jet.

---

[1] This is the whore of Babylon described in *Rev.* 17, and identified with the Roman Catholic Church.

[2] It is interesting to compare Milton's lines,
            Hither, as to their fountain, other stars
            Repairing, in their golden urns draw light.
                                        Paradise Lost VII, 364–5.

The hollowing owl, her post, prepares the way; 50
And winged dreams, as gnat swarms flutt'ring, let
   Sad sleep, who fain his eyes in rest would steep.
   Why then at death do weary mortals weep?
Sleep's but a shorter death; death's but a longer sleep.

7

And now the world, and dreams themselves, were drowned
In deadly sleep; the laborer snorteth fast,
His brawny arms unbent, his limbs unbound,
As dead, forget all toil to come, or past;
Only sad guilt and troubled greatness, crowned
With heavy gold and care, no rest can taste. 60
   Go then, vain man, go pill the live and dead,
   Buy, sell, fawn, flatter, rise; then couch thy head
In proud, but dangerous gold, in silk, but restless bed.

8

When lo! a sudden noise breaks the empty air:
A dreadful noise, which every creature daunts,
Frights home the blood, shoots up the limber hair;
For through the silent heaven hell's pursuivants,
Cutting their way, command foul spirits repair
With haste to Pluto, who their counsel wants.
   Their hoarse bass-horns like fenny bitterns sound; 70
   The earth shakes, dogs howl, and heaven itself, astound,
Shuts all his eyes; the stars in clouds their candles drowned.

9

Meantime, hell's iron gates by fiends beneath
Are open flung, which framed with wondrous art
To every guilty soul yields entrance eath; [3]
But never wight but He could thence depart,
Who, dying once, was death to endless death.

[3] Easy.

So where the liver's channel to the heart
    Pays purple tribute, with their three-forked mace
     Three Tritons stand and speed his flowing race,   80
But stop the ebbing stream if once it back would pace.

10

The porter to the infernal gate is Sin,[4]
A shapeless shape, a foul deformed thing,
Nor nothing, nor a substance, as those thin
And empty forms which through the air fling
Their wandering shapes, at length they're fastened in
The crystal sight. It serves, yet reigns as king;
    It lives, yet's death; it pleases, full of pain;
     Monster! ah, who, who can thy being feign?   89
Thou shapeless shape, live death, pain pleasing, servile reign!

11

Of that first woman and the old serpent bred,
By lust and custom nursed, whom when her mother
Saw so deformed, how fain would she have fled
Her birth, and self! But she her dam would smother,
And all her brood, had not He rescued
Who was His mother's sire, His children's brother:
    Eternity, who yet was born and died;
     His own creator, earth's scorn, heaven's pride,
Who the Deity infleshed, and man's flesh deified.

12

Her former parts her mother seems resemble,   100
Yet only seems to flesh and weaker sight,
For she with art and paint could fine dissemble
Her loathsome face. Her back parts, black as night,
Like to her horrid sire, would force to tremble

[4] Milton gets a suggestion here for Sin and Death, who guard the
gates of hell. *Paradise Lost* II, 648–89.

The boldest heart. To the eye that meets her right
   She seems a lovely sweet, of beauty rare;
   But at the parting, he that shall compare,
Hell will more lovely deem, the devil's self more fair.

13

Her rosy cheek, quick eye, her naked breast,
And whatsoe'er loose fancy might entice,   110
She bare exposed to sight, all lovely dressed
In beauty's livery and quaint device.
Thus she bewitches many a boy unblest,
Who drenched in hell, dreams all of paradise:
   Her breasts, his spheres; her arms, his circling sky;
   Her pleasures, heaven; her love, eternity.
For her he longs to live; with her he longs to die.

14

But He that gave a stone power to descry
'Twixt natures hid, and check that metal's pride
That dares aspire to gold's fair purity,   120
Hath left a touchstone erring eyes to guide,
Which clears their sight and strips hypocrisy.
They see, they loathe, they curse her painted hide;
   Her as a crawling carrion they esteem;
   Her worst of ills, and worse than that, they deem,
Yet know her worse than they can think, or she can seem.

15

Close by her sat Despair, sad ghastly sprite,
With staring looks, unmoved, fast nailed to Sin;
Her body all of earth, her soul of fright,
About her thousand deaths, but more within;   130
Pale, pined cheeks, black hair, torn, rudely dight,
Short breath, long nails, dull eyes, sharp-pointed chin;
   Light, life, heaven, earth, herself, and all she fled.

Fain would she die, but could not; yet half dead,
A breathing corse she seemed, wrapped up in living lead.

16

In the entrance Sickness and faint Languor dwelt,
Who with sad groans toll out their passing knell,
Late fear, fright, horror that already felt
The torturer's claws, preventing death and hell.
Within loud Grief and roaring Pangs that swelt   140
In sulphur flames, did weep and howl and yell.
   A thousand souls in endless dolors lie,
    Who burn, fry, hiss, and never cease to cry,
"Oh, that I ne'er had lived; oh, that I once could die!"

17

And now the infernal powers through the air driving,
For speed their leather pinions broad display;
Now at eternal death's wide gate arriving,
Sin gives them passage; still they cut their way
Till to the bottom of hell's palace diving,
They enter Dis' [5] deep conclave. There they stay,   150
   Waiting the rest, and now they all are met,
    A full foul senate; now they all are set,
The horrid court, big swoll'n with the hideous council sweat.

18

The midst, but lowest (in hell's heraldry
The deepest is the highest room) in state
Sat lordly Lucifer; [6] his fiery eye,
Much swoll'n with pride, but more with rage and hate,
As censor mustered all his company,
Who round about with awful silence sate.
   This do, this let rebellious spirits gain,   160

[5] Dis is Pluto, ruler over Hades.
[6] Compare the counsel in Pandemonium, *Paradise Lost* II, 1–505.

Change God for Satan, heaven's for hell's sovereign:
O let him serve in hell, who scorns in heaven to reign! [7]

19

Ah, wretch! who with ambitious cares oppressed,
Longest still for future, feelest no present good;
Despising to be better, wouldst be best,
Good never; who wilt serve thy lusting mood,
Yet all command: not he who raised his crest,
But pulled it down, hath high and firmly stood.
   Fool! serve thy towering lusts, grow still, still crave,
    Rule, reign; this comfort from thy greatness have,   170
Now at thy top thou art a great commanding slave.

20

Thus fell this Prince of Darkness, once a bright
And glorious star; he wilful turned away
His borrowed globe from that eternal light;
Himself he sought, so lost himself: his ray
Vanished to smoke, his morning sunk in night,
And never more shall see the springing day.
   To be in heaven the second he disdains;
    So now the first in hell and flames he reigns,
Crowned once with joy and light, crowned now with fire
        and pains.   180

21

As where the warlike Dane the scepter sways,
They crown usurpers with a wreath of lead,
And with hot steel, while loud the traitor brays,
They melt and drop it down into his head,—
Crowned he would live, and crowned he ends his days;
All so in heaven's courts this traitor sped,

[7] Satan, in *Paradise Lost* I, 263, says, "Better to reign in hell than
serve in heaven."

Who now, when he had overlooked his train,
Rising upon his throne, with bitter strain
Thus 'gan to whet their rage and chide their frustrate pain.

22

See, see, you Spirits (I know not whether more   190
Hated, or hating heaven) ah! see the earth
Smiling in quiet peace and plenteous store.
Men fearless live in ease, in love, and mirth;
Where arms did rage, the drum and cannon roar;
Where hate, strife, envy reigned, and meager dearth,
    Now lutes and viols charm the ravished ear;
    Men plow with swords; horse-heels their armors wear;
Ah! shortly scarce they'll know what war and armors were.

23

Under their sprouting vines they sporting sit.
The old tell of evils past; youth laugh and play   200
And to their wanton heads sweet garlands fit,
Roses with lilies, myrtles weaved with bay.
The world's at rest; Erinnys, forced to quit
Her strongest holds, from earth is driven away.
    Even Turks forget their empire to increase;
    War's self is slain and whips of Furies cease.
We, we ourselves, I fear, will shortly live in peace.

24

Meantime (I burn, I broil, I burst with spite)
In midst of peace that sharp two-edged sword
Cuts through our darkness, cleaves the misty night,   210
Discovers all our snares; that sacred word,
Locked up by Rome, breaks prison, spreads the light,
Speaks every tongue, paints, and points out the Lord,
    His birth, life, death, and cross; our gilded stocks,
    Our laymen's books, the boy and woman mocks;

They laugh, they fleer, and say, "Blocks teach and worship
    blocks."

25

Springtides of light divine the air surround
And bring down heaven to earth; deaf Ignorance,
Vexed with the day, her head in hell hath drowned;
Fond Superstition, frighted with the glance   220
Of sudden beams, in vain hath crossed her round;
Truth and Religion everywhere advance
    Their conquering standards; Error's lost and fled;
    Earth burns in love to Heaven; Heaven yields her bed
To earth, and common grown, smiles to be ravished.

26

That little swimming isle above the rest,
Spite of our spite and all our plots, remains
And grows in happiness; but late our nest,
Where we and Rome, and blood, and all our trains,
Monks, nuns, dead and live idols, safe did rest.   230
Now there, next the oath of God, that wrestler [8] reigns,
    Who fills the land and world with peace; his spear
    Is but a pen, with which he down doth bear
Blind ignorance, false gods, and superstitious fear.

27

There God hath framed another paradise,
Fat olives dropping peace, victorious palms;
Nor in the midst, but everywhere doth rise
That hated tree of life, whose precious balms
Cure every sinful wound, give light to the eyes,
Unlock the ear, recover fainting qualms.   240
    There richly grows what makes a people blest,

[8] The king, James I.

A garden planted by Himself and dressed,
Where He Himself doth walk, where He Himself doth rest.

28

There every star sheds his sweet influence
And radiant beams; great, little, old, and new,
Their glittering rays and frequent confluence
The milky path to God's high palace strew;
The unwearied pastors with steeled confidence,
Conquered and conquering, fresh their fight renew.
    Our strongest holds that thundering ordinance   250
    Beats down and makes our proudest turrets dance,
Yoking men's iron necks in His sweet governance.

29

Nor can the old world content ambitious light;
Virginia, our soil, our seat, and throne,
(To which so long possession gives us right,
As long as hell's) Virginia's self is gone;
That stormy isle, which the Isle of Devils' [9] hight,
Peopled with faith, truth, grace, religion.
    What's next but hell? That now alone remains,
    And that subdued, even here He rules and reigns,   260
And mortals 'gin to dream of long, but endless pains.

30

While we, good harmless creatures, sleep or play,
Forget our former loss and following pain,
Earth sweats for heaven, but hell keeps holiday.
Shall we repent, good souls, or shall we plain?
Shall we groan, sigh, weep, mourn, for mercy pray?
Lay down our spite, wash out our sinful stain?
    Maybe He'll yield, forget, and use us well, [10]

[9] Bermuda is meant.
[10] Belial makes a similar argument for "ignoble ease and peaceful sloth" in Milton's portrayal of the Council.

Forgive, join hands, restore us whence we fell;
Maybe He'll yield us heaven and fall Himself to hell.   270

31

But me, O never let me, Spirits, forget
That glorious day when I your standard bore,
And scorning in the second place to sit,
With you assaulted heaven, His yoke forswore!
My dauntless heart yet longs to bleed and sweat
In such a fray; the more I burn, the more
    I hate: should He yet offer grace and ease,
    If subject we our arms and spite surcease,
Such offer should I hate, and scorn so base a peace.

32

Where are those Spirits? Where that haughty rage   280
That durst with me invade eternal light?
What! Are our hearts fallen too? Droop we with age?
Can we yet fall from hell and hellish spite?
Can smart our wrath, can grief our hate assuage?
Dare we with heaven, and not with earth to fight?
    Your arms, allies, yourselves as strong as ever;
    Your foes, their weapons, numbers, weaker never.
For shame, tread down this earth! What wants but your
        endeavor?

33

Now by yourselves and thunder-daunted arms,
But never-daunted hate, I you implore,   290
Command, adjure, reinforce your fierce alarms;
Kindle, I pray, who never prayed before,
Kindle your darts, treble repay our harms.
Oh, our short time, too short, stands at the door!
    Double your rage; if now we do not ply,

We lone in hell, without due company,
And worse, without desert, without revenge shall lie.

34

He, Spirits, (ah, that, that's our main torment!) He
Can feel no wounds, laughs at the sword and dart,
Himself from grief, from suffering wholly free;   300
His simple nature cannot taste of smart,
Yet in His members we Him grieved see;
For, and in them, He suffers; where His heart
    Lies bare and naked, there dart your fiery steel,
    Cut, wound, burn, sear, if not the head, the heel.
Let Him in every part some pain and torment feel.

35

That light comes posting on, that cursed light,
When they as He, all glorious, all divine,
(Their flesh clothed with the sun, and much more bright,
Yet brighter spirits) shall in His image shine,   310
And see Him as He is; there no despite,
No force, no art their state can undermine:
    Full of unmeasured bliss, yet still receiving,
    Their souls still childing joy, yet still conceiving,
Delights beyond the wish, beyond quick thoughts perceiving.

36

But we fast pinioned with dark fiery chains,
Shall suffer every ill, but do no more;
The guilty spirit there feels extremest pains,
Yet fears worse than it feels; and finding store
Of present deaths, death's absence sore complains: 320
Oceans of ills without or ebb, or shore,
    A life that ever dies, a death that lives,
    And, worst of all, God's absent presence gives
A thousand living woes, a thousand dying griefs.

37

But when he sums his time and turns his eye
First to the past, then future pangs, past days
(And every day's an age of misery)
In torment spent, by thousands down he lays,
Future by millions, yet eternity
Grows nothing less, nor past to come allays.   330
   Through every pang and grief he wild doth run,
   And challenge coward death; doth nothing shun
That he may nothing be, does all to be undone.

38

Oh, let our work equal our wages, let
Our Judge fall short, and when His plagues are spent,
Owe more than He hath paid, live in our debt;
Let heaven want vengeance, hell want punishment
To give our dues; when we with flames beset,
Still dying, live in endless languishment,
   This be our comfort: we did get and win   340
   The fires and tortures we are whelmed in;
We have kept pace, outrun His justice with our sin.

39

And now you States of Hell, give your advice,
And to these ruins lend your helping hand.
This said and ceased; straight humming murmurs rise:
Some chafe, some fret, some sad and thoughtful stand,
Some chat, and some new stratagems devise;
And everyone heaven's stronger powers banned,
   And tear for madness their uncombed snakes;
   And everyone his fiery weapon shakes,   350
And everyone expects who first the answer makes.

40

So when the falling sun hangs o'er the main,
Ready to drop into the western wave
By yellow Cam, where all the Muses reign,
And with their towers his reedy head embrave,
The warlike gnat their flutt'ring armies train;
All have sharp spears, and all shrill trumpets have;
   Their files they double, loud their cornets sound,
   Now march at length, their troops now gather round;
The banks, the broken noise, and turrets fair rebound.   360

GILES FLETCHER received his early training from the famous Westminster School and proceeded to Cambridge, though not enrolled in the same college as Phineas. That he was there in 1603 is established by the fact that his verses, the most poetical of all the contributions to the Cambridge volume of that year, appeared with those of Phineas. Through university appointments the brothers were still associated after graduation until Phineas became chaplain for Sir Henry Willoughby in 1616.

Giles, unlike Phineas, published his chief work, *Christ's Victory and Triumph,* while he was still at Cambridge. His models are apparent, but in his preface he acknowledges the literary mastership of "thrice-honoured Bartas, and our (I know no name more glorious than) Edmund Spenser, two blessed soules." This poem was the first significant religious poem published in England. In an effort to prepare for the favorable consideration of this new type, Giles made a strong argument in his preface for the use of religious subjects in poetry, but the poem was not well received. Phineas, who was devoted to his frail younger brother, wrote a poem comforting him for the harsh criticism:

> Then do not thou malicious tongues esteem;
> (The glasse, through which an envious eye doth gaze,
> Can easily make a mole-hill mountain seem.)
> His praise dispraises, his dispraises praise:
> Enough, if best men best thy labors deem,
> And to the highest pitch thy merit raise.

In spite of this point of view Giles, to us so clearly the best singer of all the Spenserian followers, was forever silenced.

Two years after Phineas left Cambridge, Giles took a "college living," possibly that of St. Mary's, closely associated later with the night-vigils of Crashaw. It was not long before he was appointed rector of Alderton in Suffolk. There is an interesting story, though its truth is questionable, that Sir Francis Bacon presented him with the latter position. He did not live long after going to Alderton, and Fuller attributes his early death to an uncongenial environment, saying quaintly:

> . . . his clownish, low-parted parishioners, having nothing but their shoes high about them, valued not their pastor, according to his worth, which disposed him to melancholy and hastened his dissolution.

His great poem, divided into four cantos, takes up the Atonement, Temptation, Crucifixion, and Resurrection of Christ, and incorporates in epic pattern much of the Calvinistic theology of the seventeenth century. The second canto was particularly useful to Milton in *Paradise Regained*, and Milton's picture of Satan as an old man in "rural weeds" in the scene of the first temptation is clearly reminiscent of Fletcher's "aged sire" who "came slowly footing" to meet Christ. The poem reaches its greatest height of beauty, however, in the fourth canto. Here the poem becomes an ecstatic hymn of the bliss of paradise, reminding one of the close of Dante's *Paradiso*.

The stanza which Fletcher used is made up of eight lines, Spenser's nine lines with the seventh omitted. The omission makes an easier rhyme scheme, *ababbccc*, but forms a closing triplet which gives a finality to each stanza that interrupts the progress of the narrative.

Giles is a poet of genius. His lines sing, and his narrative is lifted up by the beauty and luxuriance of his powerful imagination. Sometimes his richness becomes cloyingly sweet, and sometimes paradox is so freely used and so strikingly emphasized by antithesis that it becomes a flaw; yet in spite of these characteristics his poem abounds in lines which are breath-taking in sheer loveliness. That he followed Spenser and was imitated by Milton are facts which become lost in the enjoyment of his melody and poetic pictures.

Christ's Triumph after Death

1

But now the second morning from her bower
Began to glister in her beams; and now
The roses of the day began to flower
In the eastern garden, for heaven's smiling brow
Half insolent for joy began to show.
  The early sun came lively dancing out,
    And the brag lambs ran wantoning about,
That heaven and earth might seem in triumph both to shout.

2

The engladded spring, forgetful now to weep,
Began to eblazon from her leafy bed;   10
The waking swallow broke her half-year's sleep;
And every bush lay deeply purpured
With violets; the wood's late-wintry head
  Wide flaming primroses set all on fire,
    And his bald trees put on their green attire,
Among whose infant leaves the joyous birds conspire.

3

And now the taller sons, whom Titan warms,
Of unshorn mountains, blown with easy winds,
Dandled the morning's childhood in their arms;
And if they chanced to slip the prouder pines,   20
The under corylets did catch the shines
  To gild their leaves; saw never happy year
    Such joyful triumph and triumphant cheer,
As though the aged world anew created were.

4

Say, earth, why hast thou got thee new attire
And stickest thy habit full of daisies red?

Seems that thou dost to some high thought aspire,
And some new-found-out bridegroom meanest to wed.
Tell me ye trees, so fresh appareled,
 So never let the spiteful canker waste you,   30
 So never let the heavens with lightning blast you,
Why go you now so trimly dressed, or whither haste you?

5

Answer me, Jordan, why thy crooked tide
So often wanders from his nearest way,
As though some other way thy stream would slide,
And fain salute the place where something lay?
And you sweet birds, that, shaded from the ray,
 Sit caroling and piping grief away,
 The while the lambs to hear you dance and play,
Tell me, sweet birds, what it is you so fain would say? 40

6

And thou fair spouse of earth that every year
Gettest such a numerous issue of thy bride,
How chance thou hotter shinest, and drawest more near?
Sure thou somewhere some worthy sight hast spied,
That in one place for joy thou canst not bide.
 And you dead swallows, that so lively now
 Through the flit air your winged passage row,
How could new life into your frozen ashes flow?

7

Ye primroses and purple violets,
Tell me why blaze ye from your leafy bed,   50
And woo men's hands to rend you from your sets,
As though you would somewhere be carried,
With fresh perfumes and velvets garnished?
 But ah! I need not ask; 'tis surely so:

You all would to your Savior's triumphs go;
There would ye all wait and humble homage do.

8

There should the earth herself with garlands new
And lovely flowers embellished adore;
Such roses never in her garland grew,
Such lilies never in her breast she wore,   60
Like beauty never yet did shine before.
    There should the sun another sun behold,
    From whence himself borrows his locks of gold
That kindle heaven and earth with beauties manifold.

9

There might the violet and the primrose sweet
Beams of more lively and more lovely grace,
Arising from their beds of incense meet;
There should the swallow see new life embrace
Dead ashes, and the grave unheal his face
    To let the living from his bowels creep,   70
    Unable longer his own dead to keep;
There heaven and earth should see their Lord awake from
        sleep.

10

Their Lord, before by other judged to die,
Now judge of all Himself; before forsaken
Of all the world, that from His aid did fly,
Now by the saints into their armies taken;
Before for an unworthy man mistaken,
    Now worthy to be God confessed; before
    With blasphemies by all the basest tore,
Nor worshiped by angels, that Him low adore.   80

11

Whose garment was before indipped in blood,
But now imbrightened into heavenly flame,
The sun itself outglitters, though he should
Climb to the top of the celestial frame
And force the stars go hide themselves for shame;
    Before that under earth was buried,
    But now about the heavens is carried,
And there forever by the angels heried.[1]

12

So fairest Phosphor, the bright morning star,
But newly washed in the green element,   90
Before the drowsy night is half aware,
Shooting his flaming locks with dew besprent,
Springs lively up into the orient;
    And the bright drove, fleeced in gold, he chases
    To drink, that on the Olympic mountain grazes,
The while the minor planets forfeit all their faces.

13

So long He wandered in our lower sphere
That heaven began his cloudy stars despise,
Half envious, to see on earth appear
A greater light than flamed in his own skies.   100
At length it burst for spite, and out there flies
    A globe of winged angels, swift as thought,
    That on their spotted feathers lively caught
The sparkling earth, and to their azure fields it brought.

14

The rest, that yet amazed stood below,
With eyes cast up, as greedy to be fed,

[1] From the Old English, *herian,* to praise.

And hands upheld, themselves to ground did throw;
So when the Trojan boy [2] was ravished,
As through the Idalian woods they say he fled,
   His aged guardians stood all dismayed,   110
   Some lest he should have fallen back afraid,
And some their hasty vows and timely prayers said.

15

Toss up your heads, ye everlasting gates,
And let the Prince of glory enter in! [3]
At whose brave volley of siderial states,
The sun to blush, and stars grow pale were seen,
When leaping first from earth, He did begin
   To climb His angel's wings; "Then open hang
   Your crystal doors," so all the chorus sang
Of heavenly birds, as to the stars they nimbly sprang.   120

16

Hark! how the floods clap their applauding hands,
The pleasant valleys singing for delight;
The wanton mountains dance about the lands; [4]
The while the fields, struck with the heavenly light,
Set all their flowers a-smiling at the sight;
   The trees laugh with their blossoms; and the sound
   Of the triumphant shout of praise that crowned
The flaming Lamb, breaking through heaven, hath passage
      found.

[2] Jupiter, disguised as an eagle, carried off Ganymede from among his playmates on Mt. Ida to become cup-bearer to the gods on Mt. Olympus.
[3] "Lift up your heads, O ye gates; and be ye lift up, ye everlasting doors; and the King of glory shall come in." *Psalm* 24:7.
[4] "Let the floods clap their hands: let the hills be joyful together." *Psalm* 98:8. ". . . the mountains and the hills shall break forth before you into singing, and all the trees of the field shall clap their hands." *Isaiah* 55:12.

17

Out leap the antique patriarchs, all in haste,
To see the powers of hell in triumph led,
And with small stars a garland interchased
Of olive leaves they bore, to crown His head,
That was before with thorns degloried.
　　After them flew the prophets, brightly stoled
　　In shining lawn, and wimpled manifold,
Striking their ivory harps, strung all in chords of gold.

18

To which the saints victorious carols sung,
Ten thousand saints at once, that with the sound
The hollow vaults of heaven for triumph rung;
The cherubim their clamors did confound
With all the rest, and clapt their wings around;
　　Down from their thrones the dominations flow,
　　And at His feet their crowns and scepters throw;
And all the princely souls fell on their faces low.

19

Nor can the martyrs' wounds them stay behind,
But out they rush among the heavenly crowd,
Seeking their heaven out of their heaven to find,
Sounding their silver trumpets out so loud
That the shrill noise broke through the starry cloud;
　　And all the virgin souls in pure array
　　Came dancing forth and making joyous play:
So Him they lead along into the courts of day.

20

So Him they lead into the courts of day,
Where never war, nor wounds abide Him more;
But in that house eternal peace doth play,

Acquieting the souls, that new before
Their way to heaven through their own blood did score,
   But now, estranged from all misery,
   As far as heaven and earth discoasted lie,
Swelter in quiet waves of immortality.   160

21

And if great things by smaller may be guessed,
So in the midst of Neptune's angry tide
Our Britain Island, like the weedy nest
Of true halcyon,[5] on the waves doth ride,
And softly sailing, scorns the water's pride;
   While all the rest, drowned on the Continent
   And tost in bloody waves, their wounds lament,
And stand to see our peace, as struck with wonderment.

22

The ship of France religious waves do toss,
And Greece itself is now grown barbarous;   170
Spain's children hardly dare the ocean cross,
And Belge's field lies waste and ruinous,
That unto those the heavens are envious,
   And unto them, themselves are strangers grown,
   And unto these, the seas are faithless known,
And unto her, alas! her own is not her own.

23

Here only shut we Janus' iron gates,
And call the welcome Muses to our springs,
And are but pilgrims from our heavenly states,
The while the trusty earth sure plenty brings,   180
And ships through Neptune safely spread their wings.
   Go, blessed Island, wander where thou please,

[5] The halcyon bird built her nest on the waves; and during the time she was brooding, the waters were calm.

Unto thy God, or men, heaven, lands, or seas;
Thou canst not lose thy way; thy king with all hath peace.

24

Dear Prince, thy subject's joy, hope of their heirs,
Picture of peace, or breathing image rather,
The certain argument of all our prayers,
Thy Harry's and thy country's lovely father,
Let peace in endless joys forever bathe her
     Within thy sacred breast, that at thy birth   190
     Brought'st her with thee from heaven to dwell on earth,
Making our earth a heaven, and paradise of mirth.

25

Let not my liege misdeem these humble lays,
As licked with soft and supple blandishment,
Or spoken to disparagon his praise;
For though pale Cynthia near her brother's tent
Soon disappears in the white firmament,
     And gives him back the beams before were his,
     Yet when he verges, or is hardly riz,
She the vive [6] image of her absent brother is.   200

26

Nor let the Prince of Peace his beadsman blame,
That with his Stewart [7] dares his Lord compare,
And heavenly peace with earthly quiet shame;
So pines to lowly plants compared are,
And lightning Phœbus to a little star.
     And well I wot, my rhyme, albe unsmooth,

[6] From the Latin *vivere,* to live.

[7] The use of "Stewart" here connotes more than the rank of steward. Walter, son of Fleance and the Welsh Princess Nesta, returned to Scotland and became Lord High Steward and the ancestor of the Scottish line of kings. The name, Stuart, was derived from this office.

Ne says but what it means, ne means but sooth,
Ne harms the good, ne good to harmful person doth.

27

Gaze but upon the house where man embowers:
With flowers and rushes paved is his way,   210
Where all the creatures are his servitors;
The winds do sweep his chambers every day,
And clouds do wash his rooms; the ceiling gay,
   Starred aloft, the gilded knobs embrave.
  If such a house God to another gave,
How shine those glittering courts He for Himself will have?

28

And if a sullen cloud as sad as night,
In which the sun may seem embodied,
Depured of all his dross, we see so white,
Burning in melted gold his wat'ry head,   220
Or round with ivory edges silvered,
   What luster super-excellent will he
   Lighten on those that all his sunshine see,
In that all-glorious court in which all glories be?

29

If but one sun, with his diffusive fires,
Can paint the stars and the whole world with light,
And joy and life in each heart inspires,
And every saint shall shine in heaven as bright
As doth the sun in his transcendent might,
   (As faith may well believe what truth once says)   230
   What shall so many suns united rays
But dazzle all the eyes, that now in heaven we praise?

30

Here let my Lord hang up His conquering lance
And bloody armor with late slaughter warm,
And looking down on His weak militants,
Behold His saints, midst of their hot alarm,
Hang all their golden hopes upon His arm;
    And in this lower field dispacing wide,
     Through windy thoughts that would their sails misguide,
Anchor their fleshly ships fast in His wounded side.   ₂₄₀

31

Here may the band that now in triumph shines,
And that, before they were invested thus,
In earthly bodies carried heavenly minds,
Pitched round about in order glorious,
Their sunny tents and houses luminous;
    All the eternal day in songs employing,
     Joying their end, without end of their joying,
While their Almighty Prince destruction is destroying.[8]

32

Full, yet without satiety, of that
Which whets and quiets greedy appetite,   ₂₅₀
Where never sun did rise, nor ever set;
But one eternal day and endless light
Gives time to those whose time is infinite;
    Speaking with thought, obtaining without fee,
     Beholding Him whom never eye could see,
And magnifying Him that cannot greater be.

33

How can such joy as this want words to speak?
And yet what words can speak such joy as this?

[8] In *Revelations* is given the account of Christ's final victory over
Satan and his works.

Far from the world, that might their quiet break,
Here the glad souls the face of beauty kiss,   260
Poured out in pleasure on their beds of bliss;
    And drunk with nectar torrents, ever hold
    Their eyes on Him, whose graces manifold,
The more they do behold, the more they would behold.

34

Their sight drinks lovely fires in at their eyes;
Their brain sweet incense with fine breath accloys,
That on God's sweating altar burning lies;
Their hungry ears feed on their heavenly noise
That angels sing, to tell their untold joys;
    Their understanding naked truth, their wills   270
    The all, and self-sufficient Goodness fills,
That nothing here is wanting, but the want of ills.

35

No sorrow now hangs clouding on their brow,
No bloodless malady empales their face,
No age drops on their hairs his silver snow,
No nakedness their bodies doth embase,
No poverty themselves and theirs disgrace,
    No fear of death the joy of life devours,
    No unchaste sleep their precious time deflowers,
No loss, no grief, no change wait on their winged hours.   280

36

But now their naked bodies scorn the cold,
And from their eyes joy looks, and laughs at pain;
The infant wonders how he came so old,
And old man how he came so young again;
Still resting, though from sleep they still refrain,
    Where all are rich, and yet no gold they owe,

And all are kings, and yet no subjects know,
All full, and yet no time on food they do bestow.

37

For things that pass are past, and in this field
The indeficient spring no winter fears;   290
The trees together fruit and blossom yield;
The unfading lily leaves of silver bears,
And crimson rose a scarlet garment wears.
   And all of these on the saints' bodies grow,
   Not, as they wont, on baser earth below;
Three rivers here of milk and wine and honey flow.

38

About the holy city rolls a flood
Of molten crystal, like a sea of glass,
On which weak stream a strong foundation stood;
Of living diamond the building was,   300
That all things else besides itself did pass;
   Her streets, instead of stones, the stars did pave,
   And little pearls for dust, it seemed to have,
On which soft-streaming manna, like pure snow, did wave.

39

In midst of this city celestial,
Where the eternal temple should have rose,
Lightened the Idea Beatifical: [9]
End and beginning of each thing that grows,
Whose self no end, nor yet beginning knows;
   That hath no eyes to see, nor ears to hear,   310
   Yet sees and hears and is all eye, all ear;
That nowhere is contained and yet is everywhere.

[9] The entire description of heaven is based upon *Revelations* 21–22. These lines are a somewhat Platonic phrasing of *Rev.* 21:22, "And I saw no temple therein: for the Lord God Almighty and the Lamb are the temple of it."

40

Changer of all things, yet immutable;
Before and after all, the first and last,
That moving all, is yet immovable;
Great without quantity, in whose forecast
Things past are present, things to come are past;
   Swift without motion, to whose open eye
   The hearts of wicked men unbreasted lie,
At once absent and present to them, far and nigh.   320

41

It is no flaming luster made of light,
No sweet consent, or well-timed harmony,
Ambrosia for to feast the appetite,
Or flowery odor mixed with spicery,
No soft embrace or pleasure bodily;
   And yet it is a kind of inward feast,
   A harmony that sounds within the breast,
An odor, light, embrace, in which the soul doth rest.

42

A heavenly feast, no hunger can consume,
A light unseen, yet shines in every place,   330
A sound no time can steal, a sweet perfume
No winds can scatter, an entire embrace
That no satiety can e'er unlace;
   Ingraced into so high a favor, there
   The saints with their beau-peers whole worlds outwear,
And things unseen do see, and things unheard do hear.

43

Ye blessed souls, grown richer by your spoil,
Whose loss, though great, is cause of greater gains.
Here may your weary spirits rest from toil,

Spending your endless evening that remains,　340
Among those white flocks and celestial trains
　　That feed upon their Shepherd's eyes, and frame
　　That heavenly music of so wondrous fame,
Psalming aloud the holy honors of His name.

44

Had I a voice of steel to tune my song,
Were every verse as smoothly filed as glass,
And every member turned to a tongue,
And every tongue were made of sounding brass,
Yet all that skill and all this strength, alas!
　　Should it presume to gild, were misadvised　350
　　The place where David hath new songs devised,
As in his burning throne he sits emparadised.

45

Most happy prince, whose eyes those stars behold,
Treading ours under feet, now mayest thou pour
That overflowing skill wherewith of old
Thou wont'st to comb rough speech; now mayest thou shower
Fresh streams of praise upon that holy bower,
　　Which well we heaven call, not that it rolls,
　　But that it is the haven of our souls:
Most happy prince, whose sight so heavenly sight beholds!　360

46

Ah, foolish shepherds, that were wont esteem
Your God all rough and shaggy-haired to be;
And yet far wiser shepherds than ye deem,
For who so poor (though who so rich) as He,
When, with us hermiting in low degree,
　　He washed His flocks in Jordan's spotless tide;
　　And, that His dear remembrance ay might bide,
Did to us come and with us lived and for us died?

47

But now so lively colors did embeam
His sparkling forehead, and so shiny rays   370
Kindled His flaming locks that down did stream
In curls along His neck, where sweetly plays
(Singing His wounds of love in sacred lays)
   His dearest spouse, spouse of the dearest Lover,
   Knitting a thousand knots over and over,
And dying still for love, but they her still recover.

48

Fair Egliset, that at His eyes doth dress
Her glorious face, those eyes from whence are shed
Infinite bel-amours, where to express
His love, high God all heaven as captive leads,   380
And all the banners of His grace dispreads,
   And in those windows doth His arms englaze,
   And on those eyes the angels all do gaze,
And from those eyes the lights of heaven do glean their blaze.

49

But let the Kentish lad that lately taught
His oaten reed the trumpet's silver sound,
Young Thyrsilis,[10] and for his music brought
The willing spheres from heaven to lead a round
Of dancing nymphs and herds, that sung and crowned
   Eclecta's hymen with ten thousand flowers   390
   Of choicest praise, and hung her heavenly bowers
With saffron garlands, dressed for nuptial paramours,

[10] Young Thyrsilis is Thirsil, by which name Phineas Fletcher represented himself. In *The Purple Island*, Canto XII, Phineas Fletcher describes the betrothal of Eclecta, the daughter of Intellect and Voletta, or the will, to Christ. The passage, like the above, is much influenced by *Revelations*.

50

Let his shrill trumpet with her silver blast,
Of fair Eclecta and her spousal bed,
Be the sweet pipe and smooth encomiast;
But my green Muse, hiding her younger head
Under old Camus' flaggy banks, that spread
   Their willow locks abroad, and all the day
    With their own wat'ry shadows wanton play,
Dares not those high amours and love-sick songs assay.   400

51

Impotent words, weak lines, that strive in vain,
In vain, alas, to tell so heavenly sight!
So heavenly sight as none can greater feign,
Feign what he can that seems of greatest might,
   Might any yet compare with Infinite?
    Infinite sure those joys, my words but light;
Light is the palace where she dwells—O blessed wight!

DRUMMOND, who, like a true Elizabethan, thought to gain immortality by his verse, is "eternized" instead by a visit from Ben Jonson. Two men more unlike can scarcely be imagined—burly Jonson with his love of canary, drinking Drummond's ancestral cellars dry, and the neat, ascetic Scotchman, rebelling somewhat at the manners of his guest. Yet Drummond was so keenly interested in Jonson's outpouring comment on the London poets that he kept a careful record of their conversations. In spite of their dissimilarities in things physical, there was a marked congeniality in their literary taste: both were scholars, men of precise and tireless reading, who held that their conquest of authors entitled them to the trophies which boldly enrich their pages.

Though many other opportunities were open to him, Drummond chose to spend his life in scholarly retirement at Hawthornden. His father had intended him for law, and after Drummond had received his master's degree from the University of Edinburgh, gave him the opportunity to study law on the Continent. Court preferment was also possible for him, both through his father's position as gentleman-usher to the king and through recognition of Drummond's complimentary verses to the king and members of the royal family. But Drummond had other ideals; the glories of the court were to him only "gilded glories which decay." The proportion of two years spent in literary Paris to one year spent at Bourges in the study of law shows us his taste. When, in the year following his return to England, his father's death left the family estate in his possession, he did not hesitate in his choice. Surrounding himself with a large library of books in Latin, French, Italian, Hebrew, and Spanish, as well as English, he established himself at the age of twenty-four at picturesque Hawthornden. He formed a lasting friendship with the leading Scotch poet, Sir William Alexander of Menstrie, and made connection with the London poets through correspondence with Michael Drayton, whom he had long admired. His quiet life seems not to have been disturbed during the wars, even though he was a Royalist and the inventor of a number of military machines.

The marked French influence shown in Drummond's poetry came both from his reading and from his residence in France. When he was in Paris, Pontus de Tyard, the last of the Pléiade, had recently died, and Ronsard was still the great literary master. Drummond's first published poem, *Tears on the Death of Mœliades* (1613), occasioned by the death of Prince Henry, is quite in the manner of Ronsard. Gosse says that his "best pieces might have been translated into French of the beginning of the seventeenth century without raising any suspicion of foreign influence." [1]

Italian influence is also very marked in the poems. In fact, Drummond is primarily an exotic poet. He says of himself, "I first began to read, then loved to write," and in both content and style he shows his literary sources. In his personal library of 552 volumes only fifty books were in English; and from lists of his reading that have been preserved, we know of his wide reading in French and Italian. Some of his sonnets are direct translations from the French and Italian, and others are in close imitation. Like Petrarch he celebrated a real love and, after the death of his sweetheart, continued his sonnet sequence as an expression of his sorrow. He points out "that he was the first in the Isle that did celebrate a mistress dead." [2]

Although the sonnets of Drummond are of literary parentage, they have deep biographical interest, for the young woman "for whom they were done, and whom only I wish should see them" [3] was Mary Cunningham, who died suddenly just before the date set for their marriage. To her Drummond was faithful for fifteen years; and when he finally married at the age of forty-five, he married a woman whose

---

[1] *Jacobean Poets,* p. 102.

[2] Quoted in Ward's introduction, p. xlii from Folio, 1711: *Memoir,* p. v.

[3] Quoted in Ward's introduction, p. xlii from *Archæologia Scotica,* vol. iv, p. 83.

resemblance to Miss Cunningham had won his affection! It is notable, also, that there was almost no poetry after this marriage. In the life of a married man and unfortunate father, who had to bury six of his nine children in their infancy, poetry was supplanted by prose which was actuated only by the king's need of support.

In his criticism made during the visit to Hawthornden, Jonson pointed out the two chief weaknesses of Drummond's poems: "They smelled too much of the schools, and were not after the fancy of the time." As a counteraction he suggested that Drummond read the classical Latin authors and especially advised Quintilian, "who, he said, would tell me the faults of my verses as if he lived with me." But Drummond never achieved the manner of the Latin and Greek classical writers. Praise of Plato in the sonnet beginning "That learned Grecian" and the adoption of the idea of the pre-existence of souls "which see, know, love in heaven's great height" is as far in this direction as he gets. He remains of France and Italy and faintly echoes the fuller songs of the Renaissance.

Drummond is a sensuous poet, and the gorgeousness of his clear colors and vivid pictures is too little known. In the fields of the sonnet and the madrigal he is best; Ward says, "It is even questionable if there be any more beautiful sonnets in the English language than the best of Drummond's." [4] He holds us by the perfection of his versification. He is a supreme artificer, formal and smooth, the poet of order and beauty, but his work is not strongly individualized even in its most personal moods. He seems most genuine in his religious poems, where we find a sensuous beauty that occasionally hints of Crashaw.

Sonnets

Sleep, Silence' child, sweet father of soft rest,
Prince, whose approach peace to all mortals brings,
Indifferent host to shepherds and to kings,

[4] Introductory *Memoir* to his edition, p. xvi.

Sole comforter of minds with grief oppressed;
Lo, by thy charming rod all breathing things
Lie slumb'ring, with forgetfulness possessed,
And yet o'er me to spread thy drowsy wings
Thou spar'st, alas! who cannot be thy guest.
Since I am thine, O come, but with that face
To inward light which thou art wont to show,   10
With feigned solace ease a true-felt woe;
Or if, deaf god, thou do deny that grace,
    Come as thou wilt, and what thou wilt bequeath,
    I long to kiss the image of my death.

My lute, be as thou wast when thou didst grow
With thy green mother in some shady grove,
When immelodious winds but made thee move,
And birds on thee their ramage [1] did bestow.
Sith that dear voice which did thy sounds approve,
Which used in such harmonious strains to flow,
Is reft from earth to tune those spheres above,
What art thou but a harbinger of woe?
Thy pleasing notes be pleasing notes no more,
But orphan wailings to the fainting ear,   10
Each stop a sigh, each sound draws forth a tear:
Be therefore silent as in woods before;
    Or if that any hand to touch thee deign,
    Like widowed turtle, still her loss complain.

Thrice happy he, who by some shady grove,
Far from the clamorous world, doth live his own;
Though solitary, who is not alone,
But doth converse with that eternal love.
O how more sweet is birds' harmonious moan,

[1] Warbling.

Or the hoarse sobbings of the widowed dove,
Than those smooth whisperings near a prince's throne,
Which good make doubtful, do the evil approve!
O how more sweet is zephyr's wholesome breath,
And sighs embalmed, which new-born flow'rs unfold,　　10
Than that applause vain honour doth bequeath!
How sweet are streams to poison drunk in gold!
　　The world is full of horrors, troubles, slights;
　　Woods' harmless shades have only true delights.

I know that all beneath the moon decays,
And what by mortals in this world is brought,
In Time's great periods shall return to nought;
That fairest states have fatal nights and days;
I know how all the Muse's heavenly lays,
With toil of sprite which are so dearly bought,
As idle sounds, of none or few are sought,
And that nought lighter is than airy praise;
I know frail beauty like the purple flower,
To which one morn oft birth and death affords;　　10
That love a jarring is of minds' accords,
Where sense and will invassal reason's power:
　　Know what I list, this all cannot me move,
　　But that, O me! I both must write and love.

That learned Grecian,[2] who did so excel
In knowledge passing sense, that he is named
Of all the after-worlds divine, doth tell
That at the time when first our souls are framed,
Ere in these mansions blind they come to dwell,
They live bright rays of that eternal light,
And others see, know, love, in heaven's great height,
[2] Plato.

Not toiled with aught to reason doth rebel.
Most true it is, for straight at the first sight
My mind me told, that in some other place   10
It elsewhere saw the idea of that face,
And lov'd a love of heavenly pure delight;
    No wonder now I feel so fair a flame,
    Sith I her lov'd ere on this earth she came.

Madrigal

This life, which seems so fair,
Is like a bubble blown up in the air
By sporting children's breath,
Who chase it everywhere,
And strive who can most motion it bequeath:
And though it sometime seem of its own might,
Like to an eye of gold, to be fixed there,
And firm to hover in that empty height,
That only is because it is so light.
But in that pomp it doth not long appear;   10
    For even when most admired, it in a thought,
    As swelled from nothing, doth dissolve in nought.

Madrigal

Unhappy light,
Do not approach to bring the woeful day,
When I must bid for aye
Farewell to her, and live in endless plight.
Fair moon, with gentle beams
The sight who never mars,
Long clear heaven's sable vault; and you, bright stars,
Your golden locks long glass in earth's pure streams;
Let Phœbus never rise
To dim your watchful eyes: 10
    Prolong, alas, prolong my short delight,
    And if ye can, make an eternal night.

Song

Phœbus, arise,
And paint the sable skies
With azure, white, and red;
Rouse Memnon's mother from her Tithon's bed,
That she thy career may with roses spread;
The nightingales thy coming each where sing;
Make an eternal spring,
Give life to this dark world which lieth dead;
Spread forth thy golden hair
In larger locks than thou wast wont before,   10
And, emperor-like, decore
With diadem of pearl thy temples fair:
Chase hence the ugly night,
Which serves but to make dear thy glorious light.
This is that happy morn,
That day, long-wished day,
Of all my life so dark
(If cruel stars have not my ruin sworn,
And fates not hope betray),
Which, only white, deserves   20
A diamond for ever should it mark:
This is the morn should bring unto this grove
My love, to hear and recompense my love.
Fair king, who all preserves,
But show thy blushing beams,
And thou two sweeter eyes
Shalt see, than those which by Peneus' streams
Did once thy heart surprise;
Nay, suns, which shine as clear
As thou when two thou didst to Rome appear.   30
Now, Flora, deck thyself in fairest guise;
If that ye, winds, would hear
A voice surpassing far Amphion's lyre,
Your stormy chiding stay;
Let Zephyr only breathe,

And with her tresses play,
Kissing sometimes those purple ports of death.
The winds all silent are,
And Phœbus in his chair,
Ensaffroning sea and air,   40
Makes vanish every star:
Night like a drunkard reels
Beyond the hills to shun his flaming wheels;
The fields with flow'rs are decked in every hue,
The clouds bespangle with bright gold their blue:
Here is the pleasant place,
And everything, save her, who all should grace.

An Hymn of the Ascension

Bright portals of the sky,
    Embossed with sparkling stars,
    Doors of eternity,
    With diamantine bars,
    Your arras rich uphold,
    Loose all your bolts and springs,
    Ope wide your leaves of gold,
    That in your roofs may come the King of kings.
Scarfed in a rosy cloud,
    He doth ascend the air: 10
    Straight doth the moon Him shroud
    With her resplendent hair;
    The next encrystalled light
    Submits to Him its beams,
    And He doth trace the height
    Of that fair lamp which flames of beauty streams.
He towers those golden bounds
    He did to sun bequeath;
    The higher wand'ring rounds
    Are found His feet beneath;   20
    The Milky Way comes near,
    Heaven's axle seems to bend,

Above each turning sphere
That, robed in glory, heaven's King may ascend.
O well-spring of this All!
Thy father's image vive;
Word, that from nought did call
What is, doth reason, live;
The soul's eternal food,
Earth's joy, delight of heaven;   30
All truth, love, beauty, good:
To Thee, to Thee be praises ever given!
What was dismarshaled late
In this Thy noble frame,
And lost the prime estate,
Hath reobtained the same,
Is now most perfect seen;
Streams which diverted were,
And troubled strayed unclean
From their first source, by Thee home turned are.   40
By Thee that blemish old
Of Eden's leprous prince,
Which on his race took hold,
And him exiled from thence,
Now put away is far:
With sword, in ireful guise,
No cherub more shall bar
Poor man the entries into paradise.
By Thee those spirits pure,
First children of the light,   50
Now fixed stand and sure
In their eternal right;
Now human companies
Renew their ruined wall;
Fallen man, as Thou mak'st rise,
Thou giv'st to angels, that they shall not fall.
By Thee that prince of sin,
That doth with mischief swell,
Hath lost what he did win,

And shall endungeoned dwell;   60
His spoils are made Thy prey,
His fanes are sacked and torn,
His altars razed away,
And what adored was late, now lies a scorn.
These mansions, pure and clear,
  Which are not made by hands,
  Which once by him joyed were,
  And his, then not stained, bands
  (Now forfeited, dispossessed,
  And headlong from them thrown).   70
  Shall Adam's heirs make blest,
  By Thee, their great Redeemer, made their own.
O well-spring of this All!
  Thy father's image vive;
  Word, that from nought did call
  What is, doth reason, live;
  Whose work is but to will,
  God's coeternal Son,
  Great banisher of ill!
  By none but Thee could these great deeds be done.   80
Now each ethereal gate
  To Him hath opened been,
  And glory's King in state
  His palace enters in;
  Now comed in this high priest
  In the most holy place,
  Not without blood addressed,
  With glory heaven, the earth to crown with grace.
Stars which all eyes were late,
  And did with wonder burn,   90
  His name to celebrate,
  In flaming tongues them turn;
  Their orby crystals move
  More active than before,
  And entheate [1] from above,
  _____
  [1] Divinely inspired.

Their sovereign Prince laud, glorify, adore,
The quires of happy souls,
  Waked with that music sweet,
  Whose descant care controls,
  Their Lord in triumph meet;
  The spotless sprites of light
  His trophies do extol,
  And, arched in squadrons bright,
  Greet their great Victor in his capitol.
O glory of the heaven!
  O sole delight of earth!
  To Thee all power be given,
  God's uncreated birth!
  Of mankind lover true,
  Indearer of his wrong,
  Who dost the world renew,
  Still be Thou our salvation and our song!
From top of Olivet such notes did rise,
When man's Redeemer did transcend the skies.

THE PASTORAL strain of Spenser embodied in the graceful octosyllabic verse-mold of Jonson is the unique contribution of George Wither to English poetry.

Wither did not find his real talent, however, until imprisonment in the Marshalsea set him yearning for the spreading beeches of his native Bentworth and the charming pastoral scenes of Hampshire. Why he was put in prison for writing *Abuses Stript and Whipt* has never been discovered. The satire is very general in scope and deals with man's moral nature rather than with the faults of individuals. Far more open satire from Donne had been disregarded. Apparently Wither's attack was interpreted as fitting certain members of the court and church, in spite of its generality, and only the interference of Princess Elizabeth, Wither's own appeal in verse to the king, and the suppression of the issue finally secured his release.

The severity with which he was treated during the early days of his imprisonment was a novel experience for Wither. He had been brought up in luxury at home, and though after two years at Oxford University, he says that he was called home by his father "to hold the plough," the expression he uses does not connote financial need. He was soon established at Lincoln's Inn, ostensibly to study law. He joined the group of young poets in the Inns of Court and formed a lasting friendship with William Browne, who probably introduced him to Michael Drayton. Through his *Nuptial Poems* for Princess Elizabeth he won the patronage of the Princess and seemed well on the way to success, but suddenly he was subjected for apparently slight cause to extremely severe punishment. He writes of his hardships: "I was for many days compelled to feed on nothing but the coarsest bread, and sometimes locked up four and twenty hours together without so much as a drop of water to cool my tongue." [1] This experience deterred Wither from further satire until he

[1] Quoted by Edmund Gosse in *Jacobean Poets*, p. 183.

turned Puritan and Parliamentarian, but it did not stop the
flow of his verse. It is to this period that we are indebted for
his loveliest poems: his contribution to the *Shepherd's Pipe*
of Browne, Christopher Brooke, and John Davies of Here-
ford and his pastoral in five eclogues, the *Shepherd's Hunt-
ing*. Of the latter Gosse says: "In all the days of James I, no
more unaffected melodies, no brighter or more aerial notes,
were poured forth by any poet than are contained in this
delicious little volume. . . ." [2] In this poem appears the best
known passage of his writing, his statement of the power of
poetry, found in the *Fourth Eclogue*.

Only two of his later works are really distinguished.
Fidelia, which followed the *Shepherd's Hunting* (c. 1617),
is an unfinished poem representing a woman's epistle to an
inconstant friend. Written largely in heroic couplets of con-
siderable finish, it contains the lyric sung in the best manner
of the Cavaliers,

> Shall I wasting in despair
> Die because a woman's fair?

Fair Virtue, or the *Mistress of Philarete*, though probably
written earlier, was not published until 1622. Here he sings
of philosophy, but places his didactic poem in a pastoral
frame. In his sincere love of nature he is less artificial than
most of the pastoral poets, and the descriptions of his own
Hampshire country are rightly famous. In presenting the
idea of nature as a consoling power, Wither anticipates
Wordsworth.

With Wither's later life and writing, students of literature
are little concerned. He left the court circles which he had
satirized in *Abuses Stript and Whipt*, sold his property to
furnish out a troop of horse, and became a captain in Crom-
well's army. During the conflict the lives of Wither and Den-
ham came into interesting contact. For a time Wither en-
joyed residence on Denham's confiscated estate; later when

[2] *Ibid.*, p. 186.

Wither's forces were overpowered by Denham, Denham saved Wither from hanging by saying to the king that "whilst [Wither] lived, he should not be the worst poet in England." Whether or not Wither's "dear Betty," whom Aubrey calls "a great wit," who "would write in verses too," encouraged her husband to production, Wither wrote far too much. After the reign of James I silence would have enhanced his reputation. His religious poetry is poor; his satire puts him back in prison (Newgate this time); and his prose is hopelessly dull.

Though Wither died in the year that *Paradise Lost* was published, he was not of this later age into which his long life had brought him. We associate him rather with the earlier times—with the period of his birth, when the Armada was making its way toward England; with Spenser, his poetic master; and with William Browne of Tavistock, his warm personal friend and literary associate.

FROM *The Shepherd's Hunting*

Philarete. Seest thou not in clearest days
Oft thick fogs cloud heaven's rays,
And that vapors which do breathe
From the earth's gross womb beneath,
Seem not to us with black steams
To pollute the sun's bright beams,
And yet vanish into air,
Leaving it unblemished fair?
So, my Willy,[1] shall it be
With detractions breath and thee.   10
It shall never rise so high
As to stain thy poesy.
As that sun doth oft exhale
Vapors from each rotten vale,
Poesy so sometime drains
Gross conceits from muddy brains,
Mists of envy, fogs of spite,

[1] William Browne.

'Twixt men's judgments and her light;
But so much her power may do,
That she can dissolve them too.   20
If thy verse do bravely tower,
As she makes wing, she gets power;
Yet the higher she doth soar,
She's affronted still the more,
Till she to the highest hath past,
Then she rests with fame at last.
Let nought therefore thee affright,
But make forward in thy flight;
For if I could match thy rhyme,
To the very stars I'd climb,   30
There begin again, and fly
Till I reached eternity.
But, alas, my Muse is slow;
For thy pace she flags too low.
Yea, the more's her hapless fate,
Her short wings were clipped of late,
And poor I, her fortune ruing,
Am myself put up a-mewing.[2]
But if I my cage can rid,
I'll fly where I never did.   40
And though for her sake I'm crossed,
Though my best hopes I have lost,
And knew she would make my trouble
Ten times more than ten times double,
I would love and keep her too
Spite of all the world could do.
For though banished from my flocks,
And, confined within these rocks,
Here I waste away the light
And consume the sullen night,   50
She doth for my comfort stay,
And keeps many cares away.

[2] *The Shepherd's Hunting* was composed while Wither was imprisoned for writing the satire, *Abuses Stript and Whipt*.

Though I miss the flowery fields,
With those sweets the springtide yields,
Though I may not see those groves
Where the shepherds chant their loves,
And the lasses more excel
Than the sweet-voiced Philomel,
Though of all those pleasures past
Nothing now remains at last,　　　　　60
But remembrance, poor relief,
That more makes than mends my grief,
She's my mind's companion still,
Maugre envy's evil will,
Whence she should be driven too,
Were it in mortal's power to do.
She doth tell me where to borrow
Comfort in the midst of sorrow,
Makes the desolatest place
To her presence be a grace,　　　　　70
And the blackest discontents
To be pleasing ornaments.
In my former days of bliss,
Her divine skill taught me this,
That from everything I saw
I could some invention draw,
And raise pleasure to her height,
Through the meanest object's sight.
By the murmur of a spring,
Or the least bough's rustling;　　　　　80
By a daisy whose leaves spread
Shut when Titan goes to bed,
Or a shady bush or tree,
She could more infuse in me
Than all nature's beauties can
In some other wiser man.
By her help I also now
Make this churlish place allow
Some things that may sweeten gladness

In the very gall of sadness. 90
The dull loneness, the black shade
That these hanging vaults have made,
The strange music of the waves
Beating on these hollow caves,
This black den which rocks emboss
Overgrown with eldest moss,
The rude portals that give light
More to terror than delight,
This my chamber of neglect,
Walled about with disrespect: 100
From all these and this dull air,
A fit object for despair,
She hath taught me by her might
To draw comfort and delight.
Therefore, thou best earthly bliss,
I will cherish thee for this.
Poesy, thou sweetest content
That e'er heaven to mortals lent,
Though they as a trifle leave thee
Whose dull thoughts cannot conceive thee, 110
Though thou be to them a scorn
That to naught but earth are born,
Let my life no longer be
Than I am in love with thee.
Though our wise ones call thee madness,
Let me never taste of gladness
If I love not thy maddest fits
More than all their greatest wits.

FROM *Fair Virtue*
or
The Mistress of Philarete

Two pretty rills do meet, and meeting make
Within one valley a large silver lake,[1]

[1] This is the Pool of Alresford, in Hampshire, near Wither's home.

About whose banks the fertile mountains stood
In ages past bravely crowned with wood,
Which, lending cold-sweet shadows, gave it grace
To be accounted Cynthia's bathing place,
And from her father Neptune's brackish court
Fair Thetis [2] thither often would resort,
Attended by the fishes of the sea,
Which in those sweeter waters came to play.   10
There would the daughter of the sea-god dive;
And thither came the land-nymphs every eve
To wait upon her, bringing for her brows
Rich garlands of sweet flowers and beechy boughs.

  For pleasant was that pool, and near it then
Was neither rotten marsh nor boggy fen.
It was nor overgrown with boisterous sedge,
Nor grew there rudely then along the edge
A bending willow nor a prickly bush,
Nor broadleafed flag, nor reed, nor knotty rush;   20
But here, well ordered, was a grove with bowers:
There grassy plots set round about with flowers.
Here you might through the water see the land
Appear, strowed o'er with white or yellow sand.
Yon, deeper was it; and the wind by whiffs
Would make it rise and wash the little cliffs,
On which oft pluming sat, unfrighted then,
The gaggling wildgoose and the snow-white swan,
With all those flocks of fowls which to this day
Upon those quiet waters breed and play.   30

  For though excellencies wanting be,
Which once it had, it is the same that we
By transposition name the Ford of Arle,
And out of which along a chalky marl
That river trills whose waters wash the fort
In which brave Arthur kept his royal court.[3]

[2] Thetis was a Nereid, daughter of Nereus, not Neptune.
[3] Winchester. Alresford was only seven or eight miles away.

North-east, not far from this great pool, there lies
A tract of beechy mountains, that arise
With leisurely-ascending to such height,
As from their tops the warlike Isle of Wight   40
You in the ocean's bosom may espy,
Though near two hundred furlongs thence it lie.
The pleasant way, as up those hills you climb,
Is strewed o'er with majoram and thyme,
Which grows unset. The hedgerows do not want
The cowslip, violet, primrose, nor a plant
That freshly scents, as birch both green and tall;
Low sallows, on whose bloomings bees do fall;
Fair woodbines, which about the hedges twine;
Smooth privet, and the sharp, sweet eglantine;   50
With many more, whose leaves and blossoms fair
The earth adorn, and oft perfume the air.
     When you unto the highest do attain,
An intermixture both of wood and plain
You shall behold, which, though aloft it lie,
Hath downs for sheep and fields for husbandry.
So much, at least, as little needeth more,
If not enough to merchandise their store.
     In every row hath nature planted there
Some banquet for the hungry passenger.   60
For here the hazel-nut and filbert grows;
There bulloes,[4] and a little further sloes;
On this hand standeth a fair wilding-tree;[5]
On that large thickets of black cherries be.
The shrubby fields are raspice-orchards there,
The new-felled woods like strawberry gardens are:
And had the king of rivers blest those hills
With some small number of such pretty rills
As flow elsewhere, Arcadia had not seen
A sweeter plot of earth than this had been.   70

[4] Both bulloes and sloes are wild plums.
[5] Crab-apple.

The Author's Resolution in a Sonnet [1]

Shall I wasting in despair
Die because a woman's fair?
Or make pale my cheeks with care
'Cause another's rosy are?
Be she fairer than the day,
Or the flowery meads in May,
   If she think not well of me,
   What care I how fair she be?

Shall my silly heart be pined
'Cause I see a woman kind?   10
Or a well-disposed nature
Joined with a lovely feature?
Be she meeker, kinder than
Turtle-dove or pelican,
   If she be not so to me,
   What care I how kind she be?

Shall a woman's virtues move
Me to perish for her love?
Or her well-deservings known
Make me quite forget mine own?   20
Be she with that goodness blest
Which may merit name of best,
   If she be not such to me,
   What care I how good she be?

'Cause her fortune seems too high,
Shall I play the fool and die?
She that bears a noble mind,
If not outward helps she find,
Thinks what with them he would do

[1] This is the earliest version of this lyric first printed at the end of *Fidelia* in 1615 and later incorporated with slight changes in *Fair Virtue*, 1622.

That without them dares her woo; 30
 And unless that mind I see,
 What care I how great she be?

Great, or good, or kind, or fair,
I will ne'er the more despair;
If she love me, this believe,
I will die, ere she shall grieve:
If she slight me when I woo,
I can scorn and let her go;
 For if she be not for me,
 What care I for whom she be? 40

THOUGH William Browne was educated at Oxford University and spent the years of his maturity in the law courts at London, his poetry is so wholly the product of his early environment that he is always spoken of as William Browne of Tavistock. The quiet beauty of the Tavy valley determines the nature of Browne's best poetry quite as much as do the pastorals of his literary masters, Sidney and Spenser. But Tavistock was also aglow with pride in Drake and its other heroes, and so it is Tavistock again that accounts for the patriotic fervor which colors the pastorals of Browne. To glorify this region he dedicates all his poetic powers and his great store of learning, enriching his references by the use of legend and history.

Britannia's Pastorals, Browne's most famous work, contains 10,000 lines of description in three books. The first book appeared shortly after Browne went to the Inner Temple in 1613; the second, in 1616; and the third, not until the manuscript was found in the Salisbury Cathedral library in 1851 and printed for the Percy Society in the following year. In spite of its great length the poem is unfinished. Its worst faults are the result of his literary discipleship. In general conception he follows Drayton's *Polyolbion,* giving a poetic geography, which is, however, restricted in scope to Devon. His rivers, like Drayton's, are populated by nymphs, and his valleys inhabited by idealized shepherds. His story is a romance so complicated and so interrupted by episodes that it is almost impossible to follow it. In devising the narrative, Browne very obviously was following the intricacies of the *Arcadia* and the *Faerie Queene;* he even imitates the archaisms of Spenser and adds allegory to his already weighted story. Strangely enough, however, he does not attempt the Spenserian stanza, but uses the heroic couplet.

The best parts of the poem are found when Browne gets away from the artificial conventions of the pastoral and writes out of his love for the scenery in which he spent his boyhood. His "shady groves" are the real forests of Devon, full of English song birds; his "enameled meadows" are actual hayfields; his "purling rills" are the river scenes he knew; and though he may marry his rivers in the most conventional manner of Drayton or of Spenser, they still flow through Devon. He brings the courtly romance into sharp contrast with a country marriage scene or adds to a conventional rosy-fingered dawn the reality of the closely observed shining track of the snail. He often makes poetic use of simple details which his accuracy of observation has given him, and he loves nature with an intensity that is unusual before Wordsworth. In London, busy with the law, his heart cries in longing,

> Devon, O Devon in wind and rain!

Browne's work has also another kind of interest for us; it influenced Milton. Milton's copy of Browne's poems, annotated in his own hand, substantiates the evidence given by his poetry. Browne is Milton's predecessor in the pastoral elegy; his elegy for William Ferrar, a friend drowned at sea (*Britannia's Pastorals* II. 1), and the monody on the death of Mr. Thomas Manwood (*Fourth Eclogue* of the *Shepherd's Pipe*) should be read in connection with *Lycidas*. Browne also wrote a masque for the Inner Temple on the story of Ulysses and Circe, a work which may have influenced *Comus*. And finally, *Britannia's Pastorals* gave suggestions for such widely differing works as *L'Allegro* and *Paradise Regained*. Both in his own right as a descriptive poet of local scenes and in his influence upon a far greater poet than himself, Browne demands our study.

Though Browne could count among his friends some of the great intellectual men of his time—such men as Chapman and Drayton among the more Elizabethan figures, or Ben Jonson, Selden, and Wither in the seventeenth century trend—he seems never to have felt the spirit of his own age. He retired more and more within himself and even broke off associations with his friends. As early as 1624 he gave up his work in the law courts and returned to Exeter College, Oxford, as tutor to Robert Dormer, later Earl of Carnarvon. Here he received his master's degree. We next hear of him in the household of the Herberts of Wilton. In 1628 he married and retired to an estate of his own in Dorking, where he could enjoy the pastoral scenes he loved. He took no part in the disturbances which swept the country. To him the new period was inferior to the old, and the golden age was in the days of Elizabeth, when Sidney and Spenser were the leading poets and Drake of Tavistock went voyaging.

FROM *The Shepherd's Pipe*

The Fourth Eclogue

THE ARGUMENT

IN THIS the author bewails the death of one whom he shadoweth under the name of Philarete, compounded of the Greek words φίλος and ἀρετή, a lover of virtue, a name well befitting him to whose memory these lines are consecrated, being sometime his truly loved (and now as much lamented) friend Mr. Thomas Manwood, son to the worthy Sir Peter Manwood, knight.

Under an aged oak was Willie laid,
Willie, the lad who whilom made the rocks
To ring with joy, whilst on his pipe he played,
And from their masters wooed the neighboring flocks.
    But now o'ercome with dolors deep
      That nigh his heart-strings rent,
    Ne cared he for his silly sheep,
      Ne cared for merriment.
    But changed his wonted walks
    For uncouth paths unknown,   10

Where none but trees might hear his plaints,
    And echo rue his moan.

Autumn it was when drooped the sweetest flowers,
And rivers, swollen with pride, o'erlooked the banks;
Poor grew the day of summer's golden hours,
And void of sap stood Ida's cedar-ranks.
      The pleasant meadows sadly lay
        In chill and cooling sweats
      By rising fountains, or as they
        Feared winter's wasteful threats.   20
    Against the broad-spread oak,
      Each wind in fury bears;
    Yet fell their leaves not half so fast
      As did the shepherd's tears.

As was his seat, so was his gentle heart,
Meek and dejected, but his thoughts as high
As those aye-wandering lights, who both impart
Their beams on us, and heaven still beautify.
      Sad was his look (O heavy fate!
        That swain should be so sad,   30
      Whose merry notes the forlorn mate
        With greatest pleasure clad);
    Broke was his tuneful pipe
      That charmed the crystal floods,
    And thus his grief took airy wings
      And flew about the woods.

Day, thou art too officious in thy place,
And night too sparing of a wished stay.
Ye wandering lamps, O be ye fixed a space!
Some other hemisphere grace with your ray.   40
      Great Phœbus! Daphne [1] is not here,
        Nor Hyacinthus [2] fair;

[1] A nymph loved by Phœbus, or Apollo, who was changed into a laurel tree to escape the pursuit of the god.
[2] A youth beloved of Apollo and accidentally killed by the discus of the god.

Phœbe! [3] Endymion and thy dear
Hath long since cleft the air.
But ye have surely seen
(Whom we in sorrow miss)
A swain whom Phœbe thought her love,
And Titan deemed his.

But he is gone; then inwards turn your light,
Behold him there: here never shall you more;   50
O'erhang this sad plain with eternal night;
Or change the gaudy green she whilom wore
To fenny black! Hyperion [4] great
To ashy paleness turn her!
Green well befits a lover's heat,
But black beseems a mourner.
Yet neither this thou canst,
Nor see his second birth,
His brightness blinds thine eye more now,
Than thine did his on earth.   60

Let not a shepherd on our hapless plains
Tune notes of glee, as used were of yore!
For Philarete is dead. Let mirthful strains
With Philarete cease for evermore!
And if a fellow-swain do live
A niggard of his tears,
The shepherdesses all will give
To store him part of theirs.
Or I would lend him some,
But that the store I have   70
Will all be spent before I pay
The debt I owe his grave.

O what is left can make me leave to moan,
Or what remains but doth increase it more?

[3] One of the names for the goddess of the moon. Endymion, a beautiful shepherd of Mt. Latmos, was beloved by this goddess.
[4] Sometimes used for Helios, god of the sun.

Look on his sheep: alas! their master's gone.
Look on the place where we two heretofore
  With locked arms have vowed our love
   (Our love which time shall see
   In shepherd's songs forever more,
    And grace their harmony),   80
 It solitary seems.
  Behold our flowery beds;
 Their beauties fade, and violets
  For sorrow hang their heads.

'Tis not a cypress' bough, a countenance sad,
A mourning garment, wailing elegy,
A standing hearse in sable vesture clad,
A tomb built to his name's eternity,
  Although the shepherds all should strive
   By yearly obsequies,   90
  And vow to keep thy fame alive
   In spite of destinies,
 That can suppress my grief:
  All these and more may be,
 Yet all in vain to recompense
  My greatest loss of thee.

Cypress may fade, the countenance be changed,
A garment rot, an elegy forgotten,
A hearse 'mongst irreligious rites be ranged,
A tomb plucked down, or else through age be rotten: 100
  All things the unpartial hand of Fate
   Can raze out with a thought,
  These have a several fixed date
   Which ended, turn to nought.
 Yet shall my truest cause
  Of sorrow firmly stay,
 When these effects the wings of time
  Shall fan and sweep away.

Look as a sweet rose fairly budding forth
Bewrays her beauties to the enamored morn,   110
Until some keen blast from the envious North
Kills the sweet bud that was but newly born;
      Or else her rarest smells delighting
        Make her herself betray,
      Some white and curious hand inviting
        To pluck her hence away:
    So stands my mournful case,
      For had he been less good,
    He yet, uncropped, had kept the stock
      Whereon he fairly stood.   120

Yet though so long he lived not as he might,
He had the time appointed to him given.
Who liveth but the space of one poor night,
His birth, his youth, his age is in that even.
      Who ever doth the period see
        Of days by heaven forth plotted,
      Dies full of age, as well as he
        That had more years allotted.
    In sad tones then my verse
      Shall with incessant tears   130
    Bemoan my hapless loss of him,
      And not his want of years.

In deepest passions of my grief-swollen breast,
Sweet soul! this only comfort seizeth me,
That so few years did make thee so much blest,
And gave such wings to reach eternity.
      Is this to die? No: as a ship,
        Well built, with easy wind,
      A lazy hulk doth far outstrip,
        And soonest harbor find,   140
    So Philarete fled;
      Quick was his passage given,

When others must have a longer time
　　To make them fit for heaven.

Then not for thee these briny tears are spent,
But as the nightingales against the breer
'Tis for myself I moan, and do lament
Not that thou left'st the world, but left'st me here:
　　　Here, where without thee all delights
　　　　Fail of their pleasing power,　　　　　150
　　　All glorious days seem ugly nights;
　　　　Methinks no April shower
　　Embroider should the earth,
　　　But briny tears distil,
　　Since Flora's beauties shall no more
　　　Be honored by thy quill.

And ye his sheep, in token of his lack,
Whilom the fairest flock on all the plain,
Yean never lamb, but be it clothed in black.
Ye shady sycamores, when any swain　　　　160
　　　To carve his name upon your rind
　　　　Doth come, where his doth stand,
　　　Shed drops, if he be so unkind
　　　　To raze it with his hand.
　　And thou, my loved Muse,
　　　No more shouldst numbers move,
　　But that his name should ever live,
　　　And after death my love.

This said, he sighed, and with o'erdrowned eyes
Gazed on the heavens for what he missed on earth.　　170
Then from the ground full sadly 'gan arise
As far from future hope as present mirth;
　　　Unto his cote with heavy pace
　　　　As ever sorrow trod,
　　　He went with mind no more to trace
　　　　Where mirthful swains abode;

And as he spent the day,
    The night he passed alone.
Was never shepherd loved more dear,
    Nor made a truer moan.   180

FROM *Britannia's Pastorals*

BOOK I, *Song 2*

Near to this wood there lay a pleasant mead,
Where fairies often did their measures tread,
Which in the meadow made such circles green,
As if with garlands it had crowned been,
Or like the circle where the signs we track,
And learned shepherds call it the zodiac.
Within one of these rounds was to be seen
A hillock rise, where oft the fairy queen
At twilight sat, and did command her elves
To pinch those maids that had not swept their shelves;   10
And further, if by maidens' oversight
Within doors water were not brought at night;
Or if they spread no table, set no bread,
They should have nips from toe unto the head;
And for the maid that had performed each thing,
She in the water-pail bade leave a ring.

        .   .   .   .   .   .

    As I have seen upon a bridal day
Full many maids clad in their best array,
In honor of the bride come with their flaskets
Filled full with flowers: others in wicker baskets   20
Bring from the marish rushes to o'erspread
The ground whereon to church the lovers tread;
Whilst that the quaintest youth of all the plain
Ushers their way with many a piping strain:
So, as in joy at this fair river's birth,
Triton [1] came up a channel with his mirth,

[1] The herald of Neptune.

And called the neighboring nymphs each in her turn
To pour their pretty rivulets from their urn.
To wait upon this new-delivered spring,
Some running through the meadows, with them bring   30
Cowslip and mint; and 'tis another's lot
To light upon some gardener's curious knot,
Whence she upon her breast, love's sweet repose,
Doth bring the queen of flowers, the English rose.
Some from the fen bring reeds, wild thyme from downs;
Some from a grove the bay that poets crowns;
Some from an aged rock the moss hath torn,
And leaves him naked unto winter's storm;
Another from her banks, in mere goodwill,
Brings nutriment for fish, the camomile.   40
Thus all bring somewhat, and do overspread
The way the spring unto the sea doth tread.

BOOK II, *Song 3*

Hail, thou my native soil! thou blessed plot
Whose equal all the world affordeth not!
Show me who can so many crystal rills,
Such sweet-clothed valleys or aspiring hills;
Such wood-ground, pastures, quarries, wealthy mines;
Such rocks in whom the diamond fairly shines;
And if the earth can show the like again,
Yet will she fail in her sea-ruling men.
Time never can produce men to o'ertake
The fames of Grenville, Davies, Gilbert, Drake,   10
Or worthy Hawkins,[2] or of thousands more
That by their power made the Devonian shore
Mock the proud Tagus;[3] for whose richest spoil
The boasting Spaniard left the Indian soil
Bankrupt of store, knowing it would quit cost
By winning this, though all the rest were lost.

[2] Distinguished naval heroes.
[3] River of Spain and Portugal.

Robert Herrick 1591-1674

HERRICK's long life began just after the first three books of the *Faerie Queene* were published and before Shakespeare's great plays were written; it lasted until the whole tone of poetry was changed, with Dryden as the great poet and Wycherly the leading playwright. But Herrick seems to have been as little aware of this change as he was of the change in the universe in which he lived. Science did not show her "lovely face" to him; no great thirst for learning fired him to that white heat that kept men studying thirteen and fourteen hours a day; loyalty to the king inspired only songs, not service. Herrick was born into a singing world, and as Swinburne says, "He is and will probably be always the first in rank and station of English song-writers." [1]

The facts of Herrick's external life have little interest for us except as they bear upon his songs. The early apprenticeship to his uncle, who was a goldsmith, his late entrance at Cambridge, his transfer to Trinity College to study law—these have little to do with the Herrick we know. Of the ten years which follow his university life we know nothing except what we can gather from the songs they have given us. This was the period when

<blockquote>
He could rehearse
A lyric verse,
And speak it with the best.
</blockquote>

It was the time of "lyric feasts" with Ben Jonson at "the Sun, the Dog, the Triple Tun," and of imitation of "Saint Ben" in his most delicate imaginative vein. Great names appear among his friends: Endymion Porter, Henry Herbert, Earl of Pembroke, and the Duke of Buckingham. The distinguished musicians, William and Henry Lawes, set his lyrics to music, and his songs were sung at Whitehall before the king and queen.

Suddenly in 1627 the gay Herrick dons the chaplain's

[1] Preface to his edition of Herrick's poems, *The Muses' Library*, p. x.

gown and is off with the Duke of Buckingham to the island
of Rhé on an expedition against the French. Two years later
he leaves the London he loves so much to become the min-
ster at Dean Prior in Devonshire. There was no acceptance
of "the collar" as in the case of Herbert and no agonized
rending of the soul as in the case of Donne. Whatever caused
the change in his way of life, the same Herrick that sang in
the taverns of London now sings in the vicarage. Though at
times he rebels against "loathed Devonshire," Devon be-
comes the substance of some of his finest songs, and his life
there seems full of gay content, only occasionally touched
by the yearning of the exiled university and city-bred man
for a more congenial scene.

He lives simply, but his threshold is worn by the poor;
his life as a bachelor is made comfortable by his faithful
servant, Prudence Baldwin, and bright by the charming girls
or dreams of girls who love him even when his hair is gray.
He attends the wassailings, the Christmas celebrations, and
the country dances, and he joins in the making of columbine
chains and cowslip balls. He learns the fairy lore of Devon
and through his verses makes the fairies live for us as only
Shakespeare has done before him. Like Horace, his poetic
master, Herrick employs the pagan feeling for ritual. Rose
Macaulay in *The Shadow Flies* has given us a vivid imag-
inary picture of the half-pagan ceremonial with which Her-
rick kept the church calendar. To him Devon is not Browne's
Devon of "wind and rain"; it is a bright Devon of birds and
flowers and gay young people bringing in the May. We hear
stories of a stern minister who can hurl the manuscript of
his sermon with curses at a sleeping parishioner, but we
really know only a poet who writes his sermon notes in
verse, brings a rose as an offering to the child Jesus, and
sees in the fleeting beauty of the flowers the message of
mortality. His childlike expressions of thanks to God are
for his simple physical comforts: his little house, his hen
that lays an egg a day, his pets. His most intimate experi-
ence of God is through nature:

> We see Him come, and know Him ours,
> Who with His sunshine and His showers
> Turns all the patient ground to flowers.

When the Roundheads came into power, they gave Dean Prior to John Syms, Puritan, for they had no sympathy with Herrick's ideas. We hear no mournful note from "Robin Red Breast," as Herrick terms himself, only the glad song:

> Ravished in spirit, I come, nay, more, I fly
> To thee, blest place of my nativity.

Back in London he seems still to have been oblivious of political events. In 1648 he was publishing his collected poems, both secular and religious, dedicated to Charles, Prince of Wales; and as Gosse comments, "People were invited to listen to little madrigals upon Julia's stomacher at the singularly inopportune moment when the eyes of the whole world were bent on the unprecedented phenomenon of the proclamation of the English republic." [2]

How he lived in the London of the Commonwealth we do not know; he may have received assistance from that great patron of literature, his friend, Endymion Porter. It was not until 1662 that the vicarage at Dean Prior was returned to him by Charles II. At above seventy years of age he went back to Devonshire for a period of thirteen years of further service in the quiet countryside. But age, the sudden plunge into reality, and the sober years in London had stilled his song.

Herrick's verse is limited to the lyric, but in that field he has tremendous range and flawless technique. He creates an amazing variety of verse forms, and he never fails to mold his thought into a delicate but firm and compact structure. He shows the shaping power of the classical Latin poets, especially of Horace; the delicacy of the Greek lyrist, Anacreon; and the polish of Ben Jonson. His poetry is his

[2] Gosse, "Robert Herrick," in *Seventeenth Century Studies*, p. 127.

"living stone," as he wished; in an artistry so perfect that it seems artless and in the exquisite simplicity of his verse he has attained enduring fame.

His Prayer to Ben Jonson

When I a verse shall make,
    Know I have prayed thee,
For old religion's sake,
    Saint Ben, to aid me.

Make the way smooth for me,
    When I, thy Herrick,
Honoring thee, on my knee
    Offer my lyric.

Candles I'll give to thee,
    And a new altar;   10
And thou, Saint Ben, shalt be
    Writ in my psalter.

An Ode for Him

Ah, Ben!
    Say how or when
    Shall we, thy guests,
Meet at those lyric feasts
    Made at the Sun,
The Dog, the Triple Tun,[1]
Where we such clusters had
As made us nobly wild, not mad;
    And yet each verse of thine
Outdid the meat, outdid the frolic wine.   10

My Ben!
Or come again,

[1] Taverns in London where Jonson and his group often assembled.

Or send to us
Thy wit's great overplus;
But teach us yet
Wisely to husband it,
Lest we that talent spend,
And having once brought to an end
That precious stock, the store
Of such a wit the world should have no more.

To the Water Nymphs Drinking at the Fountain

Reach with your whiter hands to me
Some crystal of the spring;
And I about the cup shall see
Fresh lilies flourishing.

Or else, sweet nymphs, do you but this—
To the glass your lips incline;
And I shall see by that one kiss
The water turned to wine.

Delight in Disorder

A sweet disorder in the dress
Kindles in clothes a wantonness.
A lawn about the shoulders thrown
Into a fine distraction;
An erring lace, which here and there
Enthrals the crimson stomacher;
A cuff neglectful, and thereby
Ribbons to flow confusedly;
A winning wave, deserving note,
In the tempestuous petticoat;
A careless shoe-string, in whose tie
I see a wild civility;

Do more bewitch me than when art
Is too precise in every part.

The Night Piece, to Julia

Her eyes the glowworm lend thee;
The shooting stars attend thee;
   And the elves also,
   Whose little eyes glow
Like the sparks of fire, befriend thee.

No will-o'-the-wisp mislight thee;
Nor snake or slowworm bite thee;
   But on, on thy way,
   Not making a stay,
Since ghost there's none to affright thee.   10

Let not the dark thee cumber;
What though the moon does slumber?
   The stars of the night
   Will lend thee their light,
Like tapers clear without number.

Then, Julia, let me woo thee,
Thus, thus to come unto me;
   And when I shall meet
   Thy silvery feet,
My soul I'll pour into thee.   20

The Argument of His Book

I sing of brooks, of blossoms, birds, and bowers,
Of April, May, of June, and July flowers.
I sing of Maypoles, hock-carts, wassails, wakes,
Of bridegrooms, brides, and of their bridal-cakes.
I write of youth, of love, and have access

By these to sing of cleanly wantonness.
I sing of dews, of rains, and, piece by piece,
Of balm, of oil, of spice, and ambergris.
I sing of times trans-shifting, and I write
How roses first came red and lilies white.   10
I write of groves, of twilights, and I sing
The court of Mab and of the fairy king.
I write of hell; I sing (and ever shall)
Of heaven, and hope to have it after all.

To Daffodils

Fair daffodils, we weep to see
   You haste away so soon:
As yet the early-rising sun
   Has not attained his noon.
      Stay, stay,
   Until the hasting day
      Has run
   But to the evensong;
And, having prayed together, we
   Will go with you along.   10

We have short time to stay as you;
   We have as short a spring;
As quick a growth to meet decay,
   As you or anything.
      We die,
   As your hours do, and dry
      Away
   Like to the summer's rain;
Or as the pearls of morning's dew,
   Ne'er to be found again.   20

To Blossoms

Fair pledges of a fruitful tree,
   Why do ye fall so fast?

Your date is not so past
But you may stay yet here a while,
To blush and gently smile,
And go at last.

What! were ye born to be
An hour or half's delight,
And so to bid good night?
'Twas pity nature brought ye forth   10
Merely to show your worth
And lose you quite.

But you are lovely leaves, where we
May read how soon things have
Their end, though ne'er so brave;
And after they have shown their pride
Like you a while, they glide
Into the grave.

To Primroses Filled with Morning Dew

Why do ye weep, sweet babes? Can tears
Speak grief in you,
Who were but born
Just as the modest morn
Teemed her refreshing dew?
Alas, you have not known that shower
That mars a flower;
Nor felt the unkind
Breath of a blasting wind;
Nor are ye worn with years;   10
Or warped as we,
Who think it strange to see
Such pretty flowers, like to orphans young,
To speak by tears before ye have a tongue.

Speak, whimpering younglings, and make known
The reason why

Ye droop and weep.
Is it for want of sleep?
Or childish lullaby?
Or that ye have not seen as yet   20
    The violet?
Or brought a kiss
From that sweetheart to this?
No, no, this sorrow shown
    By your tears shed
Would have this lecture read:
That things of greatest, so of meanest worth,
Conceived with grief are, and with tears brought
    forth.

Corinna's Going A-Maying

Get up! get up for shame! the blooming morn
Upon her wings presents the god unshorn.
    See how Aurora throws her fair
    Fresh-quilted colors through the air:
    Get up, sweet slug-a-bed, and see
    The dew bespangling herb and tree.
Each flower has wept and bowed toward the east
Above an hour since, yet you not dressed;
    Nay, not so much as out of bed?
    When all the birds have matins said,   10
    And sung their thankful hymns, 'tis sin,
    Nay, profanation to keep in,
Whenas a thousand virgins on this day
Spring, sooner than the lark, to fetch in May.

Rise and put on your foliage, and be seen
To come forth, like the springtime, fresh and green,
    And sweet as Flora. Take no care
    For jewels for your gown or hair;
    Fear not, the leaves will strew
    Gems in abundance upon you;   20
Besides, the childhood of the day has kept,

Against you come, some orient pearls unwept;
  Come and receive them while the light
  Hangs on the dew-locks of the night,
  And Titan on the eastern hill
  Retires himself, or else stands still
Till you come forth. Wash, dress, be brief in praying:
Few beads are best when once we go a-Maying.

Come, my Corinna, come; and, coming, mark
How each field turns a street, each street a park   30
  Made green and trimmed with trees; see how
  Devotion gives each house a bough
  Or branch: each porch, each door ere this,
  An ark, a tabernacle is,
Made up of white-thorn neatly interwove,
As if here were those cooler shades of love.
  Can such delights be in the street
  And open fields, and we not see't?
  Come, we'll abroad; and let's obey
  The proclamation made for May,   40
And sin no more, as we have done, by staying;
But, my Corinna, come, let's go a-Maying.

There's not a budding boy or girl this day
But is got up and gone to bring in May;
  A deal of youth, ere this, is come
  Back, and with white-thorn laden home.
  Some have dispatched their cakes and cream
  Before that we have left to dream;
And some have wept, and wooed, and plighted troth,
And chose their priest, ere we can cast off sloth.   50
  Many a green-gown has been given,
  Many a kiss, both odd and even;
  Many a glance, too, has been sent
  From out the eye, love's firmament;
Many a jest told of the keys betraying
This night, and locks picked; yet we're not a-Maying.

Come, let us go while we are in our prime,
And take the harmless folly of the time.
　　We shall grow old apace, and die
　　Before we know our liberty.　　　　　　　　60
　　Our life is short, and our days run
　　As fast away as does the sun;
And, as a vapor or a drop of rain
Once lost, can ne'er be found again;
　　So when or you or I are made
　　A fable, song, or fleeting shade,
　　All love, all liking, all delight
　　Lies drowned with us in endless night.
Then while time serves, and we are but decaying,
Come, my Corinna, come, let's go a-Maying.　　70

To Meadows

　　Ye have been fresh and green,
　　　　Ye have been filled with flowers,
　　And ye the walks have been
　　　　Where maids have spent their hours.

　　You have beheld how they
　　　　With wicker arks did come
　　To kiss, and bear away
　　　　The richer cowslips home.

　　You've heard them sweetly sing,
　　　　And seen them in a round:　　　　　　　10
　　Each virgin, like a spring,
　　　　With honeysuckles crowned.

　　But now, we see none here
　　　　Whose silvery feet did tread,
　　And with disheveled hair
　　　　Adorned this smoother mead.

Like unthrifts, having spent
   Your stock, and needy grown,
You're left here to lament
   Your poor estates, alone.   20

His Answer to a Question

Some would know
   Why I so
Long still do tarry,
   And ask why
Here that I
Live and not marry.
   Thus I those
   Do oppose:
What man would be here,
   Slave to thrall,   10
   If at all
He could live free here?

Upon the Loss of His Mistresses

I have lost, and lately, these
Many dainty mistresses:
Stately Julia, prime of all;
Sapho next, a principal;
Smooth Anthea, for a skin
White, and heaven-like crystalline;
Sweet Electra, and the choice
Myrha, for the lute, and voice;
Next, Corinna, for her wit,
And for the graceful use of it;   10
With Perilla: all are gone;
Only Herrick's left alone,
For to number sorrow by
Their departures hence, and die.

To the Virgins, to Make Much of Time

Gather ye rosebuds while ye may:
    Old time is still a-flying;
And this same flower that smiles to-day
    To-morrow will be dying.

The glorious lamp of heaven, the sun,
    The higher he's a-getting,
The sooner will his race be run,
    And nearer he's to setting.

That age is best which is the first,
    When youth and blood are warmer;
But being spent, the worse, and worst
    Times still succeed the former.

Then be not coy, but use your time,
    And, while ye may, go marry;
For, having lost but once your prime,
    You may forever tarry.

To Anthea
Who May Command Him Anything

Bid me to live, and I will live
    Thy protestant to be;
Or bid me love, and I will give
    A loving heart to thee.

A heart as soft, a heart as kind,
    A heart as sound and free
As in the whole world thou canst find,
    That heart I'll give to thee.

Bid that heart stay, and it will stay,
    To honor thy decree;

Or bid it languish quite away,
   And it shall do so for thee.

Bid me to weep, and I will weep
   While I have eyes to see;
And, having none, yet I will keep
   A heart to weep for thee.

Bid me despair, and I'll despair
   Under that cypress tree;
Or bid me die, and I will dare
   E'en death, to die for thee.   20

Thou art my life, my love, my heart,
   The very eyes of me;
And hast command of every part,
   To live and die for thee.

To the Rose

Song

Go, happy rose, and interwove
With other flowers, bind my love.
   Tell her, too, she must not be
   Longer flowing, longer free,
   That so oft has fettered me.

Say, if she's fretful, I have bands
Of pearl and gold, to bind her hands;
   Tell her, if she struggle still,
   I have myrtle rods, at will,
   For to tame, though not to kill.   10

Take thou my blessing thus, and go,
And tell her this—but do not so,
   Lest a handsome anger fly

Like a lightning from her eye,
And burn thee up, as well as I.

To Music, to Becalm His Fever

Charm me asleep, and melt me so
  With thy delicious numbers,
That being ravished, hence I go
  Away in easy slumbers.
    Ease my sick head,
    And make my bed,
Thou power that canst sever
    From me this ill,
    And quickly still,
    Though thou not kill,   10
      My fever.

Thou sweetly canst convert the same
  From a consuming fire
Into a gentle-licking flame,
  And make it thus expire.
    Then make me weep
    My pains asleep;
And give me such reposes
    That I, poor I,
    May think, thereby,   20
    I live and die
      'Mongst roses.

Fall on me like a silent dew,
  Or like those maiden showers
Which by the peep of day do strew
  A baptime o'er the flowers.
    Melt, melt my pains
    With thy soft strains,
That having ease me given,

With full delight,   30
I leave this light
And take my flight
    For heaven.

The Country Life

*To the Honored Mr. End. Porter, Groom of the Bed-
chamber to His Majesty*

Sweet country life, to such unknown
Whose lives are others', not their own,
But serving courts and cities, be
Less happy, less enjoying thee.
Thou never plough'st the ocean's foam
To seek and bring rough pepper home;
Nor to the Eastern Ind dost rove
To bring from thence the scorched clove;
Nor, with the loss of thy loved rest,
Bring'st home the ingot from the West.   10
No, thy ambition's masterpiece
Flies no thought higher than a fleece;
Or how to pay thy hinds, and clear
All scores, and so to end the year:
But walk'st about thine own dear bounds,
Not envying others' larger grounds,
For well thou know'st 'tis not the extent
Of land makes life, but sweet content.
When now the cock, the ploughman's horn,
Calls forth the lily-wristed morn,   20
Then to thy corn-fields thou dost go,
Which though well soiled, yet thou dost know
That the best compost for the lands
Is the wise master's feet and hands.
There at the plough thou find'st thy team,
With a hind whistling there to them,
And cheer'st them up by singing how

The kingdom's portion is the plough.
This done, then to the enameled meads
Thou go'st, and as thy foot there treads,   30
Thou seest a present godlike power
Imprinted in each herb and flower,
And smell'st the breath of great-eyed kine,
Sweet as the blossoms of the vine.
Here thou behold'st thy large sleek neat
Unto the dewlaps up in meat;
And as thou look'st, the wanton steer,
The heifer, cow, and ox draw near
To make a pleasing pastime there.
These seen, thou go'st to view thy flocks   40
Of sheep, safe from the wolf and fox,
And find'st their bellies there as full
Of short sweet grass, as backs with wool,
And leav'st them, as they feed and fill,
A shepherd piping on a hill.
For sports, for pageantry, and plays,
Thou hast thy eves and holidays,
On which the young men and maids meet
To exercise their dancing feet,
Tripping the comely country round,   50
With daffodils and daisies crowned.
Thy wakes, thy quintels, here thou hast,
Thy Maypoles too with garlands graced,
Thy morris dance, thy Whitsun ale,
Thy shearing feast, which never fail,
Thy harvest home, thy wassail bowl,
That's tossed up after fox-i'-the-hole,
Thy mummeries, thy Twelfth tide kings
And queens, thy Christmas revelings,
Thy nut-brown mirth, thy russet wit,   60
And no man pays too dear for it.
To these, thou hast thy times to go
And trace the hare i' the treacherous snow;

Thy witty wiles to draw, and get
The lark into the trammel net;
Thou hast thy cockrood and thy glade,
To take the precious pheasant made;
Thy lime twigs, snares, and pitfalls then
To catch the pilfering birds, not men.
O happy life! if that their good   70
The husbandmen but understood,
Who all the day themselves do please,
And younglings, with such sports as these,
And, lying down, have naught to affright
Sweet sleep, that makes more short the night.
            Cætera desunt—

His Content in the Country

Here, here I live with what my board
Can with the smallest cost afford;
Though ne'er so mean the viands be,
They well content my Prue and me.
Or pea, or bean, or wort, or beet,
Whatever comes, content makes sweet.
Here we rejoice because no rent
We pay for our poor tenement,
Wherein we rest, and never fear
The landlord or the usurer.   10
The quarter-day does ne'er affright
Our peaceful slumbers in the night.
We eat our own, and batten more
Because we feed on no man's score;
But pity those whose flanks grow great
Swelled with the lard of others' meat.
We bless our fortunes when we see
Our own beloved privacy;
And like our living, where we're known
To very few, or else to none.   20

His Grange, or Private Wealth

Though clock,
To tell how night draws hence, I've none,
A cock
I have, to sing how day draws on.
I have
A maid, my Prue, by good luck sent
To save
That little Fates me gave or lent.
A hen
I keep, which, creaking day by day,   10
Tells when
She goes her long, white egg to lay.
A goose
I have, which, with a jealous ear,
Lets loose
Her tongue to tell what danger's near.
A lamb
I keep, tame, with my morsels fed,
Whose dam
An orphan left him, lately dead.   20
A cat
I keep, that plays about my house,
Grown fat
With eating many a miching mouse.
To these
A Tracy I do keep, whereby
I please
The more my rural privacy.
Which are
But toys to give my heart some ease: 30
Where care
None is, slight things do lightly please.

Upon Prue, His Maid

In this little urn is laid
Prudence Baldwin, once my maid,
From whose happy spark here let
Spring the purple violet.

A Ternary of Littles

Upon a Pipkin of Jelly Sent to a Lady

A little saint best fits a little shrine,
A little prop best fits a little vine,
As my small cruse best fits my little wine.

A little seed best fits a little soil,
A little trade best fits a little toil,
As my small jar best fits my little oil.

A little bin best fits a little bread,
A little garland fits a little head,
As my small stuff best fits my little shed.

A little hearth best fits a little fire,   10
A little chapel fits a little quire,
As my small bell best fits my little spire.

A little stream best fits a little boat,
A little lead best fits a little float,
As my small pipe best fits my little note.

A little meat best fits a little belly,
As sweetly, lady, give me leave to tell ye,
This little pipkin fits this little jelly.

Ceremonies for Christmas

Come, bring with a noise,
My merry, merry boys,
The Christmas log to the firing;
While my good dame, she
Bids ye all be free,
And drink to your hearts' desiring.

With the last year's brand
Light the new block, and
For good success in his spending,
On your psalteries play,   10
That sweet luck may
Come while the log is a-teending.

Drink now the strong beer,
Cut the white loaf here;
The while the meat is a-shredding
For the rare mince pie,
And the plums stand by
To fill the paste that's a-kneading.

Ceremonies for Candlemas Eve

Down with the rosemary and bays,
Down with the mistletoe;
Instead of holly, now upraise
The greener box, for show.

The holly hitherto did sway;
Let box now domineer
Until the dancing Easter Day,
Or Easter's eve appear.

Then youthful box, which now hath grace
Your houses to renew,   10

Grown old, surrender must his place
   Unto the crisped yew.

When yew is out, then birch comes in,
   And many flowers beside,
Both of a fresh and fragrant kin,
   To honor Whitsuntide.

Green rushes then, and sweetest bents,
   With cooler oaken boughs,
Come in for comely ornaments,
   To re-adorn the house.   20
Thus times do shift; each thing his turn does hold;
New things succeed as former things grow old.

Ceremony upon Candlemas Eve

Down with the rosemary, and so
Down with the bays and mistletoe;
Down with the holly, ivy, all
Wherewith ye dressed the Christmas hall;
That so the superstitious find
No one least branch there left behind;
For look, how many leaves there be
Neglected there, maids, trust to me,
So many goblins you shall see.

The Ceremonies for Candlemas Day

Kindle the Christmas brand, and then
   Till sunset let it burn;
Which quenched, then lay it up again
   Till Christmas next return.
Part must be kept, wherewith to teend
   The Christmas log next year;
And where 'tis safely kept, the fiend
   Can do no mischief there.

The Wake

Come, Anthea, let us two
Go to feast, as others do.
Tarts and custards, creams and cakes,
Are the junkets still at wakes,
Unto which the tribes resort,
Where the business is the sport.
Morris-dancers thou shalt see,
Marian, too, in pageantry,
And a mimic to devise
Many grinning properties.   10
Players there will be, and those
Base in action as in clothes;
Yet with strutting they will please
The incurious villages.
Near the dying of the day
There will be a cudgel-play,
Where a coxcomb will be broke,
Ere a good word can be spoke;
But the anger ends all here,
Drenched in ale or drowned in beer.   20
Happy rustics! best content
With the cheapest merriment,
And possess no other fear
Than to want the wake next year.

The Hock-Cart, or Harvest Home

To the Right Honorable Mildmay, Earl of Westmorland

Come, sons of summer, by whose toil
We are the lords of wine and oil;
By whose tough labors and rough hands
We rip up first, then reap, our lands.
Crowned with the ears of corn, now come,

And, to the pipe, sing harvest home.
Come forth, my lord, and see the cart
Dressed up with all the country art.
See here a maukin,[1] there a sheet,
As spotless pure as it is sweet;   10
The horses, mares, and frisking fillies
Clad all in linen, white as lilies.
The harvest swains and wenches bound
For joy to see the hock-cart crowned.
About the cart hear how the rout
Of rural younglings raise the shout,
Pressing before, some coming after,
Those with a shout, and these with laughter.
Some bless the cart, some kiss the sheaves,
Some prank them up with oaken leaves,   20
Some cross the fill-horse, some with great
Devotion stroke the home-borne wheat;
While other rustics, less attent
To prayers than to merriment,
Run after with their breeches rent.
Well, on, brave boys, to your lord's hearth,
Glittering with fire, where for your mirth
Ye shall see first the large and chief
Foundation of your feast, fat beef;
With upper stories, mutton, veal,   30
And bacon, which makes full the meal,
With several dishes standing by,
As here a custard, there a pie,
And here all-tempting frumenty.[2]
And for to make the merry cheer,
If smirking wine be wanting here,
There's that which drowns all care, stout beer;
Which freely drink to your lord's health,
Then to the plough, the commonwealth,
Next to your flails, your fanes, your fats,   40

---

[1] Maulkin. In Devon, a cloth.
[2] Wheat which has been hulled and boiled in milk.

Then to the maids with wheaten hats;
To the rough sickle, and crook'd scythe,
Drink, frolic boys, till all be blithe.
Feed and grow fat; and, as ye eat,
Be mindful that the laboring neat,
As you, may have their fill of meat;
And know, besides, ye must revoke
The patient ox unto the yoke,
And all go back unto the plough
And harrow, though they're hanged up now.   50
And, you must know, your lord's word's true:
Feed him ye must, whose food fills you;
And that this pleasure is like rain,
Not sent ye for to drown your pain,
But for to make it spring again.

The Wassail

Give way, give way, ye gates, and win
An easy blessing to your bin
And basket, by our entering in.

May both with manchet stand replete;
Your larders, too, so hung with meat,
That though a thousand, thousand eat,

Yet, ere twelve moons shall whirl about
Their silvery spheres, there's none may doubt
But more's sent in than was served out.

Next, may your dairies prosper so   10
As that your pans no ebb may know;
But if they do, the more to flow,

Like to a solemn, sober stream
Banked all with lilies, and the cream
Of sweetest cowslips filling them.

Then, may your plants be pressed with fruit,
Nor bee or hive you have be mute,
But sweetly sounding like a lute.

Next, may your duck and teeming hen
Both to the cock's tread say amen,   20
And for their two eggs render ten.

Last, may your harrows, shares, and ploughs,
Your stacks, your stocks, your sweetest mows,
All prosper by your virgin vows.

Alas! we bless, but see none here
That brings us either ale or beer;
In a dry house all things are near.

Let's leave a longer time to wait,
Where rust and cobwebs bind the gate,
And all live here with needy fate;   30

Where chimneys do forever weep
For want of warmth, and stomachs keep
With noise the servants' eyes from sleep.

It is in vain to sing, or stay
Our free feet here, but we'll away;
Yet to the Lares this we'll say:

The time will come when you'll be sad,
And reckon this for fortune bad,
To have lost the good ye might have had.

Oberon's Feast

Shapcot! [1] to thee the fairy state
I with discretion, dedicate,

[1] Herrick's personal friend.

Because thou prizest things that are
Curious and unfamiliar.
Take first the feast; these dishes gone,
We'll see the fairy court anon.

A little mushroom table spread,
After short prayers, they set on bread;
A moon-parched grain of purest wheat,
With some small glittering grit to eat   10
His choice bits with; then in a trice
They make a feast less great than nice.
But all this while his eye is served,
We must not think his ear was sterved;
But that there was in place to stir
His spleen, the chirring grasshopper,
The merry cricket, puling fly,
The piping gnat for minstrelsy.
And now we must imagine first,
The elves present to quench his thirst   20
A pure seed-pearl of infant dew,
Brought and besweetened in a blue
And pregnant violet; which done,
His kitling eyes begin to run
Quite through the table, where he spies
The horns of papery butterflies,
Of which he eats, and tastes a little
Of that we call the cuckoo's spittle.
A little fuzz-ball pudding stands
By, yet not blessed by his hands,   30
That was too coarse; but then forthwith
He ventures boldly on the pith
Of sugared rush, and eats the sag
And well-bestrutted bee's sweet bag,
Gladding his palate with some store
Of emmets' eggs; what would he more?
But beards of mice, a newt's stewed thigh,
A bloated earwig, and a fly;

With the red-capped worm that's shut
Within the concave of a nut,   40
Brown as his tooth. A little moth,
Late fattened in a piece of cloth;
With withered cherries, mandrake's ears,
Mole's eyes; to these the slain stag's tears;
The unctuous dewlaps of a snail;
The broke-heart of a nightingale
O'ercome in music; with a wine
Ne'er ravished from the flattering vine,
But gently pressed from the soft side
Of the most sweet and dainty bride,   50
Brought in a dainty daisy, which
He fully quaffs up to bewitch
His blood to height; this done, commended
Grace by his priest; the feast is ended.

The Hag

The hag is astride
This night for to ride,
The devil and she together;
Through thick and through thin,
Now out and then in,
Though ne'er so foul be the weather.

A thorn or a burr
She takes for a spur;
With a lash of a bramble she rides now;
Through brakes and through briers,   10
O'er ditches and mires,
She follows the spirit that guides now.

No beast for his food
Dares now range the wood,
But hushed in his lair he lies lurking;

While mischiefs by these,
On land and on seas,
At noon of night are a-working.

The storm will arise
And trouble the skies;
This night, and more for the wonder,   20
The ghost from the tomb
Affrighted shall come,
Called out by the clap of thunder.

The Fairies

If ye will with Mab find grace,
Set each platter in his place;
Rake the fire up, and get
Water in ere sun be set.
Wash your pails and cleanse your dairies;
Sluts are loathsome to the fairies.
Sweep your house; who doth not so,
Mab will pinch her by the toe.

Discontents in Devon

More discontents I never had
Since I was born, than here,
Where I have been, and still am sad,
In this dull Devonshire;
Yet justly too I must confess,
I ne'er invented such
Ennobled numbers for the press,
Than where I loathed so much.

His Return to London

From the dull confines of the drooping West,
To see the day spring from the pregnant East,

Ravished in spirit, I come, nay, more, I fly
To thee, blest place of my nativity!
Thus, thus with hallowed foot I touch the ground
With thousand blessings by thy fortune crowned.
O fruitful genius! that bestowest here
An everlasting plenty, year by year;
O place! O people! Manners framed to please
All nations, customs, kindreds, languages!   10
I am a free-born Roman; suffer then
That I amongst you live a citizen.
London my home is: though by hard fate sent
Into a long and irksome banishment;
Yet since called back; henceforward let me be,
O native country, repossessed by thee!
For, rather than I'll to the West return,
I'll beg of thee first here to have mine urn.
Weak I am grown, and must in short time fall;
Give thou my sacred reliques burial.   20

His Prayer for Absolution

For those my unbaptized rhymes,
Writ in my wild, unhallowed times;
For every sentence, clause, and word
That's not inlaid with Thee, my Lord,
Forgive me, God, and blot each line
Out of my book that is not Thine.
But if, 'mongst all, Thou find'st here one
Worthy Thy benediction,
That one of all the rest shall be
The glory of my work and me.   10

Another Grace for a Child

Here a little child I stand,
Heaving up my either hand;

Cold as paddocks though they be,
Here I lift them up to Thee,
For a benison to fall
On our meat and on us all. Amen.

To Find God

Weigh me the fire; or canst thou find
A way to measure out the wind;
Distinguish all those floods that are
Mixed in that watery theater;
And taste thou them as saltless there
As in their channel first they were.
Tell me the people that do keep
Within the kingdoms of the deep;
Or fetch me back that cloud again,
Beshivered into seeds of rain;   10
Tell me the motes, dust, sands, and spears
Of corn, when summer shakes his ears;
Show me that world of stars, and whence
They noiseless spill their influence:
This if thou canst; then show me Him
That rides the glorious cherubim.

A Thanksgiving to God for His House

Lord, Thou hast given me a cell
    Wherein to dwell,
A little house, whose humble roof
    Is weather-proof;
Under the spars of which I lie
    Both soft and dry;
Where Thou, my chamber for to ward,
    Hast set a guard
Of harmless thoughts, to watch and keep
    Me while I sleep.   10

Low is my porch, as is my fate,
    Both void of state;
And yet the threshold of my door
    Is worn by the poor,
Who thither come and freely get
    Good words, or meat.
Like as my parlor, so my hall
    And kitchen's small;
A little buttery, and therein
    A little bin,   20
Which keeps my little loaf of bread
    Unchipped, unflead;
Some brittle sticks of thorn or brier
    Make me a fire,
Close by whose living coal I sit,
    And glow like it.
Lord, I confess too, when I dine,
    The pulse is Thine,
And all those other bits that be
    There placed by Thee;   30
The worts, the purslane, and the mess
    Of watercress,
Which of Thy kindness Thou hast sent;
    And my content
Makes those, and my beloved beet,
    To be more sweet.
'Tis Thou that crown'st my glittering hearth
    With guiltless mirth,
And giv'st me wassail bowls to drink,
    Spiced to the brink.   40
Lord, 'tis Thy plenty-dropping hand
    That soils my land,
And giv'st me, for my bushel sown,
    Twice ten for one;
Thou mak'st my teeming hen to lay
    Her egg each day;

Besides my healthful ewes to bear
 Me twins each year;
The while the conduits of my kine
 Run cream for wine.   50
All these, and better, Thou dost send
 Me, to this end,
That I should render, for my part,
 A thankful heart;
Which, fired with incense, I resign
 As wholly Thine;
But the acceptance, that must be,
 My Christ, by Thee.

His Litany to the Holy Spirit

In the hour of my distress,
When temptations me oppress,
And when I my sins confess,
 Sweet Spirit, comfort me!

When I lie within my bed,
Sick in heart and sick in head,
And with doubts discomforted,
 Sweet Spirit, comfort me!

When the house doth sigh and weep,
And the world is drowned in sleep, 10
Yet mine eyes the watch do keep,
 Sweet Spirit, comfort me!

When the artless doctor sees
No one hope, but of his fees,
And his skill runs on the lees,
 Sweet Spirit, comfort me!

When his potion and his pill
Has or none or little skill,

Meet for nothing but to kill,
        Sweet Spirit, comfort me!   20

When the passing-bell doth toll,
And the furies in a shoal
Come to fright a parting soul,
        Sweet Spirit, comfort me!

When the tapers now burn blue,
And the comforters are few,
And that number more than true,
        Sweet Spirit, comfort me!

When the priest his last hath prayed,
And I nod to what is said,   30
'Cause my speech is now decayed,
        Sweet Spirit, comfort me!

When, God knows, I'm tossed about,
Either with despair or doubt,
Yet, before the glass be out,
        Sweet Spirit, comfort me!

When the Tempter me pursu'th
With the sins of all my youth,
And half damns me with untruth,
        Sweet Spirit, comfort me!   40

When the flames and hellish cries
Fright mine ears and fright mine eyes,
And all terrors me surprise,
        Sweet Spirit, comfort me!

When the Judgment is revealed,
And that opened which was sealed,
When to Thee I have appealed,
        Sweet Spirit, comfort me!

The White Island, or Place of the Blest

In this world, the isle of dreams,
While we sit by sorrow's streams,
Tears and terrors are our themes
   Reciting:

But when once from hence we fly,
More and more approaching nigh
Unto young eternity,
   Uniting:

In that whiter island, where
Things are evermore sincere;   10
Candor here and luster there
   Delighting:

There no monstrous fancies shall
Out of hell an horror call,
To create, or cause at all,
   Affrighting.

There, in calm and cooling sleep
We our eyes shall never steep,
But eternal watch shall keep,
   Attending   20

Pleasures, such as shall pursue
Me immortalized, and you;
And fresh joys, as never too
   Have ending.

To Death

Thou bid'st me come away,
And I'll no longer stay
Than for to shed some tears
For faults of former years,
And to repent some crimes
Done in the present times;
And next, to take a bit

Of bread, and wine with it;
To don my robes of love,
Fit for the place above;   10
To gird my loins about
With charity throughout,
And so to travel hence
With feet of innocence:
These done, I'll only cry
God mercy, and so die.

To Robin Redbreast

Laid out for dead, let thy last kindness be
With leaves and moss-work for to cover me;
And while the wood-nymphs my cold corpse inter,
Sing thou my dirge, sweet-warbling chorister!
For epitaph, in foliage next write this:
Here, here the tomb of Robin Herrick is.

The Pillar of Fame

Fame's pillar here at last we set,
Out-during marble, brass, or jet;
  Charmed and enchanted so
  As to withstand the blow
    Of overthrow;
    Nor shall the seas,
    Or outrages
  Of storms, o'erbear
  What we uprear;
    Tho' kingdoms fall,   10
  This pillar never shall
  Decline or waste at all;
But stand for ever by his own
Firm and well-fixed foundation.

To his book's end this last line he'd have placed:
Jocund his Muse was, but his life was chaste.

LITTLE is known of the life of Francis Quarles, but two of the slighter facts that have come down to us catch the interest of students of literature: Quarles studied at Christ's College, Cambridge, which Milton was to enter later, and he was a friend of Phineas Fletcher's. So it was that the most unique of the religious poets was trained in the same college that brought forth the greatest, and two of the quaintest of all the English poets became college mates.

After college Quarles entered Lincoln's Inn to study law. Later he was connected with the court, serving as cupbearer to Princess Elizabeth and accompanying her abroad after her marriage to the Elector Palatine. More suited to his natural bent was his next position as secretary to Archbishop Ussher in Ireland. He had married in 1618, and he and his family lived in the bishop's home. His son John praises Ussher in a poem for "the example of his life" and attributes to the archbishop "that little education I dare own." How long Quarles remained in Ireland we do not know, but in 1639 he gained the office of Chronologer of the City of London, an office which had previously been held, at least nominally, by Ben Jonson. Whatever his duties were, they did not interrupt the steady output of religious works. Finally, however, loyalty to the king stirred Quarles to action, and he joined the royal party at Oxford in 1644.

Quarles's life was to an unusual degree dedicated to God and the king, and the advent of eighteen children into his home seems scarcely to have interrupted this main trend. Indeed, his wife states that "he preferred God and religion to the first place in his thoughts; his king and country to the second; his family and studies he reserved to the last." [1] She did not hold this rating against him, however, but paid a loyal tribute by saying, "His equal may be desired but can

---

[1] Quoted in the Memoir prefixed to *Emblems, Divine and Moral* (1866), pp. xvii–xviii.

hardly be met withal." His poetry was an offering to the cause of religion; his prose, to the cause of the king. For writing *The Loyal Convert*, extenuating the king's alliance with the Catholics, Quarles was deprived of his property and was accused of Catholicism. He never recovered from the ill treatment he received for this attempt to aid the king, and he died in the same year.

Quarles, in his study by three in the morning, was a voluminous writer and an exceedingly popular one. The religious content of his poems, which to-day makes against his popularity, created a demand for his works in the day when the King James Bible was the book of the people. His long poems are all paraphrases of Scripture. His first bears the startling title *A Feast of Worms Set Forth in a Poeme of the History of Jonah;* others are the *Song of Solomon, Ecclesiastes, Esther, Lamentations of Jeremiah,* and *Job*. The poems which are not Scriptural paraphrases contain a note of religious teaching and of piety, which had a general appeal. It is his *Emblems* (1635) which has won the greatest popularity and the most lasting fame.

An emblem consists of a Scripture motto, a print, and a poem illustrating and enlarging the thought of the verse and picture. It is accompanied by some suitable quotation from the Church Fathers or other religious writers and a final epigram. The entire assemblage gives a little sermon on the text, and its purpose is solely to edify. Quarles himself thus defines an emblem:

An Emblem is but a silent parable: Let not the tender eye check, to see the allusion to our blessed Saviour figured in these types. In Holy Scripture he is sometimes called a Sower; sometimes a Fisher; sometimes a Physician: And why not presented so as well to the eye as to the ear? Before the knowledge of letters, God was known by hieroglyphics. And indeed, what are the Heavens, the earth, nay, every creature, but Hieroglyphics and Emblems of his glory?

The idea of the prints, to which undoubtedly much of the popularity of the *Emblems* is due, was not original with Quarles but was taken from Herman Hugo's *Pia Desideria* (1624). The quaintness of these illustrations is the chief charm for the modern reader, although the many felicitous lines, the frequent imaginative power, and the vigor and flow of his rhythm are also to be admired.

Book I—Emblem XV

REV. 12:12

The devil is come unto you having great wrath, because he knoweth that he hath but a short time.

Lord! canst Thou see and suffer? Is Thy hand
    Still bound to the peace? Shall earth's black monarch take

A full possession of Thy wasted land?
   Oh, will Thy slumbering vengeance never wake,
   Till full-aged, law-resisting custom shake
The pillars of Thy right, by false command?
   Unlock Thy clouds, great Thunderer, and come down;
   Behold whose temples wear Thy sacred crown;
Redress, redress our wrongs; revenge, revenge Thy own.

See how the bold usurper mounts the seat   10
   Of royal majesty; how overstrawing
Perils with pleasure, pointing every threat
   With bugbear death, by torments over-awing
   Thy frighted subjects, or by favors drawing
Their tempted hearts to his unjust retreat;
   Lord, canst Thou be so mild, and he so bold?
   Or can Thy flocks be thriving when the fold
Is governed by the fox? Lord, canst Thou see and hold?

That swift-winged advocate that did commence
   Our welcome suits before the King of kings;   20
That sweet ambassador that hurries hence
   What airs the harmonious soul or signs or sings,
   See how she flutters her idle wings;
Her wings are clipt, and eyes put out by sense:
   Sense-conquering Faith is now grown blind and cold,
   And basely cravened, that in times of old
Did conquer heaven itself, do what the Almighty could.

Behold, how double Fraud does scourge and tear
   Astræa's [1] wounded sides, ploughed up and rent
With knotted cords, whose fury has no care;   30
   See how she stands a pris'ner, to be sent
   A slave into eternal banishment,
I know not whither, oh, I know not where:
   Her patent must be canceled in disgrace;

[1] Astræa: goddess of peace.

And sweet-lipped Fraud, with her divided face,
Must act Astræa's part, must take Astræa's place.

Faith's pinions clipt? and fair Astræa gone?
   Quick-seeing Faith now blind? and Justice see?
Has Justice now found wings? and has Faith none?
   What do we here? who would not wish to be
   Dissolved from earth, and with Astræa flee
From this blind dungeon to that sun-bright throne?
   Lord, is Thy sceptre lost, or laid aside?
   Is hell broke loose, and all her fiends untied?
Lord, rise, and rouse, and rule, and crush their furious pride.

        PETER RAV. IN MATTH.

The devil is the author of evil, the fountain of wickedness, the adversary of the truth, the corrupter of the world, man's perpetual enemy: he planteth snares, diggeth ditches, spurreth bodies; he goadeth souls, he suggesteth thoughts, belcheth anger, exposeth virtues to hatred, maketh vices beloved, soweth errors, nourisheth contention, disturbeth peace, and scattereth affliction.

        MACAR.

Let us suffer with those that suffer, and be crucified with those that are crucified, that we may be glorified with those that are glorified.

        SAVANAR.

If there be no enemy, no fight; if no fight, no victory; if no victory, no crown.

        EPIG. 15

My soul, sit thou a patient looker on;
Judge not the play before the play be done:
Her plot has many changes: every day
Speaks a new scene; the last act crowns the play.

Book II—Emblem IV

HOSEA 13:3

They shall be as the chaff that is driven with a whirlwind out
of the floor, and as the smoke out of the chimney.

Flint-hearted Stoics, you whose marble eyes
Contemn a wrinkle, and whose souls despise
To follow nature's too affected fashion,
Or travel in the regent walk of passion;
Whose rigid hearts disdain to shrink at fears,
Or play at fast or loose, with smiles and tears;

Come, burst your spleens with laughter to behold
A new-found vanity, which days of old
Ne'er knew: a vanity that has beset
The world and made more slaves than Mahomet;   10
That has condemned us to the servile yoke
Of slavery, and made us slaves to smoke.[1]
But stay; why tax I thus our modern times
For new-blown follies, and for new-born crimes:
Are we sole guilty, and the first age free?
No, they were smoked and slaved as well as we:
What's sweet-lipped honor's blast but smoke? What's treasure
But very smoke? And what more smoke than pleasure?
Alas! they're all but shadows, fumes, and blasts;
That vanishes, this fades, the other wastes.   20
The restless merchant, he that loves to steep
His brains in wealth, and lays his soul to sleep
In bags of bullion, sees the immortal crown,
And fain would mount, but ingots keep him down.
He brags to-day, perchance, and begs to-morrow;
He lent but now; wants credit now to borrow:
Blow, winds, the treasure's gone, the merchant's broke;
A slave to silver's but a slave to smoke.
Behold the glory-vying child of fame,
That from deep wounds sucks forth an honored name;   30
That thinks no purchase worth the style of good,
But what is sold for sweat, and sealed with blood;
That for a point, a blast of empty breath,
Undaunted gazes in the face of death;
Whose dear-bought bubble, filled with vain renown,
Breaks with a fillip, or a gen'ral's frown:
His stroke-got honor staggers with a stroke;
A slave to honor is a slave to smoke.
And that fond soul which wastes his idle days
In loose delights, and sports about the blaze   40

---

[1] The smoking of tobacco was still a novelty.

Of Cupid's candle; he that daily spies
Twin babies in his mistress' Geminies,
Whereto his sad devotion does impart
The sweet burnt-offering of a bleeding heart:
See, how his wings are singed in Cyprian fire,
Whose flames consume with youth, in age expire.
The world's a bubble; all the pleasures in it,
Like morning vapors, vanish in a minute:
The vapors vanish, and the bubble's broke;
A slave to pleasure is a slave to smoke.   50
Now, Stoic, cease thy laughter, and repast
Thy pickled cheeks with tears, and weep as fast.

ST. HIERON

That rich man is great who thinketh not himself great
because he is rich: the proud man (who is the poor man)
braggeth outwardly, but beggeth inwardly; he is blown up,
but not full.

PETR. RAV.

Vexation and anguish accompany riches and honor: the
pomp of the world, and the favor of the people are but
smoke, and a blast suddenly vanishing; which, if they com-
monly please, commonly bring repentance; and, for a minute
of joy, they bring an age of sorrow.

EPIG. 4

Cupid, thy diet's strange: it dulls, it rouses;
It cools, it heats; it binds, and then it looses:
Dull-sprightly-cold-hot fool, if e'er it winds thee
Into a looseness once, take heed; it binds thee.

Book IV—Emblem III

PSALM 17:5

Hold up my goings in thy paths, that my footsteps slip not.

Whene'er the Old Exchange of profit rings
    Her silver saints-bell of uncertain gains,
My merchant-soul can stretch both legs and wings:
    How I can run, and take unwearied pains!
       The charms of profit are so strong, that I,
       Who wanted legs to go, find wings to fly.

If time-beguiling Pleasure but advance
    Her lustful trump, and blow her bold alarms,

O how my sportful soul can frisk and dance,
    And hug that siren in her twined arms!   10
        The sprightly voice of sinew-strengthening pleasure
        Can lend my bedrid soul both legs and leisure.

If blazing Honor chance to fill my veins
    With flattering warmth, and flash of courtly fire,
My soul can take a pleasure in her pains;
    My lofty strutting steps disdain to tire;
        My antic knees can turn upon the hinges
        Of compliment, and screw a thousand cringes.

But when I come to thee, my God, that art
    The royal mine of everlasting treasure,   20
The real honor of my better part,
    And living fountain of eternal pleasure,
        How nerveless are my limbs! how faint and slow!
        I have no wings to fly, nor legs to go.

So when the streams of swift-foot Rhine convey
    Her upland riches to the Belgic shore,
The idle vessel slides the wat'ry way,
    Without the blast or tug of wind or oar;
        Her slippery keel divides the silver foam
        With ease: so facile is the way from home!   30

But when the home-bound vessel turns her sails
    Against the breast of the resisting stream,
O then she slugs; nor sail nor oar prevails;
    The stream is sturdy, and her tides extreme:
        Each stroke is loss, and ev'ry tug is vain;
        A boat-length's purchase is a league of pain.

Great All in All, Thou art my rest, my home;
    My way is tedious, and my steps are slow:
Reach forth Thy helpful hand, or bid me come;
    I am Thy child, O teach Thy child to go;   40

Conjoin Thy sweet commands to my desire,
And I will venture, though I fall or tire.

ST. AUGUST. SER. XV. DE VERB. APOST.

Be always displeased at what thou art, if thou desirest
to attain to what thou art not: for where thou hast pleased
thyself, there thou abidest. But if thou sayest, I have enough,
thou perishest; always add, always walk, always proceed;
neither stand still, nor go back, nor deviate: he that standeth
still, proceedeth not; he goeth back that continueth not;
he deviateth that revolteth; he goeth better that creepeth
in his way than he that runneth out of his way.

EPIG. 3

Fear not, my soul, to lose for want of cunning;
Weep not; heaven is not always got by running:
Thy thoughts are swift, although thy legs be slow;
True love will creep, not having strength to go.

George Herbert 1593-1633

To UNDERSTAND Herbert's poetry one must know something of his life, for the facts of his life and the personality of the man form the very substance and spirit of his poems.

Herbert's background and early training account largely for the quality of his character. He was of an old and noble family, and he spent his early years in the ancestral home on the border of Wales. His widowed mother, a woman of beautiful character and of great refinement and culture, personally supervised the early education of her sons. When George was about five, his mother established a home at Oxford, where her son Edward was attending the university, and put the education of George into the hands of tutors. Later she moved to London and entered George in Westminster School. In London she became a personal inspiration to John Donne, helped him in his difficulties, and gave to him a "warm redeeming hand." His tribute to her is found in *The Autumnal*. Further evidence of her charm lies in her happy marriage to John Danvers, a man much younger than herself. She had dedicated George to the church in his infancy; and she brought him up with the idea that he was to go into the ministry, a plan of life in which he was constantly encouraged by Donne. Perhaps this ideal, as well as his careful home training, accounts for a personal purity of both life and thought which makes one think of Milton.

Herbert's character and his inspiration worked together to develop a new literary type, the religious lyric. The first year that he was at Cambridge University, when he was not yet seventeen, he wrote a letter to his mother telling her of his ambition to become a poet and of his feeling that the poets use love in too restricted a sense when they limit it to love between men and women. As for himself, he says, "My poor Abilities in Poetry shall be all and ever consecrated to God's glory." He enclosed the sonnet entitled *The Resolve*, a New Year's gift which must have warmed the heart of Lady Herbert.

As he progressed toward his M.A. at Cambridge, constantly preparing himself in divinity, new possibilities opened up for him. He had been taught elegant manners and good taste in dress; he was fond of music and was a good conversationalist; and he had a pleasing personality. These qualifications, in addition to his excellent scholarship, led to his being chosen as Orator of the University. In the case of others this position had meant political preferment and had led to the office of Secretary of State. Herbert considered it "the finest place in the University" and in a letter to his stepfather described in detail its duties and honors:

. . . the Orator writes all the University letters, makes all the orations, be it to King, Prince, or whatever comes to the University; to requite these pains, he takes place next the doctors, is at all their assemblies and meetings, and sits above the proctors, is regent, or non-regent at his pleasure, and such like gayness, which will please a young man well.[1]

The years of his position as Orator were pleasant ones: he kept his own horse, he indulged his cultured tastes, he had a country house and entertained his friends. Through his position he gained many friends of prominence and power: the Marquis of Hamilton, the Duke of Richmond, Sir Henry Wotton, and Sir Francis Bacon. Even James I was attracted to him and made him welcome at court. His brother, Lord Herbert of Cherbury, had already entered public service and was ambassador to the French Court; one brother was Master of Revels at the English Court; three others were in public service—now the alluring way was open to him. But the feeling that the church was his calling was only dormant; and when in 1626 he was appointed Prebendary of Leighton, he became actively interested in the church instead of accepting his appointment as a sinecure. Since Leighton was only two miles from Little Gidding, where Nicholas Ferrar had established his devout religious com-

[1] Quoted in Palmer's *Life and Works of George Herbert*, I, 29.

munity, Herbert renewed his acquaintance with Ferrar and offered him the transfer of the prebend. Ferrar declined but urged upon Herbert the restoration of the church, which had fallen into disrepair. Herbert undertook this work; and with the aid of his mother, who at first objected to his project ("For, George, it is not for your weak body and empty purse to undertake to build churches"), he raised money among his friends to rebuild the church.

A conflict, which is fully recorded in his poetry, now arose in Herbert's soul. It is not the torment of Donne, torn between pleasant sin and the desire for God, but a stern battle between the lure of a brilliant public life to which all his natural tastes fitted him and the call to a quiet life of religious service. The struggle was not easily settled. Lady Herbert died with her hope of seeing him in the church unfulfilled; several of his prominent friends died without seeing him established at court. Though Herbert's ability would probably have enabled him to gain worldly preferment without the influence of these friends, their death turned his thoughts toward the religious life; the deep impression which the beautiful life at Little Gidding had made on him and the urging of Nicholas Ferrar both had weight; and Donne's influence bore down strongly upon him. Herbert resigned the oratorship, but his valiant fight against tuberculosis had already begun, and between indecision and ill health three more years elapsed. Finally he came to a decision: he accepted "the collar"; he deliberately and with open eyes rejected the gifts which learning, wealth, and glory could offer and dedicated himself to the church.

He was established at Bemerton, near Salisbury; and the record of his life there is given in his charming *Country Parson,* as well as in his poems. He had married the year before, and the parsonage seems to have been a happy place. There were daily prayers at the church, the care of his parishioners, and hours of recreation with his viol or lute. Twice a week he walked over to the cathedral at Salisbury to meet other musical friends and have an afternoon of music. There were only three years of life left to Herbert; but these were years of consecrated service, of beauty in daily living, and of established peace.

After he made his decision, Herbert's life had complete unity. He was no Puritan, renouncing beauty and the pleasures of the senses; to him all of life was "religious." Simple, homely tasks took on new beauty and value because they were done for God; the symbolism of the Anglican Church, the ritual, and the church calendar all assumed significance because they meant contact with God. There was no burning fervor as in Donne, no height of ecstasy as in Crashaw; Herbert's relationship with God was very simple and direct and unquestioning.

Herbert destroyed his secular poetry and in his last illness sent his religious poems to Ferrar with the direction to burn them unless he thought they might "turn to the advantage of any dejected poor soul." Ferrar wisely published the poems, which achieved immediate popularity—six editions in eight years—and greatly influenced both Crashaw and Vaughan. These poems show no evidence of contact with the new ideas of the period: no intellectual questioning, no interest in experimentation, and no scientific curiosity. Though Herbert knew Bacon so well that the latter dedicated to him a translation of the Psalms, his only indication of Baconian influence is found in the *Church Porch,* where he gives as an introduction to religion much sound advice on how to get along in the world.

The poems of Herbert show excellent craftsmanship. He develops the structural unity of the short poem by clearly announcing the theme, giving it emotional development, and bringing it to a logical close. He experimented widely in verse forms, devising many new forms and even carrying out figures in stanza structure, as in *Easter Wings.* Though his poems are metaphysical, showing the dominance of Donne, they have greater simplicity and clarity than Donne's. His figures are quaint rather than startling and often lie in the titles of his poems, as in *The Collar* or *The Pulley.* To the

modern reader the stylistic qualities are of interest; but the
spell of the poems lies in their utter sincerity, appealing
tenderness, and elevation of common things.

The Resolve

My God, where is that ancient heat towards Thee
    Wherewith whole shoals of martyrs once did burn,
    Beside their other flames? Doth poetry
Wear Venus' livery, only serve her turn?
Why are not sonnets made of Thee, and lays
    Upon Thine altar burnt? [1] Cannot Thy love
    Heighten a spirit to sound out Thy praise
As well as any she? Cannot Thy dove
Outstrip their Cupid easily in flight?
    Or since Thy ways are deep and still the same,   10
    Will not a verse run smooth that bears Thy name?
Why doth that fire, which by Thy power and might
    Each breast does feel, no braver fuel choose
    Than that which one day worms may chance refuse?

Love [1]

Immortal Love, author of this great frame,
    Sprung from that beauty which can never fade,
    How hath man parceled out Thy glorious name
And thrown it on that dust which Thou hast made,
While mortal love doth all the title gain!
    Which siding with invention, they together
    Bear all the sway, possessing heart and brain,
Thy workmanship, and give Thee share in neither.
Wit fancies beauty, beauty raiseth wit.
    The world is theirs; they two play out the game,   10

[1] Herbert is here indicating his rejection of the usual sonnet con-
vention. Love, really a name for God, has been applied to human re-
lationships. Cf. l. 3 below.

Thou standing by. And though Thy glorious name
Wrought our deliverance from the infernal pit,
   Who sings Thy praise? Only a scarf or glove
   Doth warm our hands and make them write of love.

Jordan [1]

When first my lines of heavenly joys made mention,
   Such was their luster, they did so excel,
That I sought out quaint words and trim invention;
   My thoughts began to burnish, sprout, and swell,
Curling with metaphors a plain intention,
   Decking the sense as if it were to sell.

Thousands of notions in my brain did run,
   Offering their service, if I were not sped.
I often blotted what I had begun;
   This was not quick enough, and that was dead.
Nothing could seem too rich to clothe the sun,
   Much less those joys which trample on his head.

As flames do work and wind when they ascend,
   So did I weave myself into the sense;
But while I bustled, I might hear a friend
   Whisper, "How wide is all this long pretense!
There is in love a sweetness ready penned;
   Copy out only that, and save expense."

Sin

   Lord, with what care hast Thou begirt us round!
      Parents first season us; then schoolmasters
   Deliver us to laws; they send us bound
      To rules of reason, holy messengers,

[1] The winding course of the Jordan River symbolizes to Herbert the intricate "metaphysical" style.

Pulpits and Sundays, sorrow dogging sin,
   Afflictions sorted, anguish of all sizes,
Fine nets and stratagems to catch us in;
   Bibles laid open, millions of surprises,
Blessings beforehand, ties of gratefulness,
   The sound of glory ringing in our ears;   10
Without, our shame; within, our consciences;
   Angels and grace, eternal hopes and fears.
Yet all these fences and their whole array
One cunning bosom-sin blows quite away.

The Pulley

When God at first made man,
Having a glass of blessings standing by,
   "Let us," said He, "pour on him all we can.
Let the world's riches, which dispersed lie,
   Contract into a span."

So strength first made a way;
Then beauty flowed, then wisdom, honor, pleasure.
   When almost all was out, God made a stay,
Perceiving that, alone of all His treasure,
   Rest in the bottom lay.   10

"For if I should," said He,
"Bestow this jewel also on my creature,
   He would adore my gifts instead of me
And rest in nature, not the God of nature;
   So both should losers be.

"Yet let him keep the rest,
But keep them with repining restlessness.
   Let him be rich and weary, that at least,
If goodness lead him not, yet weariness
   May toss him to my breast."   20

Peace

Sweet Peace, where dost thou dwell? I humbly crave,
      Let me once know.
  I sought thee in a secret cave,
      And asked if Peace were there.
A hollow wind did seem to answer, "No,
      Go seek elsewhere."

I did, and going did a rainbow note.
      "Surely," thought I,
  "This is the lace of Peace's coat;
      I will search out the matter."   10
But while I looked, the clouds immediately
      Did break and scatter.

Then went I to a garden, and did spy
      A gallant flower,
  The crown imperial. "Sure," said I,
      "Peace at the root must dwell."
But when I digged, I saw a worm devour
      What showed so well.

At length I met a reverend good old man,
      Whom when for Peace   20
  I did demand, he thus began:
      "There was a Prince of old
At Salem [1] dwelt, who lived with good increase
      Of flock and fold.

"He sweetly lived; yet sweetness did not save
      His life from foes.
  But after death out of His grave
      There sprang twelve stalks of wheat;

[1] Salem was the original name for Jerusalem and means peace. The Prince of Salem is Christ, the Prince of Peace. Christ is also "the bread of life," and the twelve stalks of wheat are the twelve apostles who spread the Christian religion. The entire figure is very much forced.

Which many wondering at, got some of those
    To plant and set.   30

"It prospered strangely, and did soon disperse
    Through all the earth;
  For they that taste it do rehearse
    That virtue lies therein,
A secret virtue bringing peace and mirth
    By flight of sin.

"Take of this grain, which in my garden grows,
    And grows for you;
  Make bread of it; and that repose
    And peace which everywhere   40
With so much earnestness you do pursue
    Is only there."

The Collar

I struck the board, and cried, "No more!
    I will abroad!
What? Shall I ever sigh and pine?
My lines and life are free, free as the road,
  Loose as the wind, as large as store.
    Shall I be still in suit?
  Have I no harvest but a thorn
  To let me blood, and not restore
What I have lost with cordial fruit?
    Sure there was wine   10
  Before my sighs did dry it. There was corn
  Before my tears did drown it.
Is the year only lost to me?
    Have I no bays to crown it?
No flowers, no garlands gay? All blasted?
    All wasted?
  Not so, my heart! But there is fruit,
    And thou hast hands.

Recover all thy sigh-blown age
On double pleasures. Leave thy cold dispute   20
Of what is fit and not. Forsake thy cage,
      Thy rope of sands,
Which petty thoughts have made, and made to thee
  Good cable, to enforce and draw,
      And be thy law,
While thou didst wink and wouldst not see.
      Away! Take heed!
      I will abroad.
Call in thy death's head there! Tie up thy fears!
      He that forbears   30
  To suit and serve his need
    Deserves his load."
But as I raved, and grew more fierce and wild
      At every word,
  Methoughts I heard one calling, "Child!"
    And I replied, "My Lord!"

The Quip

The merry world did on a day
  With his train-bands and mates agree
To meet together where I lay,
  And all in sport to jeer at me.

First Beauty crept into a rose;
  Which when I plucked not, "Sir," said she,
"Tell me, I pray, whose hands are those?"
  But Thou shalt answer, Lord, for me.

Then Money came, and chinking still,
  "What tune is this, poor man?" said he;   10
"I heard in music you had skill."
  But Thou shalt answer, Lord, for me.

Then came brave Glory puffing by
    In silks that whistled, who but he?
He scarce allowed me half an eye.
    But Thou shalt answer, Lord, for me.

Then came quick Wit and Conversation,
    And he would needs a comfort be,
And, to be short, make an oration.
    But Thou shalt answer, Lord, for me.   20

Yet when the hour of Thy design
    To answer these fine things shall come,
Speak not at large; say I am Thine;
    And then they have their answer home.

The Glance

When first Thy sweet and gracious eye
Vouchsafed even in the midst of youth and night
To look upon me, who before did lie
            Weltering in sin,
    I felt a sugared, strange delight,
Passing all cordials made by any art,
Bedew, embalm, and overrun my heart,
            And take it in.

Since that time many a bitter storm
My soul hath felt, even able to destroy,   10
Had the malicious and ill-meaning harm
            His swing and sway.
    But still Thy sweet original joy,
Sprung from Thine eye, did work within my soul,
And surging griefs, when they grew bold, control,
            And got the day.

If Thy first glance so powerful be,
A mirth but opened and sealed up again,
What wonders shall we feel when we shall see
    Thy full-eyed love!   20
When Thou shalt look us out of pain,
And one aspect of Thine spend in delight
More than a thousand suns disburse in light,
    In heaven above.

Affliction

When first Thou didst entice to Thee my heart,
    I thought the service brave;
So many joys I writ down for my part,
    Besides what I might have
Out of my stock of natural delights,
Augmented with Thy gracious benefits.

I looked on Thy furniture so fine,
    And made it fine to me;
Thy glorious household stuff did me entwine,
    And 'tice me unto Thee;   10
Such stars I counted mine; both heaven and earth
Paid me my wages in a world of mirth.

What pleasures could I want, whose King I served,
    Where joys my fellows were?
Thus argued into hopes, my thoughts reserved
    No place for grief or fear.
Therefore my sudden soul caught at the place,
And made her youth and fierceness seek Thy face.

At first Thou gavest me milk and sweetnesses;
    I had my wish and way.   20
My days were strowed with flowers and happiness;
    There was no month but May.

But with my years sorrow did twist and grow,
And made a party unawares for woe.

My flesh began unto my soul in pain,
      Sicknesses cleave my bones;
Consuming agues dwell in every vein
      And tune my breath to groans.
Sorrow was all my soul; I scarce believed,
Till grief did tell me roundly, that I lived.   30

When I got health, Thou took'st away my life,
      And more, for my friends die.
My mirth and edge was lost; a blunted knife
      Was of more use than I.
Thus thin and lean without a fence or friend,
I was blown through with every storm and wind.

Whereas my birth and spirit rather took
      The way that takes the town,
Thou didst betray me to a lingering book
      And wrap me in a gown.   40
I was entangled in the world of strife
Before I had the power to change my life.

Yet, for I threatened oft the siege to raise,
      Not simpering all mine age,
Thou often didst with academic praise
      Melt and dissolve my rage.
I took the sweetened pill till I came near;
I could not go away, nor persevere.

Yet lest perchance I should too happy be
      In my unhappiness,   50
Turning my purge to food, Thou throwest me
      Into more sicknesses.
Thus doth Thy power cross-bias me, not making
Thine own gift good, yet me from my ways taking.

Now I am here, what Thou wilt do with me
    None of my books will show.
I read, and sigh, and wish I were a tree,
    For sure then I should grow
To fruit or shade; at least some bird would trust
Her household to me, and I should be just.   60

Yet, though Thou troublest me, I must be meek;
    In weakness must be stout.
Well, I will change the service, and go seek
    Some other master out.
Ah my dear God! though I am clean forgot,
Let me not love Thee, if I love Thee not.

Discipline

    Throw away Thy rod,
    Throw away Thy wrath.
        O my God,
    Take the gentle path.

    For my heart's desire
    Unto Thine is bent;
        I aspire
    To a full consent.

    Not a word or look
    I affect to own,
        But by book,   10
    And Thy book alone.

    Though I fail, I weep;
    Though I halt in pace,
        Yet I creep
    To the throne of grace.

Then let wrath remove;
Love will do the deed,
   For with love
Stony hearts will bleed.   20

Love is swift of foot.
Love's a man of war,
   And can shoot,
And can hit from far.

Who can 'scape his bow?
That which wrought on thee,
   Brought thee low,
Needs must work on me.

Throw away Thy rod;
Though man frailties hath,   30
   Thou art God.
Throw away Thy wrath.

Love [2]

Love bade me welcome; yet my soul drew back,
  Guilty of dust and sin.
But quick-eyed Love, observing me grow slack
  From my first entrance in,
Drew nearer to me, sweetly questioning
  If I lacked anything.

"A guest," I answered, "worthy to be here."
  Love said, "You shall be he."
"I, the unkind, ungrateful? Ah my dear,
  I cannot look on Thee."   10
Love took my hand and, smiling, did reply,
  "Who made the eyes but I?"

"Truth, Lord, but I have marred them; let my shame
      Go where it doth deserve."
"And know you not," says Love, "who bore the blame?"
      "My dear, then I will serve."
"You must sit down," says Love, "and taste my meat."
      So I did sit and eat.

The Pearl

(*Matthew* 13:45) [1]

I know the ways of learning, both the head
    And pipes that feed the press,[2] and make it run;
What reason hath from nature borrowed,
    Or of itself, like a good housewife, spun
In laws and policy; what the stars conspire;
What willing nature speaks, what forced by fire; [3]
    Both the old discoveries, and the new-found seas,
The stock and surplus, cause and history;
    All these stand open, or I have the keys;
        Yet I love Thee.   10

I know the ways of honor, what maintains
    The quick returns of courtesy and wit;
In vies of favors whether party gains
    When glory swells the heart, and moldeth it
To all expressions both of hand and eye,
Which on the world a truelove knot may tie,
    And bear the bundle wheresoe'er it goes;
How many drams of spirit there must be
    To sell my life unto my friends or foes;
        Yet I love Thee.   20

---

[1] "Again, the kingdom of heaven is like unto a merchant man, seeking goodly pearls: who, when he had found one pearl of great price, went and sold all that he had, and bought it."

[2] The printing press referred to was apparently operated by water.

[3] Knowledge of alchemy.

I know the ways of pleasure, the sweet strains,
   The lullings and the relishes of it;
The propositions of hot blood and brains;
   What mirth and music mean; what love and wit
Have done these twenty hundred years and more;
I know the projects of unbridled store;
   My stuff is flesh, not brass; my senses live,
And grumble oft that they have more in me
   Than he that curbs them, being but one to five;
      Yet I love Thee.   30

I know all these, and have them in my hand;
   Therefore not seeled,[4] but with open eyes
I fly to Thee, and fully understand
   Both the main sale and the commodities; [5]
And at what rate and price I have Thy love,
With all the circumstances that may move.
   Yet through the labyrinths, not my groveling wit,
But Thy silk twist let down from heaven to me
   Did both conduct and teach me how by it
      To climb to Thee.   40

The Flower

How fresh, O Lord, how sweet and clean
Are Thy returns! Even as the flowers in spring,
   To which, besides their own demean,
The late-past frosts tributes of pleasure bring.
      Grief melts away
      Like snow in May,
As if there were no such cold thing.

Who would have thought my shriveled heart
Could have recovered greenness? It was gone

[4] When young falcons were being trained, their eyelids were sewed together.
[5] Herbert understands the terms on which he comes to God, both what he gives up and what he gains.

Quite underground, as flowers depart   10
To see their mother-root, when they have blown;
　　Where they together
　　All the hard weather,
Dead to the world, keep house unknown.

These are Thy wonders, Lord of power,
Killing and quickening, bringing down to hell
　　And up to heaven in an hour;
Making a chiming of a passing-bell.[1]
　　We say amiss
　　This or that is;   20
Thy word is all, if we could spell.

O that I once past changing were,
Fast in Thy paradise, where no flower can wither!
　　Many a spring I shoot up fair,
Offering at heaven, growing and groaning thither;
　　Nor doth my flower
　　Want a spring shower,
My sins and I joining together.

But while I grow in a straight line,
Still upwards bent, as if heaven were mine own,   30
　　Thy anger comes, and I decline.
What frost to that? What pole is not the zone
　　Where all things burn,
　　When Thou dost turn,
And the least frown of Thine is shown?[2]

And now in age I bud again;
After so many deaths I live and write;
　　I once more smell the dew and rain,
And relish versing.[3] O my only Light,
　　It cannot be   40

[1] "Turning a funeral knell into a bridal peal." (Palmer).
[2] The coldness of God's frown makes even the poles seem hot.
[3] This seems especially true of Herbert.

That I am he
On whom Thy tempests fell all night.

These are Thy wonders, Lord of love,
To make us see we are but flowers that glide;
  Which when we once can find and prove,
Thou hast a garden for us where to bide.
      Who would be more,
      Swelling through store,
  Forfeit their paradise by their pride.

The Elixir [1]

Teach me, my God and King,
  In all things Thee to see;
And what I do in anything,
  To do it as for Thee.

Not rudely, as a beast,
  To run into an action;
But still to make Thee prepossessed,
  And give it his perfection.

A man that looks on glass
  On it may stay his eye,   10
Or if he pleaseth, through it pass,
  And then the heaven espy.

All may of Thee partake;
  Nothing can be so mean
Which with his tincture, "for Thy sake,"
  Will not grow bright and clean.

A servant with this clause
  Makes drudgery divine:

[1] Alchemists hoped to transmute other metals into gold by means
of the *Elixir*. Herbert has identified this preparation with the philoso-
pher's stone, ll. 21–22.

Who sweeps a room as for Thy laws
　　Makes that and the action fine.　　20

This is the famous stone
　　That turneth all to gold;
For that which God doth touch and own
　　Cannot for less be told.

The Church Windows

Lord, how can man preach Thy eternal word?
　　He is a brittle, crazy glass;
Yet in Thy temple Thou dost him afford
　　This glorious and transcendent place,
　　To be a window, through Thy grace.

But when Thou dost anneal in glass Thy story,
　　Making Thy life to shine within
The holy preachers, then the light and glory
　　More reverend grows, and more doth win,
　　Which else shows waterish, bleak, and thin.　　10

Doctrine and life, colors and light, in one
　　When they combine and mingle, bring
A strong regard and awe; but speech alone
　　Doth vanish like a flaring thing,
　　And in the ear, not conscience ring.

Church Music

Sweetest of sweets, I thank you! When displeasure
　　Did through my body wound my mind,
You took me thence, and in your house of pleasure
　　A dainty lodging me assigned.

Now I in you without a body move,
　　Rising and falling with your wings.

We both together sweetly live and love,
   Yet say sometimes, "God help poor kings."

Comfort, I'll die; for if you post from me,
   Sure I shall do so, and much more.   10
But if I travel in your company,
   You know the way to heaven's door.

The Altar

A broken altar, Lord, Thy servant rears,
  Made of a heart and cemented with tears;
    Whose parts are as Thy hand did frame;
    No workman's tool hath touched the same.
        A heart alone
        Is such a stone
        As nothing but
        Thy power doth cut.
        Wherefore each part
        Of my hard heart   10
        Meets in this frame
        To praise Thy name;
  That if I chance to hold my peace,
  These stones to praise Thee may not cease.
O let thy blessed sacrifice be mine,
And sanctify this altar to be Thine.

Sunday

    O day most calm, most bright,
The fruit of this, the next world's bud,
    The indorsement of supreme delight,
Writ by a friend, and with his blood;
    The couch of time, care's balm and bay;
The week were dark but for thy light:
    Thy torch doth show the way.

The other days and thou
Make up one man, whose face thou art,
    Knocking at heaven with thy brow.   10
The worky-days are the back-part;
    The burden of the week lies there,
Making the whole to stoop and bow
        Till thy release appear.

    Man had straight forward gone
To endless death; but thou dost pull
    And turn us round to look on One
Whom, if we were not very dull,
    We could not choose but look on still;
Since there is no place so alone   20
        The which He doth not fill.

    Sundays the pillars are
On which heaven's palace arched lies;
    The other days fill up the spare
And hollow room with vanities.
    They are the fruitful beds and borders
In God's rich garden; that is bare
        Which parts their ranks and orders.

    The Sundays of man's life,
Threaded together on time's string,   30
    Make bracelets to adorn the wife [1]
Of the eternal glorious King.
    On Sundays heaven's gate stands ope,
Blessings are plentiful and rife,
        More plentiful than hope.

    This day my Savior rose,
And did inclose this light for His;

[1] "And I John saw the holy city, new Jerusalem, coming down from God out of heaven, prepared as a bride adorned for her husband." *Rev*. 21:2. Cf. 21:9.

That, as each beast his manger knows,
Man might not of his fodder miss.
   Christ hath took in this piece of ground   40
And made a garden there for those
   Who want herbs for their wound.

   The rest of our creation
Our great Redeemer did remove
   With the same shake which at His passion
Did the earth and all things with it move.
   As Samson bore the doors away,[2]
Christ's hands, though nailed, wrought our salvation
   And did unhinge that day.

   The brightness of that day   50
We sullied by our foul offense;
   Wherefore that robe we cast away,
Having a new at His expense
   Whose drops of blood paid the full price
That was required to make us gay,
   And fit for paradise.

   Thou art a day of mirth;
And where the week-days trail on ground,
   Thy flight is higher, as thy birth.
O let me take thee at the bound,   60
   Leaping with thee from seven to seven,
Till that we both, being tossed from earth,
   Fly hand in hand to heaven.

[2] Samson ". . . took the doors of the gate of the city, and the two posts, and went away with them, bar and all, and put them upon his shoulders, and carried them up to the top of an hill that is before Hebron." *Judges* 16:3.

Easter Wings

Lord, who createdst man in wealth and store,
  Though foolishly he lost the same,
    Decaying more and more
      Till he became
       Most poor;
       With Thee
      O let me rise
    As larks, harmoniously,
  And sing this day Thy victories;
Then shall the fall further the flight in me.   10

My tender age in sorrow did begin;
  And still with sickness and shame
    Thou didst so punish sin,
      That I became
      Most thin.
      With Thee
      Let me combine,
  And feel this day Thy victory;
For if I imp [1] my wing on Thine,
Affliction shall advance the flight in me.   20

Virtue

Sweet day, so cool, so calm, so bright,
  The bridal of the earth and sky,
The dew shall weep thy fall to-night,
    For thou must die.

Sweet rose, whose hue, angry and brave,
  Bids the rash gazer wipe his eye,
Thy root is ever in its grave,
    And thou must die.

---

[1] A term in falconry, meaning to repair an injured wing with feathers.

Sweet spring, full of sweet days and roses,
   A box where sweets compacted lie,   10
My music shows ye have your closes,[1]
    And all must die.

Only a sweet and virtuous soul,
   Like seasoned timber, never gives;
But though the whole world turn to coal,[2]
    Then chiefly lives.

[1] The music of his verses has shown that days and roses must come to an end. *"Close* is the technical name for a cadence or conclusion of a musical phrase." (Palmer)

[2] "But the day of the Lord will come as a thief in the night . . . the earth also and the works that are therein shall be burned up." *2 Peter* 3:10.

Thomas Carew

LITTLE is known of the life of Thomas Carew, and even the dates of his birth and death are uncertain. He was confused with T. Carey until Arthur Vincent, in the life of Carew prefixed to the edition of his poems for the *Muses' Library*, established the distinction between the two men. The best known episode in Carew's life is that of his losing his job as secretary to Sir Dudley Carleton, English ambassador first at Venice and later at The Hague, because he started slander against Carleton and his wife.

An irate father, made more testy by the recent loss of £12,000 and by the whispered reason for Carew's dismissal, made it impossible for Carew to secure another position. The father had undoubtedly borne much: years at Oxford University had been financed without Carew's graduation; years of the study of law at Middle Temple had been wasted; and time spent in idling about town had led to nothing. Finally, through personal influence the father had secured a secretary-ship with Carleton for Carew. When that position was lost, he wrote begging Carleton to take Carew back into service; but after these efforts failed, he seemed to lose confidence in his son and even prevented favorable consideration of him for other positions.

After the death of his father Carew secured a place in the retinue of Lord Herbert of Cherbury when the latter went as ambassador to France in 1619. The next that we know positively of Carew is that in 1628 he was made gentleman of the privy-chamber and soon thereafter sewer to the king, both positions of trust and favor. He was popular at court and famous for his wit and gallant manners. These and his deathbed repentance are the only extenuations for a dissolute life.

Carew had many friends among the great literary figures of his day. He had been a parishioner of John Donne's when the latter was priest at St. Dunstan's-in-the-West, the parish in which Carew was brought up, and no doubt he continued the acquaintance in London. He was a guest at Ben Jonson's famous suppers and added to that brilliant company of scholars and poets which frequented the hospitable library of Sir Robert Cotton. He knew Lord Clarendon and was the friend of Suckling and Davenant, and of the distinguished musician, Henry Lawes, who composed the music for many of his lyrics.

Though Carew is known as one of the "Sons of Ben," he also shows some filial resemblance to Donne. He lacks Donne's intensity of emotion, yet he often reminds one of Donne in idea and phrase. He is, however, more like Jonson than Donne, especially in polish and elegance, and his admiration for Jonson is based primarily on his "labour'd works." Suckling, who tossed off his lyrics apparently with careless ease, mocks at Carew's painstaking workmanship in *A Session of the Poets*, saying,

> His Muse was hide-bound and the issue of's brain
> Was seldom brought forth but with trouble and pain.

Carew compensated for his lack of spontaneity by perfecting his lyrical technique. No poem of his comes torn from an agonized soul; he takes a graceful idea, sets it in the first few lines, develops it, and brings it to a logical close. It is as carefully worked out as is a short story or a play, with a marked rise and fall of interest, and is complete in its narrow scope. Bliss Reed finds in *The Spring* a perfect illustration of the difference between the manner of the Elizabethans and of Carew, noting the abundance of detail of the Elizabethans and the extreme compression of Carew. Speed in presentation is gained not only by compactness but also by the flow of verse carried forward by the skilful use of the overlapped couplet. His daintiest pieces are elegantly accomplished and are like miniatures, small but perfect in detail and execution.

An Elegy upon the Death of the Dean of Paul's, Dr. John Donne

Can we not force from widowed poetry,
Now thou art dead, great Donne, one elegy
To crown thy hearse? Why yet did we not trust,
Though with unkneaded dough-baked prose, thy dust,
Such as the uncizared lect'rer from the flower
Of fading rhetoric, short-lived as his hour,
Dry as the sand that measures it, should lay
Upon the ashes on the funeral day?
Have we nor tune, nor voice? Didst thou dispense
Through all our language both words and sense?   10
'Tis sad truth. The pulpit may her plain
And sober Christian precepts still retain;
Doctrines it may, and wholesome uses, frame,
Grave homilies and lectures; but the flame
Of thy brave soul, that shot such heat and light
As burnt our earth and made our darkness bright,
Committed holy rapes upon our will,
Did through the eye the melting heart distil,
And the deep knowledge of dark truths so teach
As sense might judge what fancy could not reach,   20
Must be desired forever. So the fire
That fills with spirit and heat the Delphic quire,[1]
Which, kindled first by thy Promethean [2] breath,
Glowed here a while, lies quenched now in thy death.
The Muses' garden, with pedantic weeds
O'erspread, was purged by thee; the lazy seeds
Of servile imitation thrown away,
And fresh invention planted, thou didst pay
The debts of our penurious bankrupt age;
Licentious thefts, that make poetic rage   30
A mimic fury, when our souls must be

[1] The priestesses of Apollo at Delphi.
[2] Prometheus was the Titan who stole fire from heaven and brought it to earth.

Possessed, or with Anacreon's ecstasy,
Or Pindar's, not their own; the subtle cheat
Of sly exchanges, and the juggling feat
Of two-edged words, or whatsoever wrong
By ours was done the Greek or Latin tongue,
Thou hast redeemed, and opened us a mine
Of rich and pregnant fancy, drawn a line
Of masculine expression, which had good
Old Orpheus [3] seen, or all the ancient brood   40
Our superstitious fools admire, and hold
Their lead more precious than thy burnished gold,
Thou hadst been their exchequer, and no more
They in each other's dung had raked for ore.
Thou shalt yield no precedence, but of time
And the blind fate of language, whose tuned chime
More charms the outward sense; yet thou mayest claim
From so great disadvantage greater fame,
Since to the awe of thy imperious wit
Our troublesome language bends, made only fit   50
With her tough thick-ribbed hoops, to gird about
Thy giant fancy, which had proved too stout
For their soft melting phrases. As in time
They had the start, so did they cull the prime
Buds of invention many a hundred year,
And left the rifled fields, besides the fear
To touch their harvest; yet from those bare lands
Of what is only thine, thy only hands
(And that their smallest work) have gleaned more
Than all those times and tongues could reap before.   60
    But thou art gone, and thy strict laws will be
Too hard for libertines in poetry.
They will repeal the goodly exiled train
Of gods and goddesses, which in thy just reign
Were banished nobler poems; now with these
The silenced tales in the *Metamorphoses*

[3] A Thracian musician whose music could draw trees and rocks to
follow him.

Shall stuff their lines and swell the windy page,
Till verse, refined by thee in this last age,
Turn ballad-rhyme, or those old idols be
Adored again with new apostasy.   70

O pardon me, that break with untuned verse
The reverend silence that attends thy hearse,
Whose awful solemn murmurs were to thee,
More than these faint lines, a loud elegy,
That did proclaim in a dumb eloquence
The death of all the arts, whose influence,
Grown feeble, in these panting numbers lies
Gasping short-winded accents, and so dies:
So doth the swiftly turning wheel not stand
In the instant we withdraw the moving hand,   80
But some small time retain a faint weak course
By virtue of the first impulsive force;
And so whilst I cast on thy funeral pile
Thy crown of bays, oh, let it crack awhile
And spit disdain, till the devouring flashes
Suck all the moisture up; then turn to ashes.

I will not draw thee envy to engross
All thy perfections, or weep all the loss;
Those are too numerous for one elegy,
And this too great to be expressed by me.   90
Let others carve the rest; it shall suffice
I on thy grave this epitaph incise:

Here lies a king, that ruled as he thought fit
The universal monarchy of wit;
Here lie two flamens, and both those the best:
Apollo's first, at last the true God's priest.

To Ben Jonson

Upon Occasion of His Ode of Defiance Annexed to His Play of The New Inn [1]

'Tis true, dear Ben, thy just chastising hand
Hath fixed upon the sotted age a brand,
To their swollen pride and empty scribbling due;
It cannot judge, nor write, and yet 'tis true
Thy comic muse, from the exalted line
Touched by thy *Alchemist*, doth since decline
From that her zenith, and foretells a red
And blushing evening, when she goes to bed;
Yet such as shall outshine the glimmering light
With which all stars shall gild the following night.   10
Nor think it much, since all thy eaglets may
Endure the sunny trial, if we say
This hath the stronger wing, or that doth shine
Tricked up in fairer plumes, since all are thine.
Who hath his flock of cackling geese compared
With thy tuned quire of swans? or else who dared
To call thy births deformed? But if thou bind
By city-custom, or by gavelkind,[2]
In equal shares thy love on all thy race,
We may distinguish of their sex and place;   20
Though one hand shape them, and though one brain strike
Souls into all, they are not all alike.
Why should the follies, then, of this dull age
Draw from thy pen such an immodest rage
As seems to blast thy else immortal bays,
When thine own tongue proclaims thy itch of praise?
Such thirst will argue drought. No, let be hurled

<hr>

[1] The production of *The New Inn* in 1629 was a failure, and the
play was even violently hissed. Upon publishing the play, Jonson
prefixed an *Ode to Himself* in which he expressed his indignation at
the reception of the play.
[2] The reference is to the equal division among his sons of the
property left by a deceased man.

Upon thy works by the detracting world
What malice can suggest; let the rout say,
The running sands that, ere thou make a play,   30
Count the slow minutes, might a Goodwin frame [3]
To swallow, when thou hast done, thy shipwrecked name.
Let them the dear expense of oil upbraid,
Sucked by thy watchful lamp, that hath betrayed
To theft the blood of martyred authors, spilt
Into thy ink, whilst thou growest pale with guilt.
Repine not at the taper's thrifty waste,
That sleeks thy tersed poems; nor is haste
Praise, but excuse; and if thou overcome
A knotty writer, bring the booty home;   40
Nor think it theft if the rich spoils so torn
From conquered authors be as trophies worn.
Let others glut on the extorted praise
Of vulgar breath; trust thou to after days.
Thy labored works shall live when time devours
The abortive offspring of their hasty hours.
Thou art not of their rank; the quarrel lies
Within thine own verge; then let this suffice:
The wiser world doth greater thee confess
Than all men else, than thyself only less.   50

The Spring

Now that the winter's gone, the earth hath lost
Her snow-white robes; and now no more the frost
Candies the grass, or casts an icy cream
Upon the silver lake or crystal stream:
But the warm sun thaws the benumbed earth,
And makes it tender; gives a second birth
To the dead swallow; wakes in hollow tree
The drowsy cuckoo and the humble-bee.

[3] The reference is to Goodwin Sands, quicksands off the coast of Kent

Now do a quire of chirping minstrels sing,
In triumph to the world, the youthful spring: 10
The valleys, hills, and woods in rich array
Welcome the coming of the longed-for May.
Now all things smile; only my love doth lower;
Nor hath the scalding noonday sun the power
To melt that marble ice, which still doth hold
Her heart congealed, and makes her pity cold.
The ox, which lately did for shelter fly
Into the stall, doth now securely lie
In open field; and love no more is made
By the fireside; but in the cooler shade 20
Amyntas now doth with his Chloris sleep
Under a sycamore, and all things keep
Time with the season: only she doth carry
June in her eyes, in her heart January.

Upon a Ribbon
Tied about His Arm by a Lady

This silken wreath, which circles thus mine arm,
Is but an emblem of that mystic charm
Wherewith the magic of your beauties binds
My captive soul, and round about it winds
Fetters of lasting love: this hath entwined
My flesh alone; that hath empaled my mind.
Time may wear out these soft, weak bands; but those
Strong chains of brass, fate shall not discompose.
This holy relique may preserve my wrist,
But my whole frame doth by that power subsist; 10
To that my prayers and sacrifice, to this
I only pay a superstitious kiss.
This but the idol, that's the deity;
Religion is due there; here, ceremony;
That I receive by faith, this but in trust;
Here I may tender duty, there I must;

This order as a layman I may bear,
But I become Love's priest when that I wear;
This moves like air; that as the center [1] stands;
That knot your virtue tied; this but your hands;   20
That, nature framed; but this was made by art;
This makes my arm your prisoner; that, my heart.

A Song

    Ask me no more where Jove bestows,
    When June is past, the fading rose;
    For in your beauty's orient deep
    These flowers, as in their causes,[1] sleep.

    Ask me no more whither do stray
    The golden atoms of the day;
    For in pure love heaven did prepare
    Those powders to enrich your hair.

    Ask me no more whither doth haste
    The nightingale when May is past;   10
    For in your sweet dividing throat
    She winters, and keeps warm her note.

    Ask me no more where those stars light,
    That downwards fall in dead of night;
    For in your eyes they sit, and there
    Fixed become as in their sphere.

    Ask me no more if east or west
    The phœnix builds her spicy nest; [2]

[1] The Ptolemaic system with the earth as the fixed center was still generally accepted.

[1] Used in the Aristotelian sense of elements; the reference is to the seed or bulb in its inactive state.

[2] A mythical bird of the Arabian desert, which was supposed to burn in a bed of self-prepared spices every five hundred years. From the ashes arose a fresh phœnix. Only one phœnix existed at any one time.

For unto you at last she flies,
And in your fragrant bosom dies.   20

Mediocrity in Love Rejected

Song

Give me more love or more disdain;
   The torrid or the frozen zone
Bring equal ease unto my pain,
   The temperate affords me none:
Either extreme, of love or hate,
Is sweeter than a calm estate.

Give me a storm; if it be love,
   Like Danaë in that golden shower,
I swim in pleasure; if it prove
   Disdain, that torrent will devour   10
My vulture-hopes; and he's possessed
Of heaven that's but from hell released.
   Then crown my joys, or cure my pain:
   Give me more love or more disdain.

To My Inconstant Mistress

Song

When thou, poor excommunicate
   From all the joys of love, shalt see
The full reward and glorious fate
   Which my strong faith shall purchase me,
   Then curse thine own inconstancy.

A fairer hand than thine shall cure
   That heart which thy false oaths did wound;
And to my soul, a soul more pure
   Than thine shall by Love's hand be bound,
   And both with equal glory crowned.   10

Then shalt thou weep, entreat, complain
　　To Love, as I did once to thee;
When all thy tears shall be as vain
　　As mine were then, for thou shalt be
　　Damned for thy false apostasy.

A Cruel Mistress

We read of kings and gods that kindly took
A pitcher filled with water from the brook;
But I have daily tendered without thanks
Rivers of tears that overflowed their banks.
A slaughtered bull appeased angry Jove,
A horse the sun, a lamb the god of love;
But she disdains the spotless sacrifice
Of a pure heart that at her altar lies.
Vesta is not displeased if her chaste urn
Do with repaired fuel ever burn; [1]　　　　　　　　　　10
But my saint frowns, though to her honored name
I consecrate a never-dying flame.
The Assyrian king did none i' the furnace throw
But those that to his image did not bow; [2]
With bended knees I daily worship her,
Yet she consumes her own idolater.
Of such a goddess no times leave record,
That burnt the temple where she was adored.

Disdain Returned

He that loves a rosy cheek,
　　Or a coral lip admires,
Or from starlike eyes doth seek
　　Fuel to maintain his fires;

[1] In the temple of Vesta, goddess of the hearth, a fire was kept continually burning.

[2] Nebuchadnezzar made a decree that "whoso falleth not down and worshippeth [i. e., the golden image he had set up], that he should be cast into the midst of a burning fiery furnace." *Daniel* 3:11.

As old Time makes these decay,
So his flames must waste away.

But a smooth and steadfast mind,
   Gentle thoughts and calm desires,
Hearts with equal love combined,
   Kindle never-dying fires.   10
Where these are not, I despise
Lovely cheeks, or lips, or eyes.

No tears, Celia, now shall win
   My resolved heart to return;
I have searched thy soul within,
   And find naught but pride and scorn;
I have learned thy arts, and now
   Can disdain as much as thou.
Some power, in my revenge, convey
That love to her I cast away.   20

Persuasions to Enjoy

Song

If the quick spirits in your eye
   Now languish, and anon must die;
If every sweet and every grace
Must fly from that forsaken face;
   Then, Celia, let us reap our joys
   Ere time such goodly fruit destroys.

Or, if that golden fleece must grow
Forever free from aged snow;
If those bright suns must know no shade,
Nor your fresh beauties ever fade;   10
Then, fear not, Celia, to bestow
What, still being gathered, still must grow.
   Thus, either Time his sickle brings
   In vain, or else in vain his wings.

Ingrateful Beauty Threatened

Know, Celia, since thou art so proud,
   'Twas I that gave thee thy renown;
Thou hadst in the forgotten crowd
   Of common beauties lived unknown,
Had not my verse exhaled thy name,
And with it imped the wings of fame.

That killing power is none of thine:
   I gave it to thy voice and eyes;
Thy sweets, thy graces, all are mine;
   Thou art my star, shin'st in my skies;   10
Then dart not from thy borrowed sphere
Lightning on him that fixed thee there.

Tempt me with such affrights no more,
   Lest what I made I uncreate;
Let fools thy mystic forms adore,
   I'll know thee in thy mortal state;
Wise poets that wrapped truth in tales,
Knew her themselves through all her veils.

To A. L.

Persuasions to Love

Think not, 'cause men flattering say
You're fresh as April, sweet as May,
Bright as is the morning star,
That you are so; or, though you are,
Be not therefore proud, and deem
All men unworthy your esteem:
For, being so, you lose the pleasure
Of being fair, since that rich treasure
Of rare beauty and sweet feature
Was bestowed on you by nature   10

To be enjoyed; and 'twere a sin
There to be scarce, where she hath been
So prodigal of her best graces.
Thus common beauties and mean faces
Shall have more pastime, and enjoy
The sport you lose by being coy.
Did the thing for which I sue
Only concern myself, not you;
Were men so framed as they alone
Reaped all the pleasure, women none;   20
Then had you reason to be scant;
But 'twere a madness not to grant
That which affords (if you consent)
To you, the giver, more content
Than me, the beggar. Oh, then be
Kind to yourself, if not to me;
Starve not yourself because you may
Thereby make me pine away;
Nor let brittle beauty make
You your wiser thoughts forsake;   30
For that lovely face will fail;
Beauty's sweet, but beauty's frail;
'Tis sooner past, 'tis sooner done,
Than summer's rain, than winter's sun;
Most fleeting when it is most dear,
'Tis gone while we but say 'tis here.
These curious locks, so aptly twined,
Whose every hair a soul doth bind,
Will change their auburn hue, and grow
White and cold as winter's snow.   40
That eye, which now is Cupid's nest,
Will prove his grave, and all the rest
Will follow; in the cheek, chin, nose,
Nor lily shall be found, nor rose.
And what will then become of all
Those whom you now do servants call?
Like swallows, when the summer's done,

They'll fly, and seek some warmer sun.
Then wisely choose one to your friend,
Whose love may, when your beauties end,   50
Remain still firm: be provident,
And think, before the summer's spent,
Of following winter; like the ant,
In plenty hoard for time of scant.
Cull out, amongst the multitude
Of lovers that seek to intrude
Into your favor, one that may
Love for an age, not for a day;
One that will quench your youthful fires,
And feed in age your hot desires.   60
For when the storms of time have moved
Waves on that cheek which was beloved,
When a fair lady's face is pined,
And yellow spread where red once shined,
When beauty, youth, and all sweets leave her,
Love may return, but lovers never;
And old folks say there are no pains
Like itch of love in aged veins.
Oh, love me, then, and now begin it,
Let us not lose this present minute;   70
For time and age will work that wrack
Which time and age shall ne'er call back.
The snake each year fresh skin resumes,
And eagles change their aged plumes;
The faded rose each spring receives
A fresh red tincture on her leaves:
But if your beauties once decay,
You ne'er shall know a second May.
Oh, then, be wise, and whilst your season
Affords you days for sport, do reason;   80
Spend not in vain your life's short hour,
But crop in time your beauty's flower,
Which will away, and doth together
Both bud and fade, both blow and wither.

THAT "sweet swan," Edmund Waller, may be contrasted with Sir John Denham as the poet of "smoothness" instead of "strength" and with the greater number of the poets of the Restoration for the lack of obscenity in his poems. He himself said that he would not tolerate in his poems "any line that did not contain some motive to virtue." Didactic content embodied in polished couplets had given Denham great popularity, and no doubt it is this combination which explains Waller's being considered as late as 1766 "the most celebrated Lyric Poet that ever England produced." [1] Like Lovelace he has suffered from being generally known as the author of only two poems: *Go Lovely Rose* and *Lines on a Girdle*. These appear in all anthologies of English poetry, and, indeed, the charm of their simple directness entitles them to this prominence; but there is other work of Waller's that deserves to be known, especially the fine lines composed when he was more than eighty, *Of the Last Verses in the Book*. It is true that much of his verse is occasional; and though its appropriateness added to his popularity among his contemporaries, the particular point is often lost to the modern reader. There remains, however, enough of general interest incorporated in finished songlike form to captivate a reader of any period.

Waller is remarkably free from the faults of strained conceits and obscurity so frequent in seventeenth century poetry, and he possesses the virtue of facile and often charming expression. He has considerable technical power, and he has revised and polished his verse until the best of his poetry is so perfectly done that it illustrates the heights which the lyric can attain. In the development of versification he is famous for having shown the good qualities of the closed couplet. He started the popularity of this form by making preciseness and decorum of more interest than the outpouring of imagination. Dryden says he taught the "excellence

[1] *Biographia Britannica.*

and dignity" of rhyme and "first made writing easily an art." [2] His emphasis on rules and restraint as expressed in his poem on the Earl of Roscommon's translation of Horace sounds like the eighteenth century:

> Horace will our superfluous branches prune,
> Give us new rules, and set our harps in tune;
> Direct us how to back the winged horse,
> Favor his flight, and moderate his force.
> Though poets may of inspiration boast,
> Their rage, ill governed, in the clouds is lost.

Public life did not crush Waller's muse as it did that of Milton and Marvell. Waller's father, repenting of years spent in idleness at Beaconsfield, left written papers of advice to his son, which may have counseled the active life. At any rate, Clarendon tells us that Waller was "nursed in Parliaments." Waller says that he took his seat first when he was sixteen, in the reign of Charles I. His education at King's College, Cambridge, and his study of law at Lincoln's Inn did not prevent an early political career. He continued to hold a seat in Parliament through the reigns of Charles II and James II, becoming a sort of patriarch of the House. It was in the Parliament of 1643 that there occurred the proceedings which brought him into disgrace. Though he was related to John Hampden and Oliver Cromwell and held the confidence of the Commons, he was Royalist in sympathy and laid plans, with the aid of his brother-in-law, to capture London from the inside for the king, then at Oxford. "Waller's Plot" was discovered, and Waller's implication of his friends led to their execution. He himself, through a process of delay and flattery and possibly through a bribe of £30,000, escaped with a fine of £10,000, which he could well afford to pay, and banishment from the country. He went to France, where the renowned Hobbes became tutor to his son, and

---

[2] Dedication to *The Rival Ladies*.

Cowley, Denham, and other refugees were his pleasant companions.

The story of Waller's private life also has unusual interest, and this story is not marred by disgrace. To be wealthy and a poet was something of a paradox then as now; and to be the richest poet in England, with the exception of Rogers, is itself a title to interest. Waller added to his already large inheritance from his father by marrying the most greatly desired heiress of the day, and he thereby created the first sensation he produced in the public world. Anne Bankes was the only daughter of a wealthy London citizen, who at his death left his daughter and his fortune to the guardianship of the Court of Aldermen. These dignitaries favored another suitor, a man of great influence; but Waller succeeded in getting relatives of his to convey the desirable Anne to the country, where she would be without the bounds of the aldermen, and there he married her. In the wrath of the court it seemed for a while that Waller would have the girl but no fortune; for the court decreed that since Anne had married without the consent of her guardians, she should forfeit her patrimony. But the matter was brought before the Star Chamber, the king wrote a letter pardoning Waller, and the guardians had to turn over the fortune to him.

Though Waller seems to have esteemed Anne as an "excellent wife," her early death left him free to woo the Saccharissa of his sonnets, Lady Dorothy Sidney. If this was a serious love affair, it ended in great disappointment; for Lady Dorothy was married to Lord Spencer at Penshurst, the beautiful home of the Sidneys celebrated in verse by Ben Jonson. Waller solaced himself by furnishing a home to George Morley, later bishop of Winchester, who encouraged him in his literary efforts and, according to Clarendon, introduced him to that gathering of eminent men known as the "Club" of Lucius Carey, Lord Falkland.

Waller was not, however, left to go mourning all his days. The beautiful Mary Bracey went with him to France when he was banished for "Waller's Plot" and was hostess among the poverty-stricken refugees at meals provided by the sale of his first wife's jewels! Nor was she troubled by her stepdaughter. The latter had been left at Beaconsfield with Waller's mother, whose only concern seems to have been that "she should catch the small poxe or hir beauty should change" [3] before she could make a good marriage.

Waller was back at Beaconsfield in 1652, as we learn from a letter to his friend John Evelyn, his sentence of banishment revoked. He appears to have been friendly with Cromwell, and his *Panegyric* was well received. Under these circumstances it is not surprising that Charles II queried the sincerity of Waller's *Address of Welcome;* but when the king complained of the superiority of the *Panegyric,* Waller had a ready answer: "Sir, we poets never succeed so well in writing truth as in fiction." From 1661 until his death Waller held an honorable place in Parliament, was known for his tolerant spirit, and was famous among the courtiers for his wit.

Song

Go, lovely rose!
Tell her that wastes her time and me
  That now she knows,
When I resemble her to thee,
How sweet and fair she seems to be.

Tell her that's young,
And shuns to have her graces spied,
  That hadst thou sprung
In deserts, where no men abide,
Thou must have uncommended died.   10

Small is the worth
Of beauty from the light retired;

[3] From a letter quoted by Drury in his introduction to Waller's *Poems,* edited for the *Muses' Library,* p. lx.

Bid her come forth,
Suffer herself to be desired,
And not blush so to be admired.

Then die! that she
The common fate of all things rare
    May read in thee;
How small a part of time they share
That are so wondrous sweet and fair! 20

On a Girdle

That which her slender waist confined,
Shall now my joyful temples bind;
No monarch but would give his crown,
His arms might do what this has done.

It was my heaven's extremest [1] sphere,
The pale [2] which held that lovely deer;
My joy, my grief, my hope, my love
Did all within this circle move!

A narrow compass! and yet there
Dwelt all that's good and all that's fair; 10
Give me but what this ribbon bound,
Take all the rest the sun goes round!

The Self-banished

It is not that I love you less,
Than when before your feet I lay,
But to prevent the sad increase
Of hopeless love, I keep away.

In vain, alas! for everything
Which I have known belong to you,

[1] Outermost.
[2] Enclosure.

Your form does to my fancy bring,
And make my old wounds bleed anew.

Who in the spring, from the new sun,
Already has a fever got,   10
Too late begins these shafts to shun,
Which Phœbus through his veins has shot.

Too late he would the pain assuage,
And to thick shadows does retire;
About with him he bears the rage,
And in his tainted blood the fire.

But vowed I have, and never must
Your banished servant trouble you;
For if I break, you may mistrust
The vow I made to love you too.   20

At Penshurst

Had Sacharissa [1] lived when mortals made
Choice of their deities, this sacred shade
Had held an altar to her power, that gave
The peace and glory which these alleys have;
Embroidered so with flowers where she stood,
That it became a garden of a wood.
Her presence has such more than human grace
That it can civilize the rudest place;
And beauty too, and order, can impart,
Where nature ne'er intended it, nor art.   10
The plants acknowledge this, and her admire
No less than those of old did Orpheus' lyre;
If she sit down, with tops all towards her bowed,
They round about her into arbors crowd;
Or if she walk, in even ranks they stand,
Like some well-marshaled and obsequious band.

[1] Lady Dorothy Sidney, daughter of Robert, second Earl of Leicester. Cf. the poem on Penshurst by Jonson.

Amphion [2] so made stones and timber leap
Into fair figures from a confused heap;
And in the symmetry of her parts is found
A power like that of harmony in sound.   20
    Ye lofty beeches, tell this matchless dame
That if together ye fed all one flame,
It could not equalize the hundredth part
Of what her eyes have kindled in my heart!
Go, boy, and carve this passion on the bark
Of yonder tree, which stands the sacred mark
Of noble Sidney's birth; when such benign,
Such more than mortal making stars did shine,
That there they cannot but forever prove
The monument and pledge of humble love;   30
His humble love whose hopes shall ne'er rise higher
Than for a pardon that he dares admire.

To Mr. Henry Lawes, Who Had Then Newly Set a Song of Mine, in the Year 1635

Verse makes heroic virtue live;
But you can life to verses give.
As, when in open air we blow,
The breath, though strained, sounds flat and low;
But if a trumpet take the blast,
It lifts it high, and makes it last:
So in your airs our numbers dressed,
Make a shrill sally from the breast
Of nymphs, who, singing what we penned,
Our passions to themselves commend;   10
While love, victorious with thy art,
Governs at once their voice and heart.
    You, by the help of tune and time,
Can make that song which was but rhyme.
Noy pleading, no man doubts the cause,[1]

[2] Under the power of Amphion's music the stones took their places, self-moved, in the building of Thebes.
[1] The reference is to William Noy, who invented ship-money.

Or questions verses set by Lawes.
   As a church-window, thick with paint,
Lets in a light but dim and faint,
So others, with division,[2] hide
The light of sense, the poet's pride;   20
But you alone may truly boast
That not a syllable is lost:
The writer's and the setter's skill
At once the ravished ears do fill.
Let those which only warble long,
And gargle in their throats a song,
Content themselves with *ut, re, mi:*
Let words and sense be set by thee.

Of the Last Verses in the Book

When we for age could neither read nor write,
The subject made us able to indite;
The soul, with nobler resolutions decked,
The body stooping, does herself erect.
The mortal parts are requisite to raise
Her that, unbodied, can her Maker praise.
   The seas are quiet when the winds give o'er;
So, calm are we when passions are no more!
For then we know how vain it was to boast
Of fleeting things, so certain to be lost.   10
Clouds of affection from our younger eyes
Conceal that emptiness which age descries.
   The soul's dark cottage, battered and decayed,
Lets in new light through the chinks that time has made;
Stronger by weakness, wiser men become,
As they draw near to their eternal home.
Leaving the old, both worlds at once they view,
That stand upon the threshold of the new.

---

[2] Others conceal the meaning of the poem by the musical notation to which it is set.

John Milton 1608-1674

THE story of Milton is the story of a man who followed a fixed ideal and, in spite of almost insurmountable obstacles, finally attained it. He early knew that he must be a *great* poet, not just a poet, and he set for himself standards which he could reach only through a long period of preparation.

Milton's father, who was a well-to-do scrivener, gave his son unusual advantages and personally supervised much of his early training. He intended Milton for the ministry and with the aid of his wife, known for her charitable works, gave him careful religious training. He was a man of culture, a skilful musician and composer of songs, and he himself taught Milton to play the organ. He encouraged the boy's taste for books, allowing him, even when he was only twelve years old, to read until midnight. He not only sent him to St. Paul's School, which was conveniently near their home on Bread Street, but also provided an excellent tutor at home. At St. Paul's Milton gained an excellent foundation in Latin, Greek, and Hebrew and learned the technique of constructing verse by making metrical paraphrases of the Psalms. Here too he formed the most intimate friendship of his life. Later, when he was at Cambridge, it was to Diodati at Oxford that he confided his literary ambitions and plans, his tastes, and his ideals.

At Christ's College he did more than conform to the quadrivium and trivium of the prescribed course. From a Latin letter to his father we learn that he studied Latin and French in addition to the classical languages and that he became acquainted with science. All his work was very vital to him, for he accepted the Renaissance conception of a poet as a man of wide learning; and he was consciously preparing himself to be a poet. Latin exercises in his hands became poems; his very letters, also written in Latin, were literary compositions. He was even then beginning to write English verse; and from Cambridge came that poem which, though written when he was only twenty-one, is immortal. *The Hymn on the*

Morning of Christ's Nativity, produced as a "birthday gift to Christ," strikes the sonorous note which is Milton's peculiar genius and reveals his ability to use his learning for the enrichment of poetry. Milton was not always a model student; he had some difficulty with one of his tutors, was disciplined, and was suspended from the university for a time. During this period of "rustication" he wrote enthusiastically to Diodati of visits to the parks and theatres of London and of his extensive reading. He says, "My books— my very life—claim me wholly."

While Milton was gaining the knowledge requisite for a poet, he was also formulating high ideals of character. The poet was a priest and must therefore be chaste and temperate. The less serious students called him "the Lady of Christ's"; but they respected him for his fine swordsmanship, his learning, and his evident genius. To Milton, however, the opinion of his associates already meant little; his talents were to be used "as ever in my great Task-master's eye."

After receiving his master's degree, Milton secluded himself at his father's country home in Horton for more than five years of independent study, systematically recorded in notebooks. Since London was near, Milton often went up to the city to get books from the libraries, to see the plays of Shakespeare and Jonson, and to secure further training in mathematics and music. At this time he was a man of the Renaissance: definitely given to the contemplative life; a lover of all that is beautiful, sensuous, lyrical. Of the poems of this period, only *Comus* and *Lycidas* show the intrusion of Puritan seriousness and thus become the meeting ground of two periods. When the delicate masque became the vehicle for a lesson in virtue, then indeed a new note was sounded in literature; and when the pastoral elegy included lines on the corrupt state of the contemporary church, the shepherd's pipe was in the mouth of a Puritan.

Milton's long period of education was finally rounded out by a Continental tour. Handsome, scholarly, and at ease, he was welcomed by men as different as Hugo Grotius at Paris, the blind and exiled Galileo at Fiesole, the learned Manso at Naples, and the music-loving Cardinal Barberini at Rome. He distinguished himself in the meetings of the Academies at Florence and was praised for his fine Italian verse. Hearing of the civil strife in England, he gave up the continuation of his travels to Sicily and Greece and began his return journey. When the situation at home proved not to be critical, he retraced his steps through Italy in a leisurely fashion and in Geneva visited Diodati's uncle, from whom he learned of the death of his friend.

Upon his return from the Continent Milton established himself in London and for about seven years taught his nephews and a few other boys. His course of study was encyclopedic, and his aim was to fit a man "to perform justly, skilfully, and magnanimously all the offices, both private and public, of peace and war." During this time he had domestic troubles, which colored his attitude toward women for the remainder of his life. He impetuously married Mary Powell, a Royalist. A month after their marriage she deserted him for the gayer life to which she was accustomed at home. It was not until two years had passed that Mary, frightened by Milton's divorce pamphlets, which advocated divorce on the ground of incompatibility, returned to London to seek a reconciliation. In addition to his teaching, Milton was constantly using his learning and ability to help in the establishment of the Commonwealth. In stern pamphlets, which, however, contain many passages of great beauty, he wrote for liberty in speech, in religion, and in government.

When Cromwell came into power and Milton was appointed Latin Secretary, he supported the action of the nation in beheading the king, by writing his *Defense of the English People* and the *Second Defense*. The composition of the latter cost him his sight, but Milton felt that no sacrifice was too great for the cause of liberty.

The years of public service did not change the aim of Milton's life; he felt that his accomplishment in poetry was only deferred, not lost. In his prose he covenanted with the nation to "give something to after ages which they will not willingly let die," and he restated his ideal of the poet:

> He who would not be frustrate of his hope to write well hereafter in laudable things, ought himself to be a true poem; that is, a composition and pattern of the best and honorablest things; not presuming to sing the praises of heroic men, or famous cities unless he have in himself the experience and practice of all that is trustworthy.

He discussed forms suitable for great poems, showing that he was undecided whether to choose the classical epic, the short epic modeled on the book of Job, or a drama after the Greek or the Biblical pattern. He knew that his genius matured slowly, he was engrossed in aiding his country, and he had the patience to wait. The only poems of this period are a few very fine sonnets. These mark the return of the English sonnet to the Italian form, and enrich the field of the sonnet by introducing totally new content. Milton writes of contemporary events, of the great men of his time, of his friends, and of himself in verse that has the strength and dignity usually termed Miltonic. Landor says that Milton

> Caught the sonnet from the dainty hand
> Of Love, who cried to lose it, and he gave
> The notes to glory.

Finally, when he was fifty, Milton began his long-dreamed-of life work. The conditions, personal and public, would have discouraged a less persevering soul. He had known sorrow: he had lost an infant son; Mary Powell had died, leaving him three unloving daughters to care for; and his second wife, the tenderly loved Katherine Woodcock, had died a little more than a year after their marriage. He was totally blind from service in a cause which even then was apparently lost. He had seen liberty, in which he so ardently believed, turned into license and his ideal conception of man proved false. Style in poetry had changed: the Cavaliers had sung their light songs of inconstancy, and writers of the heroic couplet were rapidly changing the taste in poetic form. But Andrew Marvell, a young poet of the metaphysical school, had been appointed Milton's assistant in the secretaryship; and since Milton now had more leisure, he set himself to write his great poems.

There were, however, further interruptions. With the coming of the Restoration, Milton's life was in danger, and he had to go into hiding until after the Act of Oblivion was passed. He was heavily fined and would have fared worse if Marvell had not been able to save him. In 1663 he married a third time. In 1666 he had to flee the plague, but in his little cottage in Chalfont St. Giles he finally completed *Paradise Lost*.

The long epic had been written, but it was not the epic sketched in the letters to Diodati and Manso. The reasons for his giving up the Arthurian matter are very complex; it is sufficient here to note that the Fall of Man is the subject which symbolizes the failure of the Commonwealth. Man in the glory of the new freedom under Cromwell had been unable rightly to use his liberty, and the return to external authority only expressed the loss of liberty within. With a sweep of imagination that covered hell, heaven, chaos, and the newly created universe, Milton retold the story of the warring forces of good and evil.

Before the end of his life Milton was able to produce also a short epic, *Paradise Regained*, and a drama patterned after Greek plays, *Samson Agonistes*. He has, however, but one theme: the necessity for the dominance of reason in man's life. *Samson Agonistes* is both the most autobiographical of the poems and the fullest expression of Milton's philosophy. It completes the idea of *Paradise Lost* by showing that a man who has sinned can recover his power of inner control; this is the "paradise within" promised by the angel as compensation for the loss of Eden.

In *Paradise Lost* Milton speaks regretfully of "late choosing and beginning late"; but the work of his maturity is enriched with experience, meditation, and long-accumulated learning. Nowhere, however, is learning artificially super-imposed; it had become a part of Milton himself, and it forms a part of the texture of the poems. Sometimes it appears in musical groups of suggestive place names and again in figures of speech or allusions which add vistas of legend and myth and history to the story. His subjects require stateliness and dignity of style; and this he gains by Latin-ized sentences, diction consciously elevated above common speech, and rhythms sustained to form blank-verse para-graphs.

If one misses in Milton the warmer qualities of humor and tolerance, one is more than repaid by force of imagination, range and beauty of imagery, and variety and sublimity of music—powers far beyond ordinary human reach.

Song on May Morning

Now the bright morning star, day's harbinger,
Comes dancing from the east, and leads with her
The flowery May, who from her green lap throws
The yellow cowslip and the pale primrose.
Hail, bounteous May, that dost inspire
Mirth and youth and warm desire!
Woods and groves are of thy dressing;
Hill and dale doth boast thy blessing.
Thus we salute thee with our early song,
And welcome thee, and wish thee long.   10

On His Birthday

How soon hath Time, the subtle thief of youth,
Stolen on his wing my three-and-twentieth year!
My hasting days fly on with full career,
But my late spring no bud or blossom showeth.
Perhaps my semblance might deceive the truth

That I to manhood am arrived so near;
And inward ripeness doth much less appear,
That some more timely-happy spirits endueth.
Yet, be it less or more, or soon or slow,
It shall be still in strictest measure even   10
To that same lot, however mean or high,
Toward which Time leads me, and the will of heaven.
All is, if I have grace to use it so,
As ever in my great Task-master's eye.

Lycidas

Yet once more, O ye laurels, and once more,
Ye myrtles brown, with ivy never sere,
I come to pluck your berries harsh and crude,
And with forced fingers rude
Shatter your leaves before the mellowing year.[1]
Bitter constraint and sad occasion dear
Compels me to disturb your season due;
For Lycidas is dead, dead ere his prime,
Young Lycidas, and hath not left his peer.
Who would not sing for Lycidas? he knew   10
Himself to sing, and build the lofty rhyme.
He must not float upon his watery bier
Unwept, and welter to the parching wind,
Without the meed of some melodious tear.
   Begin, then, Sisters of the sacred well [2]
That from beneath the seat of Jove doth spring;

[1] Milton was asked to contribute to a memorial volume of verse to be published by Cambridge University in memory of Edward King, a student of the University, drowned that summer (1637) in the Irish Sea. He felt that he was not yet ready to write verse of distinction, represented by laurel, myrtle, ivy. He chose the form of the pastoral elegy with its classical tradition as suitable for such a volume and was influenced by the conventions of this form. *The Lament for Adonis* by Bion, *The Lament for Bion* by Moschus, and *Elegy No. I* by Theocritus should be read in this connection.

[2] The Muses. Milton, probably thinking of the River of Life flowing from beneath the throne of God, represents the Pierian spring at the foot of Mt. Olympus as springing from beneath the throne of Jove.

Begin, and somewhat loudly sweep the string.
Hence with denial vain and coy excuse:
So may some gentle Muse
With lucky words favor *my* destined urn,   20
And as he passes turn,
And bid fair peace be to my sable shroud!
 For we were nursed upon the self-same hill,
Fed the same flock, by fountain, shade, and rill;
Together both, ere the high lawns appeared
Under the opening eyelids of the Morn,
We drove a-field, and both together heard
What time the grey-fly winds her sultry horn,
Battening our flocks with the fresh dews of night,
Oft till the star that rose at evening bright   30
Toward heaven's descent had sloped his westering wheel.
Meanwhile the rural ditties were not mute;
Tempered to the oaten flute,
Rough Satyrs danced, and Fauns with cloven heel
From the glad sound would not be absent long;
And old Damœtas loved to hear our song.
 But, oh! the heavy change, now thou art gone,
Now thou art gone and never must return!
Thee, Shepherd, thee the woods and desert caves,
With wild thyme and the gadding vine o'ergrown,   40
And all their echoes, mourn.
The willows, and the hazel copses green,
Shall now no more be seen
Fanning their joyous leaves to thy soft lays.
As killing as the canker to the rose,
Or taint-worm to the weanling herds that graze,
Or frost to flowers, that their gay wardrobe wear,
When first the white-thorn blows;
Such, Lycidas, thy loss to shepherd's ear.
 Where were ye, Nymphs, when the remorseless deep   50
Closed o'er the head of your loved Lycidas?
For neither were ye playing on the steep

Where your old bards, the famous Druids, lie,
Nor on the shaggy top of Mona high,
Nor yet where Deva [3] spreads her wizard stream.
Ay me! I fondly dream
"Had ye been there"—for what could that have done?
What could the Muse herself that Orpheus bore,
The Muse herself, for her enchanting son,
Whom universal nature did lament,   60
When, by the rout that made the hideous roar,
His gory visage down the stream was sent,
Down the swift Hebrus to the Lesbian shore? [4]
  Alas! what boots it with uncessant care
To tend the homely, slighted, shepherd's trade,
And strictly meditate the thankless Muse?
Were it not better done, as others use,
To sport with Amaryllis in the shade,
Or with the tangles of Neæra's hair?
Fame is the spur that the clear spirit doth raise   70
(That last infirmity of noble mind)
To scorn delights and live laborious days;
But the fair guerdon when we hope to find,
And think to burst out into sudden blaze,
Comes the blind Fury [5] with the abhorred shears,
And slits the thin-spun life. "But not the praise,"
Phœbus [6] replied, and touched my trembling ears:
"Fame is no plant that grows on mortal soil,
Nor in the glistering foil
Set off to the world, nor in broad rumor lies,   80

[3] Deva is the river Dee, and Mona, the island of Anglesey. Dee "is called a 'wizard stream' because of a tradition that the shifting of the channel toward the Welsh or the English side portended good fortune to one or the other nation." (Moody)
[4] Orpheus, grieving for the loss of Eurydice, scorned the love of the Thracian women, who in revenge tore his body in pieces and cast his head and his lyre into the Hebrus.
[5] The *Fate* who cuts the thread of life, Atropos, is meant.
[6] Phœbus was the god of poetry. Notice the tenseness suggested by "trembling ears."

But lives and spreads aloft by those pure eyes
And perfect witness of all-judging Jove; [7]
As he pronounces lastly on each deed,
Of so much fame in heaven expect thy meed."

O fountain Arethuse, and thou honored flood,
Smooth-sliding Mincius,[8] crowned with vocal reeds,
That strain I heard was of a higher mood.
But now my oat proceeds,
And listens to the Herald of the Sea,[9]
That came in Neptune's plea.   90
He asked the waves, and asked the felon winds,
What hard mishap hath doomed this gentle swain?
And questioned every gust of rugged wings
That blows from off each beaked promontory.
They knew not of his story;
And sage Hippotades [10] their answer brings,
That not a blast was from his dungeon strayed:
The air was calm, and on the level brine
Sleek Panope, with all her sisters, played.[11]
It was that fatal and perfidious bark,   100
Built in the eclipse, and rigged with curses dark,
That sunk so low that sacred head of thine.

Next, Camus,[12] reverend sire, went footing slow,
His mantle hairy, and his bonnet sedge,
Inwrought with figures dim, and on the edge
Like to that sanguine flower inscribed with woe.[13]
"Ah, who hath reft," quoth he, "my dearest pledge?"

[7] Milton has already put fame on a higher plane than the plaudits
of the multitude.

[8] The river Mincius is associated with Virgil's pastoral poetry as
the spring Arethuse is with the Sicilian. This second invocation marks
the return to the pastoral tone after the more serious reflection on
fame.

[9] Triton.

[10] Æolus, god of the winds.

[11] The fifty Nereids.

[12] The personification of the river Cam at Cambridge.

[13] When Hyacinthus was accidentally killed by Apollo's discus, a
purple flower with petals marked "Ai! ai!" sprang up from the blood-
soaked ground.

Last came, and last did go,
The Pilot of the Galilean Lake; [14]
Two massy keys he bore of metals twain   110
(The golden opes, the iron shuts amain).
He shook his mitred locks, and stern bespake:—
"How well could I have spared for thee, young swain,
Enow of such as, for their bellies' sake,
Creep, and intrude, and climb into the fold! [15]
Of other care they little reckoning make
Than how to scramble at the shearers' feast,
And shove away the worthy bidden guest.
Blind mouths! [16] that scarce themselves know how to hold
A sheep-hook, or have learned aught else the least   120
That to the faithful herdman's art belongs!
What recks it them? What need they? They are sped;
And when they list, their lean and flashy songs
Grate on their scrannel pipes of wretched straw;
The hungry sheep look up, and are not fed,
But, swoln with wind and the rank mist they draw,
Rot inwardly, and foul contagion spread;
Besides what the grim wolf [17] with privy paw
Daily devours apace, and nothing said.
But that two-handed engine [18] at the door   130
Stands ready to smite once, and smite no more."
    Return, Alpheus; the dread voice is past

[14] Peter. "And I will give unto thee the keys of the kingdom of heaven." *Matt.* 16:19.

[15] "Verily, verily, I say unto you, He that entereth not by the door into the sheepfold, but climbeth up some other way, the same is a thief and a robber." *John* 10:1.

[16] One should see Ruskin's discussion of the passage in *Of Kings Treasuries.* A minister should be the shepherd of his flock, watching over them and feeding them. Milton says the clergy of his day is the opposite of the good shepherd. The compression of the figure is powerful.

[17] The Catholic Church.

[18] A vague figure, striking terror by its vagueness. The two houses of Parliament, the two-edged sword of St. Michael, the "sharp two-edged sword" of Christ in John's vision, *Rev.* 1:16, and other suggestions have been made.

That shrunk thy streams; return, Sicilian Muse,[19]
And call the vales, and bid them hither cast
Their bells and flowerets of a thousand hues.
Ye valleys low, where the mild whispers use
Of shades and wanton winds and gushing brooks,
On whose fresh lap the swart star sparely looks,
Throw hither all your quaint enameled eyes,
That on the green turf suck the honeyed showers,   140
And purple all the ground with vernal flowers.
Bring the rathe [20] primrose that forsaken dies,
The tufted crow-toe, and pale jessamine,
The white pink, and the pansy freaked with jet,
The glowing violet,
The musk-rose, and the well-attired woodbine,
With cowslips wan that hang the pensive head,
And every flower that sad embroidery wears;
Bid amaranthus all his beauty shed,
And daffadillies fill their cups with tears,   150
To strew the laureate hearse where Lycid lies.
For so, to interpose a little ease,
Let our frail thoughts dally with false surmise.
Ay me! whilst thee the shores and sounding seas
Wash far away, where'er thy bones are hurled;
Whether beyond the stormy Hebrides,
Where thou, perhaps, under the whelming tide
Visit'st the bottom of the monstrous world;
Or whether thou, to our moist vows denied,
Sleep'st by the fable of Bellerus old,[21]   160
Where the great Vision of the guarded mount
Looks toward Namancos and Bayona's hold.[22]
Look homeward, Angel, now, and melt with ruth:

[19] A third invocation, marking the return to the pastoral after the indictment of the church.
[20] Early.
[21] *Bellerium* was the Latin name for Land's End in Cornwall.
[22] St. Michael's Mount looking toward Spain.

And, O ye dolphins, waft the hapless youth.[23]
　　Weep no more, woeful shepherds, weep no more;
For Lycidas, your sorrow, is not dead,
Sunk though he be beneath the watery floor.
So sinks the day-star in the ocean bed,
And yet anon repairs his drooping head,
And tricks his beams, and with new-spangled ore   170
Flames in the forehead of the morning sky:
So Lycidas sunk low, but mounted high,
Through the dear might of Him that walked the waves,
Where, other groves and other streams along,
With nectar pure his oozy locks he laves,
And hears the unexpressive [24] nuptial song,[25]
In the blest kingdoms meek of joy and love.
There entertain him all the Saints above,
In solemn troops, and sweet societies,
That sing, and singing in their glory move,   180
And wipe the tears forever from his eyes.[26]
Now, Lycidas, the shepherds weep no more;
Henceforth thou art the Genius of the shore,[27]
In thy large recompense, and shalt be good
To all that wander in that perilous flood.

　　Thus sang the uncouth swain to the oaks and rills,
While the still morn went out with sandals gray:
He touched the tender stops of various quills,
With eager thought warbling his Doric lay.
And now the sun had stretched out all the hills,   190
And now was dropt into the western bay;

[23] Arion was a famous musician who was robbed and forced by the
shipmen to cast himself into the sea. His music had attracted the
dolphins, and one offered his back to convey Arion safely to shore.
[24] Inexpressible.
[25] The Church is represented in *Revelations* as the bride of Christ.
[26] ". . . And God shall wipe away all tears from their eyes." *Rev.*
*:17.
[27] The guardian spirit.

At last he rose, and twitched his mantle blue:
To-morrow to fresh woods, and pastures new.

To the Lord General Cromwell

Cromwell, our chief of men, who through a cloud,
Not of war only, but detractions rude,
Guided by faith and matchless fortitude,
To peace and truth thy glorious way hast ploughed,
And on the neck of crowned Fortune [1] proud
Hast reared God's trophies, and His work pursued,
While Darwen stream,[2] with blood of Scots imbrued,
And Dunbar field,[3] resounds thy praises loud,
And Worcester's laureate wreath: [4] yet much remains
To conquer still; peace hath her victories
No less renowned than war: new foes arise,[5]   10
Threatening to bind our souls with secular chains.
Help us to save free conscience from the paw
Of hireling wolves, whose gospel is their maw.

On the Late Massacre in Piedmont

Avenge, O Lord, Thy slaughtered saints, whose bones
Lie scattered on the Alpine mountains cold; [1]
Even them who kept Thy truth so pure of old,
When all our fathers worshiped stocks and stones,
Forget not: in Thy book record their groans
Who were Thy sheep, and in their ancient fold
Slain by the bloody Piedmontese, that rolled

[1] The Stuart regime.
[2] A small river near Preston, where Cromwell defeated the Scots
August, 1648.
[3] Here Cromwell defeated a large Scottish force, September 3, 1650
[4] By his victory at Worcester Cromwell suppressed the Royalists
September 3, 1651.
[5] Presbyterianism.
[1] The Piedmontese were Protestants. In 1655 the Duke of Savoy had
many of them put to death in the effort to put an end to Protestantism
in his domain.

Mother with infant down the rocks. Their moans
The vales redoubled to the hills, and they
To heaven. Their martyred blood and ashes sow   10
O'er all the Italian fields, where still doth sway
The triple Tyrant; [2] that from these may grow
A hundredfold, who, having learnt Thy way,
Early may fly the Babylonian woe. [3]

On His Blindness

When I consider how my light is spent
Ere half my days in this dark world and wide,
And that one talent which is death to hide
Lodged with me useless, though my soul more bent
To serve therewith my Maker, and present
My true account, lest He, returning, chide,
"Doth God exact day-labor, light denied?"
I fondly ask. But Patience, to prevent
That murmur, soon replies, "God doth not need
Either man's work or His own gifts. Who best   10
Bear His mild yoke,[1] they serve Him best. His state
Is kingly: thousands at His bidding speed,
And post o'er land and ocean without rest;
They also serve who only stand and wait."

To Cyriack Skinner [II]

Cyriack, this three years' day these eyes, though clear,
To outward view, of blemish or of spot,
Bereft of light, their seeing have forgot;
Nor to their idle orbs doth sight appear
Of sun or moon or star, throughout the year,

[2] The Pope.
[3] The fall of Babylon, interpreted as Catholicism, is related in
Revelations.
[1] Christ says, "My yoke is easy, and my burden is light." See *Matt.*
1:30.

Or man or woman. Yet I argue not
Against heaven's hand or will, nor bate a jot
Of heart or hope, but still bear up and steer
Right onward. What supports me, dost thou ask?
The conscience, friend, to have lost them overplied [1]   10
In liberty's defense, my noble task,
Of which all Europe rings from side to side.
This thought might lead me through the world's vain mask
Content, though blind, had I no better guide.

On His Deceased Wife

Methought I saw my late espoused [1] saint
Brought to me like Alcestis [2] from the grave,
Whom Jove's great son to her glad husband gave,
Rescued from Death by force, though pale and faint.
Mine, as whom washed from spot of child-bed taint
Purification in the Old Law did save,[3]
And such as yet once more I trust to have
Full sight of her in heaven without restraint,
Came vested all in white,[4] pure as her mind.
Her face was veiled; [5] yet to my fancied sight   10
Love, sweetness, goodness, in her person shined
So clear as in no face with more delight.
But, oh! as to embrace me she inclined,
I waked, she fled, and day brought back my night.

[1] Physicians warned Milton that to complete his reply to Salmasius
would cost him his sight.

[1] Katherine Woodcock, his second wife, who had died in childbirth.
[2] Alcestis had given her life to save that of her husband, King
Admetus, but Hercules overcame death and restored Alcestis to King
Admetus.
[3] This law is given in *Lev.* 12:2–8.
[4] ". . . These are they which came out of great tribulation, and
have washed their robes, and made them white in the blood of the
Lamb." *Rev.* 7:14.
[5] The face of Alcestis was veiled when she was returned to King
Admetus. Masson suggests an allusion to Milton's blindness, as Milton
had lost his sight before he married Katherine Woodcock.

Samson Agonistes

A Dramatic Poem

OF THAT SORT OF DRAMATIC POEM CALLED TRAGEDY

Tragedy, as it was anciently composed, hath been ever held the gravest, moralest, and most profitable of all other poems; therefore said by Aristotle to be of power, by raising pity and fear, or terror, to purge the mind of those and such-like passions—that is, to temper and reduce them to just measure with a kind of delight, stirred up by reading or seeing those passions well imitated. Nor is Nature wanting in her own effects to make good his assertion; for so, in physic, things of melancholic hue and quality are used against melancholy, sour against sour, salt to remove salt humors. Hence philosophers and other gravest writers, as Cicero, Plutarch, and others, frequently cite out of tragic poets, both to adorn and illustrate their discourse. The apostle Paul himself thought it not unworthy to insert a verse of Euripides into the text of Holy Scripture, *I Cor.* XV. 33; and Paræus, commenting on the *Revelation,* divides the whole book, as a tragedy, into acts, distinguished each by a chorus of heavenly harpings and song between. Heretofore men in highest dignity have labored not a little to be thought able to compose a tragedy. Of that honor Dionysius the elder was no less ambitious than before of his attaining to the tyranny. Augustus Caesar also had begun his *Ajax,* but, unable to please his own judgment with what he had begun, left it unfinished. Seneca, the philosopher, is by some thought the author of those tragedies (at least the best of them) that go under that name. Gregory Nazianzen, a Father of the Church, thought it not unbeseeming the sanctity of his person to write a tragedy, which he entitled *Christ Suffering.* This is mentioned to vindicate tragedy from the small esteem, or rather infamy, which in the account of many it undergoes at this day, with other common interludes; happening through the poet's error of intermixing comic stuff with tragic sadness and gravity, or introducing trivial and vulgar persons: which by all judicious hath been counted absurd, and brought in without discretion, corruptly to gratify the people. And, though ancient tragedy use no prologue, yet using sometimes, in case of self-defence or explanation, that which Martial calls an epistle, in behalf of this tragedy, coming forth after the ancient manner, much different from what among us passes for best, thus much beforehand may be *epistled*—that chorus is here introduced after the Greek manner, not ancient only, but modern, and still in use among the Italians. In the modeling therefore of this poem, with good reason, the ancients and Italians are rather followed, as of much more authority and fame. The measure of verse used in the chorus is of all sorts, called by the Greeks *Monostrophic,* or rather *Apolelymenon,* without regard had to Strophe, Antistrophe, or Epode,—which were a kind of stanzas framed only for the music, then used with the chorus that sung; not essential to the poem, and therefore not material; or, being divided into stanzas or pauses, they may be called *Allœostropha.* Division into act and scene, referring chiefly to the stage (to which this work never was intended), is here omitted.

It suffices if the whole drama be found not produced beyond the fifth act. Of the style and uniformity, and that commonly called the plot, whether intricate or explicit— which is nothing indeed but such economy, or disposition of the fable, as may stand best with verisimilitude and decorum —they only will best judge who are not unacquainted with Æschylus, Sophocles, and Euripides, the three tragic poets unequaled yet by any, and the best rule to all who endeavor to write tragedy. The circumscription of time, wherein the whole drama begins and ends, is, according to ancient rule and best example, within the space of twenty-four hours.

THE PERSONS

SAMSON

MANOA, the father of Samson   Public Officer
DALILA, his wife   Messenger
HARAPHA of Gath   Chorus of Danites

The Scene, before the Prison in Gaza.

Samson Agonistes [1]

Sams. A little onward lend thy guiding hand
To these dark steps, a little further on;
For yonder bank hath choice of sun or shade.
There I am wont to sit, when any chance
Relieves me from my task of servile toil,
Daily in the common prison else enjoined me,
Where I, a prisoner chained, scarce freely draw
The air, imprisoned also, close and damp,
Unwholesome draught. But here I feel amends—
The breath of heaven fresh blowing, pure and sweet,   10
With day-spring born; here leave me to respire.
This day a solemn feast the people hold
To Dagon, their sea-idol,[2] and forbid
Laborious works. Unwillingly this rest
Their superstition yields me; hence, with leave
Retiring from the popular noise, I seek
This unfrequented place to find some ease—
Ease to the body some, none to the mind
From restless thoughts, that, like a deadly swarm

[1] One should read *Judges* 13–16, before reading this drama.
[2] Dagon, the god of the Philistines, was half man and half fish.
When the Philistines captured the ark and brought it into the house
of Dagon, later in the history of the Israelites, the image of Dagon
fell on its face. When Dagon was restored to his place, he again fell,
breaking off his hands and his head. This mishap and other misfortunes
attributed to the presence of the ark led the Philistines to restore the
ark to the Israelites. See *I Samuel* 5. Milton refers to the fall of Dagon
in *On the Morning of Christ's Nativity,* and places Dagon among the
fallen angels, *Paradise Lost* I, 457–76.

Of hornets armed, no sooner found alone   20
But rush upon me thronging, and present
Times past, what once I was, and what am now.
Oh, wherefore was my birth from heaven foretold
Twice by an angel, who at last, in sight
Of both my parents, all in flames ascended
From off the altar where an offering burned,
As in a fiery column charioting
His godlike presence, and from some great act
Or benefit revealed to Abraham's race?
Why was my breeding ordered and prescribed   30
As of a person separate to God,
Designed for great exploits, if I must die
Betrayed, captived, and both my eyes put out,
Made of my enemies the scorn and gaze,
To grind in brazen fetters under task
With this heaven-gifted strength? O glorious strength,
Put to the labor of a beast, debased
Lower than bond-slave! Promise was that I
Should Israel from Philistian yoke deliver!
Ask for this great deliverer now, and find him   40
Eyeless in Gaza, at the mill with slaves,
Himself in bonds under Philistian yoke.
Yet stay; let me not rashly call in doubt
Divine prediction. What if all foretold
Had been fulfilled but through mine own default?
Whom have I to complain of but myself,
Who this high gift of strength committed to me,
In what part lodged, how easily bereft me,
Under the seal of silence could not keep,
But weakly to a woman must reveal it,   50
O'ercome with importunity and tears?
O impotence of mind in body strong!
But what is strength without a double share
Of wisdom? Vast, unwieldy, burdensome,
Proudly secure, yet liable to fall
By weakest subtleties; not made to rule,

But to subserve where wisdom bears command.
God, when he gave me strength, to show withal
How slight the gift was, hung it in my hair.
But peace! I must not quarrel with the will   60
Of highest dispensation, which herein
Haply had ends above my reach to know.
Suffices that to me strength is my bane,
And proves the source of all my miseries—
So many, and so huge, that each apart
Would ask a life to wail. But, chief of all,
O loss of sight, of thee I most complain! [3]
Blind among enemies! O worse than chains,
Dungeon, or beggary, or decrepit age!
Light, the prime work of God,[4] to me is extinct,   70
And all her various objects of delight
Annulled, which might in part my grief have eased.
Inferior to the vilest now become
Of man or worm, the vilest here excel me:
They creep, yet see; I, dark in light, exposed
To daily fraud, contempt, abuse, and wrong,
Within doors, or without, still as a fool,
In power of others, never in my own—
Scarce half I seem to live, dead more than half.
O dark, dark, dark, amid the blaze of noon,   80
Irrecoverably dark, total eclipse
Without all hope of day!
O first-created beam, and thou great Word,
"Let there be light, and light was over all,"
Why am I thus bereaved thy prime decree?
The sun to me is dark
And silent as the moon,
When she deserts the night,

[3] This passage through l. 109 is autobiographical. Other passages
to be noted in connection with this are: three sonnets—*On His Blind-
ness, On His Deceased Wife,* and the second sonnet to Cyriack Skinner;
Paradise Lost III, 21–51, and VII, 23–39.
[4] Light was the first thing created, *Gen.* 1: 3. Milton wrote a beauti-
ful hymn to light in *Paradise Lost* III, 1–55.

Hid in her vacant interlunar cave.
Since light so necessary is to life,   90
And almost life itself, if it be true
That light is in the soul,
She all in every part, why was the sight
To such a tender ball as the eye confined,
So obvious and so easy to be quenched,
And not, as feeling, through all parts diffused,
That she might look at will through every pore?
Then had I not been thus exiled from light,
As in the land of darkness, yet in light,
To live a life half dead, a living death,   100
And buried; but, O yet more miserable!
Myself my sepulchre, a moving grave;
Buried, yet not exempt
By privilege of death and burial
From worst of other evils, pains, and wrongs;
But made hereby obnoxious more
To all the miseries of life,
Life in captivity
Among inhuman foes.
But who are these? for with joint pace I hear   110
The tread of many feet steering this way;
Perhaps my enemies, who come to stare
At my affliction, and perhaps to insult—
Their daily practice to afflict me more.
    Chor. This, this is he; softly a while;
Let us not break in upon him.
O change beyond report, thought, or belief!
See how he lies at random, carelessly diffused,
With languished head unpropped
As one past hope, abandoned,   120
And by himself given over,
In slavish habit, ill-fitted weeds
O'er worn and soiled.
Or do my eyes misrepresent? Can this be he,
That heroic, that renowned,

Irresistible Samson? whom, unarmed,
No strength of man, or fiercest wild beast, could withstand;
Who tore the lion as the lion tears the kid;
Ran on embattled armies clad in iron,
And, weaponless himself,   130
Made arms ridiculous, useless the forgery
Of brazen shield and spear, the hammered cuirass,
Chalybean-tempered steel, and frock of mail
Adamantean proof:
But safest he who stood aloof,
When insupportably his foot advanced,
In scorn of their proud arms and warlike tools,
Spurned them to death by troops. The bold Ascalonite
Fled from his lion ramp; old warriors turned
Their plated backs under his heel,   140
Or groveling soiled their crested helmets in the dust.
Then with what trivial weapon came to hand,
The jaw of a dead ass, his sword of bone,
A thousand foreskins fell, the flower of Palestine,
In Ramath-lechi, famous to this day:
Then by main force pulled up, and on his shoulders bore,
The gates of Azza, post and massy bar,
Up to the hill by Hebron, seat of giants old—
No journey of a sabbath-day, and loaded so—
Like whom the Gentiles feign to bear up heaven.   150
Which shall I first bewail—
Thy bondage or lost sight,
Prison within prison
Inseparably dark?
Thou art become (O worst imprisonment!)
The dungeon of thyself; thy soul
(Which men enjoying sight oft without cause complain)
Imprisoned now indeed,
In real darkness of the body dwells,
Shut up from outward light   160
To incorporate with gloomy night;
For inward light, alas!

Puts forth no visual beam.
O mirror of our fickle state,
Since man on earth, unparalleled,
The rarer thy example stands,
By how much from the top of wondrous glory,[5]
Strongest of mortal men,
To lowest pitch of abject fortune thou art fallen.
For him I reckon not in high estate   170
Whom long descent of birth,
Or the sphere of fortune, raises;
But thee, whose strength, while virtue was her mate,
Might have subdued the earth,
Universally crowned with highest praises.

   Sams. I hear the sound of words; their sense the air
Dissolves unjointed ere it reach my ear.

   Chor. He speaks; let us draw nigh. Matchless in might,
The glory late of Israel, now the grief!
We come, thy friends and neighbors not unknown,   180
From Eshtaol and Zora's fruitful vale,
To visit or bewail thee; or, if better,
Counsel or consolation we may bring,
Salve to thy sores: apt words have power to 'suage
The tumors of a troubled mind,
And are as balm to festered wounds.

   Sams. Your coming, friends, revives me; for I learn
Now of my own experience, not by talk,
How counterfeit a coin they are who 'friends'
Bear in their superscription (of the most   190
I would be understood). In prosperous days
They swarm, but in adverse withdraw their head,
Not to be found, though sought. Ye see, O friends,
How many evils have enclosed me round;
Yet that which was the worst now least afflicts me,
Blindness; for, had I sight, confused with shame,
How could I once look up, or heave the head,

---

[5] This fall from eminence is characteristic of the hero of Greek tragedy.

Who, like a foolish pilot, have shipwrecked
My vessel trusted to me from above,
Gloriously rigged, and for a word, a tear,   200
Fool! have divulged the secret gift of God
To a deceitful woman? Tell me, friends,
Am I not sung and proverbed for a fool
In every street? Do they not say, "How well
Are come upon him his deserts"? Yet why?
Immeasurable strength they might behold
In me; of wisdom nothing more than mean.
This with the other should at least have paired;
These two, proportioned ill, drove me transverse.
    Chor. Tax not divine disposal. Wisest men   210
Have erred, and by bad women been deceived;
And shall again, pretend they ne'er so wise.
Deject not, then, so overmuch thyself,
Who hast of sorrow thy full load besides.
Yet, truth to say, I oft have heard men wonder
Why thou shouldst wed Philistian women rather
Than of thine own tribe fairer, or as fair,
At least of thy own nation, and as noble.
    Sams. The first I saw at Timna, and she pleased
Me, not my parents, that I sought to wed   220
The daughter of an infidel. They knew not
That what I motioned was of God: I knew
From intimate impulse, and therefore urged
The marriage on, that, by occasion hence,
I might begin Israel's deliverance—
The work to which I was divinely called.
She proving false, the next I took to wife
(O that I never had! fond wish too late!)
Was in the vale of Sorec, Dalila,
That specious monster, my accomplished snare.   230
I thought it lawful from my former act,
And the same end, still watching to oppress
Israel's oppressors. Of what now I suffer
She was not the prime cause, but I myself,

Who, vanquished with a peal of words, (O weakness!)
Gave up my fort of silence to a woman.

    Chor. In seeking just occasion to provoke
The Philistine, thy country's enemy,
Thou never wast remiss, I bear thee witness;
Yet Israel still serves with all his sons.   240

    Sams. That fault I take not on me, but transfer
On Israel's governors and heads of tribes,
Who, seeing those great acts which God had done
Singly by me against their conquerors,
Acknowledged not, or not at all considered,
Deliverance offered. I, on the other side,
Used no ambition to commend my deeds;
The deeds themselves, though mute, spoke loud the doer.
But they persisted deaf, and would not seem
To count them things worth notice, till at length   250
Their lords, the Philistines, with gathered powers,
Entered Judea, seeking me, who then
Safe to the rock of Etham was retired—
Not flying, but forecasting in what place
To set upon them, what advantaged best.
Meanwhile the men of Judah, to prevent
The harass of their land, beset me round;
I willingly on some conditions came
Into their hands and they as gladly yield me
To the Uncircumcised a welcome prey,   260
Bound with two cords. But cords to me were threads
Touched with the flame: on their whole host I flew
Unarmed, and with a trivial weapon felled
Their choicest youth; they only lived who fled.
Had Judah that day joined, or one whole tribe,
They had by this possessed the towers of Gath,
And lorded over them whom now they serve.
But what more oft, in nations grown corrupt,
And by their vices brought to servitude,
Than to love bondage more than liberty—   270

Bondage with ease than strenuous liberty [6]—
And to despise, or envy, or suspect,
Whom God hath of His special favor raised
As their deliverer? If he aught begin,
How frequent to desert him, and at last
To heap ingratitude on worthiest deeds!
   Chor. Thy words to my remembrance bring
How Succoth and the fort of Penuel
Their great deliverer contemned,
The matchless Gideon,[7] in pursuit   280
Of Madian, and her vanquished kings;
And how ingrateful Ephraim
Had dealt with Jephtha, who by argument,
Not worse than by his shield and spear,
Defended Israel from the Ammonite,
Had not his prowess quelled their pride
In that sore battle when so many died
Without reprieve, adjudged to death
For want of well pronouncing *Shibboleth*.[8]
   Sams. Of such examples add me to the roll.   290
Me easily indeed mine may neglect,
But God's proposed deliverance not so.
   Chor. Just are the ways of God,[9]
And justifiable to men,
Unless there be who think not God at all.
If any be, they walk obscure;
For of such doctrine never was their school,
But the heart of the fool,

[6] In *Paradise Lost* II, 255-7, Milton represents the fallen angels as

         . . . preferring
    Hard liberty before the easy yoke
    Of servile pomp.

[7] The very interesting story of Gideon is found in *Judges* 7-8: 21.
One must read this account to get the significance of Milton's passage.
[8] Jeptha's conquest and his detection of the Ephraimites by the way
they pronounced "Shibboleth" is recounted in *Judges* 12: 1-6.
[9] Milton's purpose in writing *Paradise Lost* had been to show this.

And no man therein doctor but himself.
Yet more there be who doubt his ways not just,   300
As to his own edicts found contradicting;
Then give the reins to wandering thought,
Regardless of his glory's diminution,
Till, by their own perplexities involved,
They ravel more, still less resolved,
But never find self-satisfying solution.
As if they would confine the Interminable,
And tie Him to His own prescript,
Who made our laws to bind us, not Himself,
And hath full right to exempt   310
Whomso it pleases Him by choice
From national obstriction, without taint
Of sin, or legal debt;
For with His own laws He can best dispense.
He would not else, who never wanted means,
Nor in respect of the enemy just cause,
To set His people free,
Have prompted this heroic Nazarite,
Against his vow of strictest purity,
To seek in marriage that fallacious bride,   320
Unclean, unchaste.
Down, Reason, then; at least, vain reasonings down;
Though Reason here aver
That moral verdict quits her of unclean:
Unchaste was subsequent; her stain, not his.
But see! here comes thy reverend sire,
With careful step, locks white as down,
Old Manoa: advise
Forthwith how thou ought'st to receive him.
Sams. Ay me! another inward grief, awaked   330
With mention of that name, renews the assault.
Man. Brethren and men of Dan (for such ye seem
Though in this uncouth place), if old respect,
As I suppose, towards your once gloried friend,
My son, now captive, hither hath informed

Your younger feet, while mine, cast back with age,
Came lagging after, say if he be here.
   Chor. As signal now in low dejected state
As erst in highest, behold him where he lies.
   Man. O miserable change! Is this the man,   340
That invincible Samson, far renowned,
The dread of Israel's foes, who with a strength
Equivalent to angels' walked their streets,
None offering fight; who, single combatant,
Dueled their armies ranked in proud array,
Himself an army—now unequal match
To save himself against a coward armed
At one spear's length? O ever-failing trust
In mortal strength! and, oh, what not in man
Deceivable and vain? Nay, what thing good   350
Prayed for, but often proves our woe, our bane?
I prayed for children, and thought barrenness
In wedlock a reproach; I gained a son,
And such a son as all men hailed me happy:
Who would be now a father in my stead?
Oh, wherefore did God grant me my request,
And as a blessing with such pomp adorned?
Why are his gifts desirable, to tempt
Our earnest prayers, then, given with solemn hand
As graces, draw a scorpion's tail behind?   360
For this did the angel twice descend? for this
Ordained thy nurture holy, as of a plant
Select and sacred? glorious for a while,
The miracle of men; then in an hour
Ensnared, assaulted, overcome, led bound,
Thy foes' derision, captive, poor, and blind,
Into a dungeon thrust, to work with slaves!
Alas! methinks whom God hath chosen once
To worthiest deeds, if he through frailty err,
He should not so o'erwhelm, and as a thrall   370
Subject him to so foul indignities,
Be it but for honor's sake of former deeds.

Sams. Appoint not heavenly disposition, father.
Nothing of all these evils hath befallen me
But justly; I myself have brought them on;
Sole author I, sole cause. If aught seem vile,
As vile hath been my folly, who have profaned
The mystery of God, given me under pledge
Of vow, and have betrayed it to a woman,
A Canaanite, my faithless enemy.   380
This well I knew, nor was at all surprised,
But warned by oft experience. Did not she
Of Timna first betray me, and reveal
The secret wrested from me in her height
Of nuptial love professed, carrying it straight
To them who had corrupted her, my spies
And rivals? In this other was there found
More faith, who, also in her prime of love,
Spousal embraces, vitiated with gold,
Though offered only, by the scent conceived   390
Her spurious first-born, Treason against me?
Thrice she assayed, with flattering prayers and signs,
And amorous reproaches, to win from me
My capital secret, in what part my strength
Lay stored, in what part summed, that she might know;
Thrice I deluded her, and turned to sport
Her importunity, each time perceiving
How openly and with what impudence
She purposed to betray me, and (which was worse
Than undissembled hate) with what contempt   400
She sought to make me traitor to myself.
Yet, the fourth time, when, mustering all her wiles,
With blandished parleys, feminine assaults,
Tongue-batteries, she surceased not day nor night
To storm me, over-watched and wearied out,
At times when men seek most repose and rest,
I yielded, and unlocked her all my heart,
Who, with a grain of manhood well resolved,
Might easily have shook off all her snares;

But foul effeminacy held me yoked   410
Her bond-slave. O indignity, O blot
To honor and religion! servile mind
Rewarded well with servile punishment!
The base degree to which I now am fallen,
These rags, this grinding, is not yet so base
As was my former servitude, ignoble,
Unmanly, ignominious, infamous,
True slavery; and that blindness worse than this,
That saw not how degenerately I served.

Man. I cannot praise thy marriage-choices, son—   420
Rather approve them not; but thou didst plead
Divine impulsion prompting how thou might'st
Find some occasion to infest our foes.
I state not that; this I am sure—our foes
Found soon occasion thereby to make thee
Their captive, and their triumph; thou the sooner
Temptation found'st, or over-potent charms,
To violate the sacred trust of silence
Deposited within thee—which to have kept
Tacit was in thy power. True; and thou bear'st   430
Enough, and more, the burden of that fault;
Bitterly hast thou paid, and still art paying,
That rigid score. A worse thing yet remains:
This day the Philistines a popular feast
Here celebrate in Gaza, and proclaim
Great pomp, and sacrifice, and praises loud,
To Dagon, as their god who hath delivered
Thee, Samson, bound and blind, into their hands—
Them out of thine, who slew'st them many a slain.
So Dagon shall be magnified, and God,   440
Besides whom is no god, compared with idols,
Disglorified, blasphemed, and had in scorn
By the idolatrous rout amidst their wine;
Which to have come to pass by means of thee,
Samson, of all thy sufferings think the heaviest,
Of all reproach the most with shame that ever

Could have befallen thee and thy father's house.

   Sams. Father, I do acknowledge and confess
That I this honor, I this pomp, have brought
To Dagon, and advanced his praises high   450
Among the heathen round—to God have brought
Dishonor, obloquy, and oped the mouths
Of idolists and atheists; have brought scandal
To Israel, diffidence of God, and doubt
In feeble hearts, propense enough before
To waver, or fall off and join with idols:
Which is my chief affliction, shame, and sorrow,
The anguish of my soul, that suffers not
Mine eye to harbor sleep, or thoughts to rest.
This only hope relieves me, that the strife   460
With me hath end. All the contest is now
'Twixt God and Dagon. Dagon hath presumed,
Me overthrown, to enter lists with God,
His deity comparing and preferring
Before the God of Abraham. He, be sure,
Will not connive, or linger, thus provoked,
But will arise, and His great name assert.
Dagon must stoop, and shall ere long receive
Such a discomfit as shall quite despoil him
Of all these boasted trophies won on me,   470
And with confusion blank his worshipers.

   Man. With cause this hope relieves thee; and these words
I as a prophecy receive; for God
(Nothing more certain) will not long defer
To vindicate the glory of His name
Against all competition, nor will long
Endure it doubtful whether God be Lord
Or Dagon. But for thee what shall be done?
Thou must not in the meanwhile, here forgot,
Lie in this miserable loathsome plight   480
Neglected. I already have made way
To some Philistian lords, with whom to treat
About thy ransom. Well they may by this

Have satisfied their utmost of revenge,
By pains and slaveries, worse than death, inflicted
On thee, who now no more canst do them harm.

   Sams. Spare that proposal, father; spare the trouble
Of that solicitation. Let me here,
As I deserve, pay on my punishment,
And expiate, if possible, my crime,   490
Shameful garrulity. To have revealed
Secrets of *men*, the secrets of a friend,
How heinous had the fact been, how deserving
Contempt and scorn of all—to be excluded
All friendship, and avoided as a blab,
The mark of fool set on his front!
But I *God's* counsel have not kept, His holy secret
Presumptuously have published, impiously,
Weakly at least and shamefully—a sin
That Gentiles in their parables condemn   500
To their abyss and horrid pains confined.

   Man. Be penitent, and for thy fault contrite;
But act not in thy own affliction, son.
Repent the sin; but, if the punishment
Thou canst avoid, self-preservation bids;
Or the execution leave to high disposal,
And let another hand, not thine, exact
Thy penal forfeit from thyself. Perhaps
God will relent, and quit thee all His debt;
Who ever more approves and more accepts   510
(Best pleased with humble and filial submission)
Him who, imploring mercy, sues for life,
Than who, self-rigorous, chooses death as due;
Which argues over-just, and self-displeased
For self-offence more than for God offended.
Reject not, then, what offered means who knows
But God hath set before us to return thee
Home to thy country and His sacred house,
Where thou may'st bring thy offerings to avert
His further ire, with prayers and vows renewed.   520

Sams. His pardon I implore; but, as for life,
To what end should I seek it? When in strength
All mortals I excelled, and great in hopes,
With youthful courage and magnanimous thoughts
Of birth from heaven foretold and high exploits,
Full of divine instinct, after some proof
Of acts indeed heroic, far beyond
The sons of Anak,[10] famous now and blazed,
Fearless of danger, like a petty god
I walked about, admired of all, and dreaded   530
On hostile ground, none daring my affront—
Then, swollen with pride, into the snare I fell
Of fair fallacious looks, venereal trains,
Softened with pleasure and voluptuous life,
At length to lay my head and hallowed pledge
Of all my strength in the lascivious lap
Of a deceitful concubine, who shore me,
Like a tame wether, all my precious fleece,
Then turned me out ridiculous, despoiled,
Shaven, and disarmed among my enemies.   540

Chor. Desire of wine and all delicious drinks,
Which many a famous warrior overturns,
Thou couldst repress; nor did the dancing ruby,
Sparkling out-poured, the flavor or the smell,
Or taste, that cheers the heart of gods and men,
Allure thee from the cool crystalline stream.

Sams. Wherever fountain or fresh current flowed
Against the eastern ray, translucent, pure
With touch ethereal of heaven's fiery rod,
I drank, from the clear milky juice allaying   550
Thirst, and refreshed; nor envied them the grape
Whose heads that turbulent liquor fills with fumes.

Chor. O madness! to think use of strongest wines
And strongest drinks our chief support of health,

[10] Caleb took Hebron from the three sons of Anak: *Judges* 1: 20. The Anakims were giants, and this conquest was the most difficult one undertaken.

When God with these forbidden made choice to rear
His mighty champion, strong above compare,
Whose drink was only from the liquid brook!
   Sams. But what availed this temperance, not complete
Against another object more enticing?
What boots it at one gate to make defense,   560
And at another to let in the foe,
Effeminately vanquished? by which means,
Now blind, disheartened, shamed, dishonored, quelled,
To what can I be useful? wherein serve
My nation, and the work from heaven imposed?
But to sit idle on the household hearth,
A burdenous drone; to visitants a gaze,
Or pitied object; these redundant locks,
Robustious to no purpose, clustering down,
Vain monument of strength; till length of years   570
And sedentary numbness craze my limbs
To a contemptible old age obscure.
Here rather let me drudge, and earn my bread,
Till vermin, or the draff of servile food,
Consume me, and oft-invocated death
Hasten the welcome end of all my pains.
   Man. Wilt thou then serve the Philistines with that gift
Which was expressly given thee to annoy them?
Better at home lie bed-rid, not only idle,
Inglorious, unemployed, with age outworn.   580
But God, who caused a fountain at thy prayer
From the dry ground to spring, thy thirst to allay
After the brunt of battle, can as easy
Cause light again within thy eyes to spring,
Wherewith to serve Him better than thou hast.
And I persuade me so. Why else this strength
Miraculous yet remaining in those locks?
His might continues in thee not for naught,
Nor shall His wondrous gifts be frustrate thus.
   Sams. All otherwise to me my thoughts portend—   590
That these dark orbs no more shall treat with light,

Nor the other light of life continue long,
But yield to double darkness nigh at hand;
So much I feel my genial spirits droop,
My hopes all flat: Nature within me seems
In all her functions weary of herself;
My race of glory run, and race of shame,[11]
And I shall shortly be with them that rest.

    Man. Believe not these suggestions, which proceed
From anguish of the mind, and humors black   600
That mingle with thy fancy. I, however,
Must not omit a father's timely care
To prosecute the means of thy deliverance
By ransom or how else: meanwhile be calm,
And healing words from these thy friends admit.

    Sams. Oh, that torment should not be confined
To the body's wounds and sores,
With maladies innumerable
In heart, head, breast, and reins,
But must secret passage find   610
To the inmost mind,
There exercise all his fierce accidents,
And on her purest spirits prey,
As on entrails, joints, and limbs,
With answerable pains, but more intense,
Though void of corporal sense!

    My griefs not only pain me
As a lingering disease,
But, finding no redress, ferment and rage;
Nor less than wounds immedicable   620
Rankle, and fester, and gangrene,
To black mortification.
Thoughts, my tormentors, armed with deadly stings,
Mangle my apprehensive tenderest parts,
Exasperate, exulcerate, and raise
Dire inflammation, which no cooling herb

---

[11] This line and the following form one of the finest examples of the power of the simple style.

Or medicinal liquor can assuage,
Nor breath of vernal air from snowy Alp.
Sleep hath forsook and given me o'er
To death's benumbing opium as my only cure;   630
Thence faintings, swoonings of despair,
And sense of heaven's desertion.
    I was His nursling once and choice delight,
His destined from the womb,
Promised by heavenly message twice descending.
Under His special eye
Abstemious I grew up and thrived amain;
He led me on to mightiest deeds,
Above the nerve of mortal arm,
Against the Uncircumcised, our enemies: 640
But now hath cast me off as never known,
And to those cruel enemies,
Whom I by His appointment had provoked,
Left me all helpless, with the irreparable loss
Of sight, reserved alive to be repeated
The subject of their cruelty or scorn.
Nor am I in the list of them that hope;
Hopeless are all my evils, all remediless.
This one prayer yet remains, might I be heard,
No long petition—speedy death,   650
The close of all my miseries and the balm.
    Chor. Many are the sayings of the wise,
In ancient and in modern books enrolled,
Extolling patience as the truest fortitude,
And to the bearing well of all calamities,
All chances incident to man's frail life,
Consolatories writ
With studied argument, and much persuasion sought,
Lenient of grief and anxious thought.
But with the afflicted in his pangs their sound   660
Little prevails, or rather seems a tune
Harsh, and of dissonant mood from his complaint,
Unless he feel within

Some source of consolation from above,
Secret refreshings that repair his strength
And fainting spirits uphold.

   God of our fathers! what is man,
That Thou towards him with hand so various—
Or might I say contrarious?—
Temper'st Thy providence through his short course: 67
Not evenly, as Thou rul'st
The angelic orders, and inferior creatures mute,
Irrational and brute?
Nor do I name of men the common rout,
That, wandering loose about,
Grow up and perish as the summer fly,
Heads without name, no more remembered;
But such as Thou hast solemnly elected,
With gifts and graces eminently adorned,
To some great work, Thy glory,   68
And people's safety, which in part they effect.
Yet toward these, thus dignified, Thou oft,
Amidst their height of noon,
Changest Thy countenance and Thy hand, with no regard
Of highest favors past
From Thee on them, or them to Thee of service.

   Nor only dost degrade them, or remit
To life obscured, which were a fair dismission,
But throw'st them lower than Thou didst exalt them high—
Unseemly falls in human eye,   69
Too grievous for the trespass or omission;
Oft leav'st them to the hostile sword
Of heathen and profane, their carcasses
To dogs and fowls a prey, or else captived,
Or to the unjust tribunals, under change of times,
And condemnation of the ungrateful multitude.
If these they 'scape, perhaps in poverty
With sickness and disease Thou bow'st them down,
Painful diseases and deformed,
In crude old age;   700

Though not disordinate, yet causeless suffering
The punishment of dissolute days. In fine,
Just or unjust alike seem miserable,
For oft alike both come to evil end.

　So deal not with this once Thy glorious champion,
The image of Thy strength, and mighty minister.
What do I beg? how hast Thou dealt already!
Behold him in this state calamitous and turn
His labors, for Thou canst, to peaceful end.

　But who is this? what thing of sea or land—　　　710
Female of sex it seems—
That, so bedecked, ornate, and gay,
Comes this way sailing,
Like a stately ship
Of Tarsus, bound for the isles
Of Javan or Gadire,
With all her bravery on, and tackle trim,
Sails filled, and streamers waving,
Courted by all the winds that hold them play;
An amber scent of odorous perfume　　　　　720
Her harbinger, a damsel train behind?
Some rich Philistian matron she may seem;
And now, at nearer view, no other certain
Than Dalila thy wife.

　　Sams. My wife! my traitress! let her not come near me.
　　Chor. Yet on she moves; now stands and eyes thee fixed,
About to have spoke; but now, with head declined,
Like a fair flower surcharged with dew, she weeps,
And words addressed seem into tears dissolved,
Wetting the borders of her silken veil.　　　　730
But now again she makes address to speak.

　　Dal. With doubtful feet and wavering resolution
I came, still dreading thy displeasure, Samson;
Which to have merited, without excuse,
I cannot but acknowledge. Yet, if tears
May expiate (though the fact more evil drew
In the perverse event than I foresaw),

My penance hath not slackened, though my pardon
No way assured. But conjugal affection,
Prevailing over fear and timorous doubt,   740
Hath led me on, desirous to behold
Once more thy face, and know of thy estate,
If aught in my ability may serve
To lighten what thou suffer'st, and appease
Thy mind with what amends is in my power—
Though late, yet in some part to recompense
My rash but more unfortunate misdeed.

   Sams. Out, out, hyena! These are thy wonted arts,
And arts of every woman false like thee—
To break all faith, all vows, deceive, betray;   750
Then, as repentant, to submit, beseech,
And reconcilement move with feigned remorse,
Confess, and promise wonders in her change—
Not truly penitent, but chief to try
Her husband, how far urged his patience bears,
His virtue or weakness which way to assail:
Then, with more cautious and instructed skill,
Again transgresses, and again submits;
That wisest and best men, full oft beguiled,
With goodness principled not to reject   760
The penitent, but ever to forgive,
Are drawn to wear out miserable days,
Entangled with a poisonous bosom-snake,
If not by quick destruction soon cut off,
As I by thee, to ages an example.

   Dal. Yet hear me, Samson; not that I endeavor
To lessen or extenuate my offense,
But that, on the other side, if it be weighed
By itself, with aggravations not surcharged,
Or else with just allowance counterpoised,   770
I may, if possible, thy pardon find
The easier toward me, or thy hatred less.
First granting, as I do, it was a weakness
In me, but incident to all our sex,

Curiosity, inquisitive, importune
Of secrets, then with like infirmity
To publish them—both common female faults—
Was it not weakness also to make known
For importunity, that is for naught,
Wherein consisted all thy strength and safety?   780
To what I did thou show'dst me first the way.
But I to enemies revealed, and should not!
Nor should'st thou have trusted that to woman's frailty:
Ere I to thee, thou to thyself wast cruel.
Let weakness, then, with weakness come to parle,
So near related, or the same of kind;
Thine forgive mine, that men may censure thine
The gentler, if severely thou exact not
More strength from me than in thyself was found.
And what if love, which thou interpret'st hate,   790
The jealousy of love, powerful of sway
In human hearts, nor less in mine towards thee,
Caused what I did? I saw thee mutable
Of fancy; feared lest one day thou would'st leave me
As her at Timna; sought by all means, therefore,
How to endear, and hold thee to me firmest:
No better way I saw than by importuning
To learn thy secrets, get into my power
Thy key of strength and safety. Thou wilt say,
"Why, then, revealed?" I was assured by those   800
Who tempted me that nothing was designed
Against thee but safe custody and hold.
That made for me; I knew that liberty
Would draw thee forth to perilous enterprises,
While I at home sat full of cares and fears,
Wailing thy absence in my widowed bed;
Here I should still enjoy thee, day and night,
Mine and love's prisoner, not the Philistines',
Whole to myself, unhazarded abroad,
Fearless at home of partners in my love.   810
These reasons in love's law have passed for good,

Though fond and reasonless to some perhaps;
And love hath oft, well meaning, wrought much woe,
Yet always pity or pardon hath obtained.
Be not unlike all others, not austere
As thou art strong, inflexible as steel.
If thou in strength all mortals dost exceed,
In uncompassionate anger do not so.

 Sams. How cunningly the sorceress displays
Her own transgressions, to upbraid me mine!   820
That malice, not repentance, brought thee hither
By this appears. I gave, thou say'st, the example,
I led the way—bitter reproach, but true;
I to myself was false ere thou to me.
Such pardon, therefore, as I give my folly
Take to thy wicked deed; which when thou seest
Impartial, self-severe, inexorable,
Thou wilt renounce thy seeking, and much rather
Confess it feigned. Weakness is thy excuse,
And I believe it—weakness to resist   830
Philistian gold. If weakness may excuse,
What murderer, what traitor, parricide,
Incestuous, sacrilegious, but may plead it?
All wickedness is weakness; that plea, therefore,
With God or man will gain thee no remission.
But love constrained thee! Call it furious rage
To satisfy thy lust. Love seeks to have love;
My love how couldst thou hope, who took'st the way
To raise in me inexpiable hate,
Knowing, as needs I must, by thee betrayed?   840
In vain thou striv'st to cover shame with shame,
Or by evasions thy crime uncover'st more.

 Dal. Since thou determin'st weakness for no plea
In man or woman, though to thy own condemning,
Hear what assaults I had, what snares besides,
What sieges girt me round, ere I consented;
Which might have awed the best-resolved of men,
The constantest, to have yielded without blame.

It was not gold, as to my charge thou lay'st,
That wrought with me. Thou know'st the magistrates   850
And princes of my country came in person,
Solicited, commanded, threatened, urged,
Adjured by all the bonds of civil duty
And of religion—pressed how just it was,
How honorable, how glorious, to entrap
A common enemy, who had destroyed
Such numbers of our nation: and the priest
Was not behind, but ever at my ear,
Preaching how meritorious with the gods
It would be to ensnare an irreligious   860
Dishonorer of Dagon. What had I
To oppose against such powerful arguments?
Only my love of thee held long debate,
And combated in silence all these reasons
With hard contest. At length, that grounded maxim,
So rife and celebrated in the mouths
Of wisest men, that to the public good
Private respects must yield, with grave authority
Took full possession of me and prevailed;
Virtue, as I thought, truth, duty, so enjoining.   870
     Sams. I thought where all thy circling wiles would end—
In feigned religion, smooth hypocrisy!
But, had thy love, still odiously pretended,
Been, as it ought, sincere, it would have taught thee
Far other reasonings, brought forth other deeds.
I, before all the daughters of my tribe
And of my nation, chose thee from among
My enemies, loved thee, as too well thou knew'st;
Too well; unbosomed all my secrets to thee,
Not out of levity, but overpowered   880
By thy request, who could deny thee nothing;
Yet now am judged an enemy. Why, then,
Didst thou at first receive me for thy husband—
Then, as since then, thy country's foe professed?
Being once a wife, for me thou wast to leave

Parents and country; nor was I their subject,
Nor under their protection, but my own;
Thou mine, not theirs. If aught against my life
Thy country sought of thee, it sought unjustly,
Against the law of nature, law of nations;   890
No more thy country, but an impious crew
Of men conspiring to uphold their state
By worse than hostile deeds, violating the ends
For which our country is a name so dear;
Not therefore to be obeyed. But zeal moved thee;
To please thy gods thou didst it! Gods unable
To acquit themselves and prosecute their foes
But by ungodly deeds, the contradiction
Of their own deity, gods cannot be—
Less therefore to be pleased, obeyed, or feared.   900
These false pretexts and varnished colors failing,
Bare in thy guilt, how foul must thou appear!

   Dal. In argument with men a woman ever
Goes by the worse, whatever be her cause.

   Sams. For want of words, no doubt, or lack of breath!
Witness when I was worried with thy peals.

   Dal. I was a fool, too rash, and quite mistaken
In what I thought would have succeeded best.
Let me obtain forgiveness of thee, Samson;
Afford me place to show what recompense   910
Toward thee I intend for what I have misdone,
Misguided. Only what remains past cure
Bear not too sensibly, nor still insist
To afflict thyself in vain. Though sight be lost,
Life yet hath many solaces, enjoyed
Where other senses want not their delights—
At home, in leisure and domestic ease,
Exempt from many a care and chance to which
Eyesight exposes, daily, men abroad.
I to the lords will intercede, not doubting   920
Their favorable ear, that I may fetch thee
From forth this loathsome prison-house, to abide

With me, where my redoubled love and care,
With nursing diligence, to me glad office,
May ever tend about thee to old age,
With all things grateful cheered, and so supplied
That what by me thou hast lost thou least shalt miss.

    Sams. No, no; of my condition take no care;
It fits not; thou and I long since are twain;
Nor think me so unwary or accursed   930
To bring my feet again into the snare
Where once I have been caught. I know thy trains,
Though dearly to my cost, thy gins, and toils.
Thy fair enchanted cup and warbling charms,
No more on me have power; their force is nulled;
So much of adder's wisdom I have learned,
To fence my ear against thy sorceries.
If in my flower of youth and strength, when all men
Loved, honored, feared me, thou alone could hate me,
Thy husband, slight me, sell me, and forgo me,   940
How wouldst thou use me now, blind, and thereby
Deceivable, in most things as a child
Helpless, thence easily contemned and scorned,
And last neglected! How wouldst thou insult,
When I must live uxorious to thy will
In perfect thraldom! how again betray me,
Bearing my words and doings to the lords
To gloss upon, and, censuring, frown or smile!
This jail I count the house of liberty
To thine, whose doors my feet shall never enter.   950

    Dal. Let me approach at least, and touch thy hand.

    Sams. Not for thy life, lest fierce remembrance wake
My sudden rage to tear thee joint by joint.
At distance I forgive thee; go with that;
Bewail thy falsehood, and the pious works
It hath brought forth to make thee memorable
Among illustrious women, faithful wives;
Cherish thy hastened widowhood with the gold
Of matrimonial treason: so farewell.

Dal. I see thou art implacable, more deaf 96
To prayers than winds and seas. Yet winds to seas
Are reconciled at length, and sea to shore:
Thy anger, unappeasable, still rages,
Eternal tempest never to be calmed.
Why do I humble thus myself, and suing
For peace, reap nothing but repulse and hate,
Bid go with evil omen, and the brand
Of infamy upon my name denounced?
To mix with thy concernments I desist
Henceforth, nor too much disapprove my own. 97
Fame, if not double-faced, is double-mouthed,
And with contrary blast proclaims most deeds;
On both his wings, one black, the other white,
Bears greatest names in his wild aery flight.
My name, perhaps, among the Circumcised
In Dan, in Judah, and the bordering tribes,
To all posterity may stand defamed,
With malediction mentioned, and the blot
Of falsehood most unconjugal traduced.
But in my country, where I most desire, 98
In Ecron, Gaza, Asdod, and in Gath,
I shall be named among the famousest
Of women, sung at solemn festivals,
Living and dead recorded, who, to save
Her country from a fierce destroyer, chose
Above the faith of wedlock bands; my tomb
With odors visited and annual flowers;
Not less renowned than in Mount Ephraim
Jael, who, with inhospitable guile,
Smote Sisera sleeping, through the temples nailed.[12] 99
Nor shall I count it heinous to enjoy
The public marks of honor and reward
Conferred upon me for the piety
Which to my country I was judged to have shown.
At this whoever envies or repines,

[12] See *Judges* 4:16–22.

I leave him to his lot, and like my own.

Chor. She's gone—a manifest serpent by her sting
Discovered in the end, till now concealed.

Sams. So let her go. God sent her to debase me,
And aggravate my folly, who committed   1000
To such a viper his most sacred trust
Of secrecy, my safety, and my life.

Chor. Yet beauty, though injurious, hath strange power,
After offense returning, to regain
Love once possessed, nor can be easily
Repulsed, without much inward passion felt,
And secret sting of amorous remorse.

Sams. Love-quarrels oft in pleasing concord end;
Not wedlock-treachery endangering life.

Chor. It is not virtue, wisdom, valor, wit,   1010
Strength, comeliness of shape, or amplest merit,
That woman's love can win, or long inherit;
But what it is, hard is to say,
Harder to hit,
Which way soever men refer it,
(Much like thy riddle, Samson) in one day
Or seven though one should musing sit.

If any of these, or all, the Timnian bride
Had not so soon preferred
Thy paranymph, worthless to thee compared,   1020
Successor in thy bed,
Nor both so loosely disallied
Their nuptials, nor this last so treacherously
Had shorn the fatal harvest of thy head.
Is it for that such outward ornament
Was lavished on their sex that inward gifts
Were left for haste unfinished, judgment scant,
Capacity not raised to apprehend
Or value what is best,
In choice, but oftest to affect the wrong?   1030
Or was too much of self-love mixed,
Of constancy no root infixed,

That either they love nothing, or not long?
  Whate'er it be, to wisest men and best,
Seeming at first all heavenly under virgin veil,
Soft, modest, meek, demure,
Once joined, the contrary she proves—a thorn
Intestine, far within defensive arms
A cleaving mischief, in his way to virtue
Adverse and turbulent; or by her charms   1040
Draws him awry, enslaved
With dotage, and his sense depraved
To folly and shameful deeds, which ruin ends.
What pilot so expert but needs must wreck,
Embarked with such a steers-mate at the helm?
  Favored of heaven who finds
One virtuous, rarely found,
That in domestic good combines!
Happy that house! his way to peace is smooth:
But virtue which breaks through all opposition,   1050
And all temptation can remove,
Most shines and most is acceptable above.
  Therefore God's universal law
Gave to the man despotic power
Over his female in due awe,
Nor from that right to part an hour,
Smile she or lour:
So shall he least confusion draw
On his whole life, not swayed
By female usurpation, nor dismayed.   1060
  But had we best retire? I see a storm.
  Sams. Fair days have oft contracted wind and rain.
  Chor. But this another kind of tempest brings.
  Sams. Be less abstruse; my riddling days are past.
  Chor. Look now for no enchanting voice, nor fear
The bait of honeyed words; a rougher tongue
Draws hitherward; I know him by his stride,
The giant Harapha of Gath, his look
Haughty, as is his pile high-built and proud.

Comes he in peace? What wind hath blown him hither   1070
I less conjecture than when first I saw
The sumptuous Dalila floating this way:
His habit carries peace, his brow defiance.
  Sams. Or peace or not, alike to me he comes.
  Chor. His fraught we soon shall know: he now arrives.
  Har. I come not, Samson, to condole thy chance,
At these perhaps, yet wish it had not been,
Though for no friendly intent. I am of Gath;
Men call me Harapha, of stock renowned
As Og, or Anak, and the Emims old   1080
That Kiriathaim held. Thou know'st me now,
If thou at all art known. Much I have heard
Of thy prodigious might and feats performed,
Incredible to me, in this displeased,
That I was never present on the place
Of those encounters, where we might have tried
Each other's force in camp or listed field;
And now am come to see of whom such noise
Hath walked about, and each limb to survey,
If thy appearance answer loud report.   1090
  Sams. The way to know were not to see, but taste.
  Har. Dost thou already single me? I thought
Gyves and the mill had tamed thee. O that fortune
Had brought me to the field where thou art famed
To have wrought such wonders with an ass's jaw!
I should have forced thee soon with other arms,
Or left thy carcass where the ass lay thrown;
So had the glory of prowess been recovered
To Palestine, won by a Philistine
From the unforeskinned race, of whom thou bear'st   1100
The highest name for valiant acts. That honor,
Certain to have won by mortal duel from thee,
I lose, prevented by thy eyes put out.
  Sams. Boast not of what thou wouldst have done, but do
What then thou wouldst; thou seest it in thy hand.
  Har. To combat with a blind man I disdain,

And thou hast need much washing to be touched.
   Sams. Such usage as your honorable lords
Afford me, assassinated and betrayed;
Who durst not with their whole united powers   1110
In fright withstand me single and unarmed,
Nor in the house with chamber-ambushes
Close-banded durst attack me, no, not sleeping,
Till they had hired a woman with their gold,
Breaking her marriage-faith, to circumvent me.
Therefore, without feigned shifts, let be assigned
Some narrow place enclosed, where sight may give thee,
Or rather flight, no great advantage on me;
Then put on all thy gorgeous arms, thy helmet
And brigandine of brass, thy broad habergeon,   1120
Vant-brace and greaves and gauntlet; add thy spear,
A weaver's beam, and seven-times-folded shield:
I only with an oaken staff will meet thee,
And raise such outcries on thy clattered iron,
Which long shall not withhold me from thy head,
That in a little time, while breath remains thee,
Thou oft shalt wish thyself at Gath, to boast
Again in safety what thou wouldst have done
To Samson, but shalt never see Gath more.
   Har. Thou durst not thus disparage glorious arms   1130
Which greatest heroes have in battle worn,
Their ornament and safety, had not spells
And black enchantments, some magician's art,
Armed thee or charmed thee strong, which thou from heaven
Feign'dst at thy birth was given thee in thy hair,
Where strength can least abide, though all thy hairs
Were bristles ranged like those that ridge the back
Of chafed wild boars or ruffled porcupines.
   Sams. I know no spells, use no forbidden arts;
My trust is in the Living God, Who gave me,   1140
At my nativity, this strength, diffused
No less through all my sinews, joints, and bones,
Than thine, while I preserved these locks unshorn,

The pledge of my unviolated vow.
For proof hereof, if Dagon be thy god,
Go to his temple, invocate his aid
With solemnest devotion, spread before him
How highly it concerns his glory now
To frustrate and dissolve these magic spells,
Which I to be the power of Israel's God   1150
Avow, and challenge Dagon to the test,
Offering to combat thee, his champion bold,
With the utmost of his godhead seconded:
Then thou shalt see, or rather to thy sorrow
Soon feel, whose God is strongest, thine or mine.
    Har. Presume not on thy God. Whate'er He be,
Thee He regards not, owns not, hath cut off
Quite from His people, and delivered up
Into thy enemies' hand; permitted them
To put out both thine eyes, and fettered send thee   1160
Into the common prison, there to grind
Among the slaves and asses, thy comrades,
As good for nothing else, no better service
With those thy boisterous locks; no worthy match
For valor to assail, nor by the sword
Of noble warrior, so to stain his honor,
But by the barber's razor best subdued.
    Sams. All these indignities, for such they are
From thine, these evils I deserve and more,
Acknowledge them from God inflicted on me   1170
Justly, yet despair not of his final pardon,
Whose ear is ever open, and his eye
Gracious to readmit the suppliant;
In confidence whereof I once again
Defy thee to the trial of mortal fight,
By combat to decide whose god is God,
Thine, or whom I with Israel's sons adore.
    Har. Fair honor that thou dost thy God, in trusting
He will accept thee to defend His cause,
A murderer, a revolter, and a robber!   1180

Sams. Tongue-doughty giant, how dost thou prove me
    these?
    Har. Is not thy nation subject to our lords?
Their magistrates confessed it when they took thee
As a league-breaker, and delivered bound
Into our hands; for hadst thou not committed
Notorious murder on those thirty men
At Ascalon, who never did thee harm,
Then, like a robber, stripp'dst them of their robes?
The Philistines, when thou hadst broke the league,
Went up with armed powers thee only seeking,   1190
To others did no violence nor spoil.
    Sams. Among the daughters of the Philistines
I chose a wife, which argued me no foe,
And in your city held my nuptial feast;
But your ill-meaning politician lords,
Under pretense of bridal friends and guests,
Appointed to await me thirty spies,
Who, threatening cruel death, constrained the bride
To wring from me, and tell to them, my secret,
That solved the riddle which I had proposed.   1200
When I perceived all set on enmity,
As on my enemies, wherever chanced,
I used hostility, and took their spoil,
To pay my underminers in their coin.
My nation was subjected to your lords!
It was the force of conquest; force with force
Is well ejected when the conquered can.
But I, a private person, whom my country
As a league-breaker gave up bound, presumed
Single rebellion, and did hostile acts!   1210
I was no private, but a person raised,
With strength sufficient, and command from heaven,
To free my country. If their servile minds
Me, their deliverer sent, would not receive,
But to their masters gave me up for nought,
The unworthier they; whence to this day they serve.

Ⅱ was to do my part from heaven assigned,
And had performed it if my known offense
Had not disabled me, not all your force.
These shifts refuted, answer thy appellant, 1220
Though by his blindness maimed for high attempts,
Who now defies thee thrice to single fight,
As a petty enterprise of small enforce.

Har. With thee, a man condemned, a slave enrolled,
Due by the law to capital punishment?
To fight with thee no man of arms will deign.

Sams. Cam'st thou for this, vain boaster, to survey me,
To descant on my strength, and give thy verdict!
Come nearer; part not hence so slight informed;
But take good heed my hand survey not thee. 1230

Har. O Baal-zebub! can my ears unused
Hear these dishonors, and not render death?

Sams. No man withholds thee; nothing from thy hand
Fear I incurable; bring up thy van;
My heels are fettered, but my fist is free.

Har. This insolence other kind of answer fits.

Sams. Go, baffled coward, lest I run upon thee,
Though in these chains, bulk without spirit vast,
And with one buffet lay thy structure low,
Or swing thee in the air, then dash thee down, 1240
To the hazard of thy brains and shattered sides.

Har. By Astaroth, ere long thou shalt lament
These braveries, in irons loaden on thee.

Chor. His giantship is gone somewhat crest-fallen,
Stalking with less unconscionable strides,
And lower looks, but in a sultry chafe.

Sams. I dread him not, nor all his giant brood,
Though fame divulge him father of five sons,
All of gigantic size, Goliah chief.

Chor. He will directly to the lords, I fear, 1250
And with malicious counsel stir them up
Some way or other yet further to afflict thee.

Sams. He must allege some cause, and offered fight

Will not dare mention, lest a question rise
Whether he durst accept the offer or not;
And that he durst not plain enough appeared.
Much more affliction than already felt
They cannot well impose, nor I sustain,
If they intend advantage of my labors,
The work of many hands, which earns my keeping,   126
With no small profit daily to my owners.
But come what will; my deadliest foe will prove
My speediest friend, by death to rid me hence;
The worst that he can give to me the best
Yet so it may fall out, because their end
Is hate, not help to me, it may with mine
Draw their own ruin who attempt the deed.

   Chor. O, how comely it is, and how reviving
To the spirits of just men long oppressed,
When God into the hands of their deliverer   127
Puts invincible might,
To quell the mighty of the earth, the oppressor,
The brute and boisterous force of violent men,
Hardy and industrious to support
Tyrannic power, but raging to pursue
The righteous, and all such as honor truth!
He all their ammunition
And feats of war defeats,
With plain heroic magnitude of mind
And celestial vigor armed;   128
Their armories and magazines contemns,
Renders them useless, while
With winged expedition
Swift as the lightning glance he executes
His errand on the wicked, who, surprised,
Lose their defense, distracted and amazed.

   But patience is more oft the exercise
Of saints, the trial of their fortitude,
Making them each his own deliverer,
And victor over all   129

That tyranny or fortune can inflict.
Either of these is in thy lot,
Samson, with might endued
Above the sons of men; but sight bereaved
May chance to number thee with those
Whom patience finally must crown.
 This Idol's day hath been to thee no day of rest,
Laboring thy mind
More than the working day thy hands.
And yet, perhaps, more trouble is behind; 1300
For I descry this way
Some other tending; in his hand
A sceptre or quaint staff he bears,
Comes on amain, speed in his look.
By his habit I discern him now
A public officer, and now at hand.
His message will be short and voluble.
 Off. Ebrews, the prisoner Samson here I seek.
 Chor. His manacles remark him; there he sits.
 Off. Samson, to thee our lords thus bid me say: 1310
This day to Dagon is a solemn feast,
With sacrifices, triumph, pomp, and games;
Thy strength they know surpassing human rate,
And now some public proof thereof require
To honor this great feast and great assembly.
Rise, therefore, with all speed, and come along,
Where I will see thee heartened and fresh clad,
To appear as fits before the illustrious lords.
 Sams. Thou know'st I am an Ebrew; therefore tell them
Our law forbids at their religious rites 1320
My presence; for that cause I cannot come.
 Off. This answer, be assured, will not content them.
 Sams. Have they not sword-players, and every sort
Of gymnic artists, wrestlers, riders, runners,
Jugglers and dancers, antics, mummers, mimics,
But they must pick me out, with shackles tired,
And over-labored at their public mill,

To make them sport with blind activity?
Do they not seek occasion of new quarrels,
On my refusal, to distress me more,   1330
Or make a game of my calamities?
Return the way thou cam'st; I will not come.
    Off. Regard thyself; this will offend them highly.
    Sams. Myself! my conscience, and internal peace.
Can they think me so broken, so debased
With corporal servitude, that my mind ever
Will condescend to such absurd commands?
Although their drudge, to be their fool or jester,
And, in my midst of sorrow and heart-grief,
To show them feats, and play before their god—   1340
The worst of all indignities, yet on me
Joined with extreme contempt! I will not come.
    Off. My message was imposed on me with speed,
Brooks no delay: is this thy resolution?
    Sams. So take it with what speed thy message needs.
    Off. I am sorry what this stoutness will produce.
    Sams. Perhaps thou shalt have cause to sorrow indeed.
    Chor. Consider, Samson; matters now are strained
Up to the height, whether to hold or break.
He's gone, and who knows how he may report   1350
Thy words by adding fuel to the flame?
Expect another message, more imperious,
More lordly thundering than thou well wilt bear.
    Sams. Shall I abuse this consecrated gift
Of strength, again returning with my hair
After my great transgression—so requite
Favor renewed, and add a greater sin
By prostituting holy things to idols,
A Nazarite, in place abominable,
Vaunting my strength in honor to their Dagon?   1360
Besides how vile, contemptible, ridiculous,
What act more execrably unclean, profane?
    Chor. Yet with this strength thou serv'st the Philistines,
Idolatrous, uncircumcised, unclean.

Sams. Not in their idol-worship, but by labor
Honest and lawful to deserve my food
Of those who have me in their civil power.

   Chor. Where the heart joins not, outward acts defile not.

   Sams. Where outward force constrains, the sentence holds:
But who constrains me to the temple of Dagon,   1370
Not dragging? The Philistian lords command:
Commands are no constraints. If I obey them,
I do it freely, venturing to displease
God for the fear of man, and man prefer,
Set God behind; which, in His jealousy,
Shall never, unrepented, find forgiveness.
Yet that He may dispense with me, or thee,
Present in temples at idolatrous rites
For some important cause, thou need'st not doubt.

   Chor. How thou wilt here come off surmounts my
          reach.   1380

   Sams. Be of good courage; I begin to feel
Some rousing motions in me, which dispose
To something extraordinary my thoughts.
I with this messenger will go along—
Nothing to do, be sure, that may dishonor
Our law, or stain my vow of Nazarite.
If there be aught of presage in the mind,
This day will be remarkable in my life
By some great act, or of my days the last.

   Chor. In time thou hast resolved: the man returns.   1390

   Off. Samson, this second message from our lords
To thee I am bid say: Art thou our slave,
Our captive, at the public mill our drudge,
And dar'st thou, at our sending and command,
Dispute thy coming? Come without delay;
Or we shall find such engines to assail
And hamper thee, as thou shalt come of force,
Though thou wert firmlier fastened than a rock.

   Sams. I could be well content to try their art,
Which to no few of them would prove pernicious;   1400

Yet, knowing their advantages too many,
Because they shall not trail me through their streets
Like a wild beast, I am content to go.
Masters' commands come with a power resistless
To such as owe them absolute subjection;
And for a life who will not change his purpose?
(So mutable are all the ways of men!)
Yet this be sure, in nothing to comply
Scandalous or forbidden in our law.

    Off. I praise thy resolution. Doff these links: 1410
By this compliance thou wilt win the lords
To favor, and perhaps to set thee free.

    Sams. Brethren, farewell. Your company along
I will not wish, lest it perhaps offend them
To see me girt with friends; and how the sight
Of me, as of a common enemy,
So dreaded once, may now exasperate them
I know not. Lords are lordliest in their wine;
And the well-feasted priest then soonest fired
With zeal, if aught religion seem concerned;   1420
No less the people, on their holy-days,
Impetuous, insolent, unquenchable.
Happen what may, of me expect to hear
Nothing dishonorable, impure, unworthy
Our God, our law, my nation, or myself;
The last of me or no I cannot warrant.

    Chor. Go, and the Holy One
Of Israel be thy guide
To what may serve His glory best, and spread His name
Great among the heathen round;   1430
Send thee the angel of thy birth, to stand
Fast by thy side, who from thy father's field
Rode up in flames after his message told
Of thy conception, and be now a shield
Of fire; that spirit that first rushed on thee
In the camp of Dan,
Be efficacious in thee now at need!

For never was from heaven imparted
Measure of strength so great to mortal seed,
As in thy wondrous actions hath been seen.   1440
But wherefore comes old Manoa in such haste
With youthful steps? Much livelier than erewhile
He seems: supposing here to find his son,
Or of him bringing to us some glad news?
  Man. Peace with you, brethren! My inducement hither
Was not at present here to find my son,
By order of the lords new parted hence
To come and play before them at their feast.
I heard all as I came; the city rings,
And numbers thither flock: I had no will,   1450
Lest I should see him forced to things unseemly.
But that which moved my coming now was chiefly
To give ye part with me what hope I have
With good success to work his liberty.
  Chor. That hope would much rejoice us to partake
With thee. Say, reverend sire; we thirst to hear.
  Man. I have attempted, one by one, the lords,
Either at home, or through the high street passing,
With supplication prone and father's tears,
To accept of ransom for my son, their prisoner.   1460
Some much averse I found, and wondrous harsh,
Contemptuous, proud, set on revenge and spite;
That part most reverenced Dagon and his priests:
Others more moderate seeming, but their aim
Private reward, for which both God and State
They easily would set to sale: a third
More generous far and civil, who confessed
They had enough revenged, having reduced
Their foe to misery beneath their fears;
The rest was magnanimity to remit,   1470
If some convenient ransom were proposed.
What noise or shout was that? It tore the sky.
  Chor. Doubtless the people shouting to behold
Their once great dread, captive and blind before them,

Or at some proof of strength before them shown.

Man. His ransom, if my whole inheritance
May compass it, shall willingly be paid
And numbered down. Much rather I shall choose
To live the poorest in my tribe, than richest
And he in that calamitous prison left.　　　　　　　　　1480
No, I am fixed not to part hence without him.
For his redemption all my patrimony,
If need be, I am ready to forgo
And quit. Not wanting him, I shall want nothing.

Chor. Fathers are wont to lay up for their sons;
Thou for thy son art bent to lay out all:
Sons wont to nurse their parents in old age;
Thou in old age car'st how to nurse thy son,
Made older than thy age through eye-sight lost.

Man. It shall be my delight to tend his eyes,　　　　　1490
And view him sitting in his house, ennobled
With all those high exploits by him achieved,
And on his shoulders waving down those locks
That of a nation armed the strength contained.
And I persuade me God hath not permitted
His strength again to grow up with his hair
Garrisoned round about him like a camp
Of faithful soldiery, were not his purpose
To use him further yet in some great service—
Not to sit idle with so great a gift　　　　　　　　　　1500
Useless, and thence ridiculous, about him.
And, since his strength with eye-sight was not lost,
God will restore him eye-sight to his strength.

Chor. Thy hopes are not ill founded, nor seem vain,
Of his delivery, and thy joy thereon
Conceived, agreeable to a father's love;
In both which we, as next, participate.

Man. I know your friendly minds, and—O, what noise!
Mercy of heaven! what hideous noise was that?
Horribly loud, unlike the former shout.　　　　　　　1510

Chor. Noise call you it, or universal groan,

As if the whole inhabitation perished?
Blood, death, and deathful deeds are in that noise,
Ruin, destruction at the utmost point.
   Man. Of ruin indeed methought I heard the noise.
Oh! it continues; they have slain my son.
   Chor. Thy son is rather slaying them: that outcry
From slaughter of one foe could not ascend.
   Man. Some dismal accident it needs must be.
What shall we do—stay here, or run and see?   1520
   Chor. Best keep together here, lest, running thither,
We unawares run into danger's mouth.
This evil on the Philistines is fallen:
From whom could else a general cry be heard?
The sufferers, then, will scarce molest us here;
From other hands we need not much to fear.
What if, his eye-sight (for to Israel's God
Nothing is hard) by miracle restored,
He now be dealing dole among his foes,
And over heaps of slaughtered walk his way?   1530
   Man. That were a joy presumptuous to be thought.
   Chor. Yet God hath wrought things as incredible
For His people of old; what hinders now?
   Man. He can, I know, but doubt to think He will;
Yet hope would fain subscribe, and tempts belief.
A little stay will bring some notice hither.
   Chor. Of good or bad so great, of bad the sooner;
For evil news rides post, while good news baits.
And to our wish I see one hither speeding—
An Ebrew, as I guess, and of our tribe.   1540
   Messenger. O, whither shall I run, or which way fly
The sight of this so horrid spectacle,
Which erst my eyes beheld, and yet behold?
For dire imagination still pursues me.
But providence or instinct of nature seems,
Or reason, though disturbed and scarce consulted,
To have guided me aright, I know not how,
To thee first, reverend Manoa, and to these

My countrymen, whom here I knew remaining,
As at some distance from the place of horror,   1550
So in the sad event too much concerned.
 Man. The accident was loud, and here before thee
With rueful cry; yet what it was we hear not.
No preface needs; thou seest we long to know.
 Mess. It would burst forth; but I recover breath,
And sense distract, to know well what I utter.
 Man. Tell us the sum; the circumstance defer.
 Mess. Gaza yet stands; but all her sons are fallen,
All in a moment overwhelmed and fallen.
 Man. Sad! but thou know'st to Israelites not saddest   1560
The desolation of a hostile city.
 Mess. Feed on that first; there may in grief be surfeit.
 Man. Relate by whom.
 Mess.   By Samson.
 Man.   That still lessens
The sorrow and converts it nigh to joy.
 Mess. Ah! Manoa, I refrain too suddenly
To utter what will come at last too soon,
Lest evil tidings, with too rude irruption
Hitting thy aged ear, should pierce too deep.
 Man. Suspense in news is torture; speak them out.
 Mess. Then take the worst in brief: Samson is dead.   1570
 Man. The worst indeed! O all my hope's defeated
To free him hence! but Death, who sets all free,
Hath paid his ransom now and full discharge.
What windy joy this day had I conceived,
Hopeful of his delivery, which now proves
Abortive as the first-born bloom of spring
Nipped with the lagging rear of winter's frost!
Yet, ere I give the reins to grief, say first
How died he; death to life is crown or shame.
All by him fell, thou say'st; by whom fell he?   1580
What glorious hand gave Samson his death's wound?
 Mess. Unwounded of his enemies he fell.
 Man. Wearied with slaughter, then, or how? explain.

Mess. By his own hands.

Man.   Self-violence! What cause
Brought him so soon at variance with himself
Among his foes?

Mess.   Inevitable cause—
At once both to destroy and be destroyed.
The edifice, where all were met to see him,
Upon their heads and on his own he pulled.

Man. O lastly over-strong against thyself!   1590
A dreadful way thou took'st to thy revenge.
More than enough we know; but, while things yet
Are in confusion, give us, if thou canst,
Eye-witness of what first or last was done,
Relation more particular and distinct.

Mess. Occasions drew me early to this city;
And, as the gates I entered with sunrise,
The morning trumpets festival proclaimed
Through each high street. Little I had dispatched,
When all abroad was rumored that this day   1600
Samson should be brought forth, to show the people
Proof of his mighty strength in feats and games.
I sorrowed at his captive state, but minded
Not to be absent at that spectacle.
The building was a spacious theatre,
Half round on two main pillars vaulted high,
With seats where all the lords, and each degree
Of sort, might sit in order to behold;
The other side was open, where the throng
On banks and scaffolds under sky might stand: 1610
I among these aloof obscurely stood.
The feast and noon grew high, and sacrifice
Had filled their hearts with mirth, high cheer, and wine,
When to their sports they turned. Immediately
Was Samson as a public servant brought,
In their state livery clad: before him pipes
And timbrels; on each side went armed guards;
Both horse and foot before him and behind,

Archers and slingers, cataphracts, and spears.
At sight of him the people with a shout   1620
Rifted the air, clamoring their god with praise,
Who had made their dreadful enemy their thrall.
He patient, but undaunted, where they led him,
Came to the place; and what was set before him,
Which without help of eye might be assayed,
To heave, pull, draw, or break, he still performed
All with incredible, stupendious force,
None daring to appear antagonist.
At length, for intermission sake, they led him
Between the pillars; he his guide requested   1630
(For so from such as nearer stood we heard),
As over-tired, to let him lean a while
With both his arms on those two massy pillars,
That to the arched roof gave main support.
He unsuspicious led him; which when Samson
Felt in his arms, with head a while inclined,
And eyes fast fixed, he stood, as one who prayed,
Or some great matter in his mind revolved:
At last, with head erect, thus cried aloud:—
"Hitherto, lords, what your commands imposed   1640
I have performed, as reason was, obeying,
Not without wonder or delight beheld;
Now, of my own accord, such other trial
I mean to show you of my strength yet greater
As with amaze shall strike all who behold."
This uttered, straining all his nerves, he bowed;
As with the force of winds and waters pent
When mountains tremble, those two massy pillars
With horrible convulsion to and fro
He tugged, he shook, till down they came, and drew   1650
The whole roof after them with burst of thunder
Upon the heads of all who sat beneath,
Lords, ladies, captains, counsellors, or priests,
Their choice nobility and flower, not only
Of this, but each Philistian city round,

Met from all parts to solemnize this feast.
Samson, with these immixed, inevitably
Pulled down the same destruction on himself;
The vulgar only 'scaped, who stood without,
   Chor. O dearly bought revenge, yet glorious!   1660
Living or dying thou hast fulfilled
The work for which thou wast foretold
To Israel, and now liest victorious
Among thy slain self-killed;
Not willingly, but tangled in the fold
Of dire necessity, whose law in death conjoined
Thee with thy slaughtered foes, in number more
Than all thy life had slain before.
   Semichor. While their hearts were jocund and sublime,
Drunk with idolatry, drunk with wine   1670
And fat regorged of bulls and goats,
Chanting their idol, and preferring
Before our living Dread, Who dwells
In Silo, His bright sanctuary,
Among them He a spirit of frenzy sent,
Who hurt their minds,
And urged them on with mad desire
To call in haste for their destroyer.
They, only set on sport and play,
Unweetingly importuned   1680
Their own destruction to come speedy upon them.
So fond are mortal men,
Fallen into wrath divine,
As their own ruin on themselves to invite,
Insensate left, or to sense reprobate,
And with blindness internal struck.
   Semichor. But he, though blind of sight,
Despised, and thought extinguished quite,
With inward eyes illuminated,
His fiery virtue roused   1690
From under ashes into sudden flame,
And as an evening dragon came,

Assailant on the perched roosts
And nests in order ranged
Of tame villatic fowl, but as an eagle
His cloudless thunder bolted on their heads.
So virtue, given for lost,
Depressed and overthrown, as seemed,
Like that self-begotten bird [13]
In the Arabian woods embossed,   1700
That no second knows nor third,
And lay erewhile a holocaust,
From out her ashy womb now teemed,
Revives, reflourishes, then vigorous most
When most unactive deemed;
And, though her body die, her fame survives,
A secular bird, ages of lives.

   Man. Come, come; no time for lamentation now,
Nor much more cause. Samson hath quit himself
Like Samson, and heroicly hath finished   1710
A life heroic, on his enemies
Fully revenged—hath left them years of mourning,
And lamentation to the sons of Caphtor
Through all Philistian bounds; to Israel
Honor hath left and freedom, let but them
Find courage to lay hold on this occasion;
To himself and father's house eternal fame;
And, which is best and happiest yet, all this
With god not parted from him, as was feared,
But favoring and assisting to the end.   1720
Nothing is here for tears, nothing to wail
Or knock the breast; no weakness, no contempt,
Dispraise, or blame; nothing but well and fair,
And what may quiet us in a death so noble.
Let us go find the body where it lies
Soaked in his enemies' blood, and from the stream
With lavers pure, and cleansing herbs, wash off
The clotted gore. I, with what speed the while

[13] The phœnix.

(Gaza is not in plight to say us nay),
Will send for all my kindred, all my friends,   1730
To fetch him hence, and solemnly attend,
With silent obsequy and funeral train,
Home to his father's house. There will I build him
A monument, and plant it round with shade
Of laurel ever green and branching palm,
With all his trophies hung, and acts enrolled
In copious legend, or sweet lyric song.
Thither shall all the valiant youth resort,
And from his memory inflame their breasts
To matchless valor and adventures high;   1740
The virgins also shall, on feastful days
Visit his tomb with flowers, only bewailing
His lot unfortunate in nuptial choice,
From whence captivity and loss of eyes.
   Chor. All is best, though we oft doubt
What the unsearchable dispose
Of Highest Wisdom brings about,
And ever best found in the close.
Oft He seems to hide His face,
But unexpectedly returns,   1750
And to his faithful champion hath in place
Bore witness gloriously; whence Gaza mourns,
And all that band them to resist
His uncontrollable intent.
His servants He, with new acquist
Of true experience from this great event,
With peace and consolation hath dismissed,
And calm of mind, all passion spent.[14]

[14] This line is an almost perfect definition of Greek *katharsis*.

SIR JOHN SUCKLING, "the darling of the court," had wealth, wit, and a bachelor state to establish his popularity. There was even a kind of allurement in his appearance, for according to Aubrey, "his beard turn'd up naturally, so that he had a brisk and graceful look." We can visualize him in the midst of the brilliant court circles, setting the ladies a-twitter with his easy impudence.

He had opportunities too, which would add to his popularity. Unlike the majority of the Cavaliers he had studied at Cambridge University. Like many of the other young poets he had enrolled in the Inns of Court; but inheriting a fortune at the death of his father, he gave up law and spent some time in travel, visiting France, Germany, Italy, and Spain. His unusual ability in languages enabled him to bring back the finer flavor of his experiences. He was knighted upon his return to England in 1630, and the next year distinguished himself in foreign service with the troops of the Marquis of Hamilton, which went to the aid of Gustavus Adolphus.

Back in England he was welcomed at the court as an openhanded wit and gallant, but soon one of his fine gestures brought laughter down upon him. When it became necessary for the king to send troops to Scotland, Suckling furnished a troop of one hundred select horsemen. These were gorgeously equipped at a cost of £12,000 with white doublets, scarlet coats, breeches, and hats, the latter adorned with a fine plume. These gay troops, "the finest sight" of the king's army, were soon fleeing with the remainder of the forces, and Suckling had to endure a ballad made upon him and sung with great glee by the Roundheads.

The magnificence of this display was only one of many examples of the thoroughness with which Suckling went into everything he did. He gave sumptuous assemblies, at one of which the favors for the ladies consisted of silk stockings, garters, and gloves. The production of his play *Aglaura* cost three or four hundred pounds. The costumes for the play were especially rich and were embroidered in pure silver and gold.

Suckling became a great gambler both with dice and cards and would spend much of his time in bed, the cards spread out before him, studying various methods of play and devising new ones. There is an interesting account of his two sisters coming up weeping to London in terror lest he should lose all their money. But Davenant records that when Suckling had lost heavily, "he would make himself glorious in apparel, and said that it exalted his spirits, and that he had then the best luck, when he was most gallant, and his spirits high." Apparently he could retrieve his losses, for later he had generous sums to expend for the king's cause.

When Strafford was impeached and sent to the Tower, Suckling joined a conspiracy for rescuing him, but upon the detection of the plot, he escaped to the Continent. There, with his usual high gesture, he played the closing scene of his life at the age of thirty-four, dying a suicide in preference to living an exile in dreary poverty.

Gay, with a tendency to dazzle, Suckling abandoned the Jonsonian style for a startling informality of manner and a light and casual tone. Like many other poets of the day he could not escape the influence of Donne. He parodies "I long to talk with some old lover's ghost," patterns phrases reminiscent of Donne, and writes of inconstancy in the same light-hearted way. He does not, however, become serious or intense as Donne does; it is his gaiety, audacity, and verve that charm us. Millamant's phrase in Congreve's *Way of the World* is still the best characterization we have of him: "easy, natural Suckling."

Song

[from *Aglaura*]

Why so pale and wan, fond lover?
Prithee, why so pale?

Will, when looking well can't move her,
  Looking ill prevail?
    Prithee, why so pale?

Why so dull and mute, young sinner?
  Prithee, why so mute?
Will, when speaking well can't win her,
  Saying nothing do't?
    Prithee, why so mute?   10

Quit, quit, for shame; this will not move,
  This cannot take her.
If of herself she will not love,
  Nothing can make her:
    The devil take her!

[Constancy]

Out upon it! I have loved
  Three whole days together;
And am like to love three more,
  If it prove fair weather.

Time shall molt away his wings,
  Ere he shall discover
In the whole wide world again
  Such a constant lover.

But the spite on it is, no praise
  Is due at all to me: 10
Love with me had made no stays
  Had it any been but she.

Had it any been but she,
  And that very face,
There had been at least ere this
  A dozen dozen in her place.

A Song to a Lute [1]

Hast thou seen the down in the air,
    When wanton blasts have tossed it?
Or the ship on the sea,
    When ruder waves have crossed it?
Hast thou marked the crocodile's weeping,
    Or the fox's sleeping?
Or hast viewed the peacock in his pride,
    Or the dove by his bride,
    When he courts for his lechery?
O so fickle, O so vain, O so false, so false is she!   10

Song

I prithee send me back my heart,
    Since I cannot have thine;
For, if from yours you will not part,
    Why then shouldst thou have mine?

Yet now I think on it, let it lie;
    To find it were in vain,
For thou hast a thief in either eye
    Would steal it back again.

Why should two hearts in one breast lie
    And yet not lodge together?   10
O love, where is thy sympathy,
    If thus our breasts thou sever?

But love is such a mystery,
    I cannot find it out;
For when I think I'm best resolved,
    I then am in most doubt.

[1] This is a parody of Jonson's "Her Triumph," third stanza.

Then farewell care, and farewell woe,
  I will no longer pine;
For I'll believe I have her heart
  As much as she hath mine.   20

[*The Siege*]

'Tis now, since I sat down before
  That foolish fort, a heart,
(Time strangely spent) a year and more,
  And still I did my part:

Made my approaches, from her hand
  Unto her lip did rise,
And did already understand
  The language of her eyes;

Proceeded on with no less art—
  My tongue was engineer;   10
I thought to undermine the heart
  By whispering in the ear.

When this did nothing, I brought down
  Great cannon-oaths, and shot
A thousand thousand to the town;
  And still it yielded not.

I then resolved to starve the place
  By cutting off all kisses,
Praying, and gazing on her face,
  And all such little blisses.   20

To draw her out, and from her strength,
  I drew all batteries in,
And brought myself to lie at length
  As if no siege had been.

When I had done what man could do
   And thought the place mine own,
The enemy lay quiet too,
   And smiled at all was done.

I sent to know from whence and where
   These hopes and this relief;   30
A spy informed, Honor was there,
   And did command in chief.

"March, march," quoth I; "the word straight give;
   Let's lose no time, but leave her;
That giant upon air will live,
   And hold it out forever.

"To such a place our camp remove
   As will no siege abide;
I hate a fool that starves her love
   Only to feed her pride."   40

A Doubt of Martyrdom

O for some honest lover's ghost,[1]
   Some kind unbodied post
   Sent from the shades below!
   I strangely long to know
Whether the nobler chaplets wear,
Those that their mistress' scorn did bear
   Or those that were used kindly.

For whatso'er they tell us here
   To make those sufferings dear,
   'Twill there, I fear, be found   10
   That to the being crowned
To have loved alone will not suffice,

---

[1] Compare with Donne's "I long to talk with some old lover's ghost. . . ."

Unless we also have been wise
And have our loves enjoyed.

What posture can we think him in
That, here unloved, again
Departs, and is thither gone
Where each sits by his own?
Or how can that Elysium be
Where I my mistress still must see
Circled in other's arms?

For there the judges all are just,
And Sophonisba [2] must
Be his whom she held dear,
Not his who loved her here.
The sweet Philoclea, since she died,
Lies by her Pirocles his side,
Not by Amphialus. [3]

Some bays, perchance, or myrtle bough,
For difference crowns the brow
Of those kind souls that were
The noble martyrs here;
And if that be the only odds
(As who can tell?), ye kinder gods,
Give me the woman here!

Song

Honest lover whatsoever,
If in all thy love there ever

[2] Daughter of Hasdrubal, promised in marriage by her father to the Numidian prince, Masinissa, but later awarded to his rival, Syphax. When Masinissa overcame Syphax, he took Sophonisba; and when Scipio demanded her surrender, he sent her poison, with which she ended her life.

[3] The story is found in Sidney's *Arcadia*. Amphialus loved his cousin, Philoclea, but she loved Pirocles.

Was one wavering thought, if thy flame
Were not still even, still the same,
        Know this,
    Thou lov'st amiss;
    And to love true,
Thou must begin again, and love anew.

If, when she appears i' the room,
Thou dost not quake, and art struck dumb,   10
And in striving this to cover,
Dost not speak thy words twice over,
        Know this,
    Thou lov'st amiss;
    And to love true,
Thou must begin again, and love anew.

If fondly thou dost not mistake,
And all defects for graces take,
Persuad'st thyself that jests are broken
When she hath little or nothing spoken,   20
        Know this,
    Thou lov'st amiss;
    And to love true,
Thou must begin again, and love anew.

If, when thou appear'st to be within,
Thou let'st not men ask and ask again;
And when thou answer'st, if it be
To what was asked thee, properly,
        Know this,
    Thou lov'st amiss;   30
    And to love true,
Thou must begin again, and love anew.

If, when thy stomach calls to eat,
Thou cut'st not fingers 'stead of meat,
And with much gazing on her face

Dost not rise hungry from the place,
　　Know this,
　　　Thou lov'st amiss;
　　　And to love true,
Thou must begin again, and love anew.   40

If by this thou dost discover
That thou art no perfect lover,
And, desiring to love true,
Thou dost begin to love anew,
　　Know this,
　　　Thou lov'st amiss;
　　　And to love true,
Thou must begin again, and love anew.

A Ballad upon a Wedding

I tell thee, Dick, where I have been,
Where I the rarest things have seen,
　　Oh, things without compare!
Such sights again cannot be found
In any place on English ground,
　　Be it at wake or fair.

At Charing Cross, hard by the way
Where we (thou know'st) do sell our hay,
　　There is a house with stairs;
And there did I see coming down   10
Such folk as are not in our town,
　　Forty, at least, in pairs.

Amongst the rest, one pestilent fine
(His beard no bigger, though, than thine)
　　Walked on before the rest.
Our landlord looks like nothing to him;
The king (God bless him!), 'twould undo him
　　Should he go still so dressed.

At course-a-park,[1] without all doubt,
He should have first been taken out   20
    By all the maids i' the town,
Though lusty Roger there had been,
Or little George upon the Green,
    Or Vincent of the Crown.

But wot you what? the youth was going
To make an end of all his wooing;
    The parson for him stayed.
Yet by his leave, for all his haste,
He did not so much wish all past,
    Perchance, as did the maid.   30

The maid (and thereby hangs a tale),
For such a maid no Whitsun-ale
    Could ever yet produce;
No grape, that's kindly ripe, could be
So round, so plump, so soft as she,
    Nor half so full of juice.

Her finger was so small the ring
Would not stay on, which they did bring;
    It was too wide a peck:
And to say truth (for out it must),   40
It looked like the great collar (just)
    About our young colt's neck.

Her feet beneath her petticoat,
Like little mice, stole in and out,
    As if they feared the light;
But oh, she dances such a way,
No sun upon an Easter day
    Is half so fine a sight!

[1] "A country game, in which a girl called out one of the other sex to chase her" (*New English Dictionary*).

He would have kissed her once or twice,
But she would not, she was so nice,   50
    She would not do't in sight;
And then she looked as who should say,
I will do what I list to-day;
    And you shall do't at night.

Her cheeks so rare a white was on,
No daisy makes comparison
    (Who sees them is undone),
For streaks of red were mingled there,
Such as are on a Catherine pear,
    (The side that's next the sun).   60

Her lips were red, and one was thin
Compared to that was next her chin
    (Some bee had stung it newly);
But, Dick, her eyes so guard her face
I durst no more upon them gaze
    Than on the sun in July.

Her mouth so small, when she does speak,
Thou'dst swear her teeth her words did break,
    That they might passage get;
But she so handled still the matter,   70
They came as good as ours, or better,
    And are not spent a whit.

If wishing should be any sin,
The parson himself had guilty been
    (She looked that day so purely);
And did the youth so oft the feat
At night, as some did in conceit,
    It would have spoiled him, surely.

Just in the nick the cook knocked thrice,
And all the waiters in a trice   80

His summons did obey;
Each serving-man, with dish in hand,
Marched boldly up, like our trained band,
    Presented, and away.

When all the meat was on the table,
What man of knife or teeth was able
    To stay to be entreated?
And this the very reason was,
Before the parson could say grace,
    The company was seated.   90

The business of the kitchen's great,
For it is fit that men should eat;
    Nor was it there denied.
Passion o' me, how I run on!
There's that that would be thought upon,
    I trow, besides the bride.

Now hats fly off, and youths carouse;
Healths first go round, and then the house;
    The bride's came thick and thick:
And when 'twas named another's health,   100
Perhaps he made it hers by stealth;
    And who could help it, Dick?

O' the sudden up they rise and dance;
Then sit again and sigh and glance;
    Then dance again and kiss.
Thus several ways the time did pass,
Till every woman wished her place,
    And every man wished his!

By this time all were stolen aside
To counsel and undress the bride,   110
    But that he must not know;
But yet 'twas thought he guessed her mind,

And did not mean to stay behind
Above an hour or so.

When in he came, Dick, there she lay
Like new-fallen snow melting away
    ('Twas time, I trow, to part);
Kisses were now the only stay,
Which soon she gave, as who would say,
    "God be with ye, with all my heart."

But just as heaven would have to cross it,
In came the bridesmaids with the posset.
    The bridegroom ate in spite,
For had he left the women to't,
It would have cost two hours to do't,
    Which were too much that night.

At length the candle's out, and now
All that they had not done, they do.
    What that is, who can tell?
But I believe it was no more
Than thou and I have done before
    With Bridget and with Nell.

Song

When, dearest, I but think of thee,
Methinks all things that lovely be
    Are present, and my soul delighted:
For beauties that from worth arise
Are like the grace of deities,
    Still present with us, though unsighted.

Thus whilst I sit and sigh the day
With all his borrowed lights away,
    Till night's black wings do overtake me,

Thinking on thee, thy beauties then,   10
As sudden lights do sleeping men,
  So they by their bright rays awake me.

Thus absence dies, and dying proves
No absence can subsist with loves
  That do partake of fair perfection;
Since in the darkest night they may
By love's quick motion find a way
  To see each other by reflection.

The waving sea can with each flood
Bathe some high promont that hath stood   20
  Far from the main up in the river;
O think not then but love can do
As much, for that's an ocean too,
  Which flows not every day, but ever!

Samuel Butler 1612-1680

THE author of the favorite book of Charles II is not a vivid figure; in fact, his personality was so overshadowed by his book that contemporaries spoke of Butler himself as Hudibras. We see him somewhat vaguely in positions of importance in several of the great houses in England. These positions afforded him both time and facilities for reading and for the study of painting, an art which he seems to have loved. Through diligent self-improvement he gained at this time a wide and varied learning, even though he lacked a university education. The second household in which he found service, that of Elizabeth, Countess of Kent, was especially rich in opportunities. Here were books in abundance and the companionship of the great Selden, who came to use them. Later on, however, when he was in the home of Sir Samuel Luke, his opportunity to become familiar with Puritan ideas and customs was more important for him than books. Sir Samuel Luke himself, a Presbyterian officer in Cromwell's army, provided the original for the character of Hudibras.

After the Restoration Butler received the appointment of secretary to the Earl of Carbury, who later made him steward of Ludlow castle. When and why he gave up this position we do not know. We know only that he spent some time in France and formed a low opinion of French manners; that he married a Mrs. Herbert, reputed to possess money which was afterwards lost through bad securities; that he was not suitably rewarded for his popular poem; and that he was in very meager circumstances, if not in actual need, when he died in 1680.

But as in his own day, it is *Hudibras* and not Butler that is of primary interest. In the introduction to his edition of the poem, Alexander Ramsay says, "A man of any education must not be entirely ignorant of *Hudibras*"; but no doubt many persons of education find themselves in the uncertain position of Pepys. Pepys bought the book because it was "now in the fashion for drollery," spending 2s. 6d. for it, but he found it "so silly an abuse of the Presbyter knight going to the warrs" that he sold it for 18d. In order to be in style, however, he had to get another copy, though he confesses he could never "see enough where the wit lies."

The reader of today will "miss the matter" more easily than did Pepys, for the poem is full of allusions generally understood and enjoyed by the court of Charles II but not intelligible at the present time without heavy annotation. The plot is hard to follow, for it is very loosely constructed, depending upon the dominance of the hero to afford unity. The first part portrays the religious conceptions of the Presbyterians and their attitude toward amusements; the second part shows Hudibras in love and satirizes chivalric love and foolish credulity; the third part continues the satire on chivalry and also provides ridicule of law and lawyers. The story is a conglomeration of Butler's keen observations accumulated over a long period of time, and this discursive material is made even more obscure by the length and complexity of the dialogue of the characters. Few readers survive to the end of Part III.

There are, however, compensations for the unrecognized allusions, the involved plot, and the complex dialogue. The satire, though limited in subject to Presbyterians and Independents, has permanent value, for it applies to pretense and hypocrisy and littleness in human nature in any age. Indeed, it touches almost all the insincerities of life and especially ridicules pretended love and courage, false show of learning, and false politics, morality, and religion. The seriousness of his satire is cloaked in his burlesque of the romantic heroic poem. He turns the theme of war into cudgelings and the hurling of stones and rotten eggs and the theme of love into the wooing of a widow for her money; he translates the supernatural machinery into the frauds of an astrologer; and he changes the exaltation of the hero into discredit. The "drollery" is perennially mirth-provoking in spite of its sting. The content, the characters, the ludicrous and surprising rhymes—all are welded together to serve the one purpose of ridicule.

The poem follows *Don Quixote* in design and is the nearest approach in English to this masterpiece. In adapting this pattern to English life, thought, and character, Butler has created one of the greatest mock-heroic poems in our literature and the greatest satire before *Absalom and Achitophel.*

FROM *Hudibras*

When civil dudgeon first grew high,
And men fell out, they knew not why;
When hard words, jealousies, and fears
Set folks together by the ears
And made them fight, like mad or drunk,
For Dame Religion as for punk,[1]
Whose honesty they all durst swear for,
Though not a man of them knew wherefore;
When gospel-trumpeter, surrounded
With long-eared rout,[2] to battle sounded,   10
And pulpit, drum ecclesiastic,[3]
Was beat with fist instead of a stick;—
Then did Sir Knight abandon dwelling,
And out he rode a-colonelling.

     A wight he was whose very sight would
Entitle him Mirror of Knighthood;
That never bowed his stubborn knee
To anything but chivalry,
Nor put up blow but that which laid
Right Worshipful on shoulder-blade;   20
Chief of domestic knights and errant,
Either for chartel[4] or for warrant;

[1] A mistress.

[2] The ears of the Puritans were especially noticeable because of the short hair of the Roundheads.

[3] The reference is to the pounding on the pulpit by the vehement divines.

[4] A challenge.

Great on the bench, great in the saddle,
That could as well bind o'er as swaddle: [5]
Mighty he was at both of these,
And styled of [6] war as well as peace.
(So some rats of amphibious nature
Are either for the land or water.)
But here our authors make a doubt
Whether he were more wise or stout. 30
Some hold the one and some the other;
But howsoe'er they make a pother,
The difference was so small his brain
Outweighed his rage but half a grain:
Which made some take him for a tool
That knaves do work with, called a fool.
For it has been held by many that
As Montaigne, playing with his cat,
Complains she thought him but an ass,
Much more she would Sir Hudibras 40
(For that's the name our valiant knight
To all his challenges did write):
But they're mistaken very much;
'Tis plain enough he was no such.
We grant, although he had much wit,
He was very shy of using it;
As being loth to wear it out,
And therefore bore it not about,
Unless on holidays, or so,
As men their best apparel do. 50
Beside, 'tis known he could speak Greek
As naturally as pigs squeak;
That Latin was no more difficile
Than to a blackbird 'tis to whistle.
Being rich in both, he never scanted
His bounty unto such as wanted,
But much of either would afford

[5] To cudgel.
[6] Titled by.

To many that had not one word.
For Hebrew roots, although they're found
To flourish most in barren ground,   60
He had such plenty as sufficed
To make some think him circumcised;
And truly so he was perhaps,
Not as a proselyte, but for claps.
He was in logic a great critic,
Profoundly skilled in analytic:
He could distinguish and divide
A hair 'twixt south and southwest side;
On either which he would dispute,
Confute, change hands, and still confute: 70
He'd undertake to prove, by force
Of argument, a man's no horse;
He'd prove a buzzard is no fowl,
And that a lord may be an owl,
A calf an alderman, a goose a justice,
And rooks committee-men and trustees.[7]
He'd run in debt by disputation,
And pay with ratiocination.
All this by syllogism true,
In mood and figure, he would do.   80
  For rhetoric, he could not ope
His mouth but out there flew a trope;[8]
And when he happened to break off
In the middle of his speech, or cough,
He had hard words ready to show why,
And tell what rules he did it by.
Else, when with greatest art he spoke,
You'd think he talked like other folk;
For all a rhetorician's rules
Teach nothing but to name his tools.   90
But when he pleased to show it, his speech
In loftiness of sound was rich,

[7] Men appointed to act in the counties with the power of Parliament.
[8] A figure of speech.

A Babylonish dialect,
Which learned pedants much affect.
It was a parti-colored dress
Of patched and piebald languages:
'Twas English cut on Greek and Latin,
Like fustian heretofore on satin.[9]
It had an odd promiscuous tone,
As if he had talked three parts in one;   100
Which made some think, when he did gabble,
They had heard three laborers of Babel,
Or Cerberus himself pronounce
A leash of languages at once.
This he as volubly would vent
As if his stock would ne'er be spent;
And truly, to support that charge,
He had supplies as vast and large.
For he could coin or counterfeit
New words with little or no wit;   110
Words so debased and hard no stone
Was hard enough to touch them on.
And when with hasty noise he spoke 'em,
The ignorant for current took 'em;
That had the orator,[10] who once
Did fill his mouth with pebble-stones
When he harangued, but known his phrase,
He would have used no other ways.

    In mathematics he was greater
Than Tycho Brahe, or Erra Pater:[11]   120
For he, by geometric scale,
Could take the size of pots of ale;
Resolve by sines and tangents, straight,
If bread or butter wanted weight;
And wisely tell what hour o' the day

[9] The coarse fustian was slashed so that the satin would show as an inset.
[10] The reference is to Demosthenes, who, to cure speech defect, practiced speaking with pebbles in his mouth.
[11] Butler gave this name to William Lilly, a famous astrologer.

The clock does strike, by algebra.
    Beside, he was a shrewd philosopher,
And had read every text and gloss over;
Whate'er the crabbed'st author hath,
He understood by implicit faith;   130
Whatever sceptic could inquire for;
For every why he had a wherefore;
Knew more than forty of them do,
As far as words and terms could go:
All which he understood by rote
And, as occasion served, would quote,
No matter whether right or wrong;
They might be either said or sung.
His notions fitted things so well
That which was which he could not tell,   140
But oftentimes mistook the one
For the other, as great clerks have done.
He could reduce all things to acts,
And knew their natures by abstracts;
Where entity and quiddity,[12]
The ghosts of defunct bodies, fly;
Where truth in person does appear,
Like words congealed in northern air.
He knew what's what, and that's as high
As metaphysic wit can fly.   150
In school-divinity as able
As he that hight Irrefragable;[13]
A second Thomas, or, at once
To name them all, another Duns.
For he a rope of sand could twist
As tough as learned Sarbonist.
And weave fine cobwebs, fit for skull
That's empty when the moon is full;

[12] Terms used by metaphysicians to distinguish existence or being and essence from body.

[13] Alexander Hales, so called because his arguments could not be broken down.

Such as take lodgings in a head
That's to be let unfurnished. 160
He could raise scruples dark and nice,
And after solve 'em in a trice;
As if divinity had catched
The itch on purpose to be scratched,
Or, like a mountebank, did wound
And stab herself with doubts profound,
Only to show with how small pain
The sores of faith are cured again;
Although by woeful proof we find
They always leave a scar behind. 170
He knew the seat of paradise,
Could tell in what degree it lies;
And, as he was disposed, could prove it
Below the moon, or else above it;
What Adam dreamt of when his bride
Came from her closet in his side;
Whether the devil tempted her
By a High Dutch [14] interpreter;
If either of them had a navel;
Who first made music malleable; 180
Whether the serpent at the fall
Had cloven feet or none at all:
All this without a gloss or comment
He could unriddle in a moment,
In proper terms, such as men smatter
When they throw out and miss the matter.
   For his religion, it was fit
To match his learning and his wit:
'Twas Presbyterian true blue,
For he was of that stubborn crew 190
Of errant saints whom all men grant
To be the true church militant:

[14] This is a satirical reference to the attempt of Goropius Becanus to
prove that High Dutch was spoken by Adam and Eve.

Such as do build their faith upon
The holy text of pike and gun;
Decide all controversies by
Infallible artillery,
And prove their doctrine orthodox
By apostolic blows and knocks;
Call fire, and sword, and desolation
A godly, thorough reformation,   200
Which always must be carried on
And still be doing, never done;
As if religion were intended
For nothing else but to be mended.
A sect whose chief devotion lies
In odd, perverse antipathies;
In falling out with that or this,
And finding somewhat still amiss;
More peevish, cross, and splenetic
Than dog distract or monkey sick;   210
That with more care keep holiday
The wrong, than others the right way;
Compound for sins they are inclined to
By damning those they have no mind to;
Still so perverse and opposite
As if they worshiped God for spite.
The selfsame thing they will abhor
One way and long another for.
Free-will they one way disavow,
Another, nothing else allow: 220
All piety consists therein
In them, in other men all sin.
Rather than fail, they will defy
That which they love most tenderly:
Quarrel with minced pies and disparage
Their best and dearest friend, plum-porridge;
Fat pig and goose itself oppose,
And blaspheme custard through the nose.

The apostles of this fierce religion,
Like Mahomet's, were ass[15] and widgeon,[16]   230
To whom our knight by fast instinct
Of wit and temper was so linked,
As if hypocrisy and nonsense
Had got the advowson of his conscience.

. . . . . .

A squire he had whose name was Ralph,
That in the adventure went his half.
Though writers, for more stately tone,
Do call him *Ralpho,* 'tis all one;
And when we can with metre safe,
We'll call him so, if not plain Raph;   240
(For rhyme the rudder is of verses,
With which like ships they steer their courses).
An equal stock of wit and valor
He had laid in, by birth a tailor.
The mighty Tyrian queen[17] that gained
With subtle shreds a tract of land,
Did leave it, with a castle fair,
To his great ancestor, her heir.
From him descended cross-legged knights,
Famed for their faith and warlike fights   250
Against the bloody cannibal,
Whom they destroyed, both great and small.
This sturdy squire, he had as well
As the bold Trojan knight, seen hell,

[15] The reference is to Alborach, the creature Mahomet rode upon in his journey by night to heaven.

[16] When Mahomet was hiding in a cave, pigeons laid their eggs at the entrance and a spider covered the mouth with its web, so that the pursuers inferred no one had entered the cave. Also, Mahomet taught a pigeon to take seed placed in his ear and then, according to George Sandys (*Travels,* ed. 1673, p. 42) "affirmed it to be the Holy Ghost which informed him in divine precepts."

[17] Dido, having bought as much land in Africa as an ox-hide could surround, cut the hide into strips.

Not with a counterfeited pass
Of golden bough,[18] but true gold lace.
His knowledge was not far behind
The knight's, but of another kind,
And he another way came by it;
Some call it *Gifts,* and some *New-light,*[19]   260
A liberal art, that costs no pains
Of study, industry, or brains.
His wits were sent him for a token,
But in the carriage cracked and broken
Like commendation nine-pence,[20] crooked
With—*To and from my Love*—it looked.
He ne'er considered it, as loth
To look a gift-horse in the mouth;
And very wisely would lay forth
No more upon it than 'twas worth.   270
But as he got it freely, so
He spent it frank and freely too;
For saints themselves will sometimes be,
Of gifts that cost them nothing, free.
By means of this, with hem and cough,
Prolongers to enlightened stuff,
He could deep mysteries unriddle
As easily as thread a needle;
For as of vagabonds we say
That they are ne'er beside their way,   280
Whate'er men speak by this New Light,
Still they are sure to be in the right.
'Tis a dark lantern of the spirit,
Which none see by but those that bear it;
A light that falls down from on high
For spiritual trades to cozen by;
An *ignis fatuus* that bewitches,

[18] The reference is to the gift taken by Æneas to Proserpine to gain opportunity to see Anchises in Hades.
[19] The *inspiration* claimed by the Independents and Anabaptists.
[20] The nine-pence was often bent, as a love token.

And leads men into pools and ditches
To make them dip themselves, and sound
For Christendom in dirty pond;   290
To dive, like wild fowl, for salvation,
And fish to catch regeneration.
This light inspires, and plays upon
The nose of saint, like bag-pipe drone,
And speaks through hollow, empty soul
As through a trunk or whispering hole,
Such language as no mortal ear
But spiritual eavesdroppers can hear.
So Phœbus, or some friendly Muse,
Into small poets song infuse,   300
Which they at second hand rehearse
Through reed or bag-pipe, verse for verse.
Thus Ralph became infallible
As three or four-legged oracle,[21]
The ancient cup,[22] or modern chair,[23]
Spoke truth point-blank, though unaware.
For mystic learning, wondrous able
In magic, talisman, and cabal,
Whose primitive tradition reaches
As far as Adam's first green breeches; [24]   310
Deep-sighted in intelligences,
Ideas, atoms, influences;
And much of *terra incognita,*
The intelligible world,[25] could say;
A deep occult philosopher,
As learned as the wild Irish are,
Or Sir Agrippa,[26] for profound
And solid lying much renowned:

[21] The *tripos* of the priestess at Delphi.
[22] Joseph's divining cup, *Gen.* 44:5.
[23] The Pope's chair.
[24] In the Geneva Bible *Gen.* 3: 17 reads: "And they sewed fig-tree leaves together, and made themselves breeches."
[25] The world of the philosophers.
[26] Cornelius Agrippa, Secretary to Emperor Maximilian.

He Anthroposophus,[27] and Fludd,[28]
And Jacob Behmen [29] understood;   320
Knew many an amulet and charm
That would do neither good nor harm:
In Rosicrucian lore [30] as learned
As he that *vere adeptus* [31] earned.
He understood the speech of birds
As well as they themselves do words:
Could tell what subtlest parrots mean,
That speak and think contrary clean;
What member 'tis of whom they talk
When they cry *rope,* and *walk, knave, walk.*   330
He'd extract numbers out of matter
And keep them in a glass, like water
Of sovereign power to make men wise;
For dropped in blear thick-sighted eyes,
They'd make them see in darkest night,
Like owls, though purblind in the light.
By help of these, as he professed,
He had first matter seen undressed.
He took her naked, all alone,
Before one rag of form was on.   340
The chaos, too, he had descried
And seen quite through, or else he lied:
Not that of pasteboard, which men show
For groats at fair of Barthol'mew;
But its great grandsire, first o' the name,
Whence that and Reformation came;
Both cousins-german, and right able
To inveigle and draw in the rabble.

[27] An unintelligible discourse on the state of man after death, entitled *Anthroposophia Theomagica.*

[28] A philosopher of wide learning.

[29] Jacob Boehme, a distinguished visionary, founder of a sect called Behmenists.

[30] The Rosicrucians were members of a secret philosophical society of the seventeenth and eighteenth centuries.

[31] Title given alchemists who claimed to have found the philosopher's stone.

But Reformation was, some say,
O' the younger house to puppet-play.[32]   350
He could foretell whatsoever was
By consequence to come to pass:
As death of great men, alterations,
Diseases, battles, inundations.
All this without the eclipse of sun,
Or dreadful comet, he hath done
By inward light, a way as good,
And easy to be understood,
But with more lucky hit than those
That use to make the stars depose,   350
Like knights o' the post,[33] and falsely charge
Upon themselves what others forge,
As if they were consenting to
All mischief in the world men do;
Or, like the devil, did tempt and sway 'em
To rogueries and then betray 'em.
They'll search a planet's house to know
Who broke and robbed a house below;
Examine Venus and the moon,
Who stole a thimble and a spoon;   370
And though they nothing will confess,
Yet by their very looks can guess,
And tell what guilty aspect bodes,
Who stole, and who received the goods.
They'll question Mars, and by his look
Detect who 'twas that nimmed a cloak;
Make Mercury confess and 'peach
Those thieves which he himself did teach.
They'll find in the physiognomies
O' the planets all men's destinies;   380
Like him that took the doctor's bill

---

[32] Those who claimed to act by inner light were moved by a superior force as were puppets.

[33] Those who waited around at the courts to be hired to give evidence.

And swallowed it instead o' the pill;
Cast the nativity o' the question,[34]
And from positions to be guessed on,
As sure as if they knew the moment
Of native's birth, tell what will come on't.
They'll feel the pulses of the stars
To find out agues, coughs, catarrhs,
And tell what *crisis* does divine
The rot in sheep, or mange in swine;   390
In men what gives or cures the itch,
What makes them cuckolds, poor or rich;
What gains or loses, hangs or saves;
What makes men great, what fools or knaves;
But not what wise, for only of those
The stars, they say, cannot dispose,
No more than can the astrologians:
There they say right, and like true Trojans
This Ralpho knew, and therefore took
The other course, of which we spoke.   400
Thus was the accomplished knight endued
With gifts and knowledge per'lous shrewd.
Never did trusty squire with knight,
Or knight with squire, e'er jump more right.
Their arms and equipage did fit,
As well as virtues, parts, and wit.
Their valors, too, were of a rate,
And out they sallied at the gate.[35]

[34] The reference is to the idea that astrologers could cast a nativity
from the hour and minute of the question as well as from the hour and
minute of the birth.

[35] Butler learned many of his satiric devices from Cleveland, though
by chronology of birth he precedes Cleveland.

Richard Crashaw   1613(?)-1649

RICHARD CRASHAW, the only Catholic among the famous religious poets of the seventeenth century, was baptized a Protestant by the distinguished James Ussher, later archbishop. His father, a Puritan minister, preached violently against the Catholic Church and gave his pronouncement a permanent form in his will, saying:

> I account Poperie (as nowe it is) the heape and chaos of all heresie and the channell whereinto the fowlest impieties and heresies y^t have byne in the Christian Worlde have runn and closelye emptied themselves. I beleeve the Popes seate and power to be the power of the greate Antechrist and the doctrine of the Pope (as nowe it is) to be the doctrine of Antechrist . . . and that the true and absolute Papist soe livinge and dyeinge debarrs himself of salvation for oughte that we knowe.[1]

In spite of such teachings Richard Crashaw's mystical nature and great love of beauty predisposed him toward Catholicism. This tendency was fostered by a series of contacts during his college life. When he entered Cambridge, he came under the influence of a high churchman, who was his tutor. After graduation Crashaw was elected fellow at Peterhouse, known for the Roman Catholic trend in the adornment of its new chapel. As fellow he was tutor for the nephew of Nicholas Ferrar, the ascetic leader of the Anglican Community of Little Gidding. Crashaw went frequently to Little Gidding and shared in the vigils of prayer and the monastic order of life that gave to the community the name of "Protestant Nunnery." He soon established for himself the custom of night watches in Peterhouse Chapel or in the adjoining church of Little St. Mary's, so that he was said to spend more hours in prayer at night than most people did in the day.

[1] Quoted by L. C. Martin in his edition of Crashaw's poems, pp. xviii–xix.

353

Other hours, however, were spent in writing poetry or in friendly association with fellow poets at the university. Crashaw must have come to Cambridge with some evidence of poetic ability, although, unlike Cowley, he had published nothing; for soon after his entrance he was writing funeral verses for several prominent people connected with the university. A friendship between Crashaw and Cowley, which probably stimulated production on the part of both, began, amusingly enough, by the gift of two green apricots and some verses from Crashaw to the younger poet. It is pleasant to picture Crashaw as the one congenial companion whom Cowley chose to accompany him on the walks he loved to take. Later, at Peterhouse, Crashaw's closest friend was another poet, Joseph Beaumont, whose poems definitely reflect the influence of the association.

This "little contentful kingdom," as Crashaw called his years at Peterhouse, was lost to him when the Puritan forces exacted the Covenant of all who remained at Cambridge and ruthlessly destroyed the beautiful statues and symbols in the chapel and the church. He seems to have gone with the other Royalists to Oxford for a short time before he took refuge on the Continent, and it is possible that he was there again associated with Cowley.

It is not certain when his high-church practices led Crashaw into the Catholic Church; but he had accepted Catholicism when Cowley, who had gone to Paris in 1646 to become secretary to the exiled queen, discovered him in great need. Cowley presented his friend to Henrietta Maria, who gave him a recommendation to Cardinal Palotto at Rome.

Crashaw was received by the cardinal, but he could not endure the wickedness which he saw around him among the members of the cardinal's retinue. Apparently he revealed these conditions, becoming thereby so hated by his associates that Palotto had to send him away from Rome. He chose for Crashaw the beautiful little church at Loretto, but the poet lived only four weeks after reaching his new work. There are two stories to account for his death: one, that the heat of the trip to Loretto in summer made him ill; the other, that the enemies he had made in the cardinal's household had given him a slow poison. His death deprived the Catholic Church of a zealous priest; but it gave to English literature one of its very fine elegies, Cowley's *On the Death of Mr. Crashaw.*

Crashaw's single volume of poetry contains both his slender output of secular verse, *The Delights of the Muses,* and his religious verse, the *Epigrammata Sacra* and *The Steps to the Temple.* The former seems to have been produced largely before 1635, when Crashaw accepted the Peterhouse fellow-ship and the celibacy which this acceptance entailed. The two most famous poems in this early group are *Music's Duel,* an adaptation of a poem by Strada, in which he exquisitely imitates the sound of the lute and the voice of the nightingale, and the quaintly original *Wishes to His Supposed Mistress.* The astonishing absence of amatory verse in the collection causes one to feel that Crashaw had early reached the deci-sion expressed in his poem *On Marriage:*

> I would be married, but I'd have no wife;
> I would be married to a single life.

Though *The Steps to the Temple* is influenced, at least in conception, by Herbert's *The Temple,* the content is marked by a mystical ecstasy which Herbert never knew. When Crashaw writes of the Saints or of the Virgin Mary, his poems glow with the warmth of human love and his phrase-ology often becomes that of a lover. This characteristic of the Catholic mystics definitely distinguishes him from the other religious poets. When he worships before the figure of the crucified Christ or the *Mater Dolorosa,* he is almost overcome by the vividness of his sympathetic emotion. He vicariously suffers Christ's agony to such an extent that the cry is wrung from him, "Jesu, no more! It is full tide"; and he feels re-created within himself the poignant grief of Mary as she holds in her arms the dead body of her Son. Overwhelmed by Christ's sacrifice, he strives to pay his indebtedness

> With all the powers my poor heart hath
> Of humble love and loyal faith.

In full dedication of himself to this end he prays, "Fold up my life in love. . . . Leave nothing of myself in me."

The other outstanding characteristic of Crashaw is his ability to create sense impressions with an almost startling distinctness. Crashaw was skilled in drawing, painting, and engraving; and his artistic ability enables him to produce such vivid pictures in his verse as:

> Two silken sister flowers consult, and lay
> Their bashful cheeks together, newly they
> Peeped from their buds, showed like the garden's eyes
> Scarce waked.

Other sense impressions, particularly smell and touch, are prevalent in his poems. It has been said that Crashaw is a Keats with Catholicism added. Indeed, his temper is congenial to the Romantic poets and had a definite appeal for Coleridge, who attributes the inspiration of *Christabel* to lines from *St. Theresa*.

Crashaw was not critical of his own work and is very uneven in his poetry. His lack of technique was distasteful to the eighteenth century; and although he greatly influenced the *Epistle of Eloisa to Abelard,* Pope's judgment was that "nothing regular or just can be expected from him." Crashaw enjoys the questionable distinction of being the author of the two worst lines in English literature and probably of the most distasteful poem *The Weeper*. After piling up conceits in verse after verse in his effort to represent the weeping eyes of Mary Magdalene, he comes to a climax in:

> Two walking baths, two weeping motions,
> Portable and compendious oceans.

Yet he more than compensates for some of the worst conceits of the century by lines of almost startling beauty and power:

> By thy large drafts of intellectual day . . .
> By the full kingdom of that final kiss . . .
> And whereso'er He sets His white
> Steps, walk with Him those ways of light. . . .
> Love, thou art absolute sole lord
> Of life and death.

It is for such jewels as these that we treasure Crashaw.

Wishes
To His Supposed Mistress

Whoe'er she be,
That not impossible she
That shall command my heart and me;

Where'er she lie,
Locked up from mortal eye
In shady leaves of destiny;

Till that ripe birth
Of studied fate stand forth,
And teach her fair steps to our earth;

Till that divine   10
Idea take a shrine
Of crystal flesh, through which to shine;

Meet you her, my wishes,
Bespeak her to my blisses,
And be ye called my absent kisses.

I wish her beauty
That owes not all his duty
To gaudy tire or glistering shoe-tie:

Something more than
Taffeta or tissue can,   20
Or rampant feather, or rich fan,

More than the spoil
Of shop, or silkworm's toil,
Or a bought blush, or a set smile;

A face that's best
By its own beauty dressed,
And can alone command the rest,

A face made up
Out of no other shop
Than what nature's white hand sets ope;   30

A cheek where youth
And blood, with pen of truth,
Write what the reader sweetly rueth,

A cheek where grows
More than a morning rose,
Which to no box his being owes;

Lips where all day
A lover's kiss may play,
Yet carry nothing thence away;

Looks that oppress   40
Their richest tires, but dress
And clothe their simplest nakedness;

Eyes that displace
The neighbor diamond, and out-face
That sunshine by their own sweet grace;

Tresses that wear
Jewels but to declare
How much themselves more precious are,

Whose native ray
Can tame the wanton day   50
Of gems that in their bright shades play—

Each ruby there
Or pearl that dare appear,
Be its own blush, be its own tear;

A well-tamed heart,
For whose more noble smart
Love may be long choosing a dart;

Eyes that bestow
Full quivers on love's bow,
Yet pay less arrows than they owe;   60

Smiles that can warm
The blood, yet teach a charm
That chastity shall take no harm;

Blushes that been
The burnish of no sin,
Nor flames of aught too hot within;

Joys that confess
Virtue their mistress,
And have no other head to dress;

Fears fond and slight,   70
As the coy bride's when night
First does the longing lover right;

Tears, quickly fled,
And vain, as those are shed
For a dying maidenhead;

Days that need borrow
No part of their good morrow
From a fore-spent night of sorrow,

Days that, in spite
Of darkness, by the light   80
Of a clear mind are day all night;

Nights sweet as they,
Made short by lovers' play,
Yet long by the absence of the day;

Life that dares send
A challenge to his end,
And, when it comes, say, "Welcome, friend!"

Sidneian showers
Of sweet discourse, whose powers
Can crown old winter's head with flowers;   90

Soft silken hours,
Open suns, shady bowers;
'Bove all, nothing within that lowers;

Whate'er delight
Can make day's forehead bright,
Or give down to the wings of night.

In her whole frame
Have nature all the name,
Art and ornament the shame.

Her flattery,   100
Picture and poesy;
Her counsel her own virtue be.

I wish her store
Of worth may leave her poor
Of wishes; and I wish—no more.

Now if time knows
That her whose radiant brows
Weave them a garland of my vows;

Her whose just bays
My future hopes can raise,   110
A trophy to her present praise;

Her that dares be
What these lines wish to see:
I seek no further—it is she.

'Tis she, and here
Lo! I unclothe and clear
My wishes' cloudy character.

May she enjoy it
Whose merit dare apply it,
But modesty dares still deny it.   120

Such worth as this is
Shall fix my flying wishes,
And determine them to kisses.

Let her full glory,
My fancies, fly before ye!
Be ye my fictions, but her story.

A Hymn to the Name and Honor of the Admirable Saint Teresa [1]

Foundress of the Reformation of the Discalced [2] Carmelites, both men and women; a woman for angelical height of speculation, for masculine courage of performance, more than

[1] This poem portrays the mystical religious experience which conquered the heart of Saint Teresa even when she was a child and sent her to a hard life of service and a martyr's death.

[2] Barefoot Carmelites.

a woman, who yet a child outran maturity, and durst plot a martyrdom.

Love, thou art absolute sole lord
Of life and death. To prove the word,
We'll now appeal to none of all
Those thy old soldiers, great and tall,
Ripe men of martyrdom, that could reach down
With strong arms their triumphant crown,
Such as could with lusty breath,
Speak loud into the face of death
Their great Lord's glorious name, to none
Of those whose spacious bosoms spread a throne   10
For Love at large to fill; spare blood and sweat,
And see him take a private seat,
Making his mansion in the mild
And milky soul of a soft child.
    Scarce has she learned to lisp the name
Of martyr; yet she thinks it shame
Life should so long play with that breath
Which, spent, can buy so brave a death.
She never undertook to know
What death with Love should have to do;   20
Nor has she e'er yet understood
Why, to show love, she should shed blood;
Yet, though she cannot tell you why,
She can love, and she can die.
    Scarce has she blood enough to make
A guilty sword blush for her sake;
Yet has she a heart dares hope to prove
How much less strong is death than Love.
    Be Love but there, let poor six years
Be posed with the maturest fears   30
Man trembles at, you straight shall find
Love knows no nonage, nor the mind;
'Tis Love, not years or limbs, that can
Make the martyr or the man.

Love touched her heart, and, lo, it beats
High, and burns with such brave heats,
Such thirsts to die, as dares drink up
A thousand cold deaths in one cup.
Good reason; for she breathes all fire;
Her white breast heaves with strong desire 40
Of what she may, with fruitless wishes,
Seek for amongst her mother's kisses.
    Since 'tis not to be had at home [3]
She'll travel to a martyrdom.
No home for hers confesses she,
But where she may a martyr be.
    She'll to the Moors,[4] and trade with them
For this unvalued diadem.
She'll offer them her dearest breath,
With Christ's name in it, in change for death. 50
She'll bargain with them, and will give
Them God; teach them how to live
In Him; or, if they this deny,
For Him she'll teach them how to die.
So shall she leave amongst them sown
Her Lord's blood, or at least her own.
    Farewell, then, all the world! Adieu!
Teresa is no more for you.
Farewell, all pleasures, sports, and joys
(Never till now esteemed toys); 60
Farewell, whatever dear may be,
Mother's arms, or father's knee;
Farewell, house, and farewell, home!
She's for the Moors and martyrdom.
    Sweet, not so fast! lo, thy fair spouse,
Whom thou seek'st with so swift vows,

---

[3] Coleridge said that lines 43–64 "were ever present to my mind whilst writing the second part of Christabel; if, indeed, by some subtle process of the mind they did not suggest the first thoughts of the whole poem."
[4] When St. Teresa was a child, she and her brother planned to go among the Moors, hoping to lose their lives for love of God.

Calls thee back, and bids thee come
To embrace a milder martyrdom.

Blest powers forbid thy tender life
Should bleed upon a barbarous knife,   70
Or some base hand have power to rase
Thy breast's chaste cabinet, and uncase
A soul kept there so sweet; O no,
Wise Heaven will never have it so:
Thou art Love's victim, and must die
A death more mystical and high.
Into Love's arms thou shalt let fall
A still-surviving funeral.
His is the dart must make the death [5]
Whose stroke shall taste thy hallowed breath;   80
A dart thrice dipped in that rich flame
Which writes thy spouse's radiant name
Upon the roof of heaven, where aye
It shines, and with a sovereign ray
Beats bright upon the burning faces
Of souls, which in that name's sweet graces
Find everlasting smiles. So rare,
So spiritual, pure, and fair
Must be the immortal instrument
Upon whose choice point shall be sent   90
A life so loved; and that there be
Fit executioners for thee,
The fairest and first-born sons of fire,
Blest seraphim, shall leave their quire,
And turn Love's soldiers, upon thee
To exercise their archery.

O how oft shalt thou complain
Of a sweet and subtle pain;
Of intolerable joys;
Of a death in which who dies   100

[5] She had visions of an angel with a golden spear tipped with fire; this spear he thrust into her heart, increasing thereby her already intense love of God.

Loves his death, and dies again,
And would forever so be slain,
And lives, and dies, and knows not why
To live, but that he thus may never leave to die.
　How kindly will thy gentle heart
Kiss the sweetly killing dart,
And close in his embraces keep
Those delicious wounds, that weep
Balsam to heal themselves with. Thus
When these thy deaths, so numerous, 110
Shall all at last die into one,
And melt thy soul's sweet mansion,
Like a soft lump of incense, hasted
By too hot a fire, and wasted
Into perfuming clouds, so fast
Shalt thou exhale to heaven at last
In a resolving sigh, and then,—
O what? Ask not the tongues of men.
Angels cannot tell; suffice
Thyself shall feel thine own full joys 120
And hold them fast forever there.
So soon as thou shalt first appear,
The moon of maiden stars, thy white
Mistress, attended by such bright
Souls as thy shining self, shall come,
And in her first ranks make thee room;
Where 'mongst her snowy family
Immortal welcomes wait for thee.
　O what delight, when revealed Life shall stand,
And teach thy lips heaven with His hand; 130
On which thou now may'st to thy wishes
Heap up thy consecrated kisses.
What joys shall seize thy soul when she,
Bending her blessed eyes on thee
(Those second smiles of heaven), shall dart
Her mild rays through thy melting heart!
　Angels, thy old friends, there shall greet thee,

Glad at their own home now to meet thee.
   All thy good works which went before
And waited for thee at the door
Shall own thee there; and all in one
Weave a constellation
Of crowns, with which the King, thy spouse,
Shall build up thy triumphant brows.
   All thy old woes shall now smile on thee,
And thy pains sit bright upon thee;
All thy sorrows here shall shine,
All thy sufferings be divine.
Tears shall take comfort and turn gems,
And wrongs repent to diadems.
Even thy deaths shall live, and new
Dress the soul that erst they slew.
Thy wounds shall blush to such bright scars
As keep account of the Lamb's wars.
   Those rare works where thou shalt leave writ
Love's noble history, with wit
Taught thee by none but Him, while here
They feed our souls, shall clothe thine there.
Each heavenly word by whose hid flame
Our hard hearts shall strike fire, the same
Shall flourish on thy brows, and be
Both fire to us and flame to thee,
Whose light shall live bright in thy face
By glory, in our hearts by grace.
   Thou shalt look round about, and see
Thousands of crowned souls throng to be
Themselves thy crown, sons of thy vows,
The virgin-births with which thy sovereign spouse
Made fruitful thy fair soul. Go now,
And with them all about thee, bow
To Him. "Put on," He'll say, "put on,
My rosy love, that thy rich zone
Sparkling with the sacred flames
Of thousand souls, whose happy names

Heaven keep upon thy score": thy bright
Life brought them first to kiss the light
That kindled them to stars. And so
Thou with the Lamb, thy Lord, shalt go;
And wheresoe'er He sets His white
Steps, walk with Him those ways of light,   180
Which who in death would live to see,
Must learn in life to die like thee.

FROM *The Flaming Heart* [1]

O sweet incendiary! show here thy art,
Upon this carcass of a hard, cold heart;
Let all thy scattered shafts of light, that play
Among the leaves of thy large books of day,
Combined against this breast, at once break in
And take away from me myself and sin!
This gracious robbery shall thy bounty be,
And my best fortunes such fair spoils of me.
O thou undaunted daughter of desires!
By all thy dower of lights and fires,   10
By all the eagle in thee, all the dove,
By all thy lives and deaths of love,
By thy large draughts of intellectual day,
And by thy thirsts of love more large than they,
By all thy brim-filled bowls of fierce desire,
By thy last morning's draught of liquid fire,
By the full kingdom of that final kiss
That seized thy parting soul and sealed thee His;
By all the heavens thou hast in Him,
Fair sister of the seraphim,[2]   20
By all of Him we have in thee,

[1] These fine concluding lines were added to *The Flaming Heart* four
ears after it was first printed and form almost a separate poem. The
ooks of St. Teresa had greatly stirred Crashaw even when he was still
Protestant, and her life inspired his finest poems.

[2] St. Teresa is usually pictured with a seraph beside her.

Leave nothing of myself in me!
Let me so read thy life that I
Unto all life of mine may die!

Charitas Nimia; or, The Dear Bargain

Lord, what is man? why should he cost Thee
So dear? what had his ruin lost Thee?
Lord, what is man, that thou hast over-bought
So much a thing of naught?

Love is too kind, I see, and can
Make but a simple merchant-man.
'Twas for such sorry merchandise
Bold painters have put out his eyes.[1]

Alas, sweet Lord! what were't to Thee
If there were no such worms as we?
Heaven ne'ertheless still heaven would be,
    Should mankind dwell
    In the deep hell.
What have his woes to do with Thee?   10

    Let him go weep
    O'er his own wounds;
    Seraphim will not sleep,
Nor spheres let fall their faithful rounds.

    Still would the youthful spirits sing,
And still Thy spacious palace ring;
Still would those beauteous ministers of light
    Burn all as bright,
And bow their flaming heads before Thee;   20
Still thrones and dominations would adore Thee; [2]

[1] Love is always portrayed as blind.
[2] Ranks in the hierarchy of angels.

Still would those ever-wakeful sons of fire
    Keep warm Thy praise
    Both nights and days,
And teach Thy loved name to their noble lyre.

Let froward dust then do its kind,
And give itself for sport to the proud wind.   30
Why should a piece of peevish clay plead shares
In the eternity of Thy old cares?
Why shouldst Thou bow Thy awful breast to see
What mine own madnesses have done with me?

Should not the king still keep his throne
Because some desperate fool's undone?
Or will the world's illustrious eyes
Weep for every worm that dies?

    Will the gallant sun
    E'er the less glorious run?   40
Will he hang down his golden head,
Or e'er the sooner seek his western bed,
    Because some foolish fly
    Grows wanton, and will die?

If I were lost in misery,
What was it to Thy heaven and Thee?
What was it to Thy precious blood
If my foul heart called for a flood?

What if my faithless soul and I
    Would needs fall in   50
    With guilt and sin;
What did the Lamb that He should die?
What did the Lamb that He should need,
When the wolf sins, Himself to bleed?

    If my base lust
Bargained with death and well-beseeming dust,

Why should the white
Lamb's bosom write
The purple name
Of my sin's shame?   60
Why should His unstained breast make good
My blushes with His own heart-blood?

O my Savior, make me see
How dearly Thou hast paid for me;
That, lost again, my life may prove,
As then in death, so now in love.

In the Holy Nativity of Our Lord God

A Hymn Sung As by the Shepherds

CHORUS

Come, we shepherds, whose blest sight
   Hath met love's noon in nature's night;
Come, lift we up our loftier song
And wake the sun that lies too long.

   To all our world of well-stolen joy
He slept, and dreamt of no such thing;
   While we found out heaven's fairer eye,
And kissed the cradle of our King.
   Tell him he rises now too late
To show us aught worth looking at.   10

   Tell him we now can show him more
Than he e'er showed to mortal sight,
   Than he himself e'er saw before,
Which to be seen needs not his light:
   Tell him, Tityrus, where thou hast been;
Tell him, Thyrsis, what thou hast seen.

TITYRUS

Gloomy night embraced the place
Where the noble Infant lay.
 The Babe looked up and showed His face:
In spite of darkness, it was day.   20
 It was Thy day, Sweet! and did rise,
Not from the east, but from Thine eyes.

Chorus: It was Thy day, Sweet, [etc.]

THYRSIS

Winter chid aloud, and sent
The angry North to wage his wars.
 The North forgot his fierce intent,
And left perfumes instead of scars.
 By those sweet eyes' persuasive powers,
Where he meant frost, he scattered flowers.

 Chorus: By those sweet eyes', [etc.]   30

BOTH

We saw Thee in Thy balmy nest,
Young Dawn of our eternal day!
 We saw Thine eyes break from their east,
And chase the trembling shades away.
 We saw Thee, and we blest the sight;
We saw Thee by Thine own sweet light.

 Chorus: We saw Thee, [etc.]

TITYRUS

"Poor world," said I, "what wilt thou do
To entertain this starry Stranger?
 Is this the best thou canst bestow—   40
A cold and not too cleanly manger?

Contend, the powers of heaven and earth,
To fit a bed for this huge birth!"

Chorus: Contend, the powers, [etc.]

THYRSIS

"Proud world," said I, "cease your contest,
And let the mighty Babe alone.
   The phœnix builds the phœnix' nest;
Love's architecture is his own.
   The Babe whose birth embraves this morn
Made His own bed ere He was born."   50

Chorus: The Babe whose, [etc.]

TITYRUS

I saw the curled drops, soft and slow,
Come hovering o'er the place's head,
   Offering their whitest sheets of snow
To furnish the fair Infant's bed;
   "Forbear," said I; "be not too bold;
Your fleece is white, but 'tis too cold."

Chorus: "Forbear," said I, [etc.]

THYRSIS

I saw the obsequious seraphim
Their rosy fleece of fire bestow,   60
   For well they now can spare their wings,
Since Heaven itself lies here below.
   "Well done," said I; "but are you sure
Your down, so warm, will pass for pure?"

Chorus: "Well done," said I, [etc.]

TITYRUS

No, no, your King's not yet to seek
Where to repose His royal head;

See, see how soon His new-bloomed cheek
'Twixt's mother's breasts is gone to bed.
    "Sweet choice," said we! "no way but so,   70
Not to lie cold, yet sleep in snow."

   Chorus: "Sweet choice," said we, [etc.]

BOTH

We saw Thee in Thy balmy nest,
Bright Dawn of our eternal day!
    We saw Thine eyes break from their east,
And chase the trembling shades away.
    We saw Thee, and we blest the sight;
We saw Thee by Thine own sweet light.

   Chorus: We saw Thee, [etc.]

FULL CHORUS

Welcome, all wonders in one sight!   80
Eternity shut in a span,
    Summer in winter, day in night,
Heaven in earth, and God in man!
    Great little one! whose all-embracing birth
Lifts earth to heaven, stoops heaven to earth.

Welcome, though nor to gold nor silk,
To more than Caesar's birthright is:
    Two sister-seas of virgin milk,
With many a rarely tempered kiss,
    That breathes at once both maid and mother,   90
Warms in the one, cools in the other.

She sings Thy tears asleep, and dips
Her kisses in Thy weeping eye;
    She spreads the red leaves of Thy lips,
That in their buds yet blushing lie:

She 'gainst those mother-diamonds tries
The points of her young eagle's eyes.

Welcome, though not to those gay flies,
Gilded i' the beams of earthly kings,
  Slippery souls in smiling eyes;   100
But to poor shepherds, homespun things,
  Whose wealth's their flock, whose wit, to be
Well read in their simplicity.

Yet when young April's husband-showers
Shall bless the fruitful Maia's bed,
  We'll bring the first-born of her flowers
To kiss Thy feet, and crown Thy head.
  To Thee, dread Lamb! whose love must keep
The shepherds more than they the sheep,

To Thee, meek Majesty! soft King   110
Of simple graces and sweet loves,
  Each of us his lamb will bring,
Each his pair of silver doves;
  Till burnt at last in fire of Thy fair eyes,
Ourselves become our own best sacrifice.

To the Noblest and Best of Ladies, the Countess of Denbigh [1]

Persuading her to resolution in religion, and to render herself without further delay into the communion of the Catholic church.

What heaven-entreated heart is this,
Stands trembling at the gate of bliss?
Holds fast the door, yet dares not venture

[1] One of Crashaw's patrons in his time of need. To her he dedicated the volume of his poems entitled *Carmen Deo Nostro*.

Fairly to open it and enter;
Whose definition is a doubt
'Twixt life and death, 'twixt in and out?
Say, ling'ring fair, why comes the birth
Of your brave soul so slowly forth?
Plead your pretenses, O you strong
In weakness, why you choose so long   10
In labor of yourself to lie,
Nor daring quite to live nor die.
Ah, linger not, loved soul! A slow
And late consent was a long no;
Who grants at last, long time had tried
And did his best to have denied.
What magic bolts, what mystic bars,
Maintain the will in these strange wars!
What fatal, what fantastic bands
Keep the free heart from its own hands!   20
So when the year takes cold, we see
Poor waters their own prisoners be;
Fettered, and locked up fast they lie
In a sad self-captivity.
The astonished nymphs their flood's strange fate deplore,
To see themselves their own severer shore.
Thou that alone canst thaw this cold,
And fetch the heart from its stronghold,
Almighty Love! end this long war,
And of a meteor make a star.   30
O fix this fair indefinite!
And 'mongst Thy shafts of sovereign light
Choose out that sure decisive dart,
Which has the key of this close heart,
Knows all the corners of't, and can control
The self-shut cabinet of an unsearched soul.
O let it be at last, Love's hour;
Raise this tall trophy of thy power;
Come once the conquering way; not to confute,
But kill this rebel-word "irresolute,"   40

That so, in spite of all this peevish strength
Of weakness, she may write, "Resolved at length."
Unfold at length, unfold fair flower,
And use the season of Love's shower;
Meet his well-meaning wounds, wise heart!
And haste to drink the wholesome dart,
That healing shaft, which heaven till now
Hath in Love's quiver hid for you.
O dart of Love! arrow of light.
O happy you, if it hit right!   50
It must not fall in vain, it must
Not mark the dry regardless dust.
Fair one, it is your fate; and brings
Eternal worlds upon its wings.
Meet it with wide-spread arms, and see
Its seat your soul's just center be.
Disband dull fears; give faith the day;
To save your life, kill your delay.
It is Love's siege, and sure to be
Your triumph, though his victory.   60
'Tis cowardice that keeps this field,
And want of courage not to yield:
Yield then, O yield, that Love may win
The fort at last, and let life in.
Yield quickly, lest perhaps you prove
Death's prey, before the prize of Love.
This fort of your fair self, if't be not won,
He is repulsed indeed; but you're undone.

John Cleveland 1613-1658

To "Clevelandize" became as popular in the seventeenth century as to "parly Euphuism" was in the days of Elizabeth. Cleveland prided himself on remembering all he read and was said to be able to sum up "whole books in a metaphor." His ready wit could seize upon a clever idea and, incorporating much curious learning, spin it out through a series of intricate and extravagant figures to an apt conclusion. The intellectual dexterity necessary in following him was the delight of an age which carried to an extreme the style introduced by Donne. For his cleverness he was called "the best of English poets" even in the presence of Milton's nephew; and his comparative popularity may be judged by the fact that during the time Milton's *Minor Poems* reached two editions, Cleveland's poems reached more than twenty.

Cleveland seems to have acquired his taste for books early in life. His father was a teacher and a preacher and could give Cleveland a cultural background. The schoolmaster at Hinckley, where Cleveland was reared, taught him in his early youth to "English" the "choicest elegancies in Latin and Greek." At Christ's College, Cambridge, he did well, being chosen at the beginning of his second year instead of Milton to write and deliver the speech of welcome to the visiting French Ambassador and the Chancellor of the University, the Earl of Holland. Among his works are preserved two of his speeches made when he was "Father" of the Cambridge revels, and these reveal a light cleverness wholly lacking in Milton's productions for the same office. His elegy on the death of Edward King finds a place with *Lycidas* in the book of elegies put out by the university.

After graduation Cleveland stayed on at Cambridge, studying and directing the work of undergraduates as fellow in his father's college, St. John's. Here he was said to be "a delight and ornament" to the college and gained a reputation as an orator. He received his master's degree from Cambridge in 1635 and from Oxford in 1637.

When forced by the Puritans to leave Cambridge, he took refuge at Oxford and was, according to Wood, greatly admired "for his high Panegyrics and smart Satyrs." From then on it was his "smart Satyrs" instead of his metaphysical lyrics which were important. When the Royalists fully realized their danger, it was Cleveland who took up his pen to fight in verse for the king with as much earnestness as did Milton in prose for Cromwell. This was the time when he invoked satiric verse with the couplet:

> Come, keen iambics, with your badger's feet,
> And badger-like bite till your teeth do meet.

The Rebel Scot, a powerful satire against the Scotch for deserting Charles I, is one of the most famous of his poems. He was highly praised for his writing, and it was said that with his satires he struck "blows that shaked triumphing Rebellion, reaching the soul of those not to be reached by Law or Power, striking each Traitor to a paleness beyond that of any Loyal Corpse that bled by them." [1]

Having lost his fellowship at St. John's, he was appointed Judge Advocate at Newark. After the surrender of Newark he had no position and was dependent upon Royalist friends. Finally he was discovered and thrown into Yarmouth prison, charged with "great abilities" which were considered dangerous to the Parliamentary cause. Three months later he was released at his own petition by Cromwell; but his "vile durance," as he terms it, had weakened his health. He spent the brief remainder of his life in Gray's Inn, where he and Samuel Butler are said to have been closely associated.

It is as the literary master of Butler that Cleveland is best known. From him Butler learned the effective devices of epigram, exaggeration, double rhyme, and the clever rhetorical *zeugma*, but he burlesques where Cleveland bites.

Before the time of Cleveland satires had been written by

[1] Quoted in Berdan's edition of Cleveland's poems, p. 33, from David Lloyd's *Memoirs*, London, 1668, p. 617.

Donne, Bishop Hall, George Wither, and others in imitation of the Latin satirists and were general in their nature. With Cleveland satire became personal. This change won for him the title of "first English satirist," and, together with the establishment of the closed heroic couplet as the form for satirical expression, prepared the way for Dryden and Pope.

An Elegy on Ben Jonson

Who first reformed our stage with justest laws,
And was the first best judge in his own cause;
Who, when his actors trembled for applause,

Could (with noble confidence) prefer
His own, by right, to a whole theater,
From principles which he knew could not err:

Who to his fable did his persons fit,
With all the properties of art and wit,
And above all that could be acted, writ:

Who public follies did to covert drive,   10
Which he again could cunningly retrive,
Leaving them no ground to rest on and thrive:

Here JONSON lies, whom, had I named before,
In that one word alone I had paid more
Than can be now, when plenty makes me poor.

Fuscara; or, The Bee Errant

Nature's confectioner, the bee
(Whose suckets [1] are moist alchemy,
The still of his refining mold
Minting the gardens into gold),

[1] Sweetmeats.

Having rifled all the fields
Of what dainties Flora yields,
Ambitious now to take excise
Of a more fragrant paradise,
At my Fuscara's sleeve arrived,
Where all delicious sweets are hived.   10
The airy freebooter distrains [2]
First on the violet of her veins,
Whose tincture, could it be more pure,
His ravenous kiss had made it bluer.
Here did he sit and essence quaff
Till her coy pulse had beat him off,
That pulse which he that feels may know
Whether the world's long-lived or no.
The next he preys on is her palm,
That almoner of transpiring balm;   20
So soft, 'tis air but once removed;
Tender as 'twere a jelly gloved.
Here, while his canting drone-pipe scanned
The mystic figures of her hand,
He tipples palmistry and dines
On all her fortune-telling lines.
He bathes in bliss and finds no odds
Betwixt her nectar and the gods'.
He perches now upon her wrist,
A proper hawk for such a fist,   30
Making that flesh his bill of fare
Which hungry cannibals would spare;
Where lilies in a lovely brown
Inoculate carnation.
Her *argent* skin with *or* so streamed
As if the milky way were creamed.
From hence he to the woodbine bends
That quivers at her finger's ends,
That runs division on the tree
Like a thick-branching pedigree.   40

[2] Seizes for debt.

So 'tis not her the bee devours,
It is a pretty maze of flowers;
It is the rose that bleeds, when he
Nibbles his nice phlebotomy.
About her finger he doth cling
In the fashion of a wedding-ring,
And bids his comrades of the swarm
Crawl like a bracelet 'bout her arm.
Thus when the hovering publican
Had sucked the toll of all her span,   50
Turning his draughts with drowsy hums
As Danes carouse by kettle-drums,
It was decreed, that posy gleaned,
The small familiar should be weaned.
At this the errant's courage quails;
Yet aided by his native sails,
The bold Columbus still designs
To find her undiscovered mines.
To the Indies of her arm he flies,
Fraught with the east and western prize;   60
Which when he had in vain essayed,
Armed like a dapper lancepresade [3]
With Spanish pike, he broached a pore
And so both made and healed the sore:
For as in gummy trees there's found
A salve to issue at the wound,
Of this, her breach, the like was true;
Hence trickled out a balsam, too.
But oh, what wasp was it that could prove
Ravaillac [4] to my Queen of Love!   70
The king of bees, now jealous grown
Lest her beams should melt his throne,
And finding that his tribute slacks,
His burgesses and state of wax
Turned to a hospital, the combs

[3] Lowest officer in a foot company.
[4] Assassin of Henry of Navarre.

Built rank and file like beadsmen's rooms,
And what they bleed but tart and sour
Matched with my Danae's golden shower,
Live honey all, the envious elf
Stung her 'cause sweeter than himself.   80
Sweetness and she are so allied
The bee committed parricide.

Upon Phillis Walking in a Morning before Sun-rising

The sluggish morn as yet undressed,
My Phillis brake from out her east,
As if she'd made a match to run
With Venus, usher to the sun.
The trees (like yeomen of the guard
Serving her more for pomp than ward),
Ranked on each side, with loyal duty
Weave branches to inclose her beauty.
The plants, whose luxury was lopped
Or age with crutches underpropped,   10
(Whose wooden carcasses are grown
To be but coffins of their own)
Revive, and at her general dole
Each receives his ancient soul.
The winged choristers began
To chirp their matins, and the fan
Of whistling winds like organs played,
Until their voluntaries made
The wakened earth in odors rise
To be her morning sacrifice.   20
The flowers, called out of their beds,
Start and raise up their drowsy heads;
And he that for their color seeks
May find it vaulting in her cheeks,
Where roses mix,—no civil war

Divides her York and Lancaster.
The marigold (whose courtier's face
Echoes the sun and doth unlace
Her at his rise,—at his full stop
Packs and shuts up her gaudy shop) 30
Mistakes her cue and doth display:
Thus Phillis antedates the day.
These miracles had cramped the sun,
Who, thinking that his kingdom's won,
Powders with light his frizzled locks
To see what saint his luster mocks.
The trembling leaves through which he played,
Dappling the walk with light and shade
Like lattice-windows, give the spy
Room but to peep with half an eye; 40
Lest her full orb his sight should dim
And bid us all good night in him,
Till she should spend a gentle ray
To force us a new fashioned day.
But what religious palsy's this
Which makes the boughs divest their bliss,
And that they might her footsteps straw,
Drop their leaves in shivering awe?
Phillis perceived and (lest her stay
Should wed October unto May, 50
And, as her beauty caused a spring,
Devotion might an autumn bring)
Withdrew her beams, yet made no night,
But left the sun her curate-light.

Mark Antony

When as the nightingale chanted her vespers
    And the wild forester couched on the ground,
Venus invited me in the evening whispers
    Unto a fragrant field with roses crowned,

Where she before had sent
My wishes complement;
Unto my heart's content
Played with me on the green.
    Never Mark Antony
    Dallied more wantonly   10
    With the fair Egyptian Queen.

First on her cherry cheeks I mine eyes feasted,
  Thence fear of surfeiting made me retire;
Next on her warmer lips, which, when I tasted,
  My duller spirits made me active as fire.
    Then we began to dart,
    Each at another's heart,
    Arrows that knew no smart,
    Sweet lips and smiles between.
      Never Mark Antony
      Dallied more wantonly   20
      With the fair Egyptian Queen.

Wanting a glass to plait her amber tresses,
  Which like a bracelet rich decked mine arm,
Gaudier than Juno wears when as she graces
  Jove with embraces more stately than warm,
    Then did she peep in mine
    Eyes' humor crystalline;
    I in her eyes was seen
    As if we one had been.
      Never Mark Antony
      Dallied more wantonly   30
      With the fair Egyptian Queen.

Mystical grammar of amorous glances;
  Feeling of pulses, the physic of love;
Rhetorical courtings and musical dances;
  Numbering of kisses arithmetic prove;
    Eyes like astronomy;

Straight-limbed geometry;
In her arts ingeny   40
Our wits were sharp and keen.
    Never Mark Antony
    Dallied more wantonly
    With the fair Egyptian Queen.

The Rebel Scot [1]

How, Providence? and yet a Scottish crew?
Then Madam Nature wears black patches too!
What, shall our nation be in bondage thus
Unto a land that truckles under us?
Ring the bells backward! I am all on fire.
Not all the buckets in a country quire
Shall quench my rage. A poet should be feared
When angry, like a comet's flaming beard.
And where's the stoic can his wrath appease,
To see his country sick of Pym's disease?   10
By Scotch invasion to be made a prey
To such pigwidgeon myrmidons as they?
But that there's charm in verse, I would not quote
The name of Scot without antidote;
Unless my head were red, that I might brew
Invention there that might be poison too.
Were I a drowsy judge whose dismal note
Disgorgeth halters as a juggler's throat
Doth ribbons; could I in Sir Empiric's tone
Speak pills in phrase and quack destruction;   20
Or roar like Marshall,[2] that Geneva bull,
Hell and damnation a pulpit full;
Yet to express a Scot, to play that prize,
Not all those mouth-grenadoes can suffice.

[1] The invasion of the Scots after the defeat of the Royalists at
Gloucester seemed to the English a dastardly act. This satire of Cleve-
land's is his most famous work.
[2] A leading Puritan and celebrated preacher of the time.

Before a Scot can properly be curst,
I must like Hocus swallow daggers first.
Come, keen iambics, with your badger's feet
And badger-like bite until your teeth do meet.
Help, ye tart satirists, to imp my rage
With all the scorpions that should whip this age.   30
Scots are like witches; do but whet your pen,
Scratch till the blood come, they'll not hurt you then.
Now, as the martyrs were enforced to take
The shape of beasts, like hypocrites at stake
I'll bait my Scot so, yet not cheat your eyes:
A Scot within a beast is no disguise.
No more let Ireland brag; her harmless nation
Fosters no venom since the Scot's plantation:
Nor can our feigned antiquity maintain;
Since they came in, England hath wolves again.   40
The Scot that kept the Tower might have shown,
Within the grate of his own breast alone,
The leopard and the panther, and engrossed
What all those wild collegiates had cost
The honest high-shoes in their termly fees;
First to the savage lawyer, next to these.
Nature herself doth the Scotchmen beasts confess,
Making their country such a wilderness:
A land that brings in question and suspense
God's omnipresence, but that Charles came thence,   50
But that Montrose and Crawford's loyal band
Atoned their sin and christened half the land.
Nor is it all the nation hath these spots;
There is a Church as well as Kirk of Scots:
As in a picture where the squinting paint
Shows fiend on this side, and on that side saint.
He that saw Hell in his melancholy dream
And in the twilight of his fancy's theme,
Scared from his sins, repented in a fright,
Had he viewed Scotland, had turned proselyte.   60
A land where one may pray with cursed intent,

O may they never suffer banishment!
Had Cain been Scot, God would have changed his doom;
Not forced him wander but confined him home!
Like Jews they spread and as infection fly,
As if the Devil had ubiquity.
Hence 'tis they live at rovers [3] and defy
This or that place, rags of geography.
They're citizens of the world; they're all in all;
Scotland's a nation epidemical.   70
And yet they ramble not to learn the mode,
How to be dressed, or how to lisp abroad;
To return knowing in the Spanish shrug,
Or which of the Dutch states a double jug
Resembles most in belly or in beard,
(The card by which the mariners are steered).
No, the Scots-errant fight and fight to-eat;
Their ostrich stomachs make their swords their meat.
Nature with Scots as tooth-drawers hath dealt
Who use to string their teeth upon their belt.   80
Yet wonder not at this happy choice,
The serpent's fatal still to paradise.
Sure, England hath the hemorrhoids, and these
On the north postern of the patient seize
Like leeches; thus they physically thirst
After our blood, but in the cure shall burst!
Let them not think to make us run of the score
To purchase villenage, as once before
When an act passed to stroke them on the head,
Call them good subjects, buy them gingerbread. [4]   90
Not gold, nor acts of grace, 'tis steel must tame
The stubborn Scot; a prince that would reclaim
Rebels by yielding, doth like him, or worse,
Who saddled his own back to shame his horse.

[3] A term in archery, meaning to shoot at random for distance only.
[4] Three hundred thousand pounds was voted as a gratuity to the
Scots after their invasion in 1641, merely to show the friendship of the
English!

Was it for this you left your leaner soil,
Thus to lard Israel with Egypt's spoil?
They are the Gospel's life-guard; but for them,
The garrison of New Jerusalem,
What would the brethren do? The Cause! The Cause!
Sack-possets and the fundamental laws!   100
Lord! What a godly thing is want of shirts!
How a Scotch stomach and no meat converts!
They wanted food and raiment, so they took
Religion for their seamstress and their cook.
Unmask them well; their honors and estate,
As well as conscience, are sophisticate.
Shrive but their titles and their moneys poise,
A laird and twenty pence pronounced with noise,
When construed, but for a plain yeoman go,
And a good sober two-pence, and well so.   110
Hence then, you proud imposters; get you gone,
You Picts in gentry and devotion;
You scandal to the stock of verse, a race
Able to bring the gibbet in disgrace.
Hyperbolus [5] by suffering did traduce
The ostracism and shamed it out of use.
The Indian, that heaven did forswear
Because he heard some Spaniards were there,
Had he but known what Scots in hell had been,
He would Erasmus-like have hung between.   120
My Muse hath done. A voider for the nonce.
I wrong the Devil should I pick their bones;
That dish is his; for when the Scots decease,
Hell, like their nation, feeds on barnacles.
A Scot, when from the gallow-tree got loose,
Drops into Styx and turns a solan goose. [6]

[5] Ostracism was discontinued as punishment when Aristides, who had tried to have Hyperbolus, an Athenian demagogue, ostracized, was himself banished.

[6] There was a curious belief that barnacles contained a perfectly formed bird, a sea-fowl with the bill of a goose, called a solan goose.

ALTHOUGH Pope calls Denham a "holiday-writer," he sums
up Denham's outstanding quality in the one word "strength."
The strength lay in characteristics admired by Pope: balance
and antithesis of closed couplets and didacticism. Though
Denham's work has considerable range, it was *Cooper's Hill,*
the first long descriptive poem in English, that established
his fame and influenced poets for the next hundred years.
Of it Pope said:

> On Cooper's Hill eternal wreaths shall grow
> While lasts the mountain, or while Thames shall flow.

In 1788 the *Gentleman's Magazine* satirically commented
that "readers have been used to see the Muses labouring up
. . . many hills since Cooper's and Grongar, and some gentle
Bard reclining on almost every mole-hill." [1] *Cooper's Hill*
went through five editions in about a dozen years, catching
the popular fancy not only because Denham described local
scenery, but also because he "moralized" his song in neat
quotable couplets. Indeed, Denham's style is the basis for
the praise given him by Dryden and Dr. Johnson and for his
influence on Pope; and his place with Waller in the develop-
ment of the closed heroic couplet affords him historical
importance.

It is unfortunate that the quality which makes Denham a
vivid personality is not strength but weakness. Although
Wood reports that Denham was "examined in the public
schools for the degree of Bach. of Arts" from Oxford Uni-
versity, he failed to get the degree. This failure was probably
no surprise to Denham's associates at the university, who
considered him a "slow, dreaming young man," who was
"more addicted to gaming than study." Although he wrote
The Anatomy of Play, which analyzes the evils of gambling,

---

[1] Quoted by R. D. Havens in *The Influence of Milton on English
Poetry,* p. 248.

hoping to convince his father of his penitence, the rea
nature of his repentance is shown when after his father'
death he gambled away the patrimony that he had made sur
of by his booklet. The other thing which is vivid to us is tha
he lost his mind from jealousy when his beautiful secone
wife, less than half his age, became the openly acknowledge
mistress of the Duke of York. Though himself a dissolut
member of a dissolute court, he became obsessed with th
idea that he was the Holy Ghost and hastened to tell th
king so. It was rumored that he poisoned his wife with a cu
of chocolate. The story ends with the Duchess of York'
biting off a piece of her tongue when Lady Denham's ghos
appeared to her and with an autopsy which revealed no trac
of poison.

With a sense of pity we turn from the more vivid figur
to the less vivid, which, however, won distinction as poet
wit, and courtier. Here we see a man whose eye "had a
strange piercingness, not as to shining and glory, but (lik
a Momus) when he conversed with you he look't into you
very thoughts." [2] This piercing eye was destined by Den
ham's father for the law, and Denham had been entered o
the Lincoln's Inn register before he went to Oxford. Afte
his university days he was very successful in the study o
law, in spite of the interruptions caused by his marriage an
by his growing interest in literature. The Civil War, how
ever, put an end to his legal career.

Throughout the period of the Commonwealth Denhan
suffered many hardships because of his loyalty to the king
Parliament took over his estates, he was imprisoned mor
than once, he was separated from his wife just before th
birth of their first child, and he was forced to leave th
country after the surrender of Exeter in 1646.

Denham took refuge with the queen in Paris, where h
came into contact with other literary contemporaries
Cowley, who was acting as secretary to the queen, Davenant
and Waller. Here he again took up writing. He had alread

[2] Aubrey, *Brief Lives,* I, 220.

roduced a play, *The Sophy,* and probably as early as 1636 had translated into heroic couplets the second book of the *Eneid,* a translation of much influence on both Dryden and Pope. The first draft of *Cooper's Hill* had also appeared, though in a pirated edition, in 1642. During his exile he wrote a number of shorter poems, "to divert and put off the evil hours of our banishment," he says in his dedication of these poems to the king. He was employed by the queen on a mission of importance to the king in England and is reputed to have helped the king escape from Hampton Court, and the Duke of York from St. James' Palace. That he received Royalist correspondence from Paris became known through the recognition of the handwriting of Cowley, and he was forced to return hurriedly and secretly to France. From then until the Restoration he was employed on various missions to aid the royal cause.

Upon the Restoration Denham was granted the position of Surveyor of the Works, a post left vacant by the death of Inigo Jones. He was, however, no architect and seems to have suffered some ridicule in his efforts to fulfil the obligations of his job. He did achieve a great improvement in the paving of the London streets, a work for which he was highly praised by Pepys; and he is responsible for some very creditable buildings. During this time other honors came to him: he was created a Knight of the Bath and received grants of land from the king; he was elected a member of Parliament in 1661; and he was elected a member of the Royal Society in 1663. These form a fitting close to the brighter, if more prosaic, side of Denham's strange career.

Cooper's Hill

Sure there are poets which did never dream
Upon Parnassus, nor did taste the stream
Of Helicon; we therefore may suppose
Those made not poets, but the poets those.

And as courts make not kings, but kings the court,
So where the Muses and their train resort,
Parnassus stands; if I can be to thee
A poet, thou Parnassus art to me.
Nor wonder, if (advantaged in my flight,
By taking wing from thy auspicious height)   10
Through untraced ways and airy paths I fly,
More boundless in my fancy than my eye:
My eye, which swift as thought contracts the space
That lies between, and first salutes the place
Crowned with that sacred pile, so vast, so high,
That whether 'tis a part of earth or sky
Uncertain seems, and may be thought a proud
Aspiring mountain, or descending cloud,
Paul's, the late theme of such a Muse whose flight
Has bravely reached and soared above thy height; [1]   20
Now shalt thou stand though sword, or time, or fire,
Or zeal more fierce than they, thy fall conspire,
Secure, whilst thee the best of poets sings,
Preserved from ruin by the best of kings.
Under his proud survey the city lies,
And like a mist beneath a hill doth rise,
Whose state and wealth the business and the crowd,
Seems at this distance but a darker cloud;
And is to him who rightly things esteems
No other in effect than what it seems.   30
Where, with like haste, through several ways they run,
Some to undo and some to be undone;
While luxury and wealth, like war and peace,
Are each the other's ruin and increase,
As rivers lost in seas, some secret vein
Thence reconveighs, there to be lost again.
Oh, happiness of sweet retired content!
To be at once secure and innocent.

[1] Waller, *Upon His Majesty's Repairing of Paul's.* The work was begun in 1633, but the repairs were not completed until about nine years later.

Windsor the next (where Mars with Venus dwells,
Beauty with strength) above the valley swells   40
Into my eye and doth itself present
With such an easy and unforced ascent
That no stupendous precipice denies
Access, no horror turns away our eyes;
But such a rise as doth at once invite
A pleasure and a reverence from the sight.
Thy mighty master's emblem, in whose face
Sat meekness, heightened with majestic grace;
Such seems thy gentle height, made only proud
To be the basis of that pompous load,   50
Than which a nobler weight no mountain bears,
But Atlas only that supports the spheres.
When nature's hand this ground did thus advance,
'Twas guided by a wiser power than chance,
Marked out for such a use as if 'twere meant
T'invite the builder, and his choice prevent.
Nor can we call it choice when what we choose,
Folly or blindness only could refuse.
A crown of such majestic towers doth grace
The gods' great mother [2] when her heavenly race   60
Do homage to her; yet she cannot boast
Amongst that numerous and celestial host
More heroes than can Windsor, nor doth fame's
Immortal book record more noble names.
Not to look back so far, to whom this isle
Owes the first glory of so brave a pile,
Whether to Cæsar, Albanact, or Brute,[3]
The British Arthur, or the Danish Canute
(Though this of old no less contest did move
Than when for Homer's birth seven cities strove;   70
Like him in birth, thou shouldst be like in fame,

[2] Cybele. The rim of her crown is carved in the shape of battlements
and towers.
[3] Brutus, grandson of Æneas, was the legendary founder of Britain.
After his death the kingdom was divided among his three sons: Al-
banact received Scotland; Locrine, England; and Camber, Wales.

As thine his fate, if mine had been his flame);
But whoso'er it was, nature designed
First a brave place, and then as brave a mind.
Not to recount those several kings, to whom
It gave a cradle, or to whom a tomb,
But thee, great Edward, and thy greater son,[4]
(The lilies which his father wore, he won)
And thy Bellona, who the consort came
Not only to thy bed, but to thy fame;
She to thy triumph led one captive king   80
And brought that son, which did the second bring.[5]
Then didst thou found that Order [6] (whether love
Or victory thy royal thoughts did move).
Each was a noble cause, and nothing less
Than the design has been the great success,
Which foreign kings and emperors esteem
The second honor to their diadem.
Had thy great destiny but given thee skill
To know, as well as power to act her will,   90
That from those kings, who then thy captives were,
In after-times should spring a royal pair [7]
Who should possess all that thy mighty power,
Or thy desires more mighty, did devour,
To whom their better fate reserves what ere
The victor hopes for, or the vanquished fear;
That blood, which thou and thy grandsire shed,
And all that since these sister nations bled,
Had been unspilt, had happy Edward known
That all the blood he spilt had been his own.   100
When he that patron chose [8] in whom are joined
Soldier and martyr, and his arms confined

[4] The reference is to Edward III and the Black Prince.
[5] Queen Phillippa is the *Bellona* referred to; the first "captive king" is King David II of Scotland and the second, King John II of France captured at Poitiers.
[6] The Order of the Garter.
[7] Charles I and Henrietta Maria are meant, though the genealogy is not entirely accurate.
[8] His patron was St. George.

Within the azure circle, he did seem
But to foretell and prophesy of him
Who to his realms that azure round hath joined,
Which nature for their bound at first designed;
That bound, which to the world's extremest ends,
Endless itself, its liquid arms extends:
Nor doth he need those emblems which we paint,
But is himself the soldier and the saint. 110
Here should my wonder dwell, and here my praise;
But my fixed thoughts my wandering eye betrays,
Viewing a neighboring hill, whose top of late
A chapel crowned, till in the common fate
The adjoining Abbey [9] fell (may no such storm
Fall on our times, where ruin must reform).
Tell me, my Muse, what monstrous dire offense,
What crime could any Christian king incense
To such a rage? Was't luxury, or lust?
Was he so temperate, so chaste, so just? 120
Were these their crimes? They were his own much more;
But wealth is crime enough to him that's poor,
Who having spent the treasures of his crown,
Condemns their luxury to feed his own.
And yet this act, to varnish o'er the shame
Of sacrilege, must bear devotion's name.
No crime so bold but would be understood
A real, or at least a seeming good.
Who fears not to do ill, yet fears the name,
And free from conscience, is a slave to fame. 130
Thus he the church at once protects and spoils;
But Prince's swords are sharper than their styles.[10]
And thus to the ages past he makes amends,
Their charity destroys, their faith defends.
Then did religion in a lazy cell,
In empty, airy contemplations dwell,
And like the block, unmoved lay; but ours,

[9] Chertsey Abbey.
[10] The reference is to a book by Henry VIII.

As much too active, like the stork devours.
Is there no temperate region can be known,
Betwixt their frigid, and our torrid zone?   140
Could we not wake from that lethargic dream,
But to be restless in a worse extreme?
And for that lethargy was there no cure,
But to be cast into a calenture? [11]
Can knowledge have no bound, but must advance
So far, to make us wish for ignorance?
And rather in the dark to grope our way
Than led by a false guide to err by day?
Who sees these dismal heaps, but would demand
What barbarous invader sacked the land?   150
But when he hears no Goth, no Turk did bring
This desolation, but a Christian king,
When nothing but the name of zeal appears
'Twixt our best actions and the worst of theirs,
What does he think our sacrilege would spare,
When such the effects of our devotions are?
Parting from thence 'twixt anger, shame, and fear,
Those for what's past, and this for what's too near,
My eye, descending from the hill, surveys
Where Thames amongst the wanton valleys strays.   160
Thames, the most loved of all the ocean's sons,
By his old sire, to his embraces runs,
Hasting to pay his tribute to the sea,
Like mortal life to meet eternity.
Though with those streams he no resemblance hold,
Whose foam is amber and their gravel gold;
His genuine, and less guilty wealth to explore,
Search not his bottom, but survey his shore,
O'er which he kindly spreads his spacious wing,
And hatches plenty for the ensuing spring.   170
Not then destroys it with too fond a stay,
Like mothers which their infants overlay;
Nor with a sudden and impetuous wave,

[11] A fever caused by exposure to tropical heat.

Like profuse kings, resumes the wealth he gave.
No unexpected inundations spoil
The mower's hopes, nor mock the plowman's toil;
But God-like his unwearied bounty flows;
First loves to do, then loves the good he does.
Nor are his blessings to his banks confined,
But free and common as the sea or wind;   180
When he to boast, or to disperse his stores,
Full of the tributes of his grateful shores,
Visits the world, and in his flying towers
Brings home to us, and makes the Indies ours;
Finds wealth where 'tis, bestows it where it wants,
Cities in deserts, woods in cities plants,
So that to us no thing, no place is strange,
While his fair bosom is the world's exchange.
O could I flow like thee, and make thy stream
My great example, as it is my theme!   190
Though deep, yet clear, though gentle, yet not dull,
Strong without rage, without o'er-flowing full.
Heaven her Eridanus [12] no more shall boast,
Whose fame in thine, like lesser currents lost,
Thy nobler streams shall visit Jove's abodes,
To shine amongst the stars and bathe the gods.
Here nature, whether more intent to please
Us or herself with strange varieties
(For things of wonder give no less delight
To the wise Maker's, than beholder's sight,   200
Though these delights from several causes move;
For so our children, thus our friends we love),
Wisely she knew the harmony of things,
As well as that of sounds, from discords springs.
Such was the discord which did first disperse
Form, order, beauty through the universe.
While dryness moisture, coldness heat resists,
All that we have, and that we are, subsists;

[12] Eridanus, the name of a river. Phaeton was hurled into this river
when struck by Jupiter's thunderbolt.

While the steep horrid roughness of the wood
Strives with the gentle calmness of the flood,   21
Such huge extremes when nature doth unite,
Wonder from thence results, from thence delight.
The stream is so transparent, pure, and clear,
That had the self-enamored youth gazed here,
So fatally deceived he had not been,
While he the bottom, not his face had seen.
But his proud head the airy mountain hides
Among the clouds; his shoulders and his sides
A shady mantle clothes; his curled brows
Frown on the gentle stream, which calmly flows,   22
While winds and storms his lofty forehead beat,
The common fate of all that's high or great.
Low at his foot a spacious plain is placed,
Between the mountain and the stream embraced,
Which shade and shelter from the hill derives,
While the kind river wealth and beauty gives;
And in the mixture of all these appears
Variety, which all the rest indears.
This scene had some bold Greek, or British bard
Beheld of old, what stories had we heard   23
Of fairies, satyrs, and the nymphs, their dames,
Their feasts, their revels, and their amorous flames.
'Tis the same still, although their airy shape
All but the quick poetic sight escape.
There Faunus and Sylvanus keep their courts,
And thither all the horned host resorts
To graze the ranker mead; that noble herd
On whose sublime and shady fronts is reared
Nature's great masterpiece, to show how soon
Great things are made, but sooner are undone.   24
Here have I seen the king, when great affairs
Give leave to slacken and unbend his cares,
Attended to the chase by all the flower
Of youth, whose hopes a nobler prey devour.
Pleasure with praise and danger they would buy,

And wish a foe that would not only fly.
The stag now conscious of his fatal growth,
At once indulgent to his fear and sloth,
To some dark covert his retreat had made,
Where no man's eye, nor heaven's should invade   250
His soft repose; when the unexpected sound
Of dogs and men his wakeful ear doth wound.
Roused with the noise, he scarce believes his ear,
Willing to think the illusions of his fear
Had given this alarm; but straight his view
Confirms that more than all he fears is true.
Betrayed in all his strengths, the wood beset,
All instruments, all arts of ruin met,
He calls to mind his strength and then his speed,
His winged heels, and then his armed head;   260
With these to avoid, with that his fate to meet;
But fear prevails and bids him trust his feet.
So fast he flies that his reviewing eye
Has lost the chasers, and his ear the cry;
Exulting, till he finds their nobler sense
Their disproportioned speed does recompense.
Then curses his conspiring feet, whose scent
Betrays that safety which their swiftness lent.
Then tries his friends: among the baser herd,
Where he so lately was obeyed and feared,   270
His safety seeks; the herd, unkindly wise,
Or chases him from thence, or from him flies.
Like a declining statesman left forlorn
To his friends' pity and pursuers' scorn,
With shame remembers, while himself was one
Of the same herd, himself the same had done.
Thence to the coverts and the conscious groves,
The scenes of his past triumphs and his loves,
Sadly surveying where he ranged alone,
Prince of the soil and all the herd his own,   280
And like a bold knight errant did proclaim
Combat to all, and bore away the dame,

And taught the woods to echo to the stream
His dreadful challenge and his clashing beam;
Yet faintly now declines the fatal strife,
So much his love was dearer than his life.
Now every leaf and every moving breath
Presents a foe, and every foe a death.
Wearied, forsaken, and pursued, at last
All safety in despair of safety placed,   290
Courage he thence resumes, resolved to bear
All their assaults, since 'tis in vain to fear.
And now too late he wishes for the fight
That strength he wasted in ignoble flight.
But when he sees the eager chase renewed,
Himself by dogs, the dogs by men pursued,
He straight revokes his bold resolve, and more
Repents his courage than his fear before;
Finds that uncertain ways unsafest are,
And doubt a greater mischief than despair.   300
Then to the stream, when neither friends, nor force,
Nor speed, nor art avail, he shapes his course;
Thinks not their rage so desperate to assay
An element more merciless than they.
But fearless they pursue, nor can the flood
Quench their dire thirst; alas, they thirst for blood.
So toward a ship the oarfin'd galleys ply,
Which wanting sea to ride, or wind to fly,
Stands but to fall revenged on those that dare
Tempt the last fury of extreme despair.   310
So fares the stag among the enraged hounds,
Repels their force, and wounds returns for wounds.
And as a hero, whom his baser foes
In troops surround, now these assails, now those,
Though prodigal of life, disdains to die,
By common hands; but if he can descry
Some nobler foe's approach, to him he calls
And begs his fate, and then contented falls:

So when the king a mortal shaft lets fly
From his unerring hand, then glad to die,   320
Proud of the wound, to it resigns his blood
And stains the crystal with a purple flood.
This a more innocent and happy chase
Than when of old, but in the self-same place,[13]
Fair liberty pursued, and meant a prey
To lawless power, here turned and stood at bay,
When in that remedy all hope was placed
Which was, or should have been at least, the last.
Here was that Charter sealed wherein the crown
All marks of arbitrary power lays down.   330
Tyrant and slave, those names of hate and fear,
The happier style of king and subject bear:
Happy when both to the same center move,
When kings give liberty, and subjects love.
Therefore not long in force this Charter stood;
Wanting that seal, it must be sealed in blood.
The subjects armed, the more the princes gave,
The advantage only took the more to crave.
Till kings by giving, give themselves away,
And even that power that should deny, betray.   340
"Who gives constrained, but his own fear reviles,
Not thanked, but scorned; nor are they gifts, but spoils."
Thus kings, by grasping more than they could hold,
First made their subjects by oppression bold;
And popular sway, by forcing kings to give
More than was fit for subjects to receive,
Ran to the same extremes; and one excess
Made both, by striving to be greater, less.
When a calm river, raised with sudden rains,
Or snows dissolved, o'erflows the adjoining plains,   350
The husbandmen with high-raised banks secure
Their greedy hopes, and this he can endure.
But if with bays and dams they strive to force

[13] That is, Runnymede.

His channel to a new or narrow course,
No longer then within his banks he dwells;
First to a torrent, then a deluge swells;
Stronger and fiercer by restraint he roars,
And knows no bound, but makes his power his shores.

IF Richard Lovelace had lived in the Renaissance, he would have been called a "complete gentleman." In his own day he fulfilled Milton's inclusive definition of the educated man. He was an amateur in music and painting, a scholar, poet, courtier, soldier, and statesman. To these abilities were added charm and a steadfastness of character that was unusual among the Cavaliers. Wood says of him also that he was "the most amiable and beautiful person that ever eye beheld," and Aubrey extravagantly states that he was "one of the handsomest men of England . . . an extraordinary handsome man . . . a most beautiful gentleman."

His beauty may have helped him to obtain a university degree. When the king and queen visited Oxford in 1636, "a great Lady" attending the queen requested the chancellor of the university to create Lovelace Master of Arts. Forthwith the degree was conferred, in spite of the fact that he had been a student only two years.

The Lovelace family knew little but army life: Richard's father died on the foreign field, and his brothers fought for the king. His talents, however, seemed to indicate a literary career; before the occasion of the king's visit he had written a play, which had been produced at the university. But the patriotic enthusiasm of the Royalist center seems to have turned him away from his literary aspirations to follow in the family tradition of service to the king. It was not until he was in prison as the result of his loyalty to that he produced his first poem of distinction.

The epochs in Lovelace's career are marked by famous poems. He took part in both Scottish expeditions and left a literary memorial of them in a poem to General Goring, under whom he served. A handsome and daring figure, he presented to Parliament the petition of his native section of Kent re-

---

[1] C. H. Wilkinson has established the date of Lovelace's death as 1657 instead of the long-accepted 1658. See his *Poems of Richard Lovelace,* I, xlix.

questing the restoration of the king's rights. The occasion was a very dramatic one, for Parliament had ordered a previous petition burned by the common hangman. Lovelace had to pay for his temerity by imprisonment, but during his confinement produced the beautiful lyric *To Althea, from Prison*. When he was released he was again active in the king's cause. He furnished his brothers with men and money, and he himself took up arms, serving as captain. After the fall of Oxford in 1646 he went to the aid of Louis XIV against Spain, and on this occasion wrote *To Lucasta, Going beyond the Seas*. Upon his return to England he suffered imprisonment a second time, but used his leisure to prepare his poems for the press.

His release the following year meant little to him: the king he had served had been executed; his own property had been spent for the lost cause; his singing spirit was crushed. He passed the remaining years of his life in obscurity and probably in poverty, and we know little except that he was buried in St. Bride's Church. Here, in the next century, Richardson came to worship; but his straying mind seized upon the name of Lovelace for the hero of the novel *Clarissa Harlowe,* which he was then composing. The incident is the source of one of the most curious paradoxes in literary history, for "the author of *Lucasta*—known for his modesty and virtue—became a thousand times more famous in the eighteenth century as the paragon of vice." [2]

The Lucasta of the poems was identified by Wood as Lucy Sacheverel, an identification which led to a very pretty story, resembling that told in *Enoch Arden*. Hearing that Lovelace had been killed in the battle at Dunkirk, Lucy married. But Lovelace had been only wounded and returned from the wars to find his Lucasta the wife of another man. C. H. Wilkinson thinks, however, that the grounds for this story are very unreliable and suggests a member of the family of Sir Charles Lucas as Lucasta. [3]

[2] Phelps, *The Poems of Richard Lovelace,* I, xii.
[3] Wilkinson, *op. cit.,* p. xliv.

The two lines, "I could not love thee, dear, so much" and "The devil take her," have been called the opposite poles of Cavalier poetry. The stability of Lovelace presents a striking contrast indeed to the gay flippancy of Suckling. The very title of Lovelace's volume of poems, *Lucasta—Lux Casta,* or "light of virtue"—indicates his moral quality. In composition, however, Lovelace is much more uneven than Suckling. To the former, poetry was a gentleman's pastime, fit to employ only his leisure hours. Although Lovelace prepared his poems for the press, he apparently spent little time in revision, for many of his lines are unintentionally rough and obscure.

To Althea, from Prison and *To Lucasta, Going to the Wars* have been praised so highly that they have obscured Lovelace's other poems. Though every one knows the famous lines from these two, few are acquainted with the other very lovely and musical songs in *Lucasta,* and few associate with Lovelace the close observation of nature and insect life shown in *The Grasshopper.* The two poems named, however, justly deserve their priority, for both in their beauty and in the expression of the finest spirit of the Cavaliers, they have superior merit.

To Althea, from Prison

When Love with unconfined wings
    Hovers within my gates,
And my divine Althea brings
    To whisper at the grates;
When I lie tangled in her hair
    And fettered to her eye,
The birds that wanton in the air
    Know no such liberty.

When flowing cups run swiftly round,
    With no allaying Thames,   10
Our careless heads with roses bound,

Our hearts with loyal flames;
When thirsty grief in wine we steep,
    When healths and draughts go free,
Fishes that tipple in the deep
    Know no such liberty.

When, like committed [1] linnets, I
    With shriller throat shall sing
The sweetness, mercy, majesty,
    And glories of my king;   20
When I shall voice aloud how good
    He is, how great should be,
Enlarged winds that curl the flood
    Know no such liberty.

Stone walls do not a prison make,
    Nor iron bars a cage:
Minds innocent and quiet take
    That for an hermitage.
If I have freedom in my love,
    And in my soul am free,   30
Angels alone, that soar above,
    Enjoy such liberty.

To Lucasta, Going to the Wars

Tell me not, sweet, I am unkind,
    That from the nunnery
Of thy chaste breast and quiet mind
    To war and arms I fly.

True, a new mistress now I chase,
    The first foe in the field;
And with a stronger faith embrace
    A sword, a horse, a shield.

[1] Imprisoned or caged.

Yet this inconstancy is such
    As you too shall adore;   10
I could not love thee, dear, so much,
    Loved I not honor more.

To Lucasta, Going beyond the Seas

If to be absent were to be
    Away from thee;
  Or that when I am gone,
  You or I were alone,
Then, my Lucasta, might I crave
Pity from blustering wind or swallowing wave.

But I'll not sigh one blast or gale
    To swell my sail,
  Or pay a tear to 'suage [1]
  The foaming blue-god's rage; [2]   10
For whether he will let me pass
Or no, I'm still as happy as I was.

Though seas and land betwixt us both,
    Our faith and troth,
  Like separated souls,
  All time and space controls:
Above the highest sphere we meet,
Unseen, unknown, and greet as angels greet.

So then we do anticipate
    Our after-fate,   20
  And are alive in the skies,
  If thus our lips and eyes
Can speak like spirits unconfined
In heaven, their earthly bodies left behind.

[1] Assuage.
[2] Blue hair was the symbol of the sea-gods as represented on the stage.

Gratiana Dancing and Singing

See! with what constant motion,
Even, and glorious, as the sun,
  Gratiana steers that noble frame.
Soft as her breast, sweet as her voice
That gave each winding law and poise,
  And swifter than the wings of fame,

She beat the happy pavement,
By such a star made firmament,
  Which now no more the roof envies;
But swells up high with Atlas even,   10
Bearing the brighter, nobler heaven,
  And in her, all the deities.

Each step trod out a lover's thought,
And the ambitious hopes he brought
  Chained to her brave feet with such arts,
Such sweet command, and gentle awe,
As when she ceased, we sighing saw
  The floor lay paved with broken hearts.

So did she move; so did she sing
Like the harmonious spheres that bring   20
  Unto their rounds their music's aid; [1]
Which she performed such a way,
As all the enamoured world will say,
  "The Graces danced, and Apollo played."

The Scrutiny

Why shouldst thou swear I am forsworn,
  Since thine I vowed to be?

[1] The spheres of the Ptolemaic system were supposed to make very beautiful music as they turned.

Lady, it is already morn,
   And 'twas last night I swore to thee
   That fond impossibility.

Have I not loved thee much and long?
   A tedious twelve hour's space! [1]
I should all other beauties wrong,
   And rob thee of a new embrace,
   Should I still dote upon thy face.   10

Not but all joy in thy brown hair
   By others may be found;
But I must search the black and fair,
   Like skilful mineralists that sound
   For treasure in unplowed-up ground.

Then if, when I have loved my round,
   Thou provest the pleasant she,
With spoils of meaner beauties crowned,
   I laden will return to thee,
   E'en sated with variety.   20

The Grasshopper

To My Noble Friend, Mr. Charles Cotton

O thou that swing'st upon the waving ear
   Of some well-filled oaten beard,
Drunk every night with a delicious tear
   Dropped thee from heaven, where now thou art reared;

The joys of earth and air are thine entire,
   That with thy feet and wings dost hop and fly;
And, when thy poppy works, thou dost retire
   To thy carved acorn-bed to lie.

[1] Hazlitt gives months. The reading of Cotgrave, *hours,* seems more
in keeping with the usual ideas of constancy in this period.

Up with the day, the sun thou welcom'st then,
    Sport'st in the gilt plats of his beams,   10
And all these merry days mak'st merry men,
    Thyself, and melancholy streams.[1]

But ah, the sickle! Golden ears are cropped;
    Ceres and Bacchus bid good night;
Sharp, frosty fingers all your flowers have topped,
    And what scythes spared, winds shave off quite.

Poor verdant fool, and now green ice! thy joys,
    Large and as lasting as thy perch of grass,
Bid us lay in 'gainst winter rain, and poise
    Their floods with an o'erflowing glass.   20

Thou best of men and friends! we will create
    A genuine summer in each other's breast,
And spite of this cold time and frozen fate,
    Thaw us a warm seat to our rest.

Our sacred hearths shall burn eternally,
    As vestal flames; the North Wind, he
Shall strike his frost-stretched wings, dissolve, and fly
    This Etna in epitome.

Dropping December shall come weeping in,
    Bewail the usurping of his reign;   30
But when in showers of old Greek we begin,
    Shall cry he hath his crown again!

Night, as clear Hesper, shall our tapers whip
    From the light casements where we play,
And the dark hag from her black mantle strip,
    And stick there everlasting day.

---

[1] With these three stanzas compare Cowley's "The Grasshopper," from his *Anacreontics*.

Thus richer than untempted kings are we,
  That, asking nothing, nothing need:
Though lord of all what seas embrace, yet he
  That wants himself is poor indeed.   40

Abraham Cowley 1618-1667

ALTHOUGH Cowley died before he was fifty, his career as a writer extended over almost forty years. This fact seems especially unusual since Cowley was brought up by a widowed mother (also his first teacher) who read only books of devotion. But a copy of the *Faerie Queene* adorned the parlor table. Chancing upon it at the age of ten, Cowley was made a poet "irremediably," and under its influence began writing creditable verses.

His mother was wise enough to give this seventh and most precocious child of hers a good education. He became one of "Anthony's Pigs," as the students of St. Peter's College, Westminster, were impartially named. There from five in the morning until eight at night the time was filled with many prayers and much study, especially of Latin, Greek, and in the last form, Hebrew. Although Cowley would not learn "the common rules of grammar," his masters gave encouragement in his writing and were proud of the *Poetical Blossoms,* published at the age of fifteen. It has been suggested that the fame of the young author reached the ambitious Milton, about to seclude himself at Horton for further study, making him aware of the "more timely-happy spirits" mentioned in his sonnet *On His Having Arrived at the Age of Twenty-three* and restive under his own "late spring."

Cowley arrived at Trinity College, Cambridge, with a second edition of *Poetical Blossoms* published and the completed manuscript of *Love's Riddle,* a pastoral play. The following year a third edition of *Poetical Blossoms* came out, and a year later *Love's Riddle* and a five-act Latin play written for production at the university. At twenty, then, and in his second year at the university, Cowley had published three successful works and was already famous. The other poets at Cambridge—Suckling, Cleveland, Fanshawe, Beaumont, and Crashaw—must have been half-delighted and half-envious.

Ejected from Cambridge by the Parliamentarians, he followed Crashaw to Oxford, the headquarters for the Royalists, where he remained until the queen fled to Paris. The flight of the queen plunged Cowley, the ambitious poet with a taste for a quiet pastoral life, into a long period of public activity. As secretary to the Queen's Chamberlain, Baron Jermyn, he also served as secretary to the queen and was employed in writing letters in code to Charles I and sent on many important state commissions on the Continent. The strain of state duties was relieved by pleasant associations with other literary expatriates: Davenant, Crashaw (whose financial distress he was able to relieve), Waller, and Denham. In order to continue writing, Cowley had need of the ambitious spirit which he had expressed at Cambridge in *The Motto:*

> Unpassed Alps stop me, but I'll cut through all,
> And march, the Muse's Hannibal.

He felt that "bright and delightful ideas" could scarcely flourish when the spirit was "shaken and disturbed with the storms of injurious fortune," and in the preface to the 1656 edition of his poems he comments that "a warlike, various, and a tragical age is best to write of, but worst to write in." In 1647, however, he published *The Mistress,* a volume of love poems, which in their abrupt openings and ingenious conceits show the influence of Donne.

In 1654 Cowley was back in London, where, according to Sprat's *Life,* "under pretense of privacy and retirement" he should find out "the posture of things in this nation." He was imprisoned, either by mistake for another man, as Sprat claims, or through suspicion, and was held until a large bail could be raised by his friends. In order to carry on his services to the crown without danger, Cowley took up the study of medicine, receiving his degree as "doctor of physic" from Oxford in 1657. This study bore direct results in only an interest in botany and a six-volume treatise on plants. Perhaps, however, it was the interest in science vitalized at this time that led later to his membership in the Royal Society, his *Proposition for the Advancement of Experimental Philosophy*, the fine *Ode to the Royal Society*, and the *Hymn to Light*.

In 1656 he had seen his collected poems through the press in spite of his study of medicine and a discouragement which set him yearning for "some obscure retreat in America." This volume contained several interesting types of work. There was the long, unfinished religious epic *Davideis* with which he was honest enough to confess that he had become bored, but there was also the wholly delightful *Anacreontics*, or translations and imitations of the odes of Anacreon. His great innovation was his *Pindarique Odes*. These did not pretend to be copies of Pindar but only an attempt to reproduce in English the spirit of Pindar. Cowley gave to English poetry the irregular ode, which later reached much greater heights in Collins, Gray, Dryden, Shelley, Keats, and Wordsworth.

Finally that "joyfullest funeral that ever I saw" (as described by Evelyn) enabled Cowley to return to France. He prepared an *Ode, Upon the Blessed Restoration and Return of His Sacred Majesty, Charles the Second,* but neither this nor the earlier promise of the directorship of the Savoy Hospital resulted in Cowley's receiving the position. The king suspected him of temporary defection to Cromwell because of a favorable reference to the Commonwealth in the preface to his collected poems, and held that his pardon was sufficient recompense for the years of service which Cowley had given. Queen Henrietta Maria did what she could, giving him lands in Kent. In 1663 he was established quietly at Barn Elms, where Evelyn visited him, taught him to make a salad, presented him with seeds, and instructed him in gardening. The winter climate there did not agree with Cowley; and after two years he settled at Chertsey, twenty miles farther up the Thames.

Cowley had always loved the contemplative life, and these later years were but the deferred fulfilment of his desires. As a student at Westminster he had spent his holidays "in the fields either alone with a book, or with some one companion, if I could find any of the same temper." [1] At thirteen, in *The Vote*, he had pictured his conception of the ideal life:

> Books should, not business, entertain the light,
> And sleep, as undisturb'd as death, the night.
>   My house a cottage, more
> Than palace; and should fitting be
> For all my use, no luxury.
>   My garden painted o'er
> With nature's hand, not art's; and pleasures yield,
> Horace might envy in his Sabine field.

A similar idea was repeated in *The Wish*, written while he was in France. The fulfilment of the longings set forth in both these poems was expressed in *Solitude*, a poem written after he moved to Chertsey.

Cowley won great fame as a poet and in his own day was ranked above Milton; but he is better known and loved today for his familiar essays, written as pastime in his retirement. We must not, however, overlook the importance of his poetical work: he anticipated Milton in the religious epic, he introduced the irregular ode, the type used later for some of the greatest English odes, and he helped to develop the heroic couplet, a contribution which led Dryden to say, "His authority is almost sacred to me."

The Wish

> Well then; I now do plainly see,
> This busy world and I shall ne'er agree;
> The very honey of all earthly joy
>   Does of all meats the soonest cloy;
>   And they, methinks, deserve my pity
> Who for it can endure the stings,

[1] *Of Myself.*

The crowd, and buzz, and murmurings
  Of this great hive, the city.

  Ah, yet, ere I descend to the grave
May I a small house and large garden have!   10
And a few friends, and many books, both true,
  Both wise, and both delightful too!
  And since love ne'er will from me flee,
A mistress moderately fair,
And good as guardian angels are,
  Only beloved, and loving me!

  O fountains, when in you shall I
Myself, eased of unpeaceful thoughts, espy?
O fields! O woods! when, when shall I be made
  The happy tenant of your shade?   20
  Here's the spring-head of pleasure's flood,
Where all the riches lie that she
  Has coined and stamped for good.

  Pride and ambition here
Only in far-fetched metaphors appear;
Here naught but winds can hurtful murmurs scatter,
  And naught but Echo flatter.
  The gods, when they descended, hither
From heaven did always choose their way;
And therefore we may boldly say   30
  That 'tis the way, too, thither.

  How happy here should I
And one dear she live and, embracing, die!
She who is all the world, and can exclude
  In deserts, solitude.
  I should have then this only fear,
Lest men, when they my pleasures see,
Should hither throng to live like me,
  And so make a city here.

To the Royal Society

I

Philosophy, the great and only heir
  Of all that human knowledge which has been
Unforfeited by man's rebellious sin,
  Though full of years he do appear
(Philosophy, I say, and call it "he,"
For whatsoe'er the painters' fancy be,
  It a male virtue seems to me),
Has still been kept in nonage till of late,
Nor managed or enjoyed his vast estate:
Three or four thousand years, one would have thought,   10
To ripeness and perfection might have brought
  A science so well bred and nursed,
And of such hopeful parts, too, at the first.
But, oh, the guardians and the tutors then,
Some negligent and some ambitious men,
  Would ne'er consent to set him free,
Or his own natural powers to let him see,
Lest that should put an end to their authority.

II

That his own business he might quite forget,
They amused him with the sports of wanton wit;   20
With the desserts of poetry they fed him,
Instead of solid meats to increase his force;
Instead of vigorous exercise, they led him
Into the pleasant labyrinths of ever-fresh discourse;
  Instead of carrying him to see
The riches which do hoarded for him lie
  In nature's endless treasury,
  They chose his eye to entertain,
  His curious but not covetous eye,
With painted scenes, and pageants of the brain.   30

Some few exalted spirits this latter age has shown,
That labored to assert the liberty,
From guardians who were now usurpers grown,
Of this old minor still, captived philosophy;
    But 'twas rebellion called to fight
    For such a long-oppressed right.
Bacon at last, a mighty man, arose,
    Whom a wise king and nature chose
    Lord Chancellor of both their laws,
And boldly undertook the injured pupil's cause.   40

III

Authority, which did a body boast,
Though 'twas but air condensed, and stalked about
Like some old giant's more gigantic ghost
    To terrify the learned rout,
With the plain magic of true reason's light
    He chased out of our sight,
Nor suffered living men to be misled
    By the vain shadows of the dead:
To graves, from whence it rose, the conquered phantom fled.
    He broke that monstrous god which stood   50
In midst of the orchard, and the whole did claim,
    Which, with a useless scythe of wood
    And something else not worth a name—
    Both vast for show, yet neither fit
    Or to defend or to beget;
    Ridiculous and senseless terrors!—made
Children and superstitious men afraid.
    The orchard's open now and free;
Bacon has broke that scarecrow deity;
    Come, enter, all that will;   60
Behold the ripened fruit; come, gather now your fill.
    Yet still, methinks, we fain would be
    Catching at the forbidden tree;
    We would be like the Deity

When truth and falsehood, good and evil, we
Without the senses' aid, within ourselves would see;
   For 'tis God only who can find
   All nature in His mind.

IV

From words, which are but pictures of the thought
(Though we our thoughts from them perversely drew),   70
To things, the mind's right object, he it brought:
Like foolish birds to painted grapes we flew; [1]
He sought and gathered for our use the true;
And when on heaps the chosen bunches lay,
He pressed them wisely the mechanic way,
Till all their juice did in one vessel join,
Ferment into a nourishment divine,
   The thirsty soul's refreshing wine.
Who to the life an exact piece would make,
Must not from others' work a copy take;   80
   No, not from Rubens or Vandyke;
Much less content himself to make it like
The ideas and the images which lie
In his own fancy or his memory.
   No, he before his sight must place
   The natural and living face;
   The real object must command
Each judgment of his eye and motion of his hand.

V

From these and all long errors of the way
In which our wandering predecessors went,   90
And like the old Hebrews many years did stray
   In deserts but of small extent,
Bacon, like Moses, led us forth at last;

[1] Reference is to the Grecian painter whose grapes were so naturally done that the birds came to peck them.

The barren wilderness he passed,
Did on the very border stand
Of the blest promised land,
And, from the mountain's top of his exalted wit,
    Saw it himself, and showed us it.
But life did never to one man allow
Time to discover worlds, and conquer too;   100
Nor can so short a line sufficient be
To fathom the vast depths of nature's sea.

    The work he did we ought to admire,
And were unjust if we should more require
From his few years, divided 'twixt the excess
Of low affliction and high happiness.
For who on things remote can fix his sight
That's always in a triumph or a fight?

VI

From you, great champions, we expect to get
These spacious countries but discovered yet,   110
Countries where yet instead of nature we
Her images and idols worshiped see.
These large and wealthy regions to subdue,
Though learning has whole armies at command
    Quartered about in every land,
A better troop she ne'er together drew.
    Methinks, like Gideon's little band,[2]
    God with design has picked out you,
To do these noble wonders by a few:
When the whole host He saw, "They are," said He,   120
    "Too many to o'ercome for Me."
    And now He chooses out his men

---

[2] See *Judges* 7. Those who lapped water from their hands in drinking were armed with trumpets and pitchers in which were concealed torches. The 300 thus equipped came to the outer part of the camp of the Midianites in the night and suddenly blew on their trumpets and broke their pitchers, revealing the lights. The amazed hosts of the enemy fled, destroying their own men in their terror and confusion.

Much in the way that He did then:
Not those many whom He found
Idly extended on the ground,
To drink with their dejected head
The stream just so as by their mouths it fled;
No, but those few who took the waters up,
And made of their laborious hands the cup.

VII

Thus you prepared; and in the glorious fight   130
Their wondrous pattern too you take:
Their old and empty pitchers first they brake,
And with their hands then lifted up the light.
Io! Sound too the trumpets here!
Already your victorious lights appear;
New scenes of heaven already we espy,
And crowds of golden worlds on high,
Which, from the spacious plains of earth and sea,
Could never yet discovered be
By sailor's or Chaldean's [3] watchful eye.   140
Nature's great works no distance can obscure;
No smallness her near objects can secure.[4]
You've taught the curious sight to press
Into the privatest recess
Of her imperceptible littleness.
You've learned to read her smallest hand,
And well begun her deepest sense to understand.

VIII

Mischief and true dishonor fall on those
Who would to laughter or to scorn expose

[3] The Chaldeans or Babylonians were believers in astrology.
[4] There was great development in both the telescope and the microscope in the seventeenth century, and the Royal Society was much interested in experiments with them. Hooke thought that with instruments man might be able to conquer all knowledge and bring back a golden age.

So virtuous and so noble a design,   150
So human for its use, for knowledge so divine.
The things which these proud men despise, and call
    Impertinent, and vain, and small,
Those smallest things of nature let me know,
Rather than all their greatest actions do.
Whoever would deposed truth advance
    Into the throne usurped from it,
Must feel at first the blows of ignorance
    And the sharp points of envious wit.
So when, by various turns of the celestial dance,   160
    In many thousand years
    A star, so long unknown, appears,
Though heaven itself more beauteous by it grow,
It troubles and alarms the world below,
Does to the wise a star, to fools a meteor show.

IX

With courage and success, you the bold work begin;
    Your cradle has not idle been:
None e'er but Hercules and you could be
At five years' age worthy a history.[5]
    And ne'er did fortune better yet   170
    The historian to the story fit:
    As you from all old errors free
And purge the body of philosophy,
    So from all modern follies he
Has vindicated eloquence and wit.
His candid style like a clean stream does slide,
    And his bright fancy all the way
    Does, like the sunshine, in it play;

[5] "The Royal Society of London for the Improving of Natural
Knowledge" was incorporated in 1662. This ode was written at the re-
quest of Thomas Sprat for his *History of the Royal Society,* printed
1667.

It does like Thames, the best of rivers, glide,
Where the god does not rudely overturn,   180
    But gently pour the crystal urn,
And with judicious hand does the whole current guide.
It has all the beauties nature can impart,
And all the comely dress without the paint of art.

Hymn to Light

First-born of Chaos, who so fair didst come
    From the old negro's darksome womb!
    Which, when it saw the lovely child,
The melancholy mass put on kind looks and smiled,

Thou tide of glory which no rest dost know,
    But ever ebb and ever flow!
    Thou golden shower of a true Jove,[1]
Who does in thee descend, and heaven to earth make love!

Hail, active nature's watchful life and health,
    Her joy, her ornament and wealth!   10
    Hail to thy husband heat, and thee,
Thou the world's beauteous bride, the lusty bridegroom he!

Say, from what golden quivers of the sky
    Do all thy winged arrows fly?
    Swiftness and power by birth are thine:
From thy great sire they came, thy sire the Word divine.[2]

'Tis, I believe, this archery to show,
    That so much cost in colors thou,
    And skill in painting, dost bestow
Upon thy ancient arms, the gaudy heavenly bow.   20

[1] Though the King of Argos had imprisoned his daughter, Danae, in a tower of brass, Jove, loving her, assumed the form of a shower of gold, and so reached her.
[2] *Gen.* 1:3. "And God said, Let there be light: and there was light."

Swift as light thoughts their empty career run,
     Thy race is finished when begun;
     Let a post-angel start with thee,[3]
And thou the goal of earth shalt reach as soon as he.

Thou in the moon's bright chariot, proud and gay,
     Dost thy bright wood of stars survey,
     And all the year dost with thee bring,
Of thousand flowery lights, thine own nocturnal spring.

Thou Scythian-like [4] dost round thy lands, above
     The sun's gilt tent, forever move,
     And still, as thou in pomp dost go,   30
The shining pageants of the world attend thy show.

Nor amidst all these triumphs dost thou scorn
     The humble glowworms to adorn,
     And with those living spangles gild—
O greatness without pride!—the bushes of the field.

Night and her ugly subjects thou dost fright,
     And sleep, the lazy owl of night;
     Ashamed and fearful to appear,
They screen their horrid shapes with the black hemi-
     sphere.   40

With 'em there hastes, and wildly takes the alarm,
     Of painted dreams, a busy swarm;
     At the first opening of thine eye,
The various clusters break, the antic atoms fly.

The guilty serpents and obscener beasts
     Creep conscious to their secret rests;
     Nature to thee does reverence pay;
Ill omens and ill sights removes out of thy way.

     [3] Angel-messenger.
     [4] Reference is to the nomadic life of the Scythians.

At thy appearance, grief itself is said
    To shake his wings and rouse his head.   50
    And cloudy care has often took
A gentle beamy smile reflected from thy look.

At thy appearance, fear itself grows bold;
    Thy sunshine melts away his cold.
    Encouraged at the sight of thee,
To the cheek color comes, and firmness to the knee.

Even lust, the master of a hardened face,
    Blushes if thou beest in the place;
    To darkness' curtains he retires;
In sympathizing night he rolls his smoky fires.   60

When, goddess, thou lift'st up thy wakened head
    Out of the morning's purple bed,
    Thy quire of birds about thee play,
And all the joyful world salutes the rising day.

The ghosts and monster spirits that did presume
    A body's privilege to assume
    Vanish again invisibly,
And bodies gain again their visibility.

All the world's bravery that delights our eyes
    Is but thy several liveries;   70
    Thou the rich dye on them bestow'st;
Thy nimble pencil paints this landscape as thou go'st.

A crimson garment in the rose thou wear'st;
    A crown of studded gold thou bear'st; [5]
    The virgin lilies in their white
Are clad but with the lawn of almost naked light.

The violet, spring's little infant, stands
    Girt in thy purple swaddling-bands;

[5] There was a flower called the "crown imperial."

On the fair tulip thou dost dote;
Thou cloth'st it in a gay and parti-colored coat.   80

With flame condensed thou dost the jewels fix,
   And solid colors in it mix;
   Flora herself envies to see
Flowers fairer than her own, and durable as she.

Ah, goddess! would thou couldst thy hand withhold
   And be less liberal to gold;
   Didst thou less value to it give,
Of how much care, alas, mightst thou poor man relieve!

To me the sun is more delightful far,
   And all fair days much fairer are.   90
   But few, ah wondrous few, there be
Who do not gold prefer, O goddess, even to thee.

Through the soft ways of heaven, and air, and sea,
   Which open all their pores to thee,
   Like a clear river thou dost glide,
And with thy living stream through the close channels slide.

But where firm bodies thy free course oppose,
   Gently thy source the land o'erflows,[6]
   Takes there possession, and does make,
Of colors mingled, light, a thick and standing lake.   100

But the vast ocean of unbounded day
   In the empyrean heaven does stay.[7]
   Thy rivers, lakes, and springs below
From thence took first their rise, thither at last must flow.

[6] At this time light was thought of as made up of particles which
could not pass through a solid substance.
[7] The highest heaven, thought by the ancients to be composed of
pure fire.

On the Death of Mr. Crashaw

Poet and saint! to thee alone are given
The two most sacred names of earth and heaven,
The hard and rarest union which can be
Next that of godhead with humanity.
Long did the Muses banished slaves abide,
And built vain pyramids to mortal pride;
Like Moses thou—though spells and charms withstand—
Hast brought them nobly home, back to their Holy Land.
  Ah wretched we, poets of earth! but thou
Wert, living, the same poet which thou art now   10
Whilst angels sing to thee their airs divine,
And joy in an applause so great as thine.
Equal society with them to hold,
Thou need'st not make new songs, but say the old.
And they, kind spirits! shall all rejoice to see
How little less than they exalted man may be.
Still the old heathen gods in numbers dwell;
The heavenliest thing on earth still keeps up hell.
Nor have we yet quite purged the Christian land;
Still idols here, like calves at Bethel, stand.[1]   20
And though Pan's death long since all oracles broke,
Yet still in rhyme the fiend Apollo spoke:
Nay, with the worst of heathen dotage we,
Vain men, the monster woman deify,
Find stars, and tie our fates there in a face,
And paradise in them, by whom we lost it, place.
What different faults corrupt our Muses thus?
Wanton as girls, as old wives fabulous!
  Thy spotless Muse, like Mary, did contain
The boundless godhead; she did well disdain   30

[1] *I Kings* 12:32. The reference is Jeroboam's setting up of the golden calves during the time of the divided kingdom, so that his followers would not return to Rehoboam, king of Judah, when they went to Jerusalem to worship.

That her eternal verse employed should be
On a less subject than eternity,
And for a sacred mistress scorned to take
But her whom God himself scorned not His spouse to make.
It, in a kind, her miracle did do:
A fruitful mother was, and virgin too.

How well, blest swan, did fate contrive thy death;
And made thee render up thy tuneful breath
In thy great mistress' arms, thou most divine
And richest offering of Loretto's shrine!   40
Where, like some holy sacrifice to expire,
A fever burns thee, and love lights the fire.
Angels—they say—brought the famed chapel there,[2]
And bore the sacred load in triumph through the air.
'Tis surer much they brought thee there; and they
And thou, their charge, went singing all the way.

Pardon, my mother church, if I consent
That angels led him when from thee he went,
For even in error sure no danger is
When joined with so much piety as his.   50
Ah, mighty God, with shame I speak it, and grief,
Ah, that our greatest faults were in belief!
And our weak reason were even weaker yet,
Rather than thus our wills too strong for it.
His faith perhaps in some nice tenets might
Be wrong; his life, I'm sure, was in the right.
And I myself a Catholic will be,
So far at least, great saint, to pray to thee.

Hail, bard triumphant! and some care bestow
On us, the poets militant below!   60
Opposed by our old enemy, adverse chance,
Attacked by envy, and by ignorance,
Enchained by beauty, tortured by desires,
Exposed by tyrant love to savage beasts and fires.
Thou from low earth in nobler flames didst rise,

[2] Legend recounts that angels bore the house of Mary's youth to
Loretto when Turks threatened the destruction of the house.

And like Elijah, mount alive the skies.[3]
Elisha-like (but with a wish much less,
More fit thy greatness and my littleness),
Lo, here I beg (I whom thou once didst prove
So humble to esteem, so good to love)   70
Not that thy spirit might on me doubled be,
I ask but half thy mighty spirit for me;
And when my Muse soars with so strong a wing,
'Twill learn of things divine, and first of thee to sing.

On the Death of Mr. William Hervey [1]

Immodicis brevis est aetas, & rara senectus. MART.

It was a dismal and a fearful night;
Scarce could the morn drive on the unwilling light,
When sleep, death's image, left my troubled breast,
    By something liker death possessed.
My eyes with tears did uncommanded flow,
    And on my soul hung the dull weight
    Of some intolerable fate.
What bell was that? Ah me! Too much I know.

My sweet companion, and my gentle peer,
Why hast thou left me thus unkindly here,   10
Thy end forever, and my life, to moan?
    Oh, thou hast left me all alone!
Thy soul and body, when death's agony
    Besieged around thy noble heart,
    Did not with more reluctance part
Than I, my dearest friend, do part from thee.

My dearest friend, would I had died for thee! [2]

[3] For the story of Elijah's ascension and the falling of his mantle
upon Elisha see *II Kings* 2:9, 11.
[1] A friend of Cowley's early life, not to be confused with William
Harvey, the great anatomist.
[2] *II Sam.* 18:33. David's lament for Absalom.

Life and this world henceforth will tedious be.
Nor shall I know hereafter what to do
   If once my griefs prove tedious too.
Silent and sad I walk about all day,
    As sullen ghosts stalk speechless by
    Where their hid treasures lie;
Alas, my treasure's gone; why do I stay?

He was my friend, the truest friend on earth;
A strong and mighty influence joined our birth.
Nor did we envy the most sounding name
   By friendship given of old to fame.
None but his brethren he, and sisters, knew
    Whom the kind youth preferred to me;
    And even in that we did agree,
For much above myself I loved them too.

Say, for you saw us, ye immortal lights,
How oft unwearied have we spent the nights?
Till the Ledaean stars, so famed for love,[3]
   Wondered at us from above.
We spent them not in toys, in lusts, or wine,
    But search of deep philosophy,
    Wit, eloquence, and poetry,
Arts which I loved, for they, my friend, were thine.

Ye fields of Cambridge, our dear Cambridge, say,
Have ye not seen us walking every day?
Was there a tree about, which did not know
   The love betwixt us two?
Henceforth, ye gentle trees, forever fade;
    Or your sad branches thicker join,
    And into darksome shades combine,
Dark as the grave wherein my friend is laid.

[3] The Gemini, the stars into which Jupiter changed the twin son
of Leda and the Swan (Jupiter in disguise) as a reward for their de
votion.

Henceforth no learned youths beneath you sing
Till all the tuneful birds to your boughs they bring;   50
No tuneful birds play with their wonted cheer,
    And call the learned youths to hear;
No whistling winds through the glad branches fly,
    But all with sad solemnity
    Mute and unmoved be,
Mute as the grave wherein my friend does lie.

To him my Muse made haste with every strain
Whilst it was new, and warm yet from the brain;
He loved my worthless rhymes, and like a friend
    Would find out something to commend.   60
Hence now, my Muse; thou canst not me delight;
    Be this my latest verse
    With which I now adorn his hearse,
And this my grief without thy help shall write.

Had I a wreath of bays about my brow,
I should contemn that flourishing honor now,
Condemn it to the fire, and joy to hear
    It rage and crackle there.
Instead of bays, crown with sad cypress me,
    Cypress which tombs does beautify;   70
    Not Phœbus grieved so much as I
For him who first was made that mournful tree.[4]

Large was his soul; as large a soul as e'er
Submitted to inform a body here;
High as the place 'twas shortly in heaven to have,
    But low and humble as his grave;
So high that all the virtues there did come
    As to their chiefest seat,
    Conspicuous and great;
So low that for me, too, it made a room.   80

[4] Cyparissus, a beautiful youth loved by Apollo, was heart-broken because he accidentally killed a pet stag. Apollo changed him into a cypress tree.

He scorned this busy world below, and all
That we, mistaken mortals, pleasure call;
Was filled with innocent gallantry and truth,
   Triumphant o'er the sins of youth.
He, like the stars, to which he now is gone,
   That shine with beams like flame,
   Yet burn not with the same,
Had all the light of youth, of the fire none.

Knowledge he only sought, and so soon caught
As if for him knowledge had rather sought;   90
Nor did more learning ever crowded lie
   In such a short mortality.
Whene'er the skilful youth discoursed or writ,
   Still did the notions throng
   About his eloquent tongue,
Nor could his ink flow faster than his wit.

So strong a wit did nature to him frame
As all things but his judgment overcame;
His judgment like the heavenly moon did show,
   Tempering that mighty sea below.   10
Oh had he lived in learning's world, what bound
   Would have been able to control
   His overpowering soul?
We have lost in him arts that not yet are found.

His mirth was the pure spirits of various wit,
Yet never did his God or friends forget,
And, when deep talk and wisdom came in view,
   Retired and gave to them their due.
For the rich help of books he always took,
   Though his own searching mind before   11
   Was so with notions written o'er
As if wise nature had made that her book.

So many virtues joined in him as we
Can scarce pick here and there in history,

More than old writers' practice e'er could reach,
  As much as they could ever teach.
These did religion, queen of virtues, sway,
  And all their sacred motions steer,
  Just like the first and highest sphere,
Which wheels about, and turns all heaven one way.[5]   120

With as much zeal, devotion, piety,
He always lived, as other saints do die.
Still with his soul severe account he kept,
  Weeping all debts out ere he slept.
Then down in peace and innocence he lay,
  Like the sun's laborious light,
  Which still in water sets at night,
Unsullied with his journey of the day.

Wondrous young man, why wert thou made so good,
To be snatched hence ere better understood,   130
Snatched before half of thee enough was seen!
  Thou ripe, and yet thy life but green!
Nor could thy friends take their last sad farewell,
  But danger and infectious death
  Maliciously seized on that breath,
Where life, spirit, pleasure always used to dwell.

But happy thou, ta'en from this frantic age,
Where ignorance and hypocrisy does rage!
A fitter time for heaven no soul e'er chose,
  The place now only free from those.   140
There 'mong the blest thou dost forever shine,
  And wheresoe'er thou casts thy view
  Upon that white and radiant crew,
Seest not a soul clothed with more light than thine.

And if the glorious saints cease not to know
Their wretched friends who fight with life below,

[5] The *primum mobile,* or outer sphere of the Ptolemaic system, which
set in motion the other spheres.

Thy flame to me does still the same abide,
  Only more pure and rarefied.
There whilst immortal hymns thou dost rehearse,
  Thou dost with holy pity see   150
  Our dull and earthly poesy,
Where grief and misery can be joined with verse.

Anacreontics
or
Some Copies of Verses Translated Paraphrastically Out of Anacreon

Drinking

The thirsty earth soaks up the rain,
And drinks, and gapes for drink again.
The plants suck in the earth, and are
With constant drinking fresh and fair.
The sea itself, which one would think
Should have but little need of drink,
Drinks ten thousand rivers up,
So filled that they o'erflow the cup.
The busy sun—and one would guess
By's drunken, fiery face no less—   10
Drinks up the sea, and when he's done,
The moon and stars drink up the sun.
They drink and dance by their own light;
They drink and revel all the night.
Nothing in nature's sober found,
But an eternal health goes round.
Fill up the bowl, then, fill it high,
Fill all the glasses there, for why
Should every creature drink but I?
Why, man of morals, tell me why?   20

The Epicure

Fill the bowl with rosy wine,
Around our temples roses twine,
And let us cheerfully a while
Like the wine and roses smile.
Crowned with roses, we contemn
Gyges' wealthy diadem.[1]
To-day is ours; what do we fear?
To-day is ours; we have it here.
Let's treat it kindly that it may
Wish, at least, with us to stay.   10
Let's banish business, banish sorrows;
To the gods belongs to-morrow.

The Grasshopper

Happy insect, what can be
In happiness compared to thee?
Fed with nourishment divine,
The dewy morning's gentle wine!
Nature waits upon thee still,
And thy verdant cup does fill;
'Tis filled wherever thou dost tread,
Nature self's thy Ganymede.
Thou dost drink and dance and sing,
Happier than the happiest king!   10
All the fields which thou dost see,
All the plants, belong to thee,
All that summer hours produce,
Fertile made with early juice.
Man for thee does sow and plow,
Farmer he, and landlord thou!
Thou dost innocently enjoy,

[1] Gyges. King of Lydia during the seventh century B. C., famous for his wealth.

Nor does thy luxury destroy;
The shepherd gladly heareth thee,
More harmonious than he.   20
Thee country hinds with gladness hear,
Prophet of the ripened year!
Thee Phœbus loves and does inspire;
Phœbus is himself thy sire.
To thee of all things upon earth
Life is no longer than thy mirth.
Happy insect, happy thou,
Dost neither age nor winter know.
But when thou'st drunk and danced and sung
Thy fill the flowery leaves among   30
(Voluptuous and wise withal,
Epicurean animal!),
Sated with thy summer feast,
Thou retirest to endless rest.

The Praise of Pindar
In Imitation of Horace His Second Ode,
Book 4

I

Pindar is imitable by none;
    The phœnix Pindar is a vast species alone.
Whoe'er but Dædalus with waxen wings could fly
And neither sink too low nor soar too high?
        What could he who followed claim
But of vain boldness the unhappy fame,
        And by his fall a sea to name?
        Pindar's unnavigable song,
Like a swollen flood from some steep mountain, pours along;
        The ocean meets with such a voice   10
From his enlarged mouth as drowns the ocean's noise.

II

So Pindar does new words and figures roll
Down his impetuous dithyrambic tide,
  Which in no channel deigns to abide,
  Which neither banks nor dikes control.
  Whether the immortal gods he sings
  In a no less immortal strain,
Or the great acts of god-descended kings,
Who in his numbers still survive and reign,
  Each rich embroidered line,   20
 Which their triumphant brows around
  By his sacred hand is bound,
Does all their starry diadems outshine.

III

Whether at Pisa's race he please
To carve in polished verse the conquerors' images,
Whether the swift, the skilful, or the strong
Be crowned in his nimble, artful, vigorous song,
Whether some brave young man's untimely fate
In words worth dying for he celebrate,
  Such mournful and such pleasing words 30
As joy to his mother's and his mistress' grief affords,
  He bids him live and grow in fame;
  Among the stars he sticks his name;
The grave can but the dross of him devour,
So small is death's, so great the poet's power.

Lo, how the obsequious wind and swelling air
  The Theban swan does upwards bear
Into the walks of clouds, where he does play,
And with extended wings opens his liquid way,
  Whilst, alas, my timorous Muse 40
  Unambitious tracks pursues;

Does, with weak, unballast wings,
About the mossy brooks and springs,
About the trees' new-blossomed heads,
About the gardens' painted beds,
About the fields and flowery meads
And all inferior beauteous things,
   Like the laborious bee,
For little drops of honey flee,
And there with humble sweets contents her industry.   50

Of Solitude

Hail, old patrician trees, so great and good!
   Hail, ye plebeian underwood!
   Where the poetic birds rejoice,
And for their quiet nests and plenteous food
   Pay with their grateful voice.

Hail, the poor Muse's richest manor seat!
   Ye country houses and retreat,
   Which all the happy gods so love
That for you oft they quit their bright and great
   Metropolis above.   10

Here Nature does a house for me erect,
   Nature, the fairest architect,
   Who those fond artists does despise
That can the fair and living trees neglect,
   Yet the dead timber prize.

Here let me, careless and unthoughtful lying,
   Hear the soft winds above me flying,
   With all their wanton boughs' dispute,
And the more tuneful birds to both replying,
   Nor be myself too mute.   20

A silver stream shall roll his waters near,
 Gilt with the sunbeams here and there;
 On whose enameled bank I'll walk,
And see how prettily they smile, and hear
 How prettily they talk.

Ah, wretched and too solitary he
 Who loves not his own company!
 He'll feel the weight of it many a day,
Unless he call in sin or vanity
 To help to bear it away.   30

O Solitude, first state of humankind!
 Which blest remained till man did find
 Even his own helper's company—
As soon as two, alas, together joined,
 The serpent made up three.

Though God Himself, through countless ages, thee
 His sole companion chose to be,
 Thee, sacred Solitude, alone,
Before the branchy head of number's tree
 Sprang from the trunk of One.   40

Thou, though men think thine an unactive part,
 Dost break and tame the unruly heart,
 Which else would know no settled pace,
Making it move, well managed by thy art,
 With swiftness and with grace.

Thou the faint beams of reason's scattered light
 Dost, like a burning-glass, unite,
 Dost multiply the feeble heat
And fortify the strength, till thou dost bright
 And noble fires beget.   50

Whilst this hard truth I teach, methinks I see
 The monster London laugh at me;

I should at thee too, foolish city,
If it were fit to laugh at misery,
But thy estate I pity.

Let but thy wicked men from out thee go,
And all the fools that crowd thee so,
Even thou, who dost thy millions boast,
A village less than Islington wilt grow,
A solitude almost.   60

Andrew Marvell 1621-1678

POET of gardens and Member of Parliament from Hull, metaphysical lyrist and political satirist—these express the dual nature of Andrew Marvell. His temperament was somewhat philosophical and mystical, and he had a natural inclination toward the contemplative life. His period of greatest poetic activity was at the time when he could wander in cultured leisure through one of the loveliest gardens in England, that of Nun Appleton House. But Marvell could not really give himself up to this life. There was a strength and force in his character and a keenness of interest in outside affairs which took Marvell from the quiet beauty that was his poetic inspiration and molded him into the steady, incorruptible public representative.

This "hunger-starved whelp of a country vicar," as Bishop Parker unbecomingly calls the son of the Headmaster of Charterhouse [1] (an almshouse just without the city of Hull) may have learned the rough expressions later useful in his satires from the shipmen about the wharves at Hull; but he also learned the "scanning of verses" at the grammar school, and other matter sufficient to admit him to Cambridge University at the age of twelve. Two years before he received his bachelor's degree, his verses in celebration of the birth of Princess Anne were recognized as good enough to appear with those of Richard Crashaw, Abraham Cowley, and Edward King in the *Musa Cantabrigiensis*.

Left an orphan shortly after his graduation, Marvell spent four years on the Continent, where he added Dutch, French, Italian, and Spanish to his store of languages already consisting of Latin, Greek, Hebrew, Arabic, Syrian, Chaldean, Persian, and possibly others. These new acquisitions were useful later when, upon Milton's recommendation, he was appointed, first to assist Milton in the Latin Secretaryship and later to succeed him. These years abroad (1642–6) were years of civil conflict at home; but Marvell felt no urge to

[1] Margoliouth, *Modern Language Review*, xvii (1922), 351.

return to take part in the war, for he held that the conflict should never have taken place.

At the middle of the century we find Marvell, a young man of twenty-nine, with his many languages and his knowledge of European countries, established at Nun Appleton House as tutor to a plain little girl of twelve. This child was Mary Fairfax, the daughter of the great general of the Parliamentary forces to whom Milton had addressed one of his fine sonnets.

Up to this time Marvell had published only a few poems, but the two years in the beautiful surroundings which he describes in his poem *Upon Appleton House* gave him time and inspiration for writing, and to them we are indebted for the greatest part of Marvell's lyrical verse. Here he stands "betwixt the morning and the flowers"; and with an accuracy of observation that vies with Wordsworth's perception of the mist running with the hare, he sees through the branches of the hazels "the hatching throstle's shining eye." He is the poet of the open air, a lover of meadows, with the mower singing at his work, of trees and birds and flowers, of luscious fruits and cool melons. Light, shadow, and color interest him, and green particularly attracts him. Though his accuracy of observation and his sensuousness suggest the romanticists, Marvell does more than reproduce physical sensations. He makes an intellectual analysis of their essence. In *The Garden*, for example, the mind transcends the actual sensuousness of the surroundings,

> Annihilating all that's made
> To a green thought in a green shade.

Though Marvell does not mention Donne as his master, his conceits have something of the manner, though not the grotesqueness, of many of Donne's. Like Donne also, he packs his lyrics with thought. In his one passionate love lyric he rises to an intensity of feeling comparable to Donne's; and the emotion, tearing its urgent way through word and rhythm, forces itself into the mind of the reader. Usually, however, Marvell is classical in his restraint; and with a kind of urbanity and precision of taste, he combines a Horatian charm of diction with beauty of rhythm.

The influence of Horace is best shown in *An Horatian Ode*, celebrating Cromwell's success in quelling a Royalist rebellion in Ireland in 1649. Palgrave ranks this ode as "one of the finest in the language" and says, "Better than anything else, it gives an idea of the grand Horatian measure." In this poem Marvell shows the fine tolerant spirit which made him trusted by both the Puritans and the Royalists. Though the ode is full of admiration for Cromwell, it also shows appreciation of the king and pity for his tragic end.

As early as 1653 we find Marvell interested in getting into public life. At this time Milton recommended that Marvell be made his assistant; but as nothing came of the recommendation immediately, Marvell went to Eton as tutor of Cromwell's ward, who was living at the home of John Oxenbridge, a clergyman. Oxenbridge had been for a time a minister in the Bermudas; and his accounts of the islands and the little Puritan colony there, even more than Waller's *Battle of the Summer Islands,* gave Marvell material for one of his best-known poems.

1657 marks Marvell's appointment to the Latin Secretaryship and the beginning of the close association of the only two Puritans to attain distinction by their poetry. Milton must have recognized the parallel of Marvell's life to his own: Cambridge University, travel, quiet years in rural surroundings, where pastoral poetry seemed the natural mode of expression; then public life. The year before the Restoration Marvell became member of Parliament for Hull, and he continued to hold this seat until his death. It was his influence which saved Milton from imprisonment or even death at the time of the Restoration. Public life brought an end to Marvell's lyric poetry; only stinging satires, which take the place in Marvell's career that pamphlets did in Milton's, were produced after Marvell entered the secretaryship.

Marvell's poems were not published until three years after his death; and though they were accompanied by a signed statement, allegedly from his wife, nothing is known of this Mary Marvell. The supposition long held that the Member of Parliament for Hull was a bachelor seems to stand, and Mary Marvell is generally assumed to be a fictitious creation. It is regrettable that so little is known of Marvell's life and personality. The public letters are concerned with affairs and not with the author, so that they tell little. Had the letters to his friend, Mr. William Skinner, not been turned over to "the pastry maid to put under pie bottoms," we might know more. It is to the poems themselves that we must go to find the taste and personality of this reserved man, in whom the dual desire for contemplative quiet and active participation in world affairs found satisfaction.

The Garden

How vainly men themselves amaze
To win the palm, the oak, or bays,
And their incessant labors see
Crowned from some single herb, or tree,
Whose short and narrow-verged shade
Does prudently their toils upbraid;
While all flowers and all trees do close
To weave the garlands of repose!

Fair Quiet, have I found thee here,
And Innocence, thy sister dear?   10
Mistaken long, I sought you then
In busy companies of men.
Your sacred plants, if here below,
Only among the plants will grow;
Society is all but rude
To this delicious solitude.

No white nor red was ever seen
So amorous as this lovely green.
Fond lovers, cruel as their flame,
Cut in these trees their mistress' name: 20
Little, alas, they know or heed
How far these beauties hers exceed!
Fair trees, wheresoe'er your barks I wound,
No name shall but your own be found.

When we have run our passion's heat,
Love hither makes his best retreat.
The gods, that mortal beauty chase,
Still in a tree did end their race:
Apollo hunted Daphne so,
Only that she might laurel grow;   30
And Pan did after Syrinx speed,
Not as a nymph, but for a reed.[1]

What wondrous life is this I lead!
Ripe apples drop about my head;
The luscious clusters of the vine
Upon my mouth do crush their wine;
The nectarine and curious peach
Into my hands themselves do reach;
Stumbling on melons, as I pass,
Insnared with flowers, I fall on grass.   40

Meanwhile the mind, from pleasure less
Withdraws into its happiness;
The mind, that ocean where each kind
Does straight its own resemblance find;
Yet it creates, transcending these,
Far other worlds and other seas,
Annihilating all that's made
To a green thought in a green shade.[2]

[1] Just before the gods overtook the fleeing maidens, these transformations took place.
[2] These two lines are the high point of the "metaphysical" manner.

Here at the fountain's sliding foot,
Or at some fruit-tree's mossy root,   50
Casting the body's vest aside,
My soul into the boughs does glide: [3]
There, like a bird, it sits and sings,
Then whets and combs its silver wings,
And, till prepared for longer flight,
Waves in its plumes the various light.

Such was that happy garden-state,
While man there walked without a mate:
After a place so pure and sweet,
What other help could yet be meet!   60
But 'twas beyond a mortal's share
To wander solitary there:
Two paradises 'twere in one
To live in paradise alone.

How well the skilful gardener drew
Of flowers and herbs this dial new,
Where, from above, the milder sun
Does through a fragrant zodiac run; [4]
And as it works, the industrious bee
Computes its time as well as we!   70
How could such sweet and wholesome hours
Be reckoned but with herbs and flowers?

The Nymph Complaining for the Death of Her Fawn

The wanton troopers riding by
Have shot my fawn, and it will die.
Ungentle men! they cannot thrive
To kill thee. Thou ne'er didst alive

[3] Marvell here identifies himself with nature in an almost Shelleyan manner.
[4] The garden was designed after the pattern of the sun-dial.

Them any harm, alas! nor could
Thy death yet do them any good.
I'm sure I never wished them ill,
Nor do I for all this, nor will;
But if my simple prayers may yet
Prevail with heaven to forget   10
Thy murder, I will join my tears,
Rather than fail. But, O my fears!
It cannot die so. Heaven's King
Keeps register of everything,
And nothing may we use in vain;
Even beasts must be with justice slain,
Else men are made their deodands.[1]
Though they should wash their guilty hands
In this warm life-blood, which doth part
From thine, and wound me to the heart,   20
Yet could they not be clean, their stain
Is dyed in such a purple grain.
There is not such another in
The world to offer for their sin.

    Unconstant Sylvio, when yet
I had not found him counterfeit,
One morning (I remember well)
Tied in this silver chain and bell,
Gave it to me: nay, and I know
What he said then; I'm sure I do: 30
Said he, "Look how your huntsman here
Hath taught a fawn to hunt his *dear*."
But Sylvio soon had me beguiled;
This waxed tame, while he grew wild,
And quite regardless of my smart,
Left me his fawn, but took his heart.

    Thenceforth I set myself to play
My solitary time away

---

[1] According to English law (not abolished until 1846) a personal belonging, the direct cause of the death of a person, which had to be given over to the crown to be used for alms.

With this, and very well content,
Could so mine idle life have spent;   40
For it was full of sport, and light
Of foot and heart, and did invite
Me to its game: it seemed to bless
Itself in me; how could I less
Than love it? Oh, I cannot be
Unkind to a beast that loveth me.

Had it lived long, I do not know
Whether it too might have done so
As Sylvio did; his gifts might be
Perhaps as false, or more, than he;   50
But I am sure, for aught that I
Could in so short a time espy,
Thy love was far more better than
The love of false and cruel men.

With sweetest milk and sugar, first
I it at mine own fingers nursed;
And as it grew, so every day
It waxed more white and sweet than they.
It had so sweet a breath! And oft
I blushed to see its foot more soft   60
And white, shall I say than my hand?
Nay, any lady's of the land.

It is a wondrous thing how fleet
'Twas on those little silver feet;
With what a pretty skipping grace
It oft would challenge me the race;
And when it had left me far away,
'Twould stay, and run again, and stay;
For it was nimbler much than hinds,
And trod as if on the four winds.   70

I have a garden of my own,
But so with roses overgrown,
And lilies, that you would it guess
To be a little wilderness;
And all the springtime of the year

It only loved to be there.
Among the beds of lilies I
Have sought it oft, where it should lie,
Yet could not, till itself would rise,
Find it, although before mine eyes;   &
For, in the flaxen lilies' shade,
It like a bank of lilies laid.
Upon the roses it would feed,
Until its lips e'en seemed to bleed;
And then to me 'twould boldly trip,
And print those roses on my lip.
But all its chief delight was still
On roses thus itself to fill,
And its pure virgin limbs to fold
In whitest sheets of lilies cold: 90
Had it lived long, it would have been
Lilies without, roses within.

  O help! O help! I see it faint
And die as calmly as a saint!
See how it weeps! the tears do come
Sad, slowly dropping like a gum.
So weeps the wounded balsam; so
The holy frankincense doth flow;
The brotherless Heliades [2]
Melt in such amber tears as these.   100

  I in a golden vial will
Keep these two crystal tears, and fill
It till it do o'erflow with mine;
Then place it in Diana's shrine.

  Now my sweet fawn is vanished to
Whither the swans and turtles [3] go,
In fair Elysium to endure,
With milk-white lambs and ermines pure.

[2] Phaeton, the brother of the Heliades, was unable to drive the
chariot of the sun and was killed by a thunderbolt from Jupiter in
order to save the universe. His sisters, transformed into trees, contin-
ued to weep, and their tears were turned into amber.
[3] Turtledoves.

O do not run too fast; for I
Will but bespeak thy grave, and die.　　110
　First, my unhappy statue shall
Be cut in marble, and withal,
Let it be weeping too; but there

The engraver sure his art may spare;
For I so truly thee bemoan
That I shall weep, though I be stone,
Until my tears, still dropping, wear
My breast, themselves engraving there.
There at my feet shalt thou be laid,
Of purest alabaster made;　　120
For I would have thine image be
White as I can, though not as thee.

The Picture of Little T. C. in a Prospect of Flowers

See with what simplicity
This nymph begins her golden days!
In the green grass she loves to lie,
And there with her fair aspect tames
The wilder flowers, and gives them names;
But only with the roses plays,
　　And them does tell
What color best becomes them, and what smell.

Who can foretell for what high cause
This darling of the gods was born?　　10
Yet this is she whose chaster laws
The wanton Love shall one day fear,
And, under her command severe,
See his bow broke and ensigns torn.
　　Happy who can
Appease this virtuous enemy of man!

O then let me in time compound
And parley with those conquering eyes,
Ere they have tried their force to wound;
Ere with their glancing wheels they drive   20
In triumph over hearts that strive,
And them that yield but more despise:
      Let me be laid
Where I may see thy glories from some shade.

Meantime, whilst every verdant thing
Itself does at thy beauty charm,
Reform the errors of the spring;
Make that the tulips may have share
Of sweetness, seeing they are fair;
And roses of their thorns disarm;   30
      But most procure
That violets may a longer age endure.

But, O young beauty of the woods,
Whom nature courts with fruits and flowers,
Gather the flowers, but spare the buds,
Lest Flora, angry at thy crime
To kill her infants in their prime,
Do quickly make the example yours;
      And ere we see,
Nip in the blossom all our hopes and thee.   40

The Mower to the Glowworms

Ye living lamps, by whose dear light
The nightingale does sit so late,
And studying all the summer night,
Her matchless songs does meditate;

Ye country comets, that portend
No war nor prince's funeral,[1]

---

[1] Comets were once considered portents of the death of the ruler or
of some other great disaster.

Shining unto no higher end
Than to presage the grass's fall;

Ye glowworms, whose officious flame
To wandering mowers shows the way,   10
That in the night have lost their aim,
And after foolish fires [2] do stray;

Your courteous lights in vain you waste,
Since Juliana here is come,
For she my mind hath so displaced
That I shall never find my home.

The Mower's Song

My mind was once the true survey
Of all these meadows fresh and gay,
And in the greenness of the grass
Did see its hopes as in a glass;
When Juliana came, and she,
What I do to the grass, does to my thoughts and me.

But these, while I with sorrow pine,
Grew more luxuriant still and fine,
That not one blade of grass you spied,
But had a flower on either side;   10
When Juliana came, and she,
What I do to the grass, does to my thoughts and me.

Unthankful meadows, could you so
A fellowship so true forego,
And in your gaudy May-games meet,
While I lay trodden under feet?
When Juliana came, and she,
What I do to the grass, does to my thoughts and me.

[2] Will-o'-the-wisps.

But what you in compassion ought,
Shall now by my revenge be wrought;   20
And flowers, and grass, and I, and all
Will in one common ruin fall;
For Juliana comes, and she,
What I do to the grass, does to my thoughts and me.

And thus, ye meadows, which have been
Companions of my thoughts more green,
Shall now the heraldry become
With which I shall adorn my tomb;
For Juliana comes, and she,
What I do to the grass, does to my thoughts and me.   30

The Definition of Love

My Love is of a birth as rare
As 'tis, for object, strange and high;
It was begotten by Despair
Upon Impossibility.

Magnanimous Despair alone
Could show me so divine a thing,
Where feeble Hope could ne'er have flown
But vainly flapped its tinsel wing.

And yet I quickly might arrive
Where my extended soul is fixed;   10
But Fate does iron wedges drive,
And always crowds itself betwixt.

For Fate with jealous eye does see
Two perfect loves, nor lets them close;
Their union would her ruin be,
And her tyrannic power depose.

And therefore her decrees of steel
Us as the distant poles have placed,
(Though Love's whole world on us doth wheel)
Not by themselves to be embraced,   20

Unless the giddy heaven fall,
And earth some new convulsion tear,
And, us to join, the world should all
Be cramped into a planisphere.[1]

As lines, so loves, oblique may well
Themselves in every angle greet;
But ours, so truly parallel,
Though infinite, can never meet.

Therefore the love which us doth bind,
But Fate so enviously debars,   30
Is the conjunction of the mind,
And opposition of the stars.[2]

To His Coy Mistress

Had we but world enough, and time,
This coyness, lady, were no crime.
We would sit down, and think which way
To walk, and pass our long love's day.
Thou by the Indian Ganges' side
Shouldst rubies find; I by the tide
Of Humber would complain. I would
Love you ten years before the flood,
And you should, if you please, refuse
Till the conversion of the Jews.   10
My vegetable love should grow

---

[1] A map of the world projected on a flat surface.
[2] Astronomical terms are effectively used here.

Vaster than empires and more slow;
An hundred years should go to praise
Thine eyes, and on thy forehead gaze;
Two hundred to adore each breast,
But thirty thousand to the rest;
An age at least to every part,
And the last age should show your heart.
For, lady, you deserve this state,
Nor would I love at lower rate.   20

　　But at my back I always hear
Time's winged chariot hurrying near;
And yonder all before us lie
Deserts of vast eternity.
Thy beauty shall no more be found,
Nor, in thy marble vault, shall sound
My echoing song; then worms shall try
That long-preserved virginity,
And your quaint honor turn to dust,
And into ashes all my lust: 30
The grave's a fine and private place,
But none, I think, do there embrace.

　　Now therefore, while the youthful hue
Sits on thy skin like morning dew,
And while thy willing soul transpires
At every pore with instant fires,
Now let us sport us while we may,
And now, like amorous birds of prey,
Rather at once our time devour
Than languish in his slow-chapped power.   40
Let us roll all our strength and all
Our sweetness up into one ball,
And tear our pleasures with rough strife
Thorough the iron gates of life:
Thus, though we cannot make our sun
Stand still, yet we will make him run.

Bermudas

Where the remote Bermudas ride,
In the ocean's bosom unespied,
From a small boat that rowed along,
The listening winds received this song: [1]

"What should we do but sing His praise,
That led us through the watery maze
Unto an isle so long unknown,
And yet far kinder than our own?
Where He the huge sea-monsters wracks,
That lift the deep upon their backs;   10
He lands us on a grassy stage,
Safe from the storms, and prelate's rage.
He gave us this eternal spring
Which here enamels everything,
And sends the fowls to us in care,
On daily visits through the air;
He hangs in shades the orange bright,
Like golden lamps in a green night,
And does in the pomegranates close
Jewels more rich than Ormus [2] shows;   20
He makes the figs our mouths to meet,
And throws the melons at our feet;
But apples plants of such a price,
No tree could ever bear them twice;
With cedars, chosen by His hand,
From Lebanon, [3] He stores the land;
And makes the hollow seas, that roar,
Proclaim the ambergris [4] on shore;

[1] Religious freedom was granted the colonists of Bermuda, and the singers of this poem are religious exiles from England.

[2] A wealthy Persian city. Milton in *Paradise Lost* II, 2, says that Satan's throne "Outshone the wealth of Ormus and of Ind."

[3] Lebanon, a famous mountain in the south of Syria, noted for forests of cedar.

[4] A waxy substance secured from sperm whales for use in perfumery.

He cast (of which we rather boast)
The Gospel's pearl upon our coast,   30
And in these rocks for us did frame
A temple, where to sound His name.
Oh! let our voice His praise exalt,
Till it arrive at heaven's vault,
Which, thence (perhaps) rebounding, may
Echo beyond the Mexique Bay."

   Thus sung they in the English boat,
An holy and a cheerful note;
And all the way, to guide their chime,
With falling oars they kept the time.   40

An Horatian Ode
Upon Cromwell's Return from Ireland

The forward youth that would appear
Must now forsake his Muses dear,
    Nor in the shadows sing
    His numbers languishing:

'Tis time to leave the books in dust,
And oil the unused armor's rust,
    Removing from the wall
    The corslet of the hall.

So restless Cromwell could not cease
In the inglorious arts of peace,   10
    But through adventurous war
    Urged his active star;

And like the three-forked lightning, first
Breaking the clouds where it was nursed,
    Did through his own side
    His fiery way divide.[1]

[1] Cromwell was an "Independent" and had broken away from the Presbyterians.

For 'tis all one to courage high,
The emulous or enemy;
     And with such to inclose
     Is more than to oppose.   20

Then burning through the air he went,
And palaces and temples rent;
     And Cæsar's head at last
     Did through his laurels blast.[2]

'Tis madness to resist or blame
The force of angry heaven's flame;
     And if we would speak true,
     Much to the man is due,

Who, from his private gardens, where
He lived reserved and austere   30
     (As if his highest plot
     To plant the bergamot),

Could by industrious valor climb
To ruin the great work of time,
     And cast the kingdom old
     Into another mold;

Though Justice against Fate complain,
And plead the ancient rights in vain;
     (But those do hold or break,
     As men are strong or weak).   40

Nature, that hateth emptiness,
Allows of penetration [3] less,
     And therefore must make room
     Where greater spirits come.

[2] The reference is, of course, to King Charles I.
[3] "Occupation of the same space by two bodies at the same time."
(*New English Dictionary*)

What field of all the civil war,
Where his were not the deepest scar?
    And Hampton shows what part
    He had of wiser art;

Where, twining subtle fears with hope,
He wove a net of such a scope   50
    That Charles himself might chase
    To Carisbrooke's narrow case,

That thence the royal actor borne
The tragic scaffold might adorn;
    While round the armed bands
    Did clap their bloody hands.[4]

He nothing common did, or mean,
Upon that memorable scene,
    But with his keener eye
    The axe's edge did try;   60

Nor called the gods with vulgar spite
To vindicate his helpless right;
    But bowed his comely head
    Down, as upon a bed.

This was that memorable hour
Which first assured the forced power:
    So, when they did design
    The Capitol's first line,

A bleeding head, where they begun,
Did fright the architects to run;   70
    And yet in that the state
    Foresaw its happy fate.

[4] The implication of ll. 47–56 is not now accepted.

And now the Irish are ashamed
To see themselves in one year tamed;
    So much one man can do
    That does both act and know.

They can affirm his praises best,
And have, though overcome, confessed
    How good he is, how just,
    And fit for highest trust.   80

Nor yet grown stiffer with command,
But still in the republic's hand—
    How fit he is to sway
    That can so well obey!

He to the Commons' feet presents
A kingdom for his first year's rents;
    And, what he may, forbears
    His fame, to make it theirs;

And has his sword and spoils ungirt,
To lay them at the public's skirt: 90
    So when the falcon high
    Falls heavy from the sky,

She, having killed, no more does search
But on the next green bough to perch;
    Where, when he first does lure,
    The falconer has her sure.

What may not, then, our isle presume,
While victory his crest does plume?
    What may not others fear,
    If thus he crown each year?   100

A Cæsar he, ere long, to Gaul,
To Italy an Hannibal,

And to all states not free
Shall climacteric be.

The Pict no shelter now shall find
Within his parti-colored mind,
But from this valor sad
Shrink underneath the plaid;

Happy if in the tufted brake
The English hunter him mistake,   110
Nor lay his hounds in near
The Caledonian deer.

But thou, the war's and fortune's son,
March indefatigably on!
And for the last effect,
Still keep thy sword erect;

Besides the force it has to fright
The spirits of the shady night,
The same arts that did gain
A power must it maintain.   120

Henry Vaughan 1622-1695

HENRY VAUGHAN, the mystical country doctor going his rounds in Southern Wales, was not fulfilling the early plans made for his life. He and his twin brother, Thomas, had entered Oxford at sixteen, but Henry had left, probably without his degree, because his father wanted him to study law. Established in the Inns of Court, he became acquainted with aspiring poets and interested in poetry, as did many of the law students of the time. But the Civil War, he says, "wholly frustrated" his study of law. Apparently he saw some service in the war; but at a time of which we have no record, he studied medicine. He settled down in his native section and devoted himself to medical practice and to poetry. He was proud of his section and of his descent, and in order to distinguish himself from all other Vaughans, called himself the Silurist, in reference to the Roman name for the district.

Half of his first volume of poems, published about three years before Charles was beheaded, is devoted to love poems addressed to Amoret. These were written greatly under the influence of Donne's poetry as to manner, but are so cool in content that it seems doubtful whether Amoret should be identified with Vaughan's first wife. His second volume, *Silex Scintillans* (*Sparks from the Flint*), is made up entirely of religious poetry, which he attributed to the influence of Herbert.

There were, however, other influences besides acquaintance with Herbert's poetry which brought about the change so apparent in Vaughan's outlook on life between his first poems and *Silex Scintillans*. His mystical twin brother had become a clergyman and after 1640 was in charge of the parish church near Vaughan's home; his favorite brother died; the king was executed; he himself was ill for years, and during that time his wife and some of his best friends died. He had come to feel that poetry should be devoted to "divine themes and celestial praises"; and when his brother, without Henry's consent, published *Olor Iscanus*, which had been prepared for the press several years earlier, Vaughan begged that no one read it.

In *Silex Scintillans* there are many direct imitations and frequent reminiscences of Herbert, but Vaughan is very different in spirit from Herbert. His poems are not closely bound to the church and its services as are Herbert's, but rather reflect his perception of God in nature as he observed its freshness and beauty in his long rounds, or in the elemental experiences of existence as he saw them in his work. His prayer is:

> Give him among Thy works a place
> Who in them loved and sought Thy face.

For his best figurative language he draws from nature; when he turns to medicine and the structure of clocks and watches for his figures, he is less felicitous, unable to transmute them into the strange force of Donne's maps or "stiff twin-compasses."

Though he lacks the calm steadiness of Herbert, he often reaches an ecstasy of mystical experience and an imaginative sweep which place his poems among the best of the century. Mystical perceptions were, in fact, more real to Vaughan than objective reality. He voiced the idea of the *Intimations of Immortality* two hundred years before Wordsworth wrote, and in *The Retreat* and *Childhood* portrayed "the shadows of eternity" touching the earth with strange beauty for the child but growing dimmer with the years. To Vaughan in his maturity the world is but a darkness which obscures the perfect perception of heaven. The body is an obstacle between him and the light toward which he seems eagerly to strain. Corruption and the grave hold no haunting fascination for him as they did for Donne; death is "the jewel of the just, shining nowhere, but in the dark," and it releases the spirit to soar toward the "great ring of endless light" which is eternity and to join the friends who have "all gone into the world of light."

The Retreat

Happy those early days, when I
Shined in my angel infancy; [1]
Before I understood this place
Appointed for my second race,
Or taught my soul to fancy aught
But a white, celestial thought;
When yet I had not walked above
A mile or two from my first Love,
And looking back, at that short space,
Could see a glimpse of His bright face;   10
When on some gilded cloud or flower
My gazing soul would dwell an hour,
And in those weaker glories spy
Some shadows of eternity;
Before I taught my tongue to wound
My conscience with a sinful sound,
Or had the black art to dispense
A several sin to every sense,
But felt through all this fleshly dress
Bright shoots of everlastingness.   20
Oh, how I long to travel back,
And tread again that ancient track!
That I might once more reach that plain
Where first I left my glorious train,
From whence the enlightened spirit sees
That shady city of palm trees.
But, ah! my soul with too much stay
Is drunk, and staggers in the way.
Some men a forward motion love;
But I by backward steps would move,   30
And when this dust falls to the urn,
In that state I came, return.

[1] Compare this poem with Wordsworth's *Ode on the Intimations of Immortality.*

Metrum V

Happy that first white age when we
Lived by the Earth's mere charity!
No soft luxurious diet then
Had effeminated men:
No other meat, nor wine had any
Than the coarse mast, or simple honey;
And by the parents' care laid up,
Cheap berries did the children sup.
No pompous wear was in those days,
Of gummy silks or scarlet baize.　　　　10
Their beds were on some flow'ry brink,
And clear spring-water was their drink.
The shady pine in the sun's heat
Was their cool and known retreat,
For then 'twas not cut down, but stood
The youth and glory of the wood.
The daring sailor with his slaves
Then had not cut the swelling waves,
Nor for desire of foreign store
Seen any but his native shore.　　　　20
No stirring drum scarred that age,
Nor the shrill trumpets active rage,
No wounds by bitter hatred made
With warm blood soiled the shining blade;
For how could hostile madness arm
An age of love to public harm,
When common justice none withstood,
Nor sought rewards for spilling blood?
O that at length our age would raise
Into the temper of those days!　　　　30
But—worse than Etna's fires!—debate
And avarice inflame our State.
Alas! who was it that first found
Gold, hid of purpose under ground,

That sought out pearls, and dived to find
Such precious perils for mankind!

Childhood

I cannot reach it; and my striving eye
Dazzles at it, as at eternity.

Were now that chronicle alive,
Those white designs which children drive,
And the thoughts of each harmless hour,
With their content, too, in my power,
Quickly would I make my path even,
And by mere playing go to heaven.

Why should men love
A wolf more than a lamb or dove?   10
Or choose hell-fire and brimstone streams
Before bright stars and God's own beams?
Who kisseth thorns will hurt his face,
But flowers do both refresh and grace,
And sweetly living—fie on men!—
Are, when dead, medicinal then;
If seeing much should make staid eyes,
And long experience should make wise,
Since all that age doth teach is ill,
Why should I not love childhood still?   20
Why, if I see a rock or shelf,
Shall I from thence cast down myself?
Or by complying with the world,
From the same precipice be hurled?
Those observations are but foul
Which make me wise to lose my soul.

And yet the practice worldlings call
Business, and weighty action all,
Checking the poor child for his play,
But gravely cast themselves away.   30

Dear, harmless age! the short, swift span
Where weeping virtue parts with man;
Where love without lust dwells, and bends
What way we please, without self-ends.

An age of mysteries! which he
Must live twice that would God's face see;
Which angels guard, and with it play,
Angels! which foul men drive away.

How do I study now, and scan
Thee more than e'er I studied man,   40
And only see through a long night
Thy edges and thy bordering light!
Oh, for thy center and midday!
For sure that is the narrow way!

Corruption

Sure it was so. Man in those early days
    Was not all stone and earth;
He shined a little, and by those weak rays
    Had some glimpse of his birth.
He saw heaven o'er his head, and knew from whence
    He came, condemned, hither;
And, as first love draws strongest, so from hence
    His mind sure progressed thither.
Things here were strange unto him: sweat and till,
    All was a thorn or weed: 10
Nor did those last, but—like himself—died still
    As soon as they did seed.
They seemed to quarrel with him, for that act
    That felled him foiled them all:
He drew the curse upon the world, and cracked
    The whole frame with his fall.
This made him long for home, as loth to stay

With murmurers and foes;
He sighed for Eden, and would often say,
　"Ah! what bright days were those!"　　　　　　20
Nor was heaven cold unto him; for each day
　The valley or the mountain
Afforded visits, and still paradise lay
　In some green shade or fountain.
Angels lay leiger here; each bush and cell,
　Each oak and highway knew them;
Walk but the fields, or sit down at some well,
　And he was sure to view them.
Almighty Love! where art Thou now? Mad man
　Sits down and freezeth on;　　　　　　　　30
He raves, and swears to stir nor fire, nor fan,
　But bids the thread be spun.
I see, Thy curtains are close-drawn; Thy bow
　Looks dim, too, in the cloud;
Sin triumphs still, and man is sunk below
　The center, and his shroud.
All's in deep sleep and night: thick darkness lies
　And hatcheth o'er Thy people—
But hark! what trumpet's that? what angel cries,
　"Arise! thrust in Thy sickle"?　　　　　　　40

Man [1]

Weighing the steadfastness and state
Of some mean things which here below reside,
Where birds, like watchful clocks, the noiseless date
　And intercourse of times divide,
Where bees at night get home and hive, and flowers,
　　Early as well as late,
Rise with the sun and set in the same bowers;

　I would—said I—my God would give
The staidness of these things to man! for these

[1] Compare this poem with Herbert's *The Pulley*. Vaughan has sev-
eral poems on this theme; see especially *The Pursuit*.

To His divine appointments ever cleave,   10
   And no new business breaks their peace;
The birds nor sow nor reap, yet sup and dine; [2]
    The flowers without clothes live,
Yet Solomon was never dressed so fine.[3]

  Man hath still either toys or care;
He hath no root, nor to one place is tied,
But ever restless and irregular
   About this earth doth run and ride.
He knows he hath a home, but scarce knows where;
    He says it is so far   20
That he hath quite forgot how to go there.

  He knocks at all doors, strays and roams,
Nay, hath not so much wit as some stones have,
Which in the darkest nights point to their homes,
   By some hid sense their Maker gave;
Man is the shuttle, to whose winding quest
    And passage through these looms
God ordered motion, but ordained no rest.

[*The Hidden Flower*]

I walked the other day, to spend my hour,
    Into a field,
Where I sometimes had seen the soil to yield
    A gallant flower;
But winter now had ruffled all the bower
    And curious store
    I knew there heretofore.

[2] "Behold the fowls of the air: for they sow not, neither do they reap, nor gather into barns; yet your heavenly Father feedeth them. . . ." *Matt.* 6:26. Cf. *Luke* 12:24.

[3] "Consider the lilies of the field, how they grow; they toil not, neither do they spin: And yet I say unto you, that even Solomon in all his glory was not arrayed like one of these." *Matt.* 6:28–29. Cf. *Luke* 12:27.

Yet I, whose search loved not to peep and peer
      I' the face of things,
Thought with myself, there might be other springs   10
      Besides this here,
Which, like cold friends, sees us but once a year;
      And so the flower
      Might have some other bower.

Then taking up what I could nearest spy,
      I digged about
That place where I had seen him to grow out;
      And by and by
I saw the warm recluse alone to lie,
      Where, fresh and green,   20
      He lived of us unseen.

Many a question intricate and rare
      Did I there strow;
But all I could extort was, that he now
      Did there repair
Such losses as befell him in this air,
      And would ere long
      Come forth most fair and young.

This past, I threw the clothes quite o'er his head;
      And, stung with fear   30
Of my own frailty, dropped down many a tear
      Upon his bed;
Then, sighing, whispered, "Happy are the dead!
      What peace doth now
      Rock him asleep below!"

And yet, how few believe such doctrine springs
      From a poor root,
Which all the winter sleeps here under foot,
      And hath no wings
To raise it to the truth and light of things,   40

But is still trod
By every wandering clod.

O Thou! whose spirit did at first inflame
    And warm the dead,
And by a sacred incubation fed
    With life this frame,
Which once had neither being, form, nor name,
    Grant I may so
    Thy steps track here below,

That in these masques and shadows I may see   50
    Thy sacred way;
And by those hid ascents climb to that day
    Which breaks from Thee,
Who art in all things, though invisibly;
    Show me Thy peace,
    Thy mercy, love, and ease.

And from this care, where dreams and sorrows reign,
    Lead me above,
Where light, joy, leisure, and true comforts move
    Without all pain;   60
There, hid in Thee, show me his life again,
    At whose dumb urn
    Thus all the year I mourn!

Love and Discipline

Since in a land not barren still
(Because Thou dost Thy grace distill)
My lot is fallen, blest be Thy will!

And since these biting frosts but kill
Some tares in me which choke or spill
That seed Thou sow'st, blest be Thy skill!

Blest be Thy dew, and blest Thy frost,
And happy I to be so crossed,
And cured by crosses at Thy cost.

The dew doth cheer what is distressed,　　　　　10
The frosts ill weeds nip and molest;
In both Thou work'st unto the best.

Thus while Thy several mercies plot,
And work on me now cold, now hot,
The work goes on and slacketh not;

For as Thy hand the weather steers,
So thrive I best, 'twixt joys and tears,
And all the year have some green ears.

The Bird

Hither thou com'st: the busy wind all night
Blew through thy lodging, where thy own warm wing
Thy pillow was. Many a sullen storm
(For which course man seems much the fitter born)
　　　　Rained on thy bed
　　　　And harmless head.

And now, as fresh and cheerful as the light,
Thy little heart in early hymns doth sing
Unto that Providence, whose unseen arm
Curbed them, and clothed thee well and warm.　　　10
　All things that be, praise Him, and had
　Their lesson taught them when first made.

So hills and valleys into singing break;
And though poor stones have neither speech nor tongue,
While active winds and streams both run and speak,
Yet stones are deep in admiration.
Thus praise and prayer here beneath the sun
Make lesser mornings, when the great are done.

For each inclosed spirit is a star
    Enlightning his own little sphere,   20
Whose light, though fetched and borrowed from far,
    Both mornings makes and evenings there.

But as these birds of light make a land glad,
Chirping their solemn matins on each tree,
So in the shades of night some dark fowls be,
Whose heavy notes make all that hear them sad.

    The turtle then in palm trees mourns,
        While owls and satyrs howl;
    The pleasant land to brimstone turns,
        And all her streams grow foul.   30

Brightness and mirth, and love and faith, all fly,
Till the day-spring breaks forth again from high.

Cock-crowing

    Father of lights! what sunny seed,
    What glance of day hast Thou confined
    Into this bird? To all the breed
    This busy ray Thou hast assigned;
        Their magnetism works all night,
        And dreams of paradise and light.

    Their eyes watch for the morning hue;
    Their little grain, expelling night,
    So shines and sings as if it knew
    The path unto the house of light.   10
        It seems their candle, howe'er done,
        Was tinned and lighted at the sun.

    If such a tincture, such a touch,
    So firm a longing can empower,

Shall Thy own image think it much
To watch for Thy appearing hour?
    If a mere blast so fill the sail,
    Shall not the breath of God prevail?

O Thou immortal light and heat!
Whose hand so shines through all this frame   20
That, by the beauty of the seat,
We plainly see who made the same,
    Seeing Thy seed abides in me,
    Dwell Thou in it, and I in Thee!

To sleep without Thee is to die;
Yea, 'tis a death partakes of hell:
For where Thou dost not close the eye,
It never opens, I can tell.
    In such a dark Egyptian border,
    The shades of death dwell, and disorder.   30

If joys, and hopes, and earnest throes,
And hearts whose pulse beats still for light
Are given to birds; who but Thee knows
A love-sick soul's exalted flight?
    Can souls be tracked by any eye
    But His who gave them wings to fly?

Only this veil which Thou hast broke,
And must be broken yet in me,
This veil, I say, is all the cloak
And cloud which shadows Thee from me.   40
    This veil Thy full-eyed love denies,
    And only gleams and fractions spies.

O take it off! make no delay;
But brush me with Thy light that I
May shine unto a perfect day,

And warm me at Thy glorious eye!
   O take it off, or till it flee,
   Though with no lily, stay with me!

The Timber

Sure thou didst flourish once! and many springs,
Many bright mornings, much dew, many showers
Passed o'er thy head; many light hearts and wings,
Which now are dead, lodged in thy living bowers.

And still a new succession sings and flies;
Fresh groves grow up, and their green branches shoot
Toward the old and still enduring skies,
While the low violet thrives at their root.

But thou beneath the sad and heavy line
Of death, doth waste all senseless, cold, and dark;   10
Where not so much as dreams of light may shine,
Nor any thought of greenness, leaf, or bark.

And yet (as if some deep hate and dissent,
Bred in thy growth betwixt high winds and thee,
Were still alive) thou dost great storms resent
Before they come, and know'st how near they be.

Else all at rest thou liest, and the fierce breath
Of tempests can no more disturb thy ease;
But this thy strange resentment after death
Means only those who broke in life thy peace.   20

So murdered man, when lovely life is done
And his blood freezed, keeps in the center still
Some secret sense, which makes the dead blood run
At his approach, that did the body kill.

And is there any murderer worse than sin?
Or any storms more foul than a lewd life?
Or what resentient can work more within
Than true remorse, when with past sins at strife?

He that hath left life's vain joys and vain care,
And truly hates to be detained on earth,   30
Hath got an house where many mansions are,
And keeps his soul unto eternal mirth.

But though thus dead unto the world, and ceased
From sin, he walks a narrow, private way;
Yet grief and old wounds make him sore displeased,
And all his life a rainy, weeping day.

For though he would forsake the world, and live
As mere a stranger, as men long since dead;
Yet joy itself will make a right soul grieve
To think he should be so long vainly lead.   40

But as shades set off light, so tears and grief
(Though of themselves but a sad blubbered story)
By showing the sin great, show the relief
Far greater, and so speak my Savior's glory.

If my way lies through deserts and wild woods,
Where all the land with scorching heat is curst,
Better the pools should flow with rain and floods
To fill my bottle, than I die with thirst.

Blest showers they are, and streams sent from above
Begetting virgins where they used to flow;   50
And trees of life no other water love;
These upper springs, and none else make them grow.

But these chaste fountains flow not till we die;
Some drops may fall before, but a clear spring

And ever running, till we leave to fling
Dirt in her way, will keep above the sky.

Rom. 6:7.

He that is dead, is freed from sin.

The Waterfall

With what deep murmurs through time's silent stealth
Doth thy transparent, cool, and wat'ry wealth
  Here flowing fall,
  And chide, and call,
As if his liquid, loose retinue stayed
Lingering, and were of this steep place afraid,
  The common pass
  Where, clear as glass,
  All must descend—
  Not to an end,   10
But quickened by this deep and rocky grave,
Rise to a longer course more bright and brave.

  Dear stream! dear bank, where often I
  Have sat and pleased my pensive eye,
  Why, since each drop of thy quick store
  Runs thither whence it flowed before,
  Should poor souls fear a shade or night,
  Who came, sure, from a sea of light?
  Or since those drops are all sent back
  So sure to thee, that none doth lack, 20
  Why should frail flesh doubt any more
  That what God takes He'll not restore?

  O useful element and clear!
  My sacred wash and cleanser here,
  My first consigner unto those
  Fountains of life where the Lamb goes!
  What sublime truths and wholesome themes

Lodge in thy mystical deep streams!
Such as dull man can never find
Unless that Spirit lead his mind   30
Which first upon thy face did move,
And hatched all with His quickening love.[1]
As this loud brook's incessant fall
In streaming rings restagnates all,
Which reach by course the bank, and then
Are no more seen, just so pass men.
O my invisible estate,
My glorious liberty, still late!
Thou art the channel my soul seeks,
Not this with cataracts and creeks.   40

Unprofitableness

How rich, O Lord, how fresh thy visits are!
'Twas but just now my bleak leaves hopeless hung,
          Sullied with dust and mud;
Each snarling blast shot through me, and did shear
Their youth, and beauty; cold showers nipped and wrung
          Their spiciness and blood;
But since thou didst in one sweet glance survey
Their sad decays, I flourish, and once more
          Breathe all perfumes and spice;
I smell a dew like myrrh, and all the day   10
Wear in my bosom a full sun; such store
          Hath one beam from Thy eyes.
But, ah, my God! what fruit hast Thou of this?
What one poor leaf did ever I yet fall
          To wait upon Thy wreath?
Thus Thou all day a thankless weed dost dress,
And when Thou hast done, a stench, a fog is all
          The odor I bequeath.

---

[1] "And the earth was without form, and void; and darkness was upon the face of the deep. And the Spirit of God moved upon the face of the waters." *Gen.* 1:2.

Vanity of Spirit

Quite spent with thoughts, I left my cell and lay
Where a shrill spring tuned to the early day.
  I begged here long, and groaned to know
  Who gave the clouds so brave a bow,
  Who bent the spheres, and circled in
  Corruption with this glorious ring,
  What is His name, and how I might
  Descry some part of His great light.
I summoned nature: pierced through all her store,
Broke up some seals, which none had touched before,   10
  Her womb, her bosom, and her head
  Where all her secrets lay abed,
  I rifled quite; and having past
  Through all her creatures, came at last
  To search myself, where I did find
  Traces and sounds of a strange kind.
Here of this mighty spring, I found some drills,
With echoes beaten from the eternal hills;
  Weak beams, and fires flashed to my sight,
  Like a young East, or moon-shine night,   20
  Which showed me in a nook cast by
  A piece of much antiquity,
  With hieroglyphics quite dismembered,
  And broken letters scarce remembered.
I took them up and, much joyed, went about
To unite those pieces, hoping to find out
  The mystery; but this ne'er done,
  That little light I had was gone:
  It grieved me much. At last, said I,
  Since in these veils my eclipsed eye   30
  May not approach thee (for at night
  Who can have commerce with the light?),
  I'll disapparel, and to buy
  But one half glance, most gladly die.

The Night

Through that pure virgin shrine,
That sacred veil drawn o'er Thy glorious noon,
That men might look and live, as glowworms shine,
  And face the moon,
 Wise Nicodemus saw such light
 As made him know his God by night.[1]

  Most blest believer he!
Who in that land of darkness and blind eyes
Thy long-expected healing wings could see,
  When Thou didst rise!   10
 And, what can never more be done,
 Did at midnight speak with the Sun!

  O who will tell me where
He found Thee at that dead and silent hour?
What hallowed solitary ground did bear
  So rare a flower,
 Within whose sacred leaves did lie
 The fulness of the Deity?

  No mercy-seat of gold,
No dead and dusty cherub, nor carved stone,   20
But His own living works did my Lord hold
  And lodge alone;
 Where trees and herbs did watch and peep
 And wonder, while the Jews did sleep.

  Dear night! this world's defeat;
The stop to busy fools; care's check and curb;

---

[1] *John* 3:2: "The same [Nicodemus] came to Jesus by night, and said unto him, Rabbi, we know that thou art a teacher come from God: for no man can do these miracles that thou doest, except God be with him."

The day of spirits; my soul's calm retreat
    Which none disturb!
  Christ's progress, and His prayer time; [2]
  The hours to which high heaven doth chime;   30

    God's silent, searching flight;
When my Lord's head is filled with dew, and all
His locks are wet with the clear drops of night;
    His still, soft call;
  His knocking time; [3] the soul's dumb watch,
  When spirits their fair kindred catch.

    Were all my loud, evil days
Calm and unhaunted as is thy dark tent,
Whose peace but by some angel's wing or voice
    Is seldom rent,   40
  Then I in heaven all the long year
  Would keep, and never wander here.

    But living where the sun
Doth all things wake, and where all mix and tire
Themselves and others, I consent and run
    To every mire,
  And by this world's ill-guiding light,
  Err more than I can do by night.

    There is in God—some say—
A deep but dazzling darkness, as men here   50
Say it is late and dusky, because they
    See not all clear.

[2] *Mark* 1:35: "And in the morning, rising up a great while before day, he went out, and departed into a solitary place, and there prayed."
   Luke 21:37: "And in the day time he was teaching in the temple; and at night he went out, and abode in the mount that is called the Mount of Olives."
   Luke 22:39–44, the prayer at night in the Garden of Gethsemane.
[3] *Rev.* 3:20: "Behold, I stand at the door and knock: if any man hear my voice, and open the door, I will come in to him, and will sup with him, and he with me."

O for that night! where I in Him
Might live invisible and dim!

The World

I saw eternity the other night
Like a great ring of pure and endless light,
    All calm as it was bright;
And round beneath it, time, in hours, days, years,
    Driven by the spheres,
Like a vast shadow moved, in which the world
    And all her train were hurled.
The doting lover in his quaintest strain
    Did there complain;
Near him, his lute, his fancy, and his flights,   10
    Wit's sour delights,
With gloves and knots, the silly snares of pleasure,
    Yet his dear treasure,
All scattered lay, while he his eyes did pour
    Upon a flower.

The darksome statesman, hung with weights and woe,
Like a thick midnight fog, moved there so slow
    He did nor stay nor go;
Condemning thoughts, like mad eclipses, scowl
    Upon his soul,
And clouds of crying witnesses without   20
    Pursued him with one shout.
Yet digged the mole, and, lest his ways be found,
    Worked under ground,
Where he did clutch his prey. But one did see
    That policy:
Churches and altars fed him; perjuries
    Were gnats and flies;
It rained about him blood and tears; but he
    Drank them as free.   30

The fearful miser on a heap of rust
Sat pining all his life there, did scarce trust
    His own hands with the dust;
Yet would not place one piece above, but lives
    In fear of thieves.
Thousands there were as frantic as himself,
    And hugged each one his pelf:
The downright epicure placed heaven in sense,
    And scorned pretense;
While others, slipped into a wide excess,   40
    Said little less;
The weaker sort, slight, trivial wares enslave,
    Who think them brave;
And poor, despised Truth sat counting by
    Their victory.

Yet some, who all this while did weep and sing,
And sing and weep, soared up into the ring;
    But most would use no wing.
"O fools!" said I, "thus to prefer dark night
    Before true light!   50
To live in grots and caves,[1] and hate the day
    Because it shows the way,
The way which from this dead and dark abode
    Leads up to God,
A way where you might tread the sun and be
    More bright than he!"
But, as I did their madness so discuss,
    One whispered thus:
"This ring the bridegroom did for none provide,
    But for his bride."   60

[Departed Friends]

They are all gone into the world of light,
    And I alone sit lingering here!

[1] Compare Plato's cave to which the inhabitants returned, preferring shadows reflected in mirrors to reality.

Their very memory is fair and bright,
    And my sad thoughts doth clear.

It glows and glitters in my cloudy breast
    Like stars upon some gloomy grove,
Or those faint beams in which this hill is dressed
    After the sun's remove.

I see them walking in an air of glory,
    Whose light doth trample on my days;   10
My days, which are at best but dull and hoary,
    Mere glimmering and decays.

O holy hope, and high humility,
    High as the heavens above!
These are your walks, and you have showed them me
    To kindle my cold love.

Dear, beauteous death! the jewel of the just,
    Shining nowhere but in the dark;
What mysteries do lie beyond thy dust,
    Could man outlook that mark!   20

He that hath found some fledged bird's nest may know
    At first sight if the bird be flown;
But what fair dell or grove he sings in now,
    That is to him unknown.

And yet, as angels in some brighter dreams
    Call to the soul when man doth sleep,
So some strange thoughts transcend our wonted themes,
    And into glory peep.

If a star were confined into a tomb,
    Her captive flames must needs burn there;   30
But when the hand that locked her up gives room,
    She'll shine through all the sphere.

O Father of eternal life, and all
   Created glories under Thee!
Resume Thy spirit from this world of thrall
   Into true liberty!

Either disperse these mists, which blot and fill
   My perspective still as they pass;
Or else remove me hence unto that hill
   Where I shall need no glass.   40

Peace

My soul, there is a country
   Far beyond the stars,
Where stands a winged sentry
   All skilful in the wars.
There, above noise and danger,
   Sweet Peace sits crowned with smiles,
And One born in a manger
   Commands the beauteous files.
He is thy gracious friend,
   And—O my soul, awake!—   10
Did in pure love descend
   To die here for thy sake.
If thou canst get but thither,
   There grows the flower of peace,
The rose that cannot wither,
   Thy fortress and thy ease.
Leave, then, thy foolish ranges;
   For none can thee secure
But One who never changes,
   Thy God, thy life, thy cure.   20

The Book

Eternal God! Maker of all
That have lived here since the man's fall;

The Rock of Ages! in whose shade
They live unseen, when here they fade;

Thou knew'st this paper when it was
Mere seed, and after that but grass;
Before 'twas dressed or spun, and when
Made linen, who did wear it then:
What were their lives, their thoughts, and deeds,
Whether good corn or fruitless weeds.   10

Thou knew'st this tree when a green shade
Covered it, since a cover made,
And where it flourished, grew, and spread,
As if it never should be dead.

Thou knew'st this harmless beast when he
Did live and feed by Thy decree
On each green thing; then slept—well fed—
Clothed with this skin which now lies spread
A covering o'er this aged book;
Which makes me wisely weep, and look   20
On my own dust; mere dust it is,
But not so dry and clean as this.
Thou knew'st and saw'st them all, and though
Now scattered thus, dost know them so.

O knowing, glorious Spirit! when
Thou shalt restore trees, beasts, and men,
When Thou shalt make all new again,
Destroying only death and pain,
Give him amongst Thy works a place
Who in them loved and sought Thy face!   30

IN the closing years of the Protectorate Dryden, an ambitious young man, who, like Cowley, had been educated at Westminster School and Trinity College, Cambridge, came up to London. Here he, himself of Puritan family, secured a secretaryship with his cousin Sir Gilbert Pickering, Chamberlain to Cromwell and member of his Privy Council. The *Heroic Stanzas on the Death of Cromwell* was the natural outcome of this association. In this poem the great Puritan leader was celebrated because "peace was the prize of all his toil and care." In the period of confusion which followed his death, the one hope of peace lay in returning to monarchal government. It was, therefore, *Astræa Redux* that Dryden celebrated in his poem on the Restoration and not the change from republicanism to monarchy.

Success came to Dryden with only deliberate speed. On account of financial necessity he first turned to the only literary field in which one could earn a living—drama. Since the Restoration theater was patronized chiefly by the nobility, Dryden had to devise a type of play which would appeal to a brilliant audience. He found inspiration in the popular French heroic romance and created plays with a background of war to give scope and intensity to the more intimate struggle between love and honor. He used only aristocratic characters drawn on a grand scale and distinguished by exaggerated emotions, which they expressed in lofty rhetorical verse. Partly to appeal to the taste of a court which had come under French influence and partly because he felt that freedom in dramatic art had led to excesses, Dryden conformed to the restraint imposed by the dramatic unities and the rhymed couplet. Later on, however, Dryden himself grew weary of the artificiality of heroic drama; and in *All for Love,* his adaptation of Shakespeare's *Antony and Cleopatra,* he returned to more probable situations and characters and to blank verse. A crisis in the history of London gave Dryden a chance to gain fame in another type besides drama. The plague, the fire, and the Dutch War provided content for *Annus Mirabilis,* his first poem of distinction. During the enforced idleness of his retreat from London to the country, he wrote *An Essay on Dramatic Poesy.* Before this he had discussed dramatic theory in prefaces, which, like Shaw's, are often more interesting than the plays; but this essay, through the medium of its dialogue form, presents the current literary discussions of the drama. It reveals both his power as a critic and his ability as a writer of prose. When the laureateship was left vacant by the death of Davenant, it was clear that Dryden was the man best fitted for the place. He was nearing fifty, however, when this recognition came.

There was no immediate change in his kind of work, for even the additional appointment as Historiographer Royal did not provide an adequate income. He had married the sister of his friend Sir Robert Howard in 1663 and now had a family to support. The real turning point in his career was 1681, when he produced the first of his great literary satires.

Dryden's discovery of his satirical talent came during a national crisis. The people did not want James, Duke of York, the Catholic brother of the king, to succeed to the throne. Since Charles had no legitimate heir, Shaftesbury headed a plot to depose Charles in favor of Monmouth, his charming illegitimate son. Dryden saw in the story of David and Absalom a Biblical parallel to this situation and in his satire *Absalom and Achitophel* made a telling blow against the plot. Shadwell had been imprisoned but was not indicted; and when he was released, a medal was struck in commemoration of the event. Dryden immediately produced his biting satire *The Medal.* The Whigs engaged Shadwell to reply; and Dryden retaliated by making the inferior poet ridiculous in *Mac Flecknoe,* where he is shown inheriting the kingdom of Nonsense. These satires are full of unforgettable portraits of contemporary figures. Although Dryden believed that "the true end of satire is the amendment of vices by correction," he never becomes abusive. He presents his subjects with urbane contempt, each line adding to the characterization until the portrait stands complete; and the vices are corrected by good-natured laughter. His satiric art established Dryden as the greatest political satirist in English literature.

Two poems in seeming contradiction show still further versatility in Dryden; in *Religio Laici* and the *Hind and the Panther* political-religious argument becomes dignified poetry. The former was written in support of the Established Church and the latter, of the Catholic faith. Dryden's change to Catholicism marked his acceptance of authority in the church and was only the outward demonstration of his innate distrust of individualism, whether in government or religion. Unfortunately, however, the renewal of a pension granted under Charles II but not secured by letters patent, was coincident with the publication of the *Hind and the Panther*. This fact led to insinuations that Dryden had been bribed by James II. While little had been made of Jonson's vacillation between Protestantism and Catholicism earlier in the century, Dryden was called turn-coat and opportunist. If Dryden had been an opportunist, he could have retained his laureateship when William and Mary came to the throne; but he remained true to the conviction at which he had finally arrived, and in financial difficulty turned in his old age to translating Chaucer, Boccaccio, and Virgil into modern English.

Throughout his life Dryden's temper of mind was that of the philosophical skeptic. He was therefore sympathetic with the ideas of the Royal Society, to which he was elected a member in 1662. He praises the great English scientists in his *Epistle to Dr. Charlton;* he enumerates the great fields of scientific discovery in *An Essay on Dramatic Poesy;* and he attributes the use of dialogue in the essay not only to the influence of the dialogues of the ancients but also to the method of procedure in "the modest inquisitions of the Royal Society." [1] Furthermore, the ideal of clear and accurate

[1] *Defense of an Essay on Dramatic Poesy, Essays,* ed. Ker, I, 124.

speech held up by the Society helped to formulate Dryden's conception of English prose style. In his verse also Dryden goes back to the naturalness of speech. Though Donne's attempt early in the century had likewise been to reproduce the conversational tone, his followers had developed an artificiality that Dryden now sought to overcome. In the effort to secure clarity and precision, he developed the closed couplet into a neat and polished unit.

Dryden is the supreme literary figure of his day in five fields: heroic drama, prose criticism, lyric poetry, satire, and translation. He was the first professional man of letters and one of the four great literary dictators. Pepys, stopping in at Will's Coffee House to see his former college mate, reports "very witty and pleasant discourse." But it was primarily through the younger group that Dryden's influence was transmitted. Among these were Wycherley and Congreve, the playwrights, Dennis, the critic, and Addison. Pope as a boy of twelve came to Will's to see Dryden, whom he already "venerated." From this dictator presiding at Will's came the literary ideals which were to dominate the next century, the great odes which made possible Wordsworth's *Intimations on Immortality* in the nineteenth century, and the standard of English language which after more than two and a half centuries remains unchanged.

Absalom and Achitophel [1]

In pious times, ere priestcraft did begin,
Before polygamy was made a sin;
When man on many multiplied his kind,

---

[1] Dryden applied the Biblical story of *II Samuel* 13–18 to contemporary politics. The Duke of Monmouth, Absalom, was the handsome and much-loved illegitimate son of Charles II. Led on by Shaftesbury (Achitophel), who headed the plot against the Catholic Duke of York, brother of Charles II and heir to the throne, the Duke of Monmouth attempted to usurp the throne. This satire was written at the request of the king. Charles II is King David, the English are the Jews, England is Sion, etc.

Ere one to one was cursedly confined;
When nature prompted, and no law denied
Promiscuous use of concubine and bride;
Then Israel's monarch after heaven's own heart,
His vigorous warmth did variously impart
To wives and slaves; and, wide as his command,
Scattered his Maker's image through the land.   10
Michal, of royal blood, the crown did wear,
A soil ungrateful to the tiller's care:
Not so the rest; for several mothers bore
To godlike David several sons before.
But since like slaves his bed they did ascend,
No true succession could their seed attend.
Of all this numerous progeny was none
So beautiful, so brave, as Absalom:
Whether, inspired by some diviner lust,
His father got him with a greater gust;   20
Or that his conscious destiny made way,
By manly beauty, to imperial sway.
Early in foreign fields he won renown
With kings and states allied to Israel's crown;
In peace the thoughts of war he could remove,
And seemed as he were only born for love.
Whate'er he did, was done with so much ease,
In him alone 'twas natural to please:
His motions all accompanied with grace,
And paradise was opened in his face.   30
With secret joy indulgent David viewed
His youthful image in his son renewed:
To all his wishes nothing he denied;
And made the charming Annabel [2] his bride.
What faults he had (for who from faults is free?)
His father could not, or he would not see.
Some warm excesses which the law forbore,
Were construed youth that purged by boiling o'er,
And Amnon's murder, by a specious name,

[2] Anne Scott, Countess of Buccleuch.

Was called a just revenge for injured fame.   40
Thus praised and loved the noble youth remained,
While David, undisturbed, in Sion reigned.
But life can never be sincerely blest;
Heaven punishes the bad, and proves the best.
The Jews, a headstrong, moody, murmuring race,
As ever tried the extent and stretch of grace;
God's pampered people, whom, debauched with ease,
No king could govern, nor no God could please
(Gods they had tried of every shape and size,
That god-smiths could produce, or priests devise);   50
These Adam-wits, too fortunately free,
Began to dream they wanted liberty;
And when no rule, no precedent was found,
Of men by laws less circumscribed and bound,
They led their wild desires to woods and caves,
And thought that all but savages were slaves.
They who, when Saul was dead, without a blow,
Made foolish Ishbosheth [3] the crown forego;
Who banished David did from Hebron [4] bring,
And with a general shout proclaimed him king: 60
Those very Jews, who, at their very best,
Their humor more than loyalty expressed,
Now wondered why so long they had obeyed
An idol monarch, which their hands had made;
Thought they might ruin him they could create,
Or melt him to that golden calf, a State.
But these were random bolts; no formed design,
Nor interest made the factious crowd to join:
The sober part of Israel, free from stain,
Well knew the value of a peaceful reign;   70
And, looking backward with a wise affright,
Saw seams of wounds, dishonest to the sight:
In contemplation of whose ugly scars

[3] Richard Cromwell, who succeeded Saul, Oliver Cromwell.
[4] Charles was crowned in Scotland (Hebron) before he was in London (Jerusalem).

They cursed the memory of civil wars.
The moderate sort of men, thus qualified,
Inclined the balance to the better side;
And David's mildness managed it so well,
The bad found no occasion to rebel.
But when to sin our biased nature leans,
The careful Devil is still at hand with means; 80
And providently pimps for ill desires:
The Good Old Cause revived, a plot requires.
Plots, true or false, are necessary things,
To raise up commonwealths and ruin kings.
　　The inhabitants of old Jerusalem
Were Jebusites; [5] the town so called from them;
And theirs the native right.
But when the chosen people [6] grew more strong,
The rightful cause at length became the wrong;
And every loss the men of Jebus bore, 90
They still were thought God's enemies the more.
Thus worn and weakened, well or ill content,
Submit they must to David's government:
Impoverished and deprived of all command,
Their taxes doubled as they lost their land;
And, what was harder yet to flesh and blood,
Their gods disgraced, and burnt like common wood.
This set the heathen priesthood in a flame;
For priests of all religions are the same:
Of whatsoe'er descent their godhead be, 100
Stock, stone, or other homely pedigree,
In his defense his servants are as bold,
As if he had been born of beaten gold.
The Jewish rabbins, though their enemies,
In this conclude them honest men and wise:
For 'twas their duty, all the learned think,
To espouse his cause, by whom they eat and drink.
From hence began that Plot, the nation's curse,

[5] Roman Catholics.
[6] The Protestants.

Bad in itself, but represented worse;
Raised in extremes, and in extremes descried; 110
With oaths affirmed, with dying vows denied;
Not weighed or winnowed by the multitude;
But swallowed in the mass, unchewed and crude.
Some truth there was, but dashed and brewed with lies,
To please the fools, and puzzle all the wise.
Succeeding times did equal folly call,
Believing nothing, or believing all.
The Egyptian [7] rites the Jebusites embraced,
Where gods were recommended by their taste.
Such savory deities must needs be good, 120
As served at once for worship and for food.
By force they could not introduce these gods,
For ten to one in former days was odds;
So fraud was used (the sacrificer's trade):
Fools are more hard to conquer than persuade.
Their busy teachers mingled with the Jews,
And raked for converts even the court and stews:
Which Hebrew priests [8] the more unkindly took,
Because the fleece accompanies the flock.
Some thought they God's anointed meant to slay 130
By guns, invented since full many a day:
Our author swears it not; but who can know
How far the Devil and Jebusites may go?
This Plot, which failed for want of common sense,
Had yet a deep and dangerous consequence:
For, as when raging fevers boil the blood,
The standing lake soon floats into a flood,
And every hostile humor, which before
Slept quiet in its channels, bubbles o'er;
So several factions from this first ferment 140
Work up to foam, and threat the government.
Some by their friends, more by themselves thought wise,
Opposed the power to which they could not rise.

[7] French.
[8] Priests of the Anglican church.

Some had in courts been great, and thrown from thence,
Like fiends were hardened in impenitence;
Some, by their monarch's fatal mercy, grown
From pardoned rebels kinsmen to the throne,
Were raised in power and public office high;
Strong bands, if bands ungrateful men could tie.
    Of these the false Achitophel was first;   150
A name to all succeeding ages curst:
For close designs, and crooked counsels fit;
Sagacious, bold, and turbulent of wit;
Restless, unfixed in principles and place;
In power unpleased, impatient of disgrace:
A fiery soul, which, working out its way,
Fretted the pigmy body to decay,
And o'er-informed the tenement of clay.
A daring pilot in extremity;
Pleased with the danger, when the waves went high,   160
He sought the storms; but, for a calm unfit,
Would steer too nigh the sands, to boast his wit.
Great wits are sure to madness near allied,
And thin partitions do their bounds divide;
Else why should he, with wealth and honor blest,
Refuse his age the needful hours of rest?
Punish a body which he could not please;
Bankrupt of life, yet prodigal of ease?
And all to leave what with his toil he won,
To that unfeathered two-legged thing, a son; [9]   170
Got, while his soul did huddled notions try;
And born a shapeless lump, like anarchy.
In friendship false, implacable in hate;
Resolved to ruin or to rule the State.
To compass this the triple bond [10] he broke,
The pillars of the public safety shook,

[9] This is Plato's definition of man applied to Shaftesbury's incompetent son.
[10] England, Sweden, and the Dutch Republic were allied against France.

And fitted Israel for a foreign yoke;
Then seized with fear, yet still affecting fame,
Usurped a patriot's all-atoning name.
So easy still it proves in factious times,   180
With public zeal to cancel private crimes.
How safe is treason, and how sacred ill,
Where none can sin against the people's will!
Where crowds can wink, and no offense be known,
Since in another's guilt they find their own!
Yet fame deserved no enemy can grudge;
The statesman we abhor, but praise the judge.
In Israel's courts ne'er sat an Abbethdin [11]
With more discerning eyes, or hands more clean;
Unbribed, unsought, the wretched to redress;   190
Swift of dispatch, and easy of access.
Oh, had he been content to serve the crown,
With virtues only proper to the gown;
Or had the rankness of the soil been freed
From cockle, that oppressed the noble seed;
David for him his tuneful harp had strung,
And heaven had wanted one immortal song.
But wild Ambition loves to slide, not stand,
And Fortune's ice prefers to Virtue's land.
Achitophel, grown weary to possess   200
A lawful fame, and lazy happiness,
Disdained the golden fruit to gather free,
And lent the crowd his arm to shake the tree.
Now, manifest of crimes contrived long since,
He stood at bold defiance with his prince;
Held up the buckler of the people's cause
Against the crown, and skulked behind the laws.
The wished occasion of the Plot he takes;
Some circumstances finds, but more he makes.
By buzzing emissaries fills the ears   210
Of list'ning crowds with jealousies and fears

[11] An Abbethdin was "an officer of the high court of justice of the
the Jews." (Noyes)

Of arbitrary counsels brought to light,
And proves the king himself a Jebusite.
Weak arguments! which yet he knew full well
Were strong with people easy to rebel.
For, governed by the moon, the giddy Jews
Tread the same track when she the prime renews;
And once in twenty years, their scribes record,
By natural instinct they change their lord.
Achitophel still wants a chief, and none   220
Was found so fit as warlike Absalom:
Not that he wished his greatness to create
(For politicians neither love nor hate),
But, for he knew his title not allowed,
Would keep him still depending on the crowd,
That kingly power, thus ebbing out, might be
Drawn to the dregs of a democracy.
Him he attempts with studied arts to please,
And sheds his venom in such words as these:
      "Auspicious prince, at whose nativity   230
Some royal planet ruled the southern sky;
Thy longing country's darling and desire;
Their cloudy pillar and their guardian fire:
Their second Moses, whose extended wand
Divides the seas, and shows the promised land;
Whose dawning day in every distant age
Has exercised the sacred prophet's rage:
The people's prayer, the glad diviners' theme,
The young men's vision, and the old men's dream!
Thee, savior, thee, the nation's vows confess,   240
And, never satisfied with seeing, bless:
Swift unbespoken pomps thy steps proclaim,
And stammering babes are taught to lisp thy name.
How long wilt thou the general joy detain,
Starve and defraud the people of thy reign?
Content ingloriously to pass thy days
Like one of Virtue's fools that feeds on praise;
Till thy fresh glories, which now shine so bright,

Grow stale and tarnish with our daily sight.
Believe me, royal youth, thy fruit must be   250
Or gathered ripe, or rot upon the tree.
Heaven has to all allotted, soon or late,
Some lucky revolution of their fate;
Whose motions if we watch and guide with skill
(For human good depends on human will),
Our Fortune rolls as from a smooth descent,
And from the first impression takes the bent;
But, if unseized, she glides away like wind,
And leaves repenting Folly far behind.
Now, now she meets you with a glorious prize,   260
And spreads her locks before her as she flies.
Had thus old David, from whose loins you spring,
Not dared, when Fortune called him, to be king,
At Gath [12] an exile he might still remain,
And heaven's anointing oil had been in vain.
Let his successful youth your hopes engage;
But shun the example of declining age:
Behold him setting in his western skies,
The shadows lengthening as the vapors rise.
He is not now, as when on Jordan's sand   270
The joyful people thronged to see him land,
Cov'ring the beach, and black'ning all the strand;
But, like the Prince of Angels, from his height
Comes tumbling downward with diminished light;
Betrayed by one poor plot to public scorn
(Our only blessing since his curst return),
Those heaps of people which one sheaf did bind,
Blown off and scattered by a puff of wind.
What strength can he to your designs oppose,
Naked of friends, and round beset with foes?   280
If Pharaoh's [13] doubtful succor he should use,
A foreign aid would more incense the Jews:
Proud Egypt would dissembled friendship bring;

[12] Probably Brussels. The reference is to the exile of Charles II.
[13] Louis XIV.

Foment the war, but not support the king:
Nor would the royal party e'er unite
With Pharaoh's arms to assist the Jebusite;
Or if they should, their interest soon would break,
And with such odious aid make David weak.
All sorts of men by my successful arts,
Abhorring kings, estrange their altered hearts   290
From David's rule: and 'tis the general cry,
'Religion, commonwealth, and liberty.'
If you, as champion of the public good,
Add to their arms a chief of royal blood,
What may not Israel hope, and what applause
Might such a general gain by such a cause?
Not barren praise alone, that gaudy flower
Fair only to the sight, but solid power;
And nobler is a limited command,
Given by the love of all your native land,   300
Than a successive title, long and dark,
Drawn from the moldy rolls of Noah's ark."
     What cannot praise effect in mighty minds,
When flattery soothes, and when ambition blinds!
Desire of power, on earth a vicious weed,
Yet, sprung from high, is of celestial seed;
In God 'tis glory; and when men aspire,
'Tis but a spark too much of heavenly fire.
The ambitious youth, too covetous of fame,
Too full of angels' metal in his frame,   310
Unwarily was led from virtue's ways,
Made drunk with honor, and debauched with praise.
Half loth, and half consenting to the ill
(For loyal blood within him struggled still),
He thus replied: "And what pretense have I
To take up arms for public liberty?
My father governs with unquestioned right;
The faith's defender, and mankind's delight;
Good, gracious, just, observant of the laws:
And heaven by wonders has espoused his cause.   320

Whom has he wronged in all his peaceful reign?
Who sues for justice to his throne in vain?
What millions has he pardoned of his foes,
Whom just revenge did to his wrath expose?
Mild, easy, humble, studious of our good,
Inclined to mercy, and averse from blood;
If mildness ill with stubborn Israel suit,
His crime is God's beloved attribute.
What could he gain, his people to betray,
Or change his right for arbitrary sway?   330
Let haughty Pharaoh curse with such a reign
His fruitful Nile, and yoke a servile train.
If David's rule Jerusalem displease,
The Dog-star heats their brains to this disease.
Why then should I, encouraging the bad,
Turn rebel and run popularly mad?
Were he a tyrant, who, by lawless might
Oppressed the Jews, and raised the Jebusite,
Well might I mourn; but nature's holy bands
Would curb my spirits and restrain my hands: 340
The people might assert their liberty,
But what was right in them were crime in me.
His favor leaves me nothing to require,
Prevents my wishes, and outruns desire.
What more can I expect while David lives?
All but his kingly diadem he gives:
And that"— But there he paused; then sighing, said—
"Is justly destined for a worthier head.
For when my father from his toils shall rest
And late augment the number of the blest,   350
His lawful issue shall the throne ascend,
Or the collateral line, where that shall end.
His brother, though oppressed with vulgar spite,
Yet dauntless, and secure of native right,
Of every royal virtue stands possessed;
Still dear to all the bravest and the best.
His courage foes, his friends his truth proclaim;

His loyalty the king, the world his fame.
His mercy even the offending crowd will find,
For sure he comes of a forgiving kind. 360
Why should I then repine at heaven's decree,
Which gives me no pretense to royalty?
Yet O that fate, propitiously inclined,
Had raised my birth, or had debased my mind;
To my large soul not all her treasure lent,
And then betrayed it to a mean descent!
I find, I find my mounting spirits bold,
And David's part disdains my mother's mold.
Why am I scanted by a niggard birth?
My soul disclaims the kindred of her earth; 370
And, made for empire, whispers me within,
'Desire of greatness is a godlike sin.' "

    Him staggering so when hell's dire agent found,
While fainting Virtue scarce maintained her ground,
He pours fresh forces in, and thus replies:
    "The eternal God, supremely good and wise,
Imparts not these prodigious gifts in vain:
What wonders are reserved to bless your reign!
Against your will, your arguments have shown,
Such virtue's only given to guide a throne. 380
Not that your father's mildness I contemn;
But manly force becomes the diadem.
'Tis true he grants the people all they crave;
And more, perhaps, than subjects ought to have:
For lavish grants suppose a monarch tame,
And more his goodness than his wit proclaim.
But when should people strive their bonds to break,
If not when kings are negligent or weak?
Let him give on till he can give no more,
The thrifty Sanhedrin [14] shall keep him poor; 390
And every shekel which he can receive,
Shall cost a limb of his prerogative.
To ply him with new plots shall be my care;

[14] Parliament.

Or plunge him deep in some expensive war;
Which when his treasure can no more supply,
He must, with the remains of kingship, buy.
His faithful friends, our jealousies and fears
Call Jebusites, and Pharaoh's pensioners;
Whom when our fury from his aid has torn,
He shall be naked left to public scorn.   400
The next successor, whom I fear and hate,
My arts have made obnoxious to the state;
Turned all his virtues to his overthrow,
And gained our elders to pronounce a foe.
His right, for sums of necessary gold,
Shall first be pawned, and afterward be sold;
Till time shall ever-wanting David draw,
To pass your doubtful title into law:
If not, the people have a right supreme
To make their kings; for kings are made for them.   410
All empire is no more than power in trust,
Which, when resumed, can be no longer just.
Succession, for the general good designed,
In its own wrong a nation cannot bind;
If altering that the people can relieve,
Better one suffer than a nation grieve.
The Jews well know their power: ere Saul they chose,
God was their king, and God they durst depose.
Urge now your piety, your filial name,
A father's right, and fear of future fame;   420
The public good, that universal call,
To which even heaven submitted, answers all.
Nor let his love enchant your generous mind;
'Tis Nature's trick to propagate her kind.
Our fond begetters, who would never die,
Love but themselves in their posterity.
Or let his kindness by the effects be tried,
Or let him lay his vain pretense aside.
God said he loved your father; could he bring
A better proof, than to anoint him king?   430

It surely showed he loved the shepherd well,
Who gave so fair a flock as Israel.
Would David have you thought his darling son?
What means he then, to alienate the crown?
The name of godly he may blush to bear:
'Tis after God's own heart to cheat his heir.
He to his brother gives supreme command;
To you a legacy of barren land,
Perhaps the old harp, on which he thrums his lays,
Or some dull Hebrew ballad in your praise.   440
Then the next heir, a prince severe and wise,
Already looks on you with jealous eyes;
Sees through the thin disguises of your arts,
And marks your progress in the people's hearts.
Though now his mighty soul its grief contains,
He meditates revenge who least complains;
And, like a lion, slumb'ring in the way,
Or sleep dissembling, while he waits his prey,
His fearless foes within his distance draws,
Constrains his roaring, and contracts his paws;   450
Till at the last, his time for fury found,
He shoots with sudden vengeance from the ground;
The prostrate vulgar passes o'er and spares,
But with a lordly rage his hunters tears.
Your case no tame expedients will afford:
Resolve on death, or conquest by the sword,
Which for no less a stake than life you draw;
And self-defense is nature's eldest law.
Leave the warm people no considering time;
For then rebellion may be thought a crime.   460
Prevail yourself of what occasion gives,
But try your title while your father lives;
And that your arms may have a fair pretense,
Proclaim you take them in the king's defense;
Whose sacred life each minute would expose
To plots, from seeming friends, and secret foes.
And who can sound the depth of David's soul?

Perhaps his fear his kindness may control.
He fears his brother, though he loves his son,
For plighted vows too late to be undone. 470
If so, by force he wishes to be gained,
Like women's lechery, to seem constrained.
Doubt not; but when he most affects the frown,
Commit a pleasing rape upon the crown.
Secure his person to secure your cause:
They who possess the prince, possess the laws."
 He said, and this advice above the rest,
With Absalom's mild nature suited best:
Unblamed of life (ambition set aside),
Not stained with cruelty, nor puffed with pride, 480
How happy had he been, if destiny
Had higher placed his birth, or not so high!
His kingly virtues might have claimed a throne,
And blest all other countries but his own.
But charming greatness since so few refuse,
'Tis juster to lament him than accuse.
Strong were his hopes a rival to remove,
With blandishments to gain the public love;
To head the faction while their zeal was hot,
And popularly prosecute the Plot. 490
To further this, Achitophel unites
The malcontents of all the Israelites;
Whose differing parties he could wisely join,
For several ends, to serve the same design:
The best (and of the princes some were such),
Who thought the power of monarchy too much;
Mistaken men, and patriots in their hearts;
Not wicked, but seduced by impious arts.
By these the springs of property were bent,
And wound so high, they cracked the government. 500
The next for interest sought to embroil the state,
To sell their duty at a dearer rate;
And make their Jewish markets of the throne,

Pretending public good, to serve their own.
Others thought kings an useless heavy load,
Who cost too much, and did too little good.
These were for laying honest David by,
On principles of pure good husbandry.
With them joined all the haranguers of the throng,
That thought to get preferment by the tongue.   510
Who follow next, a double danger bring,
Not only hating David, but the king:
The Solymæan rout, well-versed of old
In godly faction, and in treason bold;
Cow'ring and quaking at a conqueror's sword;
But lofty to a lawful prince restored;
Saw with disdain an Ethnic plot begun,
And scorned by Jebusites to be outdone.
Hot Levites [15] headed these; who, pulled before
From the ark, which in the Judges' days they bore,   520
Resumed their cant, and with a zealous cry
Pursued their old beloved Theocracy:
Where Sanhedrin and priest enslaved the nation,
And justified their spoils by inspiration:
For who so fit for reign as Aaron's race,
If once dominion they could found in grace?
These led the pack; though not of surest scent,
Yet deepest mouthed against the government.
A numerous host of dreaming saints succeed,
Of the true old enthusiastic breed: 530
'Gainst form and order they their power employ,
Nothing to build, and all things to destroy.
But far more numerous was the herd of such,
Who think too little, and who talk too much.
These out of mere instinct, they knew not why,
Adored their fathers' God and property;
And, by the same blind benefit of fate,
The Devil and the Jebusite did hate:

[15] The Presbyterian clergymen.

Born to be saved, even in their own despite,
Because they could not help believing right.   540
Such were the tools; but a whole Hydra more
Remains, of sprouting heads too long to score.
Some of their chiefs were princes of the land:
In the first rank of these did Zimri [16] stand;
A man so various, that he seemed to be
Not one, but all mankind's epitome:
Stiff in opinions, always in the wrong;
Was everything by starts, and nothing long;
But, in the course of one revolving moon,
Was chemist, fiddler, statesman, and buffoon: 550
Then all for women, painting, rhyming, drinking,
Besides ten thousand freaks that died in thinking.
Blest madman, who could every hour employ,
With something new to wish, or to enjoy!
Railing and praising were his usual themes;
And both (to show his judgment) in extremes:
So over-violent, or over-civil,
That every man, with him, was God or Devil.
In squand'ring wealth was his peculiar art:
Nothing went unrewarded but desert.   560
Beggared by fools, whom still he found too late,
He had his jest, and they had his estate.
He laughed himself from court; then sought relief
By forming parties, but could ne'er be chief;
For, spite of him, the weight of business fell
On Absalom and wise Achitophel:
Thus, wicked but in will, of means bereft,
He left not faction, but of that was left.
    Titles and names 'twere tedious to rehearse
Of lords, below the dignity of verse.   570
Wits, warriors, Commonwealth's men, were the best;
Kind husbands, and mere nobles, all the rest.
And therefore, in the name of dulness, be

[16] This portrait of George Villiers, Duke of Buckingham, is one of the
finest satirical characterizations in literature.

The well-hung Balaam [17] and cold Caleb,[18] free;
And canting Nadab [19] let oblivion damn,
Who made new porridge for the paschal lamb.
Let friendship's holy band some names assure;
Some their own worth, and some let scorn secure.
Nor shall the rascal rabble here have place,
Whom kings no titles gave, and God no grace: 580
Not bull-faced Jonas,[20] who could statutes draw
To mean rebellion, and make treason law.
But he, though bad, is followed by a worse,
The wretch who heaven's anointed dared to curse:
Shimei,[21] whose youth did early promise bring
Of zeal to God and hatred to his king,
Did wisely from expensive sins refrain,
And never broke the Sabbath, but for gain;
Nor ever was he known an oath to vent,
Or curse, unless against the government.   590
Thus heaping wealth, by the most ready way
Among the Jews, which was to cheat and pray,
The city, to reward his pious hate
Against his master, chose him magistrate.
His hand a vare [22] of justice did uphold;
His neck was loaded with a chain of gold.
During his office, treason was no crime;
The sons of Belial had a glorious time;
For Shimei, though not prodigal of pelf,
Yet loved his wicked neighbor as himself.   600
When two or three were gathered to declaim

[17] The Earl of Huntingdon, who changed from the party of Monmouth to that of the Duke of York.
[18] Lord Grey allowed an intrigue between Monmouth and his own wife.
[19] Lord Howard. Scott says that when he took the sacrament after declaring his innocence of "treasonable libel on the court party," he drank "ale poured on roasted apples and sugar."
[20] Sir William Jones prosecuted the members of the Popish Plot, but later turned against the court party.
[21] Slingsby Bethel, a Whig sheriff of London.
[22] Wand.

Against the monarch of Jerusalem,
Shimei was always in the midst of them;
And if they cursed the king when he was by,
Would rather curse than break good company.
If any durst his factious friends accuse,
He packed a jury of dissenting Jews;
Whose fellow-feeling in the godly cause
Would free the suff'ring saint from human laws.
For laws are only made to punish those   610
Who serve the king, and to protect his foes.
If any leisure time he had from power
(Because 'tis sin to misemploy an hour),
His business was, by writing, to persuade
That kings were useless, and a clog to trade;
And, that his noble style he might refine,
No Rechabite more shunned the fumes of wine.
Chaste were his cellars, and his shrieval board
The grossness of a city feast abhorred:
His cooks, with long disuse, their trade forgot;   620
Cool was his kitchen, though his brains were hot.
Such frugal virtue malice may accuse,
But sure 'twas necessary to the Jews;
For towns once burnt such magistrates require
As dare not tempt God's providence by fire.
With spiritual food he fed his servants well,
But free from flesh that made the Jews rebel;
And Moses' laws he held in more account,
For forty days of fasting in the mount.
To speak the rest, who better are forgot,   630
Would tire a well-breathed witness of the Plot.
Yet, Corah,[23] thou shalt from oblivion pass:
Erect thyself, thou monumental brass,[24]
High as the serpent of thy metal made,

[23] Titus Oates, instigator of the Popish Plot.

[24] This sarcastic reference is to the brazen serpent made by Moses and set up on a pole in the camp to cure the serpent bites of the children of Israel. *Numbers* 21:6–9.

While nations stand secure beneath thy shade.
What though his birth were base, yet comets rise
From earthy vapors, ere they shine in skies.
Prodigious actions may as well be done
By weaver's issue, as by prince's son.
This arch-attestor for the public good   640
By that one deed ennobles all his blood.
Who ever asked the witnesses' high race,
Whose oath with martyrdom did Stephen grace?
Ours was a Levite, and as times went then,
His tribe were God Almighty's gentlemen.
Sunk were his eyes, his voice was harsh and loud,
Sure signs he neither choleric was nor proud:
His long chin proved his wit; his saintlike grace
A church vermilion, and a Moses' face.
His memory, miraculously great,   650
Could plots, exceeding man's belief, repeat;
Which therefore cannot be accounted lies,
For human wit could never such devise.
Some future truths are mingled in his book;
But where the witness failed, the prophet spoke:
Some things like visionary flights appear;
The spirit caught him up, the Lord knows where;
And gave him his rabbinical degree,
Unknown to foreign university.
His judgment yet his memory did excel;   660
Which pieced his wondrous evidence so well,
And suited to the temper of the times,
Then groaning under Jebusitic crimes.
Let Israel's foes suspect his heavenly call,
And rashly judge his writ apocryphal;
Our laws for such affronts have forfeits made:
He takes his life, who takes away his trade.
Were I myself in witness Corah's place,
The wretch who did me such a dire disgrace,
Should whet my memory, though once forgot,   670
To make him an appendix of my plot.

His zeal to heaven made him his prince despise,
And load his person with indignities;
But zeal peculiar privilege affords,
Indulging latitude to deeds and words;
And Corah might for Agag's murder call,
In terms as coarse as Samuel used to Saul.
What others in his evidence did join
(The best that could be had for love or coin),
In Corah's own predicament will fall;   680
For *witness* is a common name to all.

    Surrounded thus with friends of every sort,
Deluded Absalom forsakes the court;
Impatient of high hopes, urged with renown,
And fired with near possession of a crown.
The admiring crowd are dazzled with surprise,
And on his goodly person feed their eyes.
His joy concealed, he sets himself to show,
On each side bowing popularly low;
His looks, his gestures, and his words he frames,   690
And with familiar ease repeats their names.
Thus formed by nature, furnished out with arts,
He glides unfelt into their secret hearts.
Then, with a kind compassionating look,
And sighs, bespeaking pity ere he spoke,
Few words he said; but easy those and fit,
More slow than Hybla-drops, and far more sweet.

    "I mourn, my countrymen, your lost estate;
Though far unable to prevent your fate:
Behold a banished man, for your dear cause   700
Exposed a prey to arbitrary laws!
Yet oh! that I alone could be undone,
Cut off from empire, and no more a son!
Now all your liberties a spoil are made;
Egypt and Tyrus intercept your trade,
And Jebusites your sacred rites invade.
My father, whom with reverence yet I name,
Charmed into ease, is careless of his fame;

And, bribed with petty sums of foreign gold,
Is grown in Bathsheba's [25] embraces old; 710
Exalts his enemies, his friends destroys,
And all his power against himself employs.
He gives, and let him give, my right away;
But why should he his own and yours betray?
He, only he, can make the nation bleed,
And he alone from my revenge is freed.
Take then my tears" (with that he wiped his eyes);
" 'Tis all the aid my present power supplies:
No court-informer can these arms accuse;
These arms may sons against their fathers use: 720
And 'tis my wish, the next successor's reign
May make no other Israelite complain."
   Youth, beauty, graceful action seldom fail;
But common interest always will prevail;
And pity never ceases to be shown
To him who makes the people's wrongs his own.
The crowd, that still believe their kings oppress,
With lifted hands their young Messiah bless:
Who now begins his progress to ordain
With chariots, horsemen, and a num'rous train; 730
From east to west his glories he displays,
And, like the sun, the promised land surveys.
Fame runs before him as the morning star,
And shouts of joy salute him from afar:
Each house receives him as a guardian god,
And consecrates the place of his abode.
But hospitable treats did most commend
Wise Issachar,[26] his wealthy western friend.
This moving court, that caught the people's eyes,
And seemed but pomp, did other ends disguise: 740
Achitophel had formed it, with intent

[25] The Duchess of Portsmouth, mistress of Charles II.
[26] Thomas Thynne, who entertained Monmouth when he made a
showy expedition through western England in 1680 after he had been
ordered out of the country by the council.

To sound the depths, and fathom, where it went,
The people's hearts; distinguish friends from foes,
And try their strength, before they came to blows.
Yet all was colored with a smooth pretense
Of specious love, and duty to their prince.
Religion and redress of grievances,
Two names that always cheat and always please,
Are often urged; and good King David's life
Endangered by a brother and a wife.[27]   750
Thus in a pageant show a plot is made,
And peace itself is war in masquerade.
O foolish Israel! never warned by ill!
Still the same bait, and circumvented still!
Did ever men forsake their present ease,
In midst of health imagine a disease;
Take pains contingent mischiefs to foresee,
Make heirs for monarchs, and for God decree?
What shall we think! Can people give away,
Both for themselves and sons, their native sway?   760
Then they are left defenseless to the sword
Of each unbounded, arbitrary lord:
And laws are vain, by which we right enjoy,
If kings unquestioned can those laws destroy.
Yet if the crowd be judge of fit and just,
And kings are only officers in trust,
Then this resuming cov'nant was declared
When kings were made, or is for ever barred.
If those who gave the scepter could not tie
By their own deed their own posterity,   770
How then could Adam bind his future race?
How could his forfeit on mankind take place?
Or how could heavenly justice damn us all,
Who ne'er consented to our father's fall?
Then kings are slaves to those whom they command,
And tenants to their people's pleasure stand.

[27] Queen Catherine's failure to bear children left the king's brother heir to the throne and led to the Popish Plot.

Add, that the power for property allowed
Is mischievously seated in the crowd;
For who can be secure of private right,
If sovereign sway may be dissolved by might?   780
Nor is the people's judgment always true:
The most may err as grossly as the few;
And faultless kings run down, by common cry,
For vice, oppression, and for tyranny.
What standard is there in a fickle rout,
Which, flowing to the mark, runs faster out?
Nor only crowds, but Sanhedrins may be
Infected with this public lunacy,
And share the madness of rebellious times,
To murder monarchs for imagined crimes.   790
If they may give and take whene'er they please,
Not kings alone (the Godhead's images),
But government itself at length must fall
To nature's state, where all have right to all.
Yet, grant our lords the people kings can make,
What prudent men a settled throne would shake?
For whatsoe'er their sufferings were before,
That change they covet makes them suffer more.
All other errors but disturb a state,
But innovation is the blow of fate.   800
If ancient fabrics nod, and threat to fall,
To patch the flaws, and buttress up the wall,
Thus far 'tis duty: but here fix the mark;
For all beyond it is to touch our ark.
To change foundations, cast the frame anew,
Is work for rebels who base ends pursue,
At once divine and human laws control,
And mend the parts by ruin of the whole.
The tamp'ring world is subject to this curse,
To physic their disease into a worse.   810
    Now what relief can righteous David bring?
How fatal 'tis to be too good a king!
Friends he has few, so high the madness grows:

Who dare be such, must be the people's foes.
Yet some there were, ev'n in the worst of days;
Some let me name, and naming is to praise.

In this short file Barzillai [28] first appears;
Barzillai, crowned with honor and with years.
Long since, the rising rebels he withstood
In regions waste, beyond the Jordan's flood:　　　　820
Unfortunately brave to buoy the State;
But sinking underneath his master's fate:
In exile with his godlike prince he mourned;
For him he suffered, and with him returned.
The court he practiced, not the courtier's art:
Large was his wealth, but larger was his heart,
Which well the noblest objects knew to choose,
The fighting warrior and recording Muse.
His bed could once a fruitful issue boast;
Now more than half a father's name is lost.　　　　830
His eldest hope, with every grace adorned,
By me (so heaven will have it) always mourned,
And always honored, snatched in manhood's prime
By unequal fates, and Providence's crime;
Yet not before the goal of honor won,
All parts fulfilled of subject and of son:
Swift was the race, but short the time to run.
O narrow circle, but of power divine,
Scanted in space, but perfect in thy line!
By sea, by land, thy matchless worth was known,　　　　840
Arms thy delight, and war was all thy own:
Thy force, infused, the fainting Tyrians propped;
And haughty Pharaoh found his fortune stopped.
O ancient honor! O unconquered hand,
Whom foes unpunished never could withstand!
But Israel was unworthy of thy name;
Short is the date of all immoderate fame.

---

[28] The Duke of Ormond, a faithful Royalist. He shared the exile of
Charles II and proved himself a loyal friend and subject. His eldest son
distinguished himself in the Dutch wars.

It looks as heaven our ruin had designed,
And durst not trust thy fortune and thy mind.
Now, free from earth, thy disencumbered soul   850
Mounts up, and leaves behind the clouds and starry pole:
From thence thy kindred legions may'st thou bring,
To aid the guardian angel of thy king.
Here stop, my Muse, here cease thy painful flight;
No pinions can pursue immortal height:
Tell good Barzillai thou canst sing no more,
And tell thy soul she should have fled before:
Or fled she with his life, and left this verse
To hand on her departed patron's hearse?
Now take thy steepy flight from heaven, and see   860
If thou canst find on earth another *he:*
Another *he* would be too hard to find;
See then whom thou canst see not far behind.
Zadoc [29] the priest, whom, shunning power and place,
His lowly mind advanced to David's grace.
With him the Sagan of Jerusalem,[30]
Of hospitable soul, and noble stem;
Him of the western dome,[31] whose weighty sense
Flows in fit words and heavenly eloquence.
The prophets' sons, by such example led,   870
To learning and to loyalty were bred:
For colleges on bounteous kings depend,
And never rebel was to arts a friend.
To these succeed the pillars of the laws,
Who best could plead, and best can judge a cause.
Next them a train of loyal peers ascend:
Sharp-judging Adriel,[32] the Muses' friend,
Himself a Muse—in Sanhedrin's debate
True to his prince, but not a slave of state,

[29] The Archbishop of Canterbury, Sancroft.
[30] The Bishop of London.
[31] The Dean of Westminster. The "prophets' sons" are the boys of Westminster School.
[32] The Earl of Mulgrave, Dryden's patron, was given two of the offices which were formerly held by the Duke of Monmouth.

Whom David's love with honors did adorn, 880
That from his disobedient son were torn.
Jotham [33] of piercing wit and pregnant thought,
Endued by nature, and by learning taught
To move assemblies, who but only tried
The worse a while, then chose the better side:
Nor chose alone, but turned the balance too;
So much the weight of one brave man can do.
Hushai, [34] the friend of David in distress;
In public storms, of manly steadfastness:
By foreign treaties he informed his youth, 890
And joined experience to his native truth.
His frugal care supplied the wanting throne;
Frugal for that, but bounteous of his own:
'Tis easy conduct when exchequers flow,
But hard the task to manage well the low;
For sovereign power is too depressed or high,
When kings are forced to sell, or crowds to buy.
Indulge one labor more, my weary Muse,
For Amiel: [35] who can Amiel's praise refuse?
Of ancient race by birth, but nobler yet 900
In his own worth, and without title great:
The Sanhedrin long time as chief he ruled,
Their reason guided, and their passion cooled:
So dext'rous was he in the crown's defense,
So formed to speak a loyal nation's sense,
That, as their band was Israel's tribes in small,
So fit was he to represent them all.
Now rasher charioteers the seat ascend,
Whose loose careers his steady skill commend:
They, like the unequal ruler of the day, 910
Misguide the seasons, and mistake the way;

[33] George Saville, the Marquis of Halifax, though related by marriage to Shaftesbury and in sympathy with his political principles, opposed the bill to exclude the Duke of York from succession to the throne.

[34] Lawrence Hyde, later Earl of Rochester, a patron of Dryden and the holder of various diplomatic offices.

[35] Edward Seymour, Speaker of the House of Commons.

While he withdrawn at their mad labor smiles,
And safe enjoys the sabbath of his toils.
  These were the chief, a small but faithful band
Of worthies, in the breach who dared to stand
And tempt the united fury of the land.
With grief they viewed such powerful engines bent,
To batter down the lawful government:
A numerous faction, with pretended frights,
In Sanhedrins to plume the regal rights;   920
The true successor from the court removed;
The Plot, by hireling witnesses, improved.
These ills they saw, and, as their duty bound,
They showed the king the danger of the wound;
That no concessions from the throne would please,
But lenitives fomented the disease;
That Absalom, ambitious of the crown,
Was made the lure to draw the people down;
That false Achitophel's pernicious hate
Had turned the Plot to ruin Church and State;   930
The council violent, the rabble worse;
That Shimei taught Jerusalem to curse.
  With all these loads of injuries oppressed,
And long revolving in his careful breast
The event of things, at last, his patience tired,
Thus from his royal throne, by heaven inspired,
The godlike David spoke; with awful fear
His train their Maker in their master hear.
  "Thus long have I, by native mercy swayed,
My wrongs dissembled, my revenge delayed: 940
So willing to forgive the offending age;
So much the father did the king assuage.
But now so far my clemency they slight,
The offenders question my forgiving right.
That one was made for many, they contend;
But 'tis to rule, for that's a monarch's end.
They call my tenderness of blood, my fear;
Though manly tempers can the longest bear.

Yet, since they will divert my native course,
'Tis time to show I am not good by force.   950
Those heaped affronts that haughty subjects bring,
Are burdens for a camel, not a king.
Kings are the public pillars of the State,
Born to sustain and prop the nation's weight;
If my young Samson will pretend a call
To shake the column, let him share the fall:
But O that yet he would repent and live!
How easy 'tis for parents to forgive!
With how few tears a pardon might be won
From nature, pleading for a darling son!   960
Poor pitied youth, by my paternal care
Raised up to all the height his frame could bear!
Had God ordained his fate for empire born,
He would have given his soul another turn:
Gulled with a patriot's name, whose modern sense
Is one that would by law supplant his prince;
The people's brave, the politician's tool;
Never was patriot yet, but was a fool.
Whence comes it that religion and the laws
Should more be Absalom's than David's cause?   970
His old instructor, ere he lost his place,
Was never thought indued with so much grace.
Good heavens, how faction can a patriot paint!
My rebel ever proves my people's saint.
Would *they* impose an heir upon the throne?
Let Sanhedrins be taught to give their own.
A king's at least a part of government,
And mine as requisite as their consent;
Without my leave a future king to choose,
Infers a right the present to depose.   980
True, they petition me to approve their choice,
But Esau's hands suit ill with Jacob's voice.
My pious subjects for my safety pray,
Which to secure, they take my power away.
From plots and treasons heaven preserve my years,

But save me most from my petitioners!
Unsatiate as the barren womb or grave;
God cannot grant so much as they can crave.
What then is left, but with a jealous eye
To guard the small remains of royalty?   990
The law shall still direct my peaceful sway,
And the same law teach rebels to obey:
Votes shall no more established power control—
Such votes as make a part exceed the whole:
No groundless clamors shall my friends remove,
Nor crowds have power to punish ere they prove;
For gods and godlike kings their care express,
Still to defend their servants in distress.
O that my power to saving were confined!
Why am I forced, like heaven, against my mind,   1000
To make examples of another kind?
Must I at length the sword of justice draw?
O curst effects of necessary law!
How ill my fear they by my mercy scan!
Beware the fury of a patient man.
Law they require, let Law then show her face;
They could not be content to look on Grace,
Her hinder parts, but with a daring eye
To tempt the terror of her front and die.
By their own arts, 'tis righteously decreed,   1010
Those dire artificers of death shall bleed.
Against themselves their witnesses will swear,
Till viper-like their mother Plot they tear;
And suck for nutriment that bloody gore,
Which was their principle of life before.
Their Belial with their Belzebub will fight;
Thus on my foes, my foes shall do me right.
Nor doubt the event; for factious crowds engage
In their first onset, all their brutal rage.
Then let 'em take an unresisted course;   1020
Retire, and traverse, and delude their force;
But, when they stand all breathless, urge the fight,

And rise upon 'em with redoubled might;
For lawful power is still superior found;
When long driven back, at length it stands the ground."
　He said. The Almighty, nodding, gave consent;
And peals of thunder shook the firmament.
Henceforth a series of new time began,
The mighty years in long procession ran:
Once more the godlike David was restored,　　　　　1030
And willing nations knew their lawful lord.

To the Pious Memory of the Accomplished Young Lady
Mrs. Anne Killigrew
Excellent in the Two Sister Arts of Poesy and Painting

An Ode

I

Thou youngest virgin-daughter of the skies,
　Made in the last promotion of the blest,
Whose palms, new plucked from paradise,
In spreading branches more sublimely rise,
　Rich with immortal green above the rest;
Whether, adopted to some neighboring star,
Thou roll'st above us in thy wandering race,
　Or in procession fixed and regular,
　Moved with the heaven's majestic pace,
　Or called to more superior bliss,　　　　　10
Thou tread'st with seraphim the vast abyss:
Whatever happy region is thy place,
Cease thy celestial song a little space;
Thou wilt have time enough for hymns divine,
　Since heaven's eternal year is thine.
Hear, then, a mortal Muse thy praise rehearse
　In no ignoble verse,
But such as thy own voice did practice here,

When thy first fruits of poesy were given,
To make thyself a welcome inmate there, 20
While yet a young probationer,
And candidate of heaven.

II

If by traduction came thy mind,
Our wonder is the less to find
A soul so charming from a stock so good;
Thy father was transfused into thy blood:
So wert thou born into the tuneful strain,
An early, rich, and inexhausted vein.
But if thy pre-existing soul
Was formed at first with myriads more, 30
It did through all the mighty poets roll
Who Greek or Latin laurels wore,
And was that Sappho last, which once it was before.
If so, then cease thy flight, O heaven-born mind!
Thou hast no dross to purge from thy rich ore,
Nor can thy soul a fairer mansion find
Than was the beauteous frame she left behind:
Return, to fill or mend the quire of thy celestial kind!

III

May we presume to say that at thy birth
New joy was sprung in heaven as well as here on earth? 40
For sure the milder planets did combine
On thy auspicious horoscope to shine,
And even the most malicious were in trine.[1]
Thy brother-angels at thy birth
Strung each his lyre, and tuned it high,
That all the people of the sky
Might know a poetess was born on earth;
And then, if ever, mortal ears

[1] A good omen.

Had heard the music of the spheres.
And if no clustering swarm of bees   50
On thy sweet mouth distilled their golden dew,[2]
'Twas that such vulgar miracles
Heaven had not leisure to renew;
For all the blest fraternity of love
Solemnized there thy birth, and kept thy holiday above.

IV

O gracious God! how far have we
Profaned thy heavenly gift of poesy!
Made prostitute and profligate the Muse,
Debased to each obscene and impious use,
Whose harmony was first ordained above   60
For tongues of angels and for hymns of love!
O wretched we! why were we hurried down
    This lubric and adulterate age
(Nay, added fat pollutions of our own)
    To increase the steaming ordures of the stage?
What can we say to excuse our second fall?
Let this thy vestal, heaven, atone for all:
Her Arethusian stream remains unsoiled,
Unmixed with foreign filth, and undefiled;
Her wit was more than man; her innocence a child.   70

V

Art she had none, yet wanted none,
    For nature did that want supply;
So rich in treasures of her own,
    She might our boasted stores defy:
Such noble vigor did her verse adorn
That it seemed borrowed where 'twas only born.
Her morals too were in her bosom bred,
    By great examples daily fed,

---

[2] The allusion is to the settling of bees on the lips of the sleeping infant Plato, foretelling his eloquence.

What in the best of books, her father's life, she read.
   And to be read herself she need not fear;   80
   Each test and every light her Muse will bear,
   Though Epictetus with his lamp were there.[3]
   Even love (for love sometimes her Muse expressed)
Was but a lambent flame which played about her breast,
     Light as the vapors of a morning dream;
   So cold herself, whilst she such warmth expressed,
     'Twas Cupid bathing in Diana's stream.

VI

   Born to the spacious empire of the Nine,
     One would have thought she should have been content
     To manage well that mighty government;   90
   But what can young, ambitious souls confine?
     To the next realm she stretched her sway,
     For Painture near adjoining lay,
   A plenteous province and alluring prey:
   A chamber of dependences was framed
     (As conquerors will never want pretense,
     When armed, to justify the offense),
And the whole fief in right of Poetry she claimed.
   The country open lay without defense,
   For poets frequent inroads there had made,   100
     And perfectly could represent
   The shape, the face, with every lineament;
And all the large demesnes which the dumb Sister swayed,
     All bowed beneath her government,
   Received in triumph wheresoe'er she went.
   Her pencil drew whate'er her soul designed,
And oft the happy draught surpassed the image in her mind:
     The sylvan scenes of herds and flocks
     And fruitful plains and barren rocks;
     Of shallow brooks that flowed so clear   110

---

[3] Epictetus, a Greek Stoic philosopher, had an earthenware lamp, which after his death was sold for a large sum of money.

The bottom did the top appear;
Of deeper too and ampler floods,
Which, as in mirrors, showed the woods;
Of lofty trees, with sacred shades
And perspectives of pleasant glades,
Where nymphs of brightest form appear,
And shaggy satyrs standing near,
Which them at once admire and fear;
The ruins, too, of some majestic piece,
Boasting the power of ancient Rome or Greece,   120
Whose statues, friezes, columns, broken lie,
And, though defaced, the wonder of the eye.
What nature, art, bold fiction, e'er durst frame,
Her forming hand gave feature to the name;
So strange a concourse ne'er was seen before
But when the peopled ark the whole creation bore.

VII

The scene then changed: with bold, erected look
Our martial king [4] the sight with reverence strook,
For, not content to express his outward part,
Her hand called out the image of his heart;   130
His warlike mind, his soul devoid of fear,
His high designing thoughts were figured there,
As when by magic, ghosts are made appear.
Our phœnix queen was portrayed, too, so bright
Beauty alone could beauty take so right:
Her dress, her shape, her matchless grace,
Were all observed, as well as heavenly face;
With such a peerless majesty she stands
As in that day she took the crown from sacred hands;
Before, a train of heroines was seen—   140
In beauty foremost, as in rank, the queen.
Thus nothing to her genius was denied,
But, like a ball of fire, the farther thrown,

[4] James II.

Still with a greater blaze she shone,
And her bright soul broke out on every side.
What next she had designed, heaven only knows:
To such immoderate growth her conquest rose
That fate alone its progress could oppose.

VIII

Now all those charms, that blooming grace,
The well-proportioned shape, and beauteous face,   150
Shall never more be seen by mortal eyes;
In earth the much-lamented virgin lies.
Not wit nor piety could fate prevent;
Nor was the cruel destiny content
To finish all the murder at a blow,
To sweep at once her life and beauty too;
But, like a hardened felon, took a pride
    To work more mischievously slow,
    And plundered first, and then destroyed.
Oh, double sacrilege on things divine,   160
To rob the relic and deface the shrine!
        But thus Orinda died: [5]
Heaven, by the same disease, did both translate;
As equal were their souls, so equal was their fate.

IX

Meantime her warlike brother on the seas
His waving streamers to the winds displays,
And vows for his return with vain devotion pays.
    Ah, generous youth, that wish forbear;
    The winds too soon will waft thee here!
    Slack all thy sails, and fear to come;   170
Alas! thou know'st not thou art wrecked at home!
No more shalt thou behold thy sister's face;

[5] The poetess, Katherine Philips. Both Katherine Philips and Anne
Killigrew died of smallpox.

Thou hast already had her last embrace.
But look aloft; and if thou ken'st from far,
Among the Pleiads, a new-kindled star,
If any sparkles than the rest more bright,
'Tis she that shines in that propitious light.

X

When in mid-air the golden trump shall sound,
  To raise the nations under ground;
When in the Valley of Jehoshaphat [6]   180
The judging God shall close the book of fate,
  And there the last assizes keep
  For those who wake and those who sleep;
  When rattling bones together fly
  From the four corners of the sky;
When sinews o'er the skeletons are spread,
Those clothed with flesh, and life inspires the dead; [7]
The sacred poets first shall hear the sound,
  And foremost from the tomb shall bound,
For they are covered with the lightest ground,   190
And straight, with inborn vigor, on the wing,
Like mounting larks, to the new morning sing.
There thou, sweet saint, before the quire shalt go,
As harbinger of heaven, the way to show,
The way which thou so well hast learned below.

Alexander's Feast; or, The Power of Music
An Ode in Honor of St. Cecilia's Day

I

'Twas at the royal feast, for Persia won
By Philip's warlike son:

[6] "Let the heathen be wakened and come up to the valley of Jehosha-phat: for there will I sit to judge all the heathen round about." *Joel* 3:12.
[7] For the story of the dry bones clothed with flesh see *Ezekiel* 37: 1–14.

Aloft in awful state,
The godlike hero sate
On his imperial throne;
His valiant peers were placed around,
Their brows with roses and with myrtles bound
(So should desert in arms be crowned).
The lovely Thais,[1] by his side,
Sat like a blooming Eastern bride,   10
In flower of youth and beauty's pride.
    Happy, happy, happy pair!
      None but the brave,
      None but the brave,
    None but the brave deserves the fair.

CHORUS

Happy, happy, happy pair!
    None but the brave,
    None but the brave,
None but the brave deserves the fair.

II

    Timotheus,[2] placed on high   20
      Amid the tuneful quire,
With flying fingers touched the lyre:
    The trembling notes ascend the sky,
      And heavenly joys inspire.
    The song began from Jove,
Who left his blissful seats above
(Such is the power of mighty love).
A dragon's fiery form belied the god;
    Sublime on radiant spires he rode,

[1] An Athenian courtesan accompanying Alexander the Great back to Asia.
[2] Not the great musician who died B.C. 357, but a musician of such skill that he could control the moods of Alexander.

When he to fair Olympia [3] pressed;   30
And while he sought her snowy breast,
Then round her slender waist he curled,
And stamped an image of himself, a sovereign of the world.
The listening crowd admire the lofty sound:
"A present deity!" they shout around;
"A present deity!" the vaulted roofs rebound.
                    With ravished ears
                    The monarch hears;
                    Assumes the god,
                    Affects to nod,   40
                And seems to shake the spheres.

CHORUS

                    With ravished ears
                    The monarch hears;
                    Assumes the god,
                    Affects to nod,
                And seems to shake the spheres.

III

The praise of Bacchus then the sweet musician sung,
                Of Bacchus ever fair and ever young.
                    The jolly god in triumph comes:
                    Sound the trumpets, beat the drums!   50
                        Flushed with a purple grace,
                        He shows his honest face:
Now give the hautboys breath! he comes, he comes!
                    Bacchus, ever fair and young,
                        Drinking joys did first ordain:
                    Bacchus' blessings are a treasure;
                    Drinking is the soldier's pleasure;
                        Rich the treasure,
                        Sweet the pleasure,
                    Sweet is pleasure after pain.   60

[3] Olympia for Olympias, the mother of Alexander. Heroes liked to derive their ancestry from the gods.

CHORUS

Bacchus' blessings are a treasure;
Drinking is the soldier's pleasure;
Rich the treasure,
Sweet the pleasure,
Sweet is pleasure after pain.

IV

Soothed with the sound, the king grew vain,
Fought all his battles o'er again,
And thrice he routed all his foes, and thrice he slew the slain.
The master saw the madness rise,
His glowing cheeks, his ardent eyes;   70
And while he heaven and earth defied,
Changed his hand and checked his pride.
He chose a mournful Muse,
Soft pity to infuse:
He sung Darius great and good,
By too severe a fate,
Fallen, fallen, fallen, fallen,
Fallen from his high estate,
And weltering in his blood;
Deserted at his utmost need   80
By those his former bounty fed,
On the bare earth exposed he lies,
With not a friend to close his eyes.[4]
With downcast looks the joyless victor sate,
Revolving in his altered soul
The various turns of chance below;
And now and then a sigh he stole,
And tears began to flow.

[4] Darius, conquered by Alexander, was stabbed by his own companions.

CHORUS

    Revolving in his altered soul
      The various turns of chance below;   90
    And now and then a sigh he stole,
      And tears began to flow.

V

    The mighty master smiled to see
    That love was in the next degree;
    'Twas but a kindred sound to move,
    For pity melts the mind to love.
    Softly sweet, in Lydian [5] measures,
    Soon he soothed his soul to pleasures.
    "War," he sung, "is toil and trouble;
    Honor, but an empty bubble;   100
      Never ending, still beginning,
    Fighting still, and still destroying:
      If the world be worth thy winning,
    Think, O think it worth enjoying.
      Lovely Thais sits beside thee;
      Take the good the gods provide thee."
The many rend the skies with loud applause;
So Love was crowned, but Music won the cause.
    The prince, unable to conceal his pain,
      Gazed on the fair   110
      Who caused his care,
    And sighed and looked, sighed and looked,
    Sighed and looked, and sighed again;
At length, with love and wine at once oppressed,
The vanquished victor sunk upon her breast.

CHORUS

    The prince, unable to conceal his pain,
      Gazed on the fair

[5] Sensuous music, distinguished from the sterner Doric measures.

Who caused his care,
And sighed and looked, sighed and looked,
Sighed and looked, and sighed again;   120
At length, with love and wine at once oppressed,
The vanquished victor sunk upon her breast.

VI

Now strike the golden lyre again:
A louder yet, and yet a louder strain.
Break his bands of sleep asunder,
And rouse him, like a rattling peal of thunder.
Hark, hark! the horrid sound
Has raised up his head;
As awaked from the dead,
And amazed, he stares around.   130
"Revenge, revenge!" Timotheus cries;
"See the Furies arise!
See the snakes that they rear,
How they hiss in their hair,
And the sparkles that flash from their eyes!
Behold a ghastly band,
Each a torch in his hand!
Those are Grecian ghosts, that in battle were slain,
And unburied remain
Inglorious on the plain: 140
Give the vengeance due
To the valiant crew!
Behold how they toss their torches on high,
How they point to the Persian abodes,
And glittering temples of their hostile gods!" [6]
The princes applaud with a furious joy,
And the king seized a flambeau with zeal to destroy;
Thais led the way,

[6] After capturing Persepolis, Alexander destroyed the palaces by fire.
There is only very slight authority for the story that Thais incited the
deed.

To light him to his prey,
And, like another Helen, fired another Troy.   150

CHORUS

And the king seized a flambeau with zeal to destroy;
Thais led the way,
To light him to his prey,
And, like another Helen, fired another Troy.

VII

Thus, long ago,
Ere heaving bellows learned to blow,
While organs yet were mute,
Timotheus, to his breathing flute
And sounding lyre,
Could swell the soul to rage or kindle soft desire.   160
At last divine Cecilia came,
Inventress of the vocal frame:
The sweet enthusiast, from her sacred store,
Enlarged the former narrow bounds,
And added length to solemn sounds,
With nature's mother-wit, and arts unknown before.
Let old Timotheus yield the prize,
Or both divide the crown:
He raised a mortal to the skies;
She drew an angel down.   170

GRAND CHORUS

At last divine Cecilia came,
Inventress of the vocal frame:
The sweet enthusiast, from her sacred store,
Enlarged the former narrow bounds,
And added length to solemn sounds,

With nature's mother-wit, and arts unknown before.
    Let old Timotheus yield the prize,
      Or both divide the crown:
    He raised a mortal to the skies;
      She drew an angel down.   180

Thomas Traherne 1636-1674

Traherne's poems and his prose *Centuries of Meditation*
have come to us in a dramatic way. One day in 1897 a man
with some knowledge of literature found on a London book-
stall two interesting manuscripts priced at a few pence each.
He later sold them to the learned Dr. Grosart, who identified
the poems as the work of Vaughan. Before Dr. Grosart com-
pleted the edition of Vaughan which he was preparing, he
died; and by good fortune the manuscripts came into the
hands of Bertram Dobell, the publisher. Mr. Dobell did a
clever piece of detective work which definitely proved the
poems to be by Traherne, and published them separately in
1903.

In thought many of Traherne's poems might well be taken
for Vaughan's, for they show the same conception of child-
hood as a state but little removed from a heavenly pre-
existence. Traherne, however, draws a philosophy from the
recollection of his own childhood which goes deeper than
Vaughan's or that of any other poet of childhood except
Blake. What he knew by intuition in his childhood he feels
to be real; false values originating in warped social and eco-
nomic systems have been taught to him. The natural atti-
tude toward nature and people is that which he felt as a child
and described in the third meditation of the "Third Century"
of his prose meditations:

> The corn was orient and immortal wheat, which never
> should be reaped, nor was ever sown. I thought it had
> stood from everlasting to everlasting. The dust and stones
> of the street were as precious as gold: the gates were at
> first the end of the world. The green trees when I saw
> them first through one of the gates transported and
> ravished me, their sweetness and unusual beauty made
> my heart to leap, and almost mad with ecstasy, they
> were such strange and wonderful things. The Men! O
> what venerable and reverend creatures did the aged

seem! Immortal Cherubim! And young men glittering and sparkling angels, and maids strange seraphic pieces of life and beauty! Boys and girls tumbling in the street, and playing, were moving jewels.

Traherne's problem was how man could regain this child-like attitude and so find true happiness. He came to the conclusion that happiness was a mental state and that to establish it one must have such inner resources as the *active* enjoyment of nature, people, and God. He argued that every-thing was of God; that God is love; and that therefore nature is good and beautiful and true, itself a revelation of God. He found happiness in identifying himself with nature, feeling that, "You never enjoy the world aright till the sea itself floweth in your veins, till you are clothed with the heavens, and crowned with the stars." He was surer than Vaughan that God could be found in man at his best. He could not, therefore, be happy when others were unhappy and was charitable far beyond his means. Enjoyment of God, he felt, was through the pleasure to be found in the universe and in mankind; he went even further and said that God Himself could not enjoy His own creation except through man, for God's happiness consisted in seeing man happy. Felicity for Traherne lay in an attitude and in the intellectual perception of the highest values, not in a physical state. Un-like Rousseau he did not demand a return to primitivism. He admired the simplicity of "those barbarous people that go naked," but not their lack of knowledge. One could find a more genuine happiness by exerting "the highest reason" to discover a true scale of values for life within a complex civilization.

Traherne, like Vaughan, was of Welsh descent, though he was born and reared in Hereford. His father was a shoemaker, and his family was poor; but he had a happy childhood, filled with an ecstatic joy in nature which reminds one of Words-worth's boyhood experiences. Though he complains of his early education, he had excellent training at Oxford University. He received his B.A. in 1656, his M.A. in 1661, and his B.D. in 1669. He decided sometime during this period to pursue "felicity," even if it meant living in poverty, rather than to devote his time and strength to an effort to gain wealth or fame. He entered the ministry, and he had been country rector at Credenhill for ten years and private chaplain to Sir Orlando Bridgman, Keeper of the Seals, for two years before he took his B.D. When Sir Orlando lost his office three years later, he kept Traherne with him in his retirement. Both died in the same year, Traherne being only thirty-eight. That his manuscript was preserved from 1674 to the present century is one of the pleasant miracles of literary history.

Wonder

How like an angel came I down!
How bright are all things here!
When first among His works I did appear
Oh, how their glory me did crown!
The world resembled His eternity,
In which my soul did walk;
And everything that I did see
Did with me talk.

The skies in their magnificence,
The lively, lovely air,
Oh, how divine, how soft, how sweet, how fair!   10
The stars did entertain my sense,
And all the works of God, so bright and pure,
So rich and great did seem,
As if they must endure
In my esteem.

A native health and innocence
Within my bones did grow;
And while my God did all His glories show,

I felt a vigor in my sense   20
That was all spirit. I within did flow
    With seas of life, like wine;
    I nothing in the world did know
        But 'twas divine.

    Harsh ragged objects were concealed,
        Oppressions, tears, and cries,
Sins, griefs, complaints, dissensions, weeping eyes
    Were hid, and only things revealed
Which heavenly spirits and the angels prize.
        The state of innocence   30
    And bliss, not trades and poverties,
        Did fill my sense.

    The streets were paved with golden stones
        The boys and girls were mine,
Oh, how did all their lovely faces shine!
    The sons of men were holy ones,
In joy and beauty they appeared to me,
        And everything which here I found,
    While like an angel I did see,
        Adorned the ground.   40

    Rich diamond and pearl and gold
        In every place was seen;
Rare splendors, yellow, blue, red, white, and green,
    Mine eyes did everywhere behold.
Great wonders clothed with glory did appear,
        Amazement was my bliss,
    That and my wealth was everywhere;
        No joy to this!

    Cursed and devised proprieties,
        With envy, avarice,   50
And fraud, those fiends that spoil even paradise,
    Flew from the splendor of mine eyes;

And so did hedges, ditches, limits, bounds:
    I dreamed not aught of those,
  But wandered over all men's grounds,
    And found repose.

  Proprieties themselves were mine,
    And hedges ornaments;
Walls, boxes, coffers, and their rich contents
  Did not divide my joys, but all combine.   60
Clothes, ribbons, jewels, laces, I esteemed
    My joys by others worn:
For me they all to wear them seemed
    When I was born.

Innocence

I

But that which most I wonder at, which most
I did esteem my bliss, which most I boast,
And ever shall enjoy, is that within
    I felt no stain nor spot of sin.

  No darkness then did overshade,
  But all within was pure and bright;
  No guilt did crush nor fear invade,
  But all my soul was full of light.

  A joyful sense and purity
    Is all I can remember;   10
  The very night to me was bright,
  'Twas summer in December.

II

A serious meditation did employ
My soul within, which taken up with joy

Did seem no outward thing to note, but fly
    All objects that do feed the eye,

    While it those very objects did
    Admire and prize and praise and love,
    Which in their glory most are hid,
    Which presence only doth remove.   *20*

    Their constant daily presence I
        Rejoicing at, did see,
    And that which takes them from the eye
    Of others offered them to me.

III

No inward inclination did I feel
To avarice or pride; my soul did kneel
In admiration all the day. No lust, nor strife,
    Polluted then my infant life.

    No fraud nor anger in me moved,
    No malice, jealousy, or spite;   *30*
    All that I saw I truly loved:
    Contentment only and delight

    Were in my soul. O heaven! what bliss
        Did I enjoy and feel!
    What powerful delight did this
    Inspire! for this I daily kneel.

IV

Whether it be that nature is so pure,
And custom only vicious; or that sure
God did by miracle the guilt remove,
    And made my soul to feel His love   *40*

So early; or that 'twas one day,
Wherein this happiness I found,
Whose strength and brightness so do ray,
That still it seems me to surround—

Whate'er it is, it is a light
   So endless unto me
That I a world of true delight
Did then, and to this day do see.

V

That prospect was the gate of heaven, that day
The ancient light of Eden did convey   50
Into my soul: I was an Adam there,
   A little Adam in a sphere

Of joys! Oh, there my ravished sense
Was entertained in paradise,
And had a sight of innocence,
Which was beyond all bound and price.

An antepast of heaven sure!
I on the earth did reign;
Within, without me, all was pure:
I must become a child again.   60

On News

News from a foreign country came,
As if my treasure and my wealth lay there:
So much it did my heart inflame!
'Twas wont to call my Soul into my ear,
   Which thither went to meet
    The approaching sweet,
   And on the threshold stood,
To entertain the unknown Good.

It hovered there
As if 'twould leave mine ear,   10
And was so eager to embrace
The joyful tidings as they came,
'Twould almost leave its dwelling-place,
  To entertain the same.

As if the tidings were the things,
My very joys themselves, my foreign treasure,
  Or else did bear them on their wings;
With so much joy they came, with so much pleasure.
    My Soul stood at that gate
      To recreate   20
    Itself with bliss and to
Be pleased with speed. A fuller view
    It fain would take,
    Yet journeys back would make
Unto my heart: as if 'twould fain
Go out to meet, yet stay within
To fit a place, to entertain,
  And bring the tidings in.

What sacred instinct did inspire
My Soul in childhood with a hope so strong?   30
  What secret force moved my desire
To expect my joys beyond the seas, so young?
    Felicity I knew
      Was out of view:
    And being here alone,
I saw that happiness was gone
      From me! For this,
    I thirsted absent bliss,
And thought that sure beyond the seas,
Or else in something near at hand   40
I knew not yet (since nought did please
  I knew), my bliss did stand.

But little did the infant dream
That all the treasures of the world were by,
    And that himself was so the cream
And crown of all which round about did lie.
        Yet thus it was: the gem,
            The diadem,
        The ring enclosing all
That stood upon this earthly ball;   50
            The Heavenly Eye,
        Much wider than the sky,
Wherein they all included were,
The glorious Soul that was the king
Made to possess them did appear
        A small and little thing!

The Salutation

        These little limbs,
    These eyes and hands which here I find,
These rosy cheeks wherewith my life begins,
        Where have ye been? behind
What curtain were ye from me hid so long,
Where was, in what abyss, my speaking tongue?

        When silent I
    So many thousand, thousand years
Beneath the dust did in a chaos lie,
        How could I smiles or tears,   10
Or lips or hands or eyes or ears perceive?
Welcome ye treasures which I now receive.

        I that so long
    Was nothing from eternity,
Did little think such joys as ear or tongue
        To celebrate or see:
Such sounds to hear, such hands to feel, such feet,
Beneath the skies on such a ground to meet.

New burnished joys,
  Which yellow gold and pearls excel!   20
Such sacred treasures are the limbs in boys,
  In which a soul doth dwell;
Their organized joints and azure veins
More wealth include than all the world contains.

    From dust I rise,
  And out of nothing now awake;
These brighter regions which salute mine eyes,
  A gift from God I take.
The earth, the seas, the light, the day, the skies,
The sun and stars are mine if those I prize.   30

    Long time before
  I in my mother's womb was born,
A God, preparing, did this glorious store,
  The world, for me adorn.
Into this Eden so divine and fair,
So wide and bright, I come His son and heir.

    A stranger here
  Strange things doth meet, strange glories see;
Strange treasures lodged in this fair world appear,
  Strange all and new to me;   40
But that they mine should be, who nothing was,
That strangest is of all, yet brought to pass.

Desire

  For giving me desire,
An eager thirst, a burning ardent fire,
  A virgin infant flame,
A love with which into the world I came,
  An inward hidden heavenly love,
  Which in my soul did work and move,
  And ever, ever me inflame

With restless longing, heavenly avarice,
   That never could be satisfied,
That did incessantly a paradise   10
Unknown suggest, and something undescried
   Discern, and bear me to it; be
   Thy Name for ever praised by me.

     My parched and withered bones
Burnt up did seem; my soul was full of groans;
   My thoughts extensions were:
Like paces, reaches, steps they did appear;
   They somewhat hotly did pursue,
   Knew that they had not all their due,
     Nor ever quiet were,   20
But made my flesh like hungry, thirsty ground,
   My heart a deep profound abyss,
And every joy and pleasure but a wound,
So long as I my blessedness did miss.
   O happiness! A famine burns,
   And all my life to anguish turns!

     Where are the silent streams,
The living waters and the glorious beams,
   The sweet reviving bowers,
The shady groves, the sweet and curious flowers,   30
   The springs and trees, the heavenly days,
   The flow'ry meads, and glorious rays,
     The gold and silver towers?
Alas! all these are poor and empty things!
   Trees, waters, days, and shining beams,
Fruits, flowers, bowers, shady groves, and springs,
No joy will yield, no more than silent streams;
   Those are but dead material toys,
   And cannot make my heavenly joys.

     O love! Ye amities,   40
And friendships that appear above the skies!

Ye feasts and living pleasures!
Ye senses, honors, and imperial treasures!
  Ye bridal joys! ye high delights
  That satisfy all appetites!
    Ye sweet affections, and
Ye high respects! Whatever joys there be
  In triumphs, whatsoever stand
In amicable sweet society,
Whatever pleasures are at His right hand,   50
  Ye must before I am divine,
  In full propriety be mine.

    This soaring, sacred thirst,
Ambassador of bliss, approached first,
    Making a place in me
That made me apt to prize, and taste, and see.
  For not the objects, but the sense
  Of things [1] doth bliss to our souls dispense,
    And make it, Lord, like Thee.
Sense, feeling, taste, complacency, and sight,   60
  These are the true and real joys,
The living, flowing, inward, melting, bright,
And heavenly pleasures; all the rest are toys:
  All which are founded in desire,
  As light in flame and heat in fire.

The Choice

When first eternity stooped to nought
  And in the earth its likeness sought,
When first it out of nothing framed the skies,
  And formed the moon and sun
That we might see what it had done,
    It was so wise,
    That it did prize

[1] Notice the Platonism of this statement.

Things truly greatest, brightest, fairest, best,
    All which it made, and left the rest.

Then did it take such care about the truth,   10
    Its daughter, that even in her youth,
Her face might shine upon us and be known,
      That by a better fate,
      It other toys might antedate
        As soon as shown;
        And be our own,
While we were hers: and that a virgin love
    Her best inheritance might prove.

Thoughts undefiled, simple, naked, pure;
    Thoughts worthy ever to endure,   20
Our first and disengaged thoughts it loves,
      And therefore made the truth,
      In infancy and tender youth
        So obvious to
        Our easy view
That it doth prepossess our soul, and proves
    The cause of what it all ways moves.

By merit and desire it doth allure;
    For truth is so divine and pure,
So rich and acceptable, being seen   30
      (Not parted, but in whole),
      That it doth draw and force the soul,
        As the great queen
        Of bliss, between
Whom and the soul, no one pretender ought
    Thrust in to captivate a thought.

Hence did eternity contrive to make
    The truth so fair for all our sake,
That being truth, and fair and easy too,
    While it on all doth shine,   40

We might by it become divine,
  Being led to woo
  The thing we view,
And as chaste virgins early with it join,
  That with it we might likewise shine.

Eternity doth give the richest things
  To every man, and makes all kings.
The best and richest things it doth convey
   To all, and every one;
  It raised me unto a throne!   50
    Which I enjoy
    In such a way,
That truth her daughter is my chiefest bride,
  Her daughter truth's my chiefest pride.

All mine! And seen so easily! How great, how blest!
  How soon am I of all possessed!
My infancy no sooner opes its eyes,
   But straight the spacious earth
  Abounds with joy, peace, glory, mirth,
    And being wise   60
    The very skies,
And stars do mine become; being all possessed
  Even in that way that is the best.

The Recovery

  To see us but receive, is such a sight
  As makes His treasures infinite!
  Because His goodness doth possess
In us, His own, and our own blessedness.
  Yea more, His love doth take delight
  To make our glory infinite;
   Our blessedness to see
   Is even to the Deity
A beatific vision! He attains
His ends while we enjoy. In us He reigns.   10

For God enjoyed is all His end.
Himself He then doth comprehend
When He is blessed, magnified,
Extolled, exalted, praised, and glorified,
Honored, esteemed, beloved, enjoyed,
Admired, sanctified, obeyed,
That is received. For He
Doth place His whole felicity
In that: who is despised and defied,
Undeified almost if once denied.   20

In all His works, in all His ways,
We must His glory see and praise;
And since our pleasure is the end,
We must His goodness and His love attend.
If we despise His glorious works,
Such sin and mischief in it lurks
That they are all made in vain;
And this is even endless pain
To Him that sees it: whose diviner grief
Is hereupon (ah me!) without relief.   30

We please His goodness that receive;
Refusers Him of all bereave,
As bridegrooms know full well that build
A palace for their bride. It will not yield
Any delight to him at all
If she for whom he made the hall
Refuse to dwell in it,
Or plainly scorn the benefit.
Her act that's wooed yields more delight and pleasure
If she receives, than all the pile of treasure.   40

But we have hands, and lips, and eyes,
And hearts and souls can sacrifice;
And souls themselves are made in vain
If we our evil stubbornness retain.

Affections, praises, are the things
For which He gave us all those springs;
 They are the very fruits
 Of all those trees and roots,
The fruits and ends of all His great endeavors,
Which he abolisheth whoever severs. 50

'Tis not alone a lively sense,
A clear and quick intelligence,
A free, profound, and full esteem;
Though these elixirs all and ends do seem:
 But gratitude, thanksgiving, praise,
 A heart returned for all those joys,
  These are the things admired,
  These are the things by Him desired:
These are the nectar and the quintessence,
The cream and flower that most affect His sense. 60

The voluntary act whereby
These are repaid is in His eye
More precious than the very sky.
All gold and silver is but empty dross,
 Rubies and sapphires are but loss,
 The very sun, and stars, and seas
  Far less His spirit please:
  One voluntary act of love
Far more delightful to His soul doth prove,
And is above all these as far as love. 70

John Wilmot, EARL OF ROCHESTER 1647-1680

THE POETS of the "Comic opera of the Restoration" had as their model Ovid, both in the smoothness of his verse and in his immorality. Their business was to be cynical, amusing, impudent, and amorous; they were interrupted by serious affairs. They vied with each other in wickedness, admitting only the king to superiority. Indeed, the amusing anecdote of the King and Shaftesbury may well be true:

"I believe thou art the wickedest dog in England," the king accused Shaftesbury.

Shaftesbury quickly replied, "May it please your Majesty, of a *subject,* I believe I am."

John Wilmot succeeded his father as second Earl of Rochester when he was about ten years old. He was very precocious in both learning and social life. He contributed to the university collections of verse, and he received his M.A. from Oxford shortly before he was fifteen. He gained further education by foreign travel with a tutor, who made him "perfectly in love with knowledge, by engaging him in books suitable to his inclinations." Whether through his tutor or through influential friends, he was received into the Court of Louis XIV at Versailles, and in spite of his youth was much favored by the French ladies.

Upon his return to England he was established at the Court of Charles II, where boredom was the chief crime. Here flourished the witty courtiers and poets: Killigrew, Sedley, Savile, Etheredge, Dorset, and Buckingham, vying with each other in clever verse—a group which Pepys called "cursed loose company . . . though full of wit; and worth a man's being in once to know the nature of it, and their manner of talk, and lives." Rochester was a leader in this group and a companion of the king in spite of the fact that his scandalous behavior and effrontery led the king to dismiss him in disgrace on the average of once a year. He was a lover of practical jokes, usually directed toward the seduction of women but characterized by humor and fine acting.

Rochester was not at this time wholly engrossed in the life at court and was still sensitive to noble impulses. During the wars with the Dutch Fleet this gay, handsome courtier, whom all considered a trifler, showed a different side of his character by his loyal response to his country's need. He won the regard of his new set of associates and made a record of real bravery that stands out in sharp relief against its background of frivolity.

Although this adventure was only an episode in the story of a life filled with trivialities, it so moved the heiress who had previously disdained Rochester that she relented and married him. His previous attempt to win her had failed. In need of money he had set out to win Elizabeth Mallet. When his suit was scorned, he devised a plan to kidnap her as she returned from a supper at Whitehall, accompanied by her grandfather. In the height of success in carrying out his plan, he himself was taken and imprisoned in the Tower by order of the king, to whom the grandfather had fled for aid; while the rescued Miss Mallet was returned home. Without the revelation of unsuspected nobility in Rochester, the heiress would probably have never been won.

Upon his return from the wars, Rochester was given a seat in the House of Lords and made Gentleman of the King's Bedchamber. His life became a sordid tale of drunkenness (he boasted once that he had been drunk for five years); of assistance to the king in illicit amours; of many intrigues of his own; and finally of a long illness, the result of his dissipated life. His intimacy with the king had only one value: he was able to become a patron of letters at court and to assist other poets and young playwrights.

His own verse was rated high by his contemporaries, and the elegance and music of his lyrics have always been much praised. It is as a writer of songs, whether love songs or drinking songs, that Rochester has won a place of distinction among the poets of the century. In an age of witty satire he was also admitted to possess superior satirical talent. His satires are upon political life, the manners of the time, contemporary people in literature and in court circles, and even the king himself. It is said that *The History of Insipids*, which summarizes the political life of the Restoration up to the time of its composition, caused the king to banish Rochester from the court. The *Satire against Man*, written in imitation of Boileau, is one of his best satires and illustrates his power of concentrated cleverness, which can sting as well as amuse.

Other poems of Rochester's are marked in Horace Walpole's words by "more poetry than politeness," and though widely circulated in the outspoken Restoration period, violate good taste and decency. Rochester's deathbed repentance has led to the story of a request that all of his obscene verse be destroyed. If he made such a request, it was not carried out. Since much of his verse is licentious, many other indecent poems have been attributed to Rochester, with the result that it is almost impossible to establish an authentic edition of his poems.

Upon Drinking in a Bowl

Vulcan, contrive me such a cup
    As Nestor [1] used of old:
Show all thy skill to trim it up;
    Damask it round with gold.

Make it so large that, filled with sack
    Up to the swelling brim,
Vast toasts on the delicious lake,
    Like ships at sea, may swim.

Engrave not battle on his cheek;
    With war I've nought to do: 10
I'm none of those that took Maestrick,
    Nor Yarmouth Leaguer knew.

[1] A Greek king of Pylos who in his old age fought with the Greeks against Troy. He was renowned for his wisdom.

Let it no name of planets tell,
    Fixed stars, or constellations;
For I am no Sir Sindrophel,
    Nor none of his relations.

But carve thereon a spreading vine;
    Then add two lovely boys;
Their limbs in amorous folds intwine,
    The type of future joys.   20

Cupid and Bacchus my saints are;
    May drink and love still reign:
With wine I wash away my cares,
    And then to love again.

The Mistress. A Song

An age in her embraces passed,
    Would seem a winter's day,
Where life and light with envious haste
    Are torn and snatched away.

But, oh! how slowly minutes roll,
    When absent from her eyes,
That fed my love, which is my soul;
    It languishes and dies.

For then no more a soul but shade,
    It mournfully does move;   10
And haunts my breast, by absence made
    The living tomb of love.

You wiser men despise me not,
    Whose love-sick fancy raves
On shades of souls, and heaven knows what;
    Short ages live in graves.

Whene'er those wounding eyes, so full
    Of sweetness, you did see,
Had you not been profoundly dull,
    You had gone mad like me.   20

Nor censure us; you who perceive
    My best beloved and me,
Sigh and lament, complain and grieve,
    You think we disagree.

Alas! 'tis sacred jealousy,
    Love raised to an extreme;
The only proof 'twixt them and me,
    We love, and do not dream.

Fantastic fancies fondly move
    And in frail joys believe,   30
Taking false pleasure for true love;
    But pain can ne'er deceive.

Kind jealous doubts, tormenting fears,
    And anxious cares, when past,
Prove our heart's treasure fixed and dear,
    And make us blest at last.

A Song

Absent from thee I languish still;
    Then ask me not, when I return.
The straying fool 'twill plainly kill,
    To wish all day, all night to mourn.

Dear, from thine arms then let me fly,
    That my fantastic mind may prove
The torments it deserves to try,
    That tears my fixed heart from my love.

When wearied with a world of woe,
    To thy safe bosom I retire,   10
Where love and peace and truth does flow,
    May I contented there expire.

Lest, once more wand'ring from that heaven,
    I fall on some base heart unblest;
Faithless to thee, false, unforgiven,
    And lose my everlasting rest.

Love and Life. A Song

All my past life is mine no more;
    The flying hours are gone,
Like transitory dreams given o'er,
Whose images are kept in store
    By memory alone.

The time that is to come is not;
    How can it then be mine?
The present moment's all my lot;
And that, as fast as it is got,
    Phillis, is only thine.   10

Then talk not of inconstancy,
    False hearts, and broken vows;
If I by miracle can be
This live-long minute true to thee,
    'Tis all that heaven allows.

A Song

Give me leave to rail at you;
I ask nothing but my due:
To call you false, and then to say
You shall not keep my heart a day.
But, alas! against my will,

I must be your captive still.
Ah! be kinder then; for I
Cannot change, and would not die.

Kindness has resistless charms;
All besides but weakly move: 10
Fiercest anger it disarms,
And clips the wings of flying love.
Beauty does the heart invade;
Kindness only can persuade:
It gilds the lovers servile chain,
And makes the slaves grow pleased again.

The Answer

Nothing adds to your fond fire
    More than scorn and cold disdain:
I, to cherish your desire,
    Kindness used, but 'twas in vain.

You insisted on your slave;
    Humble love you soon refused:
Hope not then a power to have,
    Which ingloriously you used.

Think not, Thirsis, I will e'er
    By my love my empire lose: 10
You grow constant through despair;
    Love returned you would abuse.

Though you still possess my heart,
    Scorn and rigor I must feign:
Ah! forgive that only art
    Love has left your love to gain.
You that could my heart subdue,
    To new conquests ne'er pretend:

Let the example make me true,
 And of a conquered foe a friend.   20

Then, if e'er I should complain
 Of your empire, or my chain,
Summon all the powerful charms,
 And kill the rebel in your arms.

Constancy. A Song

I cannot change as others do,
 Though you unjustly scorn,
Since that poor swain that sighs for you,
 For you alone was born.
No, Phillis, no; your heart to move
 A surer way I'll try;
And to revenge my slighted love,
 Will still love on, will still love on, and die.

When killed with grief Amintas lies,
 And you to mind shall call   10
The sighs that now unpitied rise,
 The tears that vainly fall,
That welcome hour that ends this smart,
 Will then begin your pain:
For such a faithful tender heart
 Can never break, can never break in vain.

I

Cambridge History of English Literature. Vols. III and VII.

Courthope, W. J. *History of English Poetry.* 6 vols. New York, 1904–11. Vol. III.

Jusserand, J. J. *A Literary History of the English People.* 3 vols. New York, 1926. Vols. II and III.

Reed, E. B. *English Lyrical Poetry.* New Haven, 1912.

Saintsbury, George. *A History of English Prosody.* 2 vols. New York, 1908. Vol. II.

Schelling, Felix E. *The English Lyric.* New York, 1913.

Spingarn, J. E. Editor. *Critical Essays of the Seventeenth Century.* 3 vols. Oxford, 1908.

II

Hebel, J. W. and Patterson, F. A. *English Seventeenth Century Literature: a Brief Working Bibliography.* New York, 1929.

Bennett, Joan. *Four Metaphysical Poets: Donne, Herbert, Vaughan, Crashaw.* New York, 1934.

Boulenger, J. R. *The Seventeenth Century.* New York, 1920.

Charlanne, Louis. *L'Influence française en Angleterre au xviie siècle.* Paris, 1906.

Clark, G. N. *The Seventeenth Century.* Oxford, 1929.

Crum, R. B. *Scientific Thought in Poetry.* New York, 1931.

Dent, E. J. *Foundations of English Opera. A Study of Musical Drama in England during the Seventeenth Century.* Cambridge, 1928.

Dowden, Edward. *Puritan and Anglican.* New York, 1901.

Duncan, Carson S. *The New Science and English Literature in the Classical Period.* Menasha, Wis., 1913.

Eliot, T. S. *Homage to John Dryden: Three Essays on the Poetry of the Seventeenth Century.* London, 1924.

Gosse, Edmund. *From Shakespeare to Pope.* New York, 1885.

    The Jacobean Poets. New York, 1894.

    Seventeenth Century Studies. New York, 1897.

Greenlaw, Edwin. "The New Science and English Literature in the Seventeenth Century," in the *Johns Hopkins Alumni Magazine*, XIII (1925), 331–59.

Grierson, H. J. C. *Cross Currents in English Literature of the Seventeenth Century*. London, 1929.

The First Half of the Seventeenth Century. New York, 1906.

Metaphysical Poetry: Donne to Butler. Oxford, 1921.

Jones, R. F. "The Background of the Battle of the Books," [1] in *Washington University Studies, Humanistic Series*, VII, 1920.

Leishman, J. B. *The Metaphysical Poets: Donne, Herbert, Vaughan, and Traherne*. Oxford, 1934.

Parry, C. H. *The Music of the Seventeenth Century*. The Oxford History of Music, Vol. III. Oxford, 1902.

Read, Herbert. "The Nature of Metaphysical Poetry," in *Reason and Romanticism*. London, 1926.

Reynolds, Myra. *The Learned Lady in England, 1650–1700*. New York, 1920.

Ustick, W. L. "Changing Ideals of Aristocratic Character and Conduct in Seventeenth Century England," in *Modern Philology*, XXX (1932), 147–66.

Wendell, Barrett. *The Temper of the Seventeenth Century in English Literature*. New York, 1904.

Whibley, Charles. "The Court Poets," in *Literary Studies*. New York, 1919.

Willey, Basil. *The Seventeenth Century Background*. London, 1934.

Williamson, George. *The Nature of the Donne Tradition*. Cambridge, Mass., 1930.

Willmott, R. A. *Lives of the Sacred Poets*. 2 vols. 2nd edition. London, 1839.

---

[1] As this anthology goes to press, there comes to hand Mr. Jones's new book *Ancients and Moderns: a Study of the Background of the Battle of the Books*, Washington University Studies, New Series, Language and Literature, No. 6, 1936. This is an expansion of the material in the earlier treatment and contains valuable additions. The editor regrets that she did not have the advantage of the use of this book.

III

Harrison, J. S. *Platonism in the English Poetry of the Sixteenth and Seventeenth Centuries*. New York, 1903.

Inge, W. R. *Christian Mysticism*. London, 1899.

The Platonic Tradition in English Religious Thought. New York, 1926.

Jones, R. M. *Spiritual Reformers in the Sixteenth and Seventeenth Centuries*. London, 1928.

Nicolson, Marjorie. "Milton and Hobbes," in *Studies in Philology*, XXIII (1926), 405–33.

"The Early Stage of Cartesianism in England," in *Studies in Philology*, XXVI (1929), 356–74.

Spurgeon, Caroline. *Mysticism in English Literature*. New York, 1913.

Thompson, E. N. S. "Mysticism in English Literature," in *Studies in Philology*, XVIII (1921), 170–231.

Tulloch, John. *Rational Theology and Christian Philosophy in England in the Seventeenth Century*. 2 vols. Edinburgh and London, 1874.

IV

Bury, J. B. *A History of Freedom of Thought*. New York, 1913.

The Idea of Progress. New York, 1932.

Gooch, G. P. *English Democratic Ideas in the Seventeenth Century*. 2nd edition. Cambridge, 1927.

Randall, J. H. *The Making of the Modern Mind*. New York, 1926.

V

Nicolson, Marjorie. "The Telescope and Imagination," in *Modern Philology*, XXXII (1935), 233–60.

"The 'New Astronomy' and English Literary Imagination," in *Studies in Philology*, XXXII (1935), 428–62.

Ornstein, Martha. *The Rôle of the Scientific Societies in the Seventeenth Century*. New York, 1913.

Sedgwick, W. T. and Tyler, H. W. *A Short History of Science*. New York, 1929.

Singer, C. J. *From Magic to Science*. London, 1928.
  Greek Science and Modern Science. London, 1920.
Sprat, Thomas. *History of the Royal Society*. London, 1667.
Stimson, Dorothy. *The Gradual Acceptance of the Coperni-
  can Theory of the Universe*. New York, 1917.
Whitehead, A. N. *Science and the Modern World*. Cam-
  bridge, 1930.

VI

PASTORAL

Chambers, E. K. "The English Pastoral," in *Sir Thomas
  Wyatt and Some Collected Studies*. London, 1933.
Greg, W. W. *Pastoral Poetry and Pastoral Drama*. London,
  1906.
Hanford, J. H. "The Pastoral Elegy and Milton's Lycidas,"
  in *Publications of the Modern Language Association*,
  XXV (1910), 403–47.
Norlin, G. "The Conventions of the Pastoral Elegy," in
  American Journal of Philology, XXV (1911), 294–312.

EPIC

Cory, Herbert. "Spenser, the School of the Fletchers, and
  Milton," in *University of California Publications in
  Modern Philology*, II, No. 5, 1912.
Dixon, W. M. *English Epic and Heroic Poetry*. New York,
  1912.

MASQUE

Campbell, L. B. *Scenes and Machines on the English Stage
  during the Renaissance*. Cambridge, 1923.
Hereford, C. H. and Simpson, Percy. "Masques and Enter-
  tainments," in *Ben Jonson* II. Oxford, 1925, pp. 247–
  334.
Lawrence, W. J. "The Mounting of the Carolan Masques,"
  in *The Elizabethan Playhouse and Other Studies*. Strat-
  ford-on-Avon, 1912.
Reyher, Paul. *Les Masques anglais (1512–1640)*. Paris,
  1909.
Sullivan, Mary. *Court Masques of James I*. London, 1913.
Welsford, Enid. *The Court Masque*. Cambridge, 1927.

SATIRE

Alden, Raymond. *The Rise of Formal Satire in England*. Philadelphia, 1899.

Previté-Orton, C. W. *Political Satire in English Poetry*. New York, 1910.

Walker, Hugh. *English Satire and Satirists*. London, 1925.

SONNET

Crosland, T. W. H. *The English Sonnet*. New York. n. d.

Crow, M. F. Editor. *English Sonnet Cycles*. 4 vols. London, 1896–8. Vol. I. (See Introduction.)

Smart, J. S. *The Sonnets of John Milton*. Glasgow, 1921.

ODE

Shafer, Robert. *The English Ode to 1660*. Princeton, 1918.

𝕬𝖕𝖕𝖊𝖓𝖉𝖎𝖝 𝕭 Bibliography of Authors

Modern Editions and Important Criticism

JOHN DONNE

Poems. Ed. by E. K. Chambers. Muses' Library. 2 vols. New York, 1896.

Poetical Works. Ed. by H. J. C. Grierson. 2 vols. Oxford, 1912. (Vol. II has important Introduction.)

Keynes, Geoffrey L. *A Bibliography of Dr. John Donne.* 2nd edition. Cambridge, 1930.

Bredvold, L. I. "The Religious Thought of Donne in Relation to Medieval and Later Traditions," in *Studies in Shakespeare, Milton, and Donne.* New York, 1925.

Dowden, Edward. "The Poetry of John Donne," in *New Studies in Literature.* London, 1895.

Fausset, H. l'A. *John Donne. A Study in Discord.* London, 1924.

George, R. E. G. *Outflying Philosophy, a Literary Study of the Religious Element in the Poems and Letters of John Donne and in the Works of Sir Thomas Browne and of Henry Vaughan the Silurist.* London, 1925.

Gosse, Edmund. *The Life and Letters of John Donne.* 2 vols. London, 1899.

Praz, Mario. *Secentismo e marinismo in Inghilterra: John Donne—Richard Crashaw.* Florence, 1925.

Ramsay, M. P. *Les Doctrines médiévales chez Donne.* Oxford, 1917.

Schelling, F. E. "Donne and His Place among Lyrical Poets," in *English Literature during the Lifetime of Shakespeare.* New York, 1910.

BEN JONSON

Masques and Entertainments. Ed. by Henry Morley. London, 1895.

Works. Ed. by Francis Cunningham. 3 vols. London, 1816 (?).

Castelain, M. *Ben Jonson; l'homme et l'œuvre.* Paris, 1907.

Eliot, T. S. "Ben Jonson," in *Elizabethan Essays.* London, 1934.

"Ben Jonson," in *The Sacred Wood*. London, 1920.

Hereford, C. H. and Simpson, Percy. *Ben Jonson. The Man and His Work*. Oxford, 1925. (Vol. I contains a biography and Vol. II criticism of masques and poems.)

Schelling, F. E. "Ben Jonson and the Classical School," in *Publications of the Modern Language Association,* XIII (1898), 221–49.

Smith, Gregory. *Ben Jonson*. London, 1919.

Swinburne, A. C. *A Study of Ben Jonson*. London, 1889.

PHINEAS FLETCHER

The Poems of Phineas Fletcher. Ed. by A. B. Grosart. Fuller Worthies' Library. 4 vols. London, 1869. Vol. II.

Giles and Phineas Fletcher, Poetical Works. Ed. by F. S. Boas. 2 vols. Cambridge, 1908–9.

GILES FLETCHER

The Poems of Giles Fletcher. Ed. by A. B. Grosart. Fuller Worthies' Library. London, 1868.

Giles and Phineas Fletcher, Poetical Works. Ed. by F. S. Boas. 2 vols. Cambridge, 1908–9. Vol. I.

WILLIAM DRUMMOND

The Poems. Ed. by W. C. Ward. Muses' Library. 2 vols. New York, 1894.

The Poetical Works. Ed. by L. E. Kastner. 2 vols. Manchester, 1913.

Masson, David. *Drummond of Hawthornden*. London, 1873.

GEORGE WITHER

The Poetry. Ed. by F. Sidgwick. 2 vols. London, 1902.

Lamb, Charles. "On the Poetical Works of George Wither," in *Critical Essays*. Ed. by William Macdonald. New York, 1914, pp. 172–8.

WILLIAM BROWNE

Poems, Ed. by G. Goodwin. Muses' Library. 2 vols. New York, 1894.

Works. Ed. by W. C. Hazlitt. 2 vols. London, 1868.
Moorman, F. W. *William Browne. His Britannia's Pastorals and the Pastoral Poetry of the Elizabethan Age.* Strassburg, 1897.

ROBERT HERRICK

The Hesperides and Noble Numbers. Ed. by A. W. Pollard. Muses' Library. 2 vols. New York, 1891.
The Poetical Works. Ed. by F. W. Moorman. Oxford, 1915.
The Poetical Works of Robert Herrick, with preface by Humbert Wolf. 4 vols. London, 1928.
Delattre, Floris. *Robert Herrick.* Paris, 1912.
Moorman, F. W. *Robert Herrick, A Biographical and Critical Study.* London, 1910.
Reed, Edward B. "Herrick's Indebtedness to Ben Jonson," in *Modern Language Notes,* XVII (1902), 478–84.

FRANCIS QUARLES

Complete Works. Ed. by A. B. Grosart. Chertsey Worthies' Library. 3 vols. Vol. III, 1881.
Emblems, Divine and Moral. Ed. by Rev. Augustus Toplady and Rev. John Ryland. London, 1839.

GEORGE HERBERT

The English Works. Ed. by G. H. Palmer. 3 vols. Boston, 1907.
The Poems. Ed. by A. Waugh. Oxford, 1907.
Hyde, A. G. *George Herbert and His Times.* London, 1906.

THOMAS CAREW

Poems. Ed. by Arthur Vincent. Muses' Library. New York, 1899.
Poems. Ed. by W. C Hazlitt. London, 1870.

EDMUND WALLER

Poems. Ed. by G. Thorn Drury. Muses' Library. New York, 1893.

JOHN MILTON

Complete Poems. Ed. by W. V. Moody. The Cambridge Poets. New York, 1899.

Poems. Ed. by F. A. Patterson. New York, 1930.

Works. Ed. by F. A. Patterson, general editor. New York, Columbia University Press, 1931–.

Hanford, James Holly. *A Milton Handbook*. Rev. ed. New York, 1933.

Stevens, David H. *Reference Guide to Milton*. Chicago, 1930.

Bailey, John. *Milton*. London, 1915.

Bridges, Robert S. *Milton's Prosody*. Rev. final ed. Oxford, 1921.

Havens, R. D. *The Influence of Milton on English Poetry*. Cambridge, Mass., 1922.

Masson, David. *The Life of John Milton Narrated in Connection with the Political, Ecclesiastical, and Literary History of His Time*. 7 vols. London, 1859–94.

Saurat, Denis. *Milton, Man and Thinker*. New York, 1925.

Thompson, E. N. S. *Essays on Milton*. New Haven, 1915.

Tillyard, E. M. W. *Milton*. London, 1930.

Hanford, J. H. "The Pastoral Elegy and Milton's *Lycidas*," in *Publications of the Modern Language Association* XXV (1910), 403–47.

"Samson Agonistes and Milton in Old Age," in *Studies in Shakespeare, Milton, and Donne*. New York, 1925.

Jebb, R. C. "*Samson Agonistes* and the Hellenic Drama," in *Proceedings of the British Academy*, 1907–8, pp. 341–8.

Parker, William R. "The Greek Spirit in Milton's *Samson Agonistes*," in *Essays and Studies* by Members of the English Association. Oxford, 1935.

SIR JOHN SUCKLING

The Poems. Ed. by Frederick A. Stokes. New York, 1886.

The Poems, Plays, and Other Remains. Ed. by W. C. Hazlitt. 2 vols. London, 1874.

The Works. Ed. by A. H. Thompson. London, 1910.

SAMUEL BUTLER

Hudibras. Ed. by Henry G. Bohn, London, 1885.

Hudibras. Ed. by Zachary Grey. The Chandos Classics. London, 1892.

Ramsay, A. R. *Samuel Butler and His Hudibras and Other Works*. London, 1846.

"Samuel Butler," in *Seventeenth Century Studies*. Ed. by Robert Shafer. Princeton, 1933.

Veldkamp, Jan. *Samuel Butler, the Author of Hudibras*. Hilversum, 1923.

RICHARD CRASHAW

Complete Works. Ed. by A. B. Grosart. Fuller Worthies' Library. 2 vols. London, 1872–3.

Poems. Ed. by L. C. Martin. Oxford, 1927.

Poems. Ed. by J. R. Tutin, with Introduction by H. C. Beeching. Muses' Library. New York, 1905.

Poems. Ed. by A. R. Waller. Cambridge, 1904.

JOHN CLEVELAND

Poems. Ed. by J. M. Berdan. New Haven, 1911.

SIR JOHN DENHAM

Poetical Works. Ed. by T. H. Banks, Jr. New Haven, 1928.

RICHARD LOVELACE

Lucasta. Ed. by W. C. Hazlitt. London, 1864.

Poems. Ed. by C. H. Wilkinson. 2 vols. Oxford, 1925.

Hartmann, C. H. *The Cavalier Spirit and Its Influence on the Life and Work of Richard Lovelace*. London, 1925.

ABRAHAM COWLEY

English Writings. Ed. by A. R. Waller. 2 vols. Cambridge, 1905–6.

The Mistress, with Other Select Poems. Ed. by John Sparrow. London, 1926.

Nethercot, A. H. *Abraham Cowley: the Muses' Hannibal.* Oxford, 1931.

"The Reputation of the 'Metaphysical' Poets during the Seventeenth Century," in *Journal of English and Germanic Philology,* XXVIII (1924), 173–98.

"The Reputation of Abraham Cowley (1660–1800)," in *Publications of the Modern Language Association,* XXXVIII (1923), 588–641.

ANDREW MARVELL

Poems and Satires. Ed. by G. A. Aitken. Muses' Library. 2 vols. New York, 1892.

Poems. Ed. by H. M. Margoliouth. 2 vols. Oxford, 1927.

Birrell, Augustine. *Andrew Marvell.* New York, 1905.

Andrew Marvell, Tercentenary Tributes. Ed. by W. H. Bagguley. Oxford, 1922.

Legouis, Pierre. *André Marvell.* Paris, 1928.

Sackville-West, Hon. V. M. *Andrew Marvell.* London, 1929.

HENRY VAUGHAN

Poems. Ed. by E. K. Chambers. Muses' Library. 2 vols. New York, 1896.

Works. Ed. by L. C. Martin. 2 vols. Oxford, 1914.

Blunden, Edmund. *On the Poems of Henry Vaughan.* London, 1927.

Guiney, L. I. "Henry Vaughan," in *A Little English Gallery.* New York, 1894, pp. 56–118.

Judson, A. C. "Henry Vaughan as a 'Nature Poet,' " in *Publications of the Modern Language Association,* XLII (1927), 146–56.

Vaughan, J. "Henry Vaughan Silurist," in *Nineteenth Century,* LXVII (1910), 492–504.

Wells, H. A. *The Tercentenary of Henry Vaughan.* New York, 1922.

JOHN DRYDEN

Works. Ed. by Sir Walter Scott and George Saintsbury. 18 vols. Edinburgh, 1882–93.

The Poems of John Dryden. Ed. by John Sargeaunt. Oxford, 1910.

The Poetical Works of John Dryden. Ed. by George R. Noyes. Boston, 1908.

Bredvold, L. I. *The Intellectual Milieu of John Dryden.* University of Michigan Publications in Language and Literature, XII, 1934.

Eliot, T. S. *John Dryden.* New York, 1932.

Hollis, Christopher. *Dryden.* London, 1933.

Lubbock, Alan. *The Character of John Dryden.* London, 1925.

Masson, David. "Dryden and the Literature of the Restoration," in *The Three Devils: Luther's, Milton's, and Goethe's.* London, 1874.

Nicoll, Allardyce. *Dryden and His Poetry.* London, 1923.

Saintsbury, George. *Dryden.* English Men of Letters Series. New York, 1887.

Van Doren, Mark. *The Poetry of John Dryden.* New York, 1920.

Verrall, A. W. *Lectures on Dryden.* Cambridge, 1914.

THOMAS TRAHERNE

Poetical Works. Ed. by Bertram Dobell. 2nd edition. London, 1906.

Willett, G. E. *Traherne, an Essay.* Cambridge, 1919.

JOHN WILMOT, EARL OF ROCHESTER

Collected Works. Ed. by John Hayward. London, 1926.

Poetical Works. Ed. by Quilter Johns. Haworth Press, Caxton House, Halifax, Yorkshire, England, 1933.

Longueville, Thomas. *Rochester and Other Literary Rakes of the Court of Charles II.* 2nd and revised edition. New York, 1903.

Pinto, Vivian de Sola. *Rochester: Portrait of a Restoration Poet.* London, 1935.

Prinz, Johannes. *John Wilmot, Earl of Rochester, His Life and Writings.* Leipzig, 1927.

Williams, Charles. *Rochester.* London, 1935.

Index

Authors' names are printed in SMALL CAPITALS, titles of poems in *italics*, and first lines of poems in roman.

DATE DUE
